THE WESTERN CHURCH IN THE
MIDDLE AGES

THE WESTERN CHURCH
IN THE MIDDLE AGES

JOHN A.F. THOMSON

Professor of Medieval History, University of Glasgow

A member of the Hodder Headline Group
LONDON

First published in Great Britain in 1998 by
Arnold, a member of the Hodder Headline Group
338 Euston Road, London NW1 3BH
175 Fifth Avenue, New York, NY10010

http://www.arnoldpublishers.com

Co-published in the United States of America by
Oxford University Press Inc.,
198 Madison Avenue, New York 10016

British Library Cataloguing in Publication Data
A catalogue entry for this book is available from the British Library

Library of Congress Cataloging-in-Publication Data
A catalog record for this book is available from the Library of Congress

Production Editor: Wendy Rooke
Production Controller: Priya Gohil
Cover designer: Terry Griffiths

ISBN 0 340 60118 3 (pb)

Composition by Phoenix Photosetting, Chatham, Kent

Contents

Preface

The writing of a new textbook on the medieval Church may require some justification, as numerous existing studies of it might well be used to demonstrate the prophetic character of the author of *Ecclesiastes,* when he wrote that of making many books there is no end, and the writers of them might well continue the quotation endorsing the view that much study is a weariness to the flesh. Yet the role of the Church in medieval society makes it essential for any student to understand how it developed and how it related to the world in which it was situated. Furthermore, because the Church set the moral agenda of society and dominated the intellectual world for the best part of a thousand years, a study of the Church should not be confined simply to institutional changes but should also examine how it affected, and was affected by, the mental outlook of lay society. This book attempts to provide an introduction to these various aspects of the Church's life, and some bibliographical guidance to students to explore them further, incorporating new work and changing perceptions of the subject in recent years. The bibliography includes all works cited in the text, and a number of others which have explored important aspects of the Church's life. More particularly, because a life of university teaching has convinced me that the best way for students to find a way into the mental world of the past is to read what the people of various periods wrote themselves, I have tried, wherever possible, to refer them to original source material which has recently become available in numerous translations, although the quantity of this does vary from period to period. My impression is that it is more common for the early and central Middle Ages than it is for the fourteenth and fifteenth centuries.

To condense so long a period of history into a single volume has made it necessary to take a selective approach to the topic, and while I have tried to cover all major aspects of the Church's life, other historians might well make a different choice of the themes which they would wish to highlight. It may be politically incorrect (and even worse, unfashionable) to say little about the part played by women in the medieval Church, but as it was essentially a male-dominated society, I believe that the omission of any lengthy discussion of this is justified. I do not underrate the importance of the topic, which has received significant attention since the 1960s, but believe that it is more important as a part of gender studies than of ecclesiastical history. I have tried, too, to write this work from a non-denominational standpoint, an approach which has become more common in recent years than it would have been even in the 1950s, when there was still a certain tendency to use the historical past to justify a particular point of view. Another problem which has, of course, to be accepted is that more new works may appear, even while this book is at the press, which will make some of my conclusions out of date, and I apologise in advance to their authors for my inability to draw on them.

Many of the debts which I owe to earlier workers in the field can be identified from the Bibliography, but I also owe more immediate thanks to friends in the Department of Medieval History in the University of Glasgow, Stuart Airlie, Marilyn Dunn, Andrew Roach and Graeme Small, who have read sections of the text and given me the benefit of their expertise on particular topics. The errors which remain are, of course, my own responsibility. Generations of students in the same department have raised questions for me to consider, and I hope that this book will assist their successors and encourage them to examine new problems. My family have always given me support and encouragement through the years of writing, and as always the greatest thanks are due to them.

Abbreviations

BAR	British Archaeological Reports
BAR-I	British Archaeological Reports, International Series
Bede, *EH*	Bede, *Ecclesiastical History*
EHD	*English Historical Documents*
EHR	*English Historical Review*
JEH	*Journal of Ecclesiastical History*
New CMH	*New Cambridge Modern History*
PIMS	Pontifical Institute of Medieval Studies
RHE	*Revue d'histoire ecclésiastique*
SCH	*Studies in Church History*
TRHS	*Transactions of the Royal Historical Society*

THE AGE OF CONVERGENCE
(*c.* 450–1050)

|1|

The spread and consolidation
of Christianity

The legacy of the ancient world

The disintegration of the Roman Empire in the West under the pressure of barbarian invasions was a protracted process. Although kingdoms under barbarian rulers were established in areas which had previously been part of the Empire from the early fifth century onwards, some vestiges of imperial power remained in Italy until the deposition of the last emperor in 476, and the old imperial tradition led to the continuance of Byzantine intervention in Italy well into the future. By about 500 the political structures of the West had been fundamentally altered from what they had been a century earlier and this had profound repercussions on the Church.

Under the Roman Empire, Christianity had developed unrecognisably from its Jewish origins; very soon after the crucifixion of Jesus of Nazareth, his disciples had begun to preach to the Gentile world, and local churches had sprung up throughout the Empire. The early centuries had been a time of struggle; Christianity with its exclusive claims to the truth could not compromise with the officially sponsored cult of the divine emperor, and there were continual persecutions until the beginning of the fourth century, when the Emperor Constantine issued an edict of toleration and was eventually himself baptised. From then on, apart from one brief spell under the Emperor Julian in the mid-fourth century, Christianity had the status of an acceptable religion within the Empire, and from the time of Theodosius I (379–95) it was regarded as the official religion, with the practice of paganism being banned. In fact one sees the survival of vestigial pagan cults, often in the form of folk customs, and this makes it impossible to estimate how far the people as a whole were genuinely Christianised. One may suspect that in most cases they simply accepted the formulae and rituals of the new faith as a substitute for, or as a supplement to, their traditional practices.

Imperial patronage had transformed the Church, bestowing advantages on it, but also creating problems. The leaders of the Church could now meet

in council to resolve disputed questions of theology, and the credal state-
ments formulated in the century and a half after Constantine determined
some of the main doctrines of future Christian orthodoxy. The fourth and
fifth centuries were an age when the Mediterranean world was still a cultured society with intellectual traditions which had been continuously preserved for almost a thousand years, and beliefs were subjected to the
scrutiny of minds trained in the subtleties of philosophy which wished to
clarify the precise nature of what the Church believed. The Council of
Nicaea (324) declared that God the Father and God the Son were of the
same substance, and the Council of Chalcedon (451) laid down the doctrine
of the two natures of Christ, both human and divine. But as with any formal definition of a doctrine as orthodox, alternative views remained, and
dissenting churchmen were left outside the ecclesiastical mainstream. The
Arians affirmed that the Son was of like, but not of the same, substance as
the Father, while the Monophysites declared that Christ had only a single
nature. The latter made little impression in the West, although they
remained powerful in parts of the Eastern Mediterranean world, but Arian
Christianity had some influence in the West. Indeed it even had support
from some emperors, but its main influence was among some of the barbarian tribes which had been converted to that form of Christianity. When they
invaded the Empire, they brought it with them, and for a time Arian and
Nicaean Christianity were opposed to each other in the new kingdoms
which arose on the ruins of the Empire. As late as the time of Gregory of
Tours, at the end of the sixth century, references are found to Arianism, but
when Visigothic Spain turned to orthodoxy, Arianism became less of a
problem. Not all barbarian Christianity was Arian; the missionary activities
of St Nynia in southern Scotland and of St Patrick in Ireland spread Nicaean
orthodoxy beyond the bounds of the Empire. And, of course, some barbarian tribes remained unconverted, although once they settled within the old
imperial lands, their leaders were willing to come to terms with the Church
as one part of the more civilised world which they were taking over.

There were various ways in which the invasions affected the character of
the Western Church. Most notably they drove a wedge between East and
West, for the tribal movements had tended to bypass the surviving empire at
Byzantium. The ties were only broken gradually, because Italy remained
linked to the East longer and more closely than other parts of the former
Western Empire, which itself had disintegrated into a number of distinct
kingdoms. Ecclesiastically, ties remained between the Eastern and the
Western churches, for the decisive schism did not come until 1054, but the
disappearance of effective imperial authority in the West gave the Church
there freedom to develop in different ways from those which its Eastern
counterpart followed. Most notably, the Western Church, at least outside
Italy, where Rome provided a bridge to the Byzantine world, did not possess
a comparable level of intellectual sophistication, so some of the later theological controversies which continued to affect the Byzantine Church were

not echoed in the West. There are some allusions to Monophysitism and Monotheletism (see Glossary) in the *Liber Pontificalis*, the official history of the popes, and in an Andalusian chronicle from the late eighth century, but there is no evidence of widespread controversies or schisms within the local churches.[1] The English eighth-century historian Bede was aware of heresies such as Arianism and Pelagianism (see Glossary), but purely in a historical sense and not as current issues.[2] Significantly, the first great theological controversy in Byzantium which did create repercussions in the West was one which focussed on a matter of worship, the rights and wrongs of reverencing images, not one which was concerned with a philosophical issue of doctrine. The disputes over when Easter should be celebrated, which occurred in seventh-century England, again had no theological implications, but simply affected the practice of worship.

Another consequence of this division of East and West was the enhanced ecclesiastical standing of Rome. In the late Roman world, the Church had looked for guidance to five main centres, Jerusalem, Alexandria, Antioch, Constantinople and Rome, but the first four of these all lay in the East. Rome therefore could provide a focal point for the development of church life in the West, although initially this was predominantly emotional, as the place where many of the early martyrs had died. Only gradually, and under the influence of a few popes, most notably Gregory I, was this transformed into a more administrative and jurisdictional role.

The medieval Western Church derived four main legacies from the Roman world. The canon of Scripture was established in the early centuries, not without disputes, and there had been various translations of the Bible into Latin, of which the most influential was that of St Jerome, which came to be known as the Vulgate. There was an established tradition of theology in the writings of the Church Fathers, of whom the most distinguished was St Augustine of Hippo, whose contribution to Christian theology over the centuries was second only to that of St Paul. Various forms of worship had become formalised in liturgies, although there were still divergences among different Christian communities, and one also saw the development of monasteries, organised communities whose fundamental task was prayer and worship. Finally, the organisational structure of the Church, under the rule of local bishops, who were based in the cities, reflected in many cases the administrative structure of the late Roman Empire.

The churches in the new kingdoms

The fortunes of the Church in Frankish Gaul were bound up with surviving influential families from imperial times. The historian Gregory of Tours was the nineteenth bishop of the see, and over two-thirds of his predecessors in it were blood relations, while other kinsmen held bishoprics elsewhere. His great-grandfather, who became a churchman after his wife's death, had been bishop of Langres, where one of his sons, Tetricus, succeeded him.[3] Such great churchmen could offer support to the barbarian kings, who could use their city bases to exercise effective territorial power.[4] The fact that the early sixth-century Frankish king Clovis had embraced the Nicaean form of Christianity, when most of his barbarian contemporaries were Arian, probably made him more acceptable as a ruler to the Christian families of sub-Roman Gaul. The prominence of such families reflects social continuity from Roman times, something which did not occur in the British Isles, where the invasions of the pagan Anglo-Saxons had driven the survivors of Christianity to the Celtic West, Cornwall, Wales, Ireland and Scotland, and destroyed the Roman foundations of society. (Possibly some isolated pockets of Christianity survived elsewhere in England, but they do not appear to have had any significance when a mission was sent to Kent from the Continent in 597.)

The early geographical basis of the Church was in the lands which had been part of the Empire, although there were some variations. The Christian areas of the Celtic West lay outside the old Roman world, and for much of the fifth and sixth centuries the lands of the Iberian peninsula were under the rule of Arian kings. Arianism, however, was essentially the religion of a Gothic ruling class, and the old Hispano-Romans, if they were Christian rather than pagan, adhered to the Catholic tradition. Relations between Catholics and Arians were not always totally hostile; it was possible for Catholic bishops to carry out church-building programmes, King Theudis allowed them to meet in council at Toledo, and regular synods met in the first half of the sixth century. There may have been some oppression after 550, because no synods seem to have met between 549 and 586. Although the last of the Arian kings, Leofgild, has sometimes been seen as a persecutor, the evidence for this is slight, and he certainly was able to appoint bishops to both communities. Indeed, he himself tried to secure the adoption of a modified Arian creed, which accepted the equality of the Father and the Son, but regarded the Holy Spirit as inferior. There had been some drift to Catholicism among the Visigoths even before King Reccared finally abandoned the Arian cause, for one of the prominent bishops of the mid-sixth century, Masona of Mérida, was of Gothic origin. Masona strongly opposed the new doctrinal formula, although some bishops were willing to accept it. There was some resistance to Reccared's conversion, but it was not long before it collapsed.[5]

Even in Italy some of the invading tribes such as the Ostrogoths and the Lombards were Arian, and built churches in some of the major centres. (Different baptisteries still survive in Ravenna for Arian and Orthodox.) The greatest of the Ostrogoth rulers, Theodoric, in fact discouraged the conversion of Romans to Arianism in Italy, because he wished to preserve a clear distinction between Goths and Romans, something which the religious distinctions provided.[6] Christianity at this period was predominantly centred on the Mediterranean world, something which remained until the emergence and spread of Islam from the seventh century. There was little spread of Christianity to the lands east of the Rhine and north of the Danube, where the tribes were predominantly pagan, until the eighth century, and it is probably fair to say that until this time the main concern of the Church was survival rather than expansion, although there was some piecemeal expansion east of the Rhine directed by Frankish bishops and abbots in the seventh century.[7] The only major area which was recovered for Christianity before 700 was England, which attracted missions from Rome at the end of the sixth century and from Iona a third of a century later. It was only after the conversion of the German tribes from the eighth century, and the contemporary loss to the Church of the southern shore of the Mediterranean and large parts of Spain to Islam, that its centre of gravity became more pronouncedly 'European', although this term is clearly anachronistic.

Traditional cults and conversion

One reason for this lack of missionary activity may be found in the lack of any strong central organisation which could take the initiative in it. Power in the Church lay with the bishops in their dioceses and their principal concerns were local. Although Christianity had been the official religion of the late Roman Empire, only a small minority of the total population was recognisably Christian. In the country particularly, the worship of nature was still rife, and the main concern of the authorities was to convert the populace as a whole rather than to spread the faith outside their own immediate areas. This had been the concern of the bishops of the late Roman period, such as St Martin of Tours. In one story of him there was a holy tree near a temple which he had destroyed, and the tree itself was a cult object. Martin allowed himself to be bound in a place where the locals could try to cut down the tree so that it would fall on him, but in fact it fell in the opposite direction, an event which was taken as a miracle. When he destroyed such sites of worship, he replaced them with churches or monasteries, a procedure which was followed by others. One Frankish bishop found in his diocese a lake to which the local rustics made offerings, so he built a church on the shore dedicated to St Hilary, and told his flock not to stain their souls with vain rites, for there was no religion in a lake, but instead to adore the relics of the saint.[8] The monasteries generally seem to have played a prominent part in converting the people, as indeed they had done in the later Roman Empire.[9] But it is still doubtful how successful such measures were in eradicating folk beliefs and practices which were seen as pagan worship. In the countryside this was bound up with seasonal changes, and the indigenous paganism of Gaul was based on fertility rites and the desire for good luck with the weather.[10] Pope Gregory the Great found peasants in Sardinia practising traditional cults, and Gallic and Spanish councils of the sixth and early seventh centuries denounced continuing worship of holy trees and holy springs. As late as 693 the Spanish Visigothic king Egica commanded his bishops to deal with rustics who made offerings to idols, and to have the offerings handed over to the neighbouring church, and measures were taken against worshippers of stones, fountains and trees.[11] In the seventh century two bishops, St Audoen of Rouen and St Eligius of Noyon, were active in preaching in rural areas, in some of which at any rate such pagan traditions were still followed.[12]

Even later, the Lombard laws of King Liutprand (727) and various laws of Charlemagne from the end of the eighth century provided penalties for those who had recourse to springs or trees.[13] Some compromises were seen as necessary – Gregory the Great advised Augustine of Canterbury that pagan temples should be converted to Christian use, and one of his successors, Boniface IV, secured the building in Rome called the Pantheon from the emperor and had it converted into a church.[14] Similar approaches can be traced through into later centuries as Christianity expanded among the pagan peoples of Europe, and attempts were made to adapt traditional imagery to Christian purposes, sometimes by drawing parallels and at others by emphasising contrasts. The account of Christ's baptism in the ninth-century Saxon *Heliand* poem depicts the dove of the Holy Spirit on the Lord's shoulder in the same manner as images of Woden with ravens similarly perched, and in the tenth-century Ragnarok stone in the Isle of Man, Christ is shown as the supplanter of the old gods; on one side Odin is depicted, gripped by the wolf which was destined to destroy him, while on the other there is a figure with a cross and a book trampling on a serpent.[15] In the early eleventh century Archbishop Unwan of Bremen had new churches built in place of sacred groves.[16] Behind this form of missionary activity lay the idea of places which had particularly holy character, a topic which will be considered in the next chapter. Pagan enclaves may have survived even in Western Europe, however, because in the *Life* of the seventh-century saint Rictrude, written in the early tenth century, the Basques were described as pagan, and may still have been so at the time of writing.[17]

Strategies of conversion

The conversion of Europe took place in two ways: the spreading of Christian worship throughout society in areas where the Church had been established in Roman times, and the expansion of Christianity and similar consolidation in areas which had previously been pagan. This outward movement of the Church to lands where it had disappeared or where it had never previously taken root was often closely linked to the political expansion of lay powers. In Scotland the spread of Christianity from Iona after the arrival of St Columba from Ireland in 565 was closely bound up with the increasing power of the Scoto-Irish kings of Dalriada, and the expansion of

Christianity into parts of Germany from the late eighth century was given strong support by Charlemagne's campaigns against the Saxons. The Roman mission to southern England in 597, however, was directed first to Kent, whose king had married a Christian princess from Frankish Gaul, whose presence provided a foothold for the mission, but the initiative seems to have come primarily from Pope Gregory I. While one need not doubt that he was zealous for spreading the faith, his action may have been prompted in part by a desire to increase the prestige of his see by recovering for the Church one of the few areas of the Western Roman Empire which had been lost to Christianity. (His retrospective view to the Roman past is suggested by the fact that in his original plan for an English Church he envisaged it having two provinces based on London and York, the two main centres of Roman Britain, rather than having centres in the chief towns of the small Anglo-Saxon kingdoms.) Once Christianity had taken root in England, it established other contacts with the Continent, but it still preserved close ties with the Roman see, closer indeed than those between Rome and other parts of Europe where the indigenous Church had a continuous existence from Roman times.

The policy pursued by these missionaries was one of conversion from the top downwards, securing the approval of the lay rulers for the new religion, and following it up with mass baptisms. This was in marked contrast to the growth of the Church in the Roman period when acceptance of the faith was an individual rather than a corporate action, and baptism followed a long period of instruction. It is therefore hardly surprising that the missionaries did not succeed in eradicating pagan folk customs and traditional rites, which had to be either incorporated or destroyed. As the pagan world was fundamentally polytheistic, their real problem was not to secure the recognition of the divinity of Christ – a polytheist can easily accept the existence of a god hitherto unknown – but rather to assert the exclusive claims of the new religion, which claimed a monopoly of the truth, and which affirmed that the deities who had previously been worshipped were at best lifeless idols and at worst demons. The English evidence demonstrates this problem clearly. Bede tells how King Redwald of East Anglia set up an altar to Christ in his temple alongside another on which he could sacrifice to the pagan gods.[18] The ship burial at Sutton Hoo in Suffolk contained a large quantity of luxurious grave goods, which would at first sight suggest the burial (or perhaps commemoration, as there is some dispute as to whether the site was a burial or a cenotaph) of a pagan who hoped to carry his possessions into the next world. But among the grave goods were two spoons marked *Saulos* and *Paulos,* an evident Christian motif, celebrating the most dramatic conversion recorded in the New Testament. Unless these spoons were simply booty, it suggests that the area must have been partially Christianised. Such an ambiguity reflects the character of a conversion which may often have been politically inspired.

There were other problems too in the nature of the conversion. The pagan gods were often bound up with tribal traditions and ancestral loyalties; the Frisian king Radbod pulled back from baptism at the last moment, refusing to join a small number in heaven and lose the company of his ancestors.[19] There was a danger after the conversion that the Christian god might be similarly viewed as a tribal god. Subject kings could be compelled to accept the religion of their overlord, as an acknowledgement that the latter possessed supernatural support. When the imposed religion was Christianity, it had to deliver the goods and demonstrate that the Christian god was more powerful than his pagan rivals. (It was not accidental that an outbreak of plague in the late seventh century which carried away many of the leaders of the clergy was followed by widespread relapses into paganism – people doubted the power of the Christian god, who had not protected his followers.) The support given to the Roman mission by Aethelberht of Kent, the most powerful Saxon king of his day, undoubtedly gave it an initial impetus, but when after his death in 616 the Kentish hegemony declined there was a pagan reaction and Christianity was driven out of those sub-kingdoms which recovered their independence. Kent still counted politically, however, and it was the marriage of a Kentish princess to Edwin of Northumbria that brought the Roman mission north at a debated date but possibly in 619, for a short-lived conversion. The defeat and death of Edwin at the hands of the powerful pagan king, Penda of Mercia, in 633 was a setback, but when Penda in turn was defeated by another Northumbrian ruler, Oswald, who had been in exile in the North, the latter appealed to Scotland for missionary support, which was forthcoming. The main thrust of Irish influence on the English Church was transmitted through Scotland to Northumbria, but one should not forget that other Irish monks may have arrived independently in southern England – Malmesbury in Wessex seems to have been an Irish foundation.

The consolidation of Northumbrian Christianity depended largely on the fortunes of war, and by the mid-seventh century the death of Penda marked an opportunity for the Church to consolidate its position throughout northern and central England. At the Synod of Whitby in 664 some differences of practice between the Roman and the Iona traditions were resolved in favour of the former, and from then on the Church in England was basically unified, far before the achievement of any political unity in the country. In this a key role was played by the last great missionary archbishop sent to England by the Papacy, the Greek Theodore of Tarsus, who came to England in 669 and proved a dynamic leader, who called together councils of the whole English Church. There were still some pagan areas in the South – Sussex and the Isle of Wight were slow to be converted, probably because they lay outside the main areas of English political activity.

To what did Christianity owe its success? The experience of England provides a useful model, not least because its early fortunes are well recorded. The most famous of its early historians, Bede, the monk of Jarrow, would have explained it as the will of God and therefore inevitable, but this is a theological rather than a historical explanation. In more mundane terms, it had to offer something more than existing society did to the influential kings who extended their patronage to it. It brought the skills of literacy, which were rapidly exploited by the lay rulers, and cultural associations with a higher level of civilisation and with memories of the Roman past. When Wilfrid converted the pagan South Saxons, he brought to them not only spiritual knowledge, but also skills in fishing.[20] But one should not overlook that the spiritual values of Christianity also had an appeal. Bede's famous story of the council which Edwin of Northumbria held with his great men on the subject of welcoming the mission of Paulinus may be more of a literary topos than a literal account of events, but two episodes in it may reflect the underlying outlook of pre-Christian society. The comparison of the life of man with the flight of a sparrow into a building on a winter night and its later departure into the dark unknown demonstrates vividly that the deepest human concerns of life and death were very real to the speaker, and the action of the pagan priest Coifi who was persuaded by Paulinus's preaching and led the way in profaning the temple which he had formerly served should remind us that men of intelligence can exist in a pre-literate society and that they might be amenable to a reasoned exposition of the new faith.[21] Significantly, about a century later Bishop Daniel of Winchester, writing to the great missionary to Germany, St Boniface, assumed that the heathen there would respond to reasoned argument, and that if he were questioning them about their gods, he should do so calmly rather than offensively, and that once they had compared Christian teachings with their own beliefs they would be converted by the former's superiority.[22]

If the missionaries pursued a strategy of persuasion rather than of confrontation, and tried to take over pagan holy places rather than overthrowing them, their approach may well explain why they did not have to face vigorous resistance. It is significant that one does not find occasions when missionaries in England were martyred specifically for their faith, nor does one see opposition to Christianity as such. In Bede's *Ecclesiastical History* Penda of Mercia is cast in the role of the pagan villain, but his hostility towards Christian Northumbria was more directed against a rival kingdom than against its religion – after all, in his campaigns he was allied with the Welsh Christian king, Cadwallon of Gwynedd. On the other hand, the willingness to compromise with aspects of the past left residual pagan practices in English society. A seventh-century handbook of penance, associated with Archbishop Theodore of Canterbury, and another attributed to Bede, contained provisions against various offences such as the eating of food which had been sacrificed to demons, and the making of incantations or the taking of auguries.[23]

The English Church recognised its origin in the activity of two groups of missionaries, the Irish and the Roman, and this probably prompted its own later zeal in the conversion of the pagan areas on the Continent. The Irish missions began early – St Columbanus, from Leinster, went to the Continent in 590 and secured assistance from various Frankish kings rather than from other ecclesiastical authorities in propagating a predominantly monastic style of religious life. His foundations at Luxeuil in Gaul and Bobbio in Italy were in areas where Christianity was already established – such attempts to consolidate Christianity were often also attempts to curb backsliding – but he also ventured into previously pagan areas in the upper reaches of the Rhine valley. His followers had connections with the Frankish missions which began to penetrate into Westphalia, Franconia and Thuringia, and these certainly prepared the way for the missions of the eighth century. The Irish monk St Kilian was traditionally martyred at Würzburg in 689, and the fact that the cathedral there is dedicated to him suggests that there is some foundation to the story. The cult of Kilian, however, was not instituted until the mid-eighth century, by one of the followers of St Boniface.[24] Although the English mission played a prominent part in the conversion of Germany, considerable areas east of the Rhine had seen some Christian activity before it began. Eustasius, who preached in some of the Frankish lands, including Bavaria, was a follower of Columbanus.[25] What the Irish missionaries, however, failed to do was to consolidate the conversions which they had made into an organised church.

Willibrord and Boniface

The first important English missionary to the Continent was the Northumbrian Willibrord, who had spent a number of years in an Irish monastery before going to Frisia in 690. There had been earlier Anglo-Saxon visitors there – Wilfrid had passed through Frisia *en route* to Rome in 678 and two others, the Hewalds, had been martyred, because the local chieftains saw the threat to their gods as a threat to their people. Willibrord's importance lay in the facts that he both looked to the Papacy for support, an action which probably reflected his English background, and sought material assistance from the powerful family of the Frankish mayors of the palace. He also maintained links with England, where he was sufficiently regarded for his deeds to be recorded by Bede, and for a life of him to be written half a century after his death. His main achievement was the establishment of a see at Utrecht, which provided a springboard for further missionary activity.[26] In some places he and his followers had to face violent opposition, and one of his followers was martyred in Heligoland for violating a pagan shrine.[27]

More important than Willibrord was the Wessex-born missionary Winfrith, later known as Boniface. Willibrord had probably been his inspiration, for his first effort at missionary activity was in Frisia in 716, but this was unsuccessful. In 718, however, he went first to Rome, where Pope Gregory II entrusted him with a mission to investigate the state of Christianity in the German lands and report back on it, just at the time when the Frankish mayor of the palace, Charles Martel, was trying to establish his authority in the Saxon lands.[28] Boniface's later activities were effectively made possible by his co-operation with the lay power. Initially, he joined Willibrord in Frisia, where Frankish protection provided the basis for re-establishing the Church, but later he went south into Hesse, where he achieved further success. This was followed by another visit to Rome, where he was ordained as a bishop in 722, but without any specific see, with a somewhat ill-defined sphere of authority east of the Rhine. The pope reinforced this by requesting Charles Martel to extend his protection to Boniface, and this gave him the opportunity both to make Christian foundations in pagan territory and to organise and reinforce existing Christian communities. He did not shirk from confrontation if this seemed desirable, as when he cut down an oak at Geismar, which was sacred to Woden, and used the wood to build an oratory. In 732 the pope appointed him as an archbishop, and he eventually set up his see at Mainz. (In fact it took time before Mainz was finally recognised as an archbishopric – Boniface's successor there was not granted archiepiscopal status immediately.) From this time he became increasingly involved in organising the German Church, setting up a framework of dioceses in Bavaria and later in central Germany to provide the infrastructure for it, although not all of these survived. Also, and characteristic of his mission, he established a number of monasteries, following the Benedictine rule, to act as centres of spiritual and intellectual activity. The evangelising of the Saxons, however, proved impossible, because the Frankish rulers had not yet sufficient power in the region.[29]

There were many ways in which Boniface seems to have found his work an uphill struggle, and for a man who achieved so much, he at times showed a surprising lack of self-confidence. Missionary work was in many ways a good deal simpler than administration and church reform, for he had problems with churchmen who did not share his ideals, and from whom he wished to keep apart, something which he had promised to do in his oath of obedience to the pope in 722. In 742 he wrote to the pope complaining that Frankish bishoprics had been given into the hands of avaricious laymen and asked for permission to take disciplinary actions against debauched deacons and priests. This last may not reflect as serious a position as might appear, for it could merely be hostile description of married clergy or of Irish and Breton priests who followed their own national customs, drifting from one diocese to another without being subject to any recognised ecclesiastical authority.[30] He attempted to strengthen links with Rome, perhaps because these gave him a measure of psychological support, and in the 740s held a series of synods to uphold discipline in the Frankish Church, with the support of successive mayors of the palace. When in 751 the last of these, Pippin, replaced the last Merovingian king, with papal approval, Boniface may have anointed him.[31] Towards the end of his life he resumed missionary activity in Frisia, where he was killed in 754, probably in an attack by brigands rather than by a consciously heathen reaction. In general he does not seem to have faced militant pagan opposition, for he was only jeered at and was not attacked when he began to cut down a sacred oak, although there may have been some reaction to the new religion, for in a letter of 752 he alluded to the heathen burning down churches. His legacy was a better organised and more dynamic Church in the Frankish lands, which was concerned with spreading the faith into lands on their eastern borders, a closer association with the lay power – in his later years he asked the abbot of St Denis to intervene with Pippin to provide support for his companions, as he feared for the future[32] – and the strengthening of ties with the Papacy.

The ninth and tenth centuries

The expansion of Carolingian political power, notably in Charlemagne's campaigns against the Saxons, provided further scope for the eastward expansion of Christendom. Einhard's *Life of Charlemagne* described the Saxons as devil worshippers who were hostile to Christianity, but noted that after they were defeated in war, they gave up their ancestral religion and accepted Christianity.[33] This description glosses over the ruthlessness of the conversion, which was imposed by the sword of pious warlords, who buttressed their political authority with the supernatural support of religion. Charlemagne's law code of 797 laid down the death penalty for those who refused conversion and for those who had their dead cremated in accordance with pagan rituals. Children had to be presented for baptism within a year of their birth, under penalty of fines.[34] The Christian advance, however, was not unbroken, for Western Europe was threatened in the eighth and ninth centuries by hostile non-Christian powers. The most serious danger was probably the advance of Islam, particularly in the Iberian peninsula, which was attacked in 711, and where the Visigothic kingdom fell before it. The Moslem advance continued into the Frankish kingdom, but was defeated by Charles Martel near Poitiers in 732, after which the frontier of the faiths was established in Spain, where some Christian rulers survived in the north. A further Moslem attack in the Rhone valley was also rebuffed, but intermittent threats continued for a long time. Rome was sacked in the mid-ninth century and in the late tenth century a group of Saracens established a base in the Alps from which they preyed on travellers.[35] In northeast Europe the explosion of Viking attacks did considerable damage to Christian foundations from the late eighth century onwards, and in Central Europe further advances of heathen tribes from Asia led to large-scale devastation in some areas. But neither the Vikings nor the Slav and Magyar attacks posed an alternative to Christianity as such, and they were at least open to conversion in a way that the Moslems were not.

The conversion of the Slavs faced a further complication which had not been found in the Germanic lands, namely the fact that they faced missionary activity not only from the Western Church but also from the Eastern.

Although the two had not yet formally split, there had been tensions between them, with disputes over both missionary methods and spheres of influence. Furthermore, these were exacerbated by the political ambitions of the Frankish and Byzantine emperors. In the second half of the ninth century, there had already been Frankish missionaries in Moravia when Prince Rostislav asked the Byzantine Emperor Michael III (842–67) to send a teacher to explain the Christian faith to his people.[36] The prince may well have been prompted to appeal to Byzantium to try to assert his independence of Frankish power, for the *Annals of Fulda* record frontier warfare between Slavs and Franks around this time.[37] Michael sent a missionary called Constantine, later and better known by his monastic name of Cyril, who translated the Scriptures and the Offices of the Church into Slavonic, an action which provoked opposition from clergy of the Latin tradition, even though Pope Hadrian II (c.867–8) was willing to accept the Slav liturgy.[38] After Cyril's death his brother Methodius returned to Moravia, but this time he held a commission from the pope, which strengthened him in dealing with Frankish opposition, and when he was carried into exile in Swabia for two years, his release was enforced by the imposition of a papal interdict from John VIII (872–82).

The Moravians undoubtedly were opposed to Frankish influence, for they drove out the German priests, but the Roman influence worked in favour of the Franks. When Methodius tried to name one of his Moravian disciples, Gorazd, as a possible successor, Rome refused to accept him, and the diocese was entrusted to a Frankish bishop, Wiching, who expelled the supporters of the Slavonic liturgy.[39] Although the churches of Moravia and Bohemia were drawn into the Western orbit, there was some continuing Greek influence and of Church Slavonic there until the eleventh century, for the earliest *Life* of Wenceslas of Bohemia stated that he learned Latin, Greek and Slavic letters and the Czech Archbishop Adalbert of Prague encouraged the vernacular liturgy.[40] Bohemia indeed had also seen substantial pagan opposition to the missionaries, for although much of the material in the early saints' lives from the country is conventional hagiography, the struggle between paganism and Christianity, even within the royal house, is a recurrent theme. Allegedly Borivoj, the first ruler to be converted (c.874), was driven out in a pagan reaction in which his wife was strangled.[41] The military advance of the Germans created a springboard for missionary activity, and the establishment of an archbishopric at Magdeburg in 968 assisted in the spread of Christianity further east. The association of the new religion with German colonialism led to a Slav revolt after the death of Otto III, which destroyed Christianity east of the Elbe. Adam of Bremen indeed suggested that the avarice of princes hindered the conversion of the people.[42] The conversion was piecemeal, and depended on the activity of individual bishops, and the absence of rigid lines of demarcation between dioceses reflects some of the uncertainty.[43] Poland and Hungary were eventually drawn into the orbit of the Western Church, with the marriage of a sister of

the Emperor Henry II to King Stephen being an important factor in the latter's conversion.[44] Bulgaria and Serbia, however, continued to look to the
East, and even although the patriarch Ignatius of Constantinople had
Roman support against his rival Photius, he was prepared to consecrate an
archbishop and various bishops to establish the Byzantine church in
Bulgaria.[45] The one area where a Slav liturgy survived in a church which
owed obedience to Rome was Croatian Dalmatia.[46] The conversions of the
kings, like those of their English predecessors earlier, were probably
prompted by the realisation that the Church could offer them practical
administrative support to buttress their authority. Nevertheless, even in the
late eleventh century, Adam of Bremen said that some of the Slavs were still
pagans, although he did not specify which.[47]

The Scandinavians proved slow to convert. The first missions, under St
Anskar, were in the first half of the ninth century, but his achievements were
fairly limited, perhaps because the gods of the Viking pantheon were closely
bound up with the military lifestyle of their followers. Churches were established in three trading centres, Birka, Hedeby and Ribe, but these may well
have been founded more to meet the needs of visiting Christian traders than
to provide a springboard for conversion of the locals.[48] It is worth remembering that the Danish invaders of England in the 870s were still heathen,
and the victory of Alfred of Wessex over Guthrum was followed by the latter's enforced baptism. The Danish settlers in England were rapidly converted, but in the mid-tenth century a pagan Norwegian king, Eric
Bloodaxe, was to take control of York. In the Scandinavian homelands, the
advance of Christianity was closely linked with the attitudes of individual
rulers, and their political preoccupations. Adam of Bremen noted varying
attitudes of early kings who 'permitted' their subjects to become Christians,
whether or not they themselves had been baptised. A later king, however,
'ordered' his followers to become Christian.[49] Politics and Christianisation
were inextricably intermingled. Missionary activity in Denmark faced a setback in the early tenth century under the militantly pagan Harthacnut Gorm
but his defeat by the emperor Henry the Fowler gave it an opportunity to
resume. Otto I also actively supported the spread of Christianity, probably
using the claims to authority of the archbishop of Hamburg over the Danish
dioceses as a means of extending his own suzerainty. Certainly when Harald
Bluetooth accepted Christianity it helped to secure his southern frontier
with the Empire.[50]

Native paganism was deeply rooted, however, and the pagan shrine at
Uppsala in Sweden survived until the twelfth century. The king had to reach
a compromise with the pagans that while he himself might accept
Christianity, he would not force his followers to abandon the traditional
gods. (An English missionary, Wolfred, who broke an image of Thor, possibly at Uppsala, was martyred about 1030. A further pair of missionaries,
about a quarter of a century later, who wished to destroy the Uppsala
shrine, were discouraged by a Christian king, because he feared that they

would be killed and he himself driven out, with a full-scale pagan reaction.[51]) The entrenchment of traditional paganism is reflected in the greater number of missionaries who suffered martyrdom in Scandinavia than in, for example, Anglo-Saxon England and in the relapse of alleged converts. Adam of Bremen noted that even nominal Christians still took part in pagan rites at Uppsala, and elsewhere stated that some inhabitants of the Swedish islands had a stubborn devotion to idolatry.[52]

It was not until the eleventh century that one begins to see the effective imposition of Christianity in Norway. The Viking leader Olaf Tryggvason was baptised in England about 995, perhaps as a pledge of good conduct not to return after receiving a large payment of Danegeld. How loyal he was to his new faith is doubtful, but he certainly made some efforts to combat traditional heathenism in the Trondelag and in Halogaland.[53] It was a later Olaf, Olaf Haraldsson, who was more responsible for destroying Norwegian paganism. His methods were direct; he executed the recalcitrant, destroyed the sacred places of the pagan gods and built churches. After his death in 1030 there was no question of Norway reverting to heathenism, and indeed a carefully propagated cult of the dead king as a saint was developed.[54] The fact that the man who succeeded to dominance in the North Sea world, Cnut, was also committed to supporting Christianity meant that in superficial terms at any rate there was no turning back. What the people may actually have believed is another matter, as can be seen in Adam of Bremen's strictures on continuing Scandinavian paganism. These are borne out by a letter of Adam's contemporary, Pope Gregory VII, in 1080, in which he warned the king of Denmark against the continuation of various (but unfortunately unspecified) heathen practices. Other letters of the same pope, however, suggest that Christianity was gaining ground, for he requested kings in both Norway and Sweden to send men to Rome for training in the Christian faith.[55]

The end of European paganism

Gradual though the spread of Christianity was, by the beginning of the twelfth century paganism had been effectively eradicated in the West, and the only remaining heathen area in Europe was Lithuania, sandwiched between the Western Church in Germany and Poland on the one hand and the Eastern Church which had been established in Western Russia. Political factors were as important here as elsewhere in bringing about the eventual conversion, and the Lithuanian princes were willing to accept baptism as a means of obtaining alliances. In the mid-thirteenth century Mindaugas was baptised, and named the Teutonic Order as his heir, although he still followed some pagan customs, and after his death there was a more general relapse into paganism.[56] Another prince, Kenstutis, offered the Emperor Charles IV that he would accept baptism if the Order would return the lands which it had conquered from him and his brothers, but Charles was firmly committed to supporting the Order. Indeed Charles was well aware of the situation in the Eastern Baltic even before his accession to the throne, for he mentioned campaigns against the Lithuanians in his autobiography.[57] Pope Gregory XI tried to persuade the Lithuanians to convert, telling them that their war with the Teutonic Knights would end if they did so, but he was dealing with a people who had long used the prospect of conversion as a diplomatic bargaining counter. Kenstutis's son Witold indeed allowed himself to be baptised five times, alternating between the Catholic and the Orthodox churches as particular political circumstances made desirable.[58] Eventually, in 1385 Prince Jogailo did convert for good when he married Jadwiga of Poland and was crowned king of the two countries, changing his name to Wladyslaw. This conversion marked the end of European paganism, and established the eastern frontier of the Western Church.

Moslems and Jews

The only other area where Christendom had a fluctuating frontier was in the Mediterranean world and in the south-west, where it faced the world of Islam. The Moors were defeated in southern Italy and Sicily in the late eleventh and early twelfth centuries and about the same period the Spanish kingdoms counter-attacked against Islam. The *Reconquista* was slow and uncoordinated, but it was steady, and by the later Middle Ages only the kingdom of Granada in the south remained in Moslem hands. Its history is bound up with the growth of the crusading movement and will be considered later in that context.[59]

Effectively, the advance of Christianity saw it securing a 'closed shop' on European society, because only one minority group in the population, the Jews, remained outside the Church. Their religious distinctiveness had been recognised in pagan Roman times, when they were allowed to follow their own rites, but the part which they had played in the crucifixion may well have meant that they became vulnerable to even greater hostility when Christianity became the official religion of the Empire. Nevertheless, they were generally allowed to survive, although subject to restrictions and discrimination which left them as an inferior group within society as a whole. The early sixth-century Burgundian law code imposed sanctions on Jews who assaulted Christians – those who raised their hands against Christian laity were to lose a hand, although this penalty could be commuted for cash. An assault on a priest, however, incurred the death penalty.[60] There were some periods of persecution in the Dark Ages; the church councils which met at Toledo under the auspices of the Visigothic kings passed substantial numbers of anti-Jewish measures. King Sisebut tried to impose a forced conversion in the early seventh century, although the greatest Spanish churchman of the day, Isidore of Seville, was critical on the grounds that people should be called to faith by reason rather than by force.[61] The Frankish chronicler Fredegar claimed that Sisebut's Merovingian contemporary Dagobert had the Jews of his kingdom baptised, at the request of the Byzantine emperor Heraclius.[62] This story is not confirmed elsewhere, although Heraclius is known to have persecuted the Jews.

The main focus of anti-Jewish measures was directed against proselytising by them. In Visigothic Spain the code of Alaric II in fact left them with considerable religious freedom,[63] but, after the conversion of the Visigoths from Arianism to Catholicism, persecution was intensified. From the seventh century royal legislation, confirmed by church councils, became increasingly savage. Sisebut laid down that a Jew who converted a Christian to Judaism was to be put to death, and if the convert refused to return to the Church, he was to be publicly whipped and reduced to slavery. The fourth Council of Toledo, however, which met at the end of 633, disowned Sisebut's policy of forcible conversion, but it banned Jews from holding public office, as this might give them authority over Christians, and forbade them to own Christian slaves. The pressures were increased in 638, when a formula was published for the abjuration of Jews. Policies varied with individual kings; Chindasuinth took action against Christians who followed Jewish rites, while Reccesuinth not only banned these as such, but even laid down that Jews must marry by Christian rites. Later kings again tried to enforce baptism on Jews, and to deprive them of means of earning a living. It is uncertain how effective these measures were, and the very survival of various Jewish communities suggests that they were not thoroughly implemented, possibly because anti-Semitism was more a matter of royal and ecclesiastical policy than a popular sentiment. Certainly the Spanish kings were more viciously anti-Jewish than their Frankish counterparts, and it was not until the conquest of most of the peninsula by the Moslems that active persecutions ceased.[64] Elsewhere the fortunes of the Jews were to take a turn for the worse after the start of the crusading movement which was to highlight adversely the distinctiveness of religions other than Christianity.

2

Religion and ideas of holiness

Holy places and holy objects

In the last chapter, we saw that one of the problems encountered by church-men who were trying to convert pagans to Christianity was the attachment of the latter to their holy places and that one of the strategies employed to counter this was to take them over for the new faith. This association of the holy with something visible or tangible lies behind many of the develop-ments in the Church, for it was only through such objects that popular beliefs could be focussed on spiritual realities. As old pagan holy places became shrines of saints and martyrs, the ecclesiastical authorities were able to exercise control over them and over the cults which they housed. This could pose problems for conscientious bishops, who might be sceptical of the genuineness of a cult. In one such case, St Martin of Tours had doubts as to whether martyrs were buried at a particular place, although previous bishops had erected an altar there. When he investigated the evidence (which his biographer says he did open-mindedly), and discovered that the body buried had been one of a brigand rather than a saint, he had the altar removed.[1]

It was above all the remains of martyrs which were popularly revered, not least because the doctrine of the Ascension of Christ made it impossible to have direct physical remains of him, although this was to some extent com-pensated by the veneration of alleged fragments from the Holy Cross or from the Crown of Thorns. The association of objects with the places hal-lowed by the saints gave them protection, as can be seen in a story from Orosius, reported by Isidore of Seville, of how during the sack of Rome in 410 the Goths refused to take certain precious vases from the sanctuary of St Peter. Even although they were Arians, they shared respect for the Holy Places.[2] The converse of this was that the saint could take vengeance on those who profaned his holy place; a Flemish chronicler in the ninth century saw the shipwreck of a Saracen fleet in 847 as a judgement for the sacking of St Peter's in the previous year.[3] And if such associated places or objects benefited from the protection of the saint, anything that was an actual physical relic was seen as having even greater power. The relic, indeed, exemplified the power of the saint, which could be demonstrated in miracles of healing, and the shrine was a point of contact between the present world and the divine world. The relic might be the actual corporeal remains of the saint, or something which had come in contact with them. Gregory of Tours describes how relics of St Peter were provided for the faithful:

> If someone wishes to take away a blessed relic, he weighs a little piece of cloth on a pair of scales and lowers it into the tomb: then he keeps vigils, fasts, and earnestly prays that the power of the apostle will assist his piety.

The divine power was seen as possessing a physical manifestation, for Gregory continues:

> If a man's faith is strong, when the piece of cloth is raised from the tomb it will be so soaked with divine power that it will weigh more than it weighed previously.[4]

These strips of cloth, which were called *brandea,* were regularly manufactured and circulated, possibly being inserted into altars.[5] Even where no such conscious creation of secondary relics is recorded, as in Anglo-Saxon England, there are numerous references to their incidental occurrence.[6] Increasingly relics were seen as an essential element of an altar, and in 787 at the second Council of Nicaea, the seventh general council of the Church, it was laid down that in churches consecrated without the relics of martyrs, these should be installed in them, and that a bishop who consecrated a church without them should be deposed for flouting ecclesiastical traditions.[7] In 801 and 813, it was enacted in the Frankish Empire that altars lacking relics should be destroyed. The development of the cult of the Eucharist as the real body and blood of Christ, however, provided an alternative to the remains of saints, and at the Council of Chelsea in 816 it was declared that the deposition of the consecrated host in a newly hallowed altar at its dedication was sufficient to sanctify it.[8] Similarly, the cult of the Virgin Mary could be supported only by secondary relics, but these too were produced, such as a piece of silk, allegedly worn by her at the time of the Nativity, which was given to Chartres by Charles the Bald in 876 and was enclosed in a reliquary about 1000.[9]

It is important to stress that the veneration of relics was something which permeated religious attitudes of the period at all levels, affecting the sophisticated and the simple alike. The acceptance of the possibility of miracles and the immediate intervention of God in human affairs was an essential part of people's mental world. In the ninth century, Paschasius Radbertus, one of the leading scholars of the age, noted the proliferation of miracles in his day, declaring that the relics of saints had never done so many great things since the beginning of the world, for the saints excited each other to song like cocks at cockcrow, and even as late as the twelfth century as sophisticated a scholar as John of Salisbury was anxious to acquire relics.[10] Nor was the miraculous confined to relics, for visions of the saints intervening in support of the faithful were also recorded. The *Royal Frankish Annals* tell how, when pagan Saxons were attacking a church, the defenders and indeed some of the attackers had a vision of two young men on white horses who protected it from attempts to set it on fire.[11]

Rome was undoubtedly the greatest source of martyrs' relics in the Middle Ages and it derived great advantages from the appeal it had as the holy place where many of the early heroes of the Church had suffered death. When, in the late seventh century, St Wilfrid visited Rome, he obtained, 'much to the comfort of the churches of Britain', a large supply of relics, duly labelled with the name of the saint and a precise description of the object.[12] The Saxon missionaries to the Continent in the eighth century, Willibrord and Boniface, both collected relics from Rome to assist them in their missions.[13] In the ninth century St Gerald of Aurillac did the same, and in the tenth Archbishop Adaldag of Bremen, who had visited Rome with the Emperor Otto the Great, collected relics which he distributed among the churches in his diocese.[14]

There was some ambiguity in attitudes to such objects, with a curious blend of naive piety and a measure of critical scepticism. When Queen Emma of England, in the eleventh century, purchased a bone of St Bartholomew from the bishop of Benevento, she insisted on having a letter attesting its authenticity.[15] The queen clearly was concerned that it was genuine, so that it would possess the power appropriate to it, for such objects had definite functions to fulfil, as representing the saints who were the protectors and patrons of the community. She was not the only person who was aware of the possibility of false relics, for Rodulfus Glaber in the same century noted both a concern among church builders that their relics were genuine and that false relics which had been enshrined in a church still attracted a popular cult, and operated miracles of healing.[16] This latter case demonstrates very clearly that popular attachment to relics, rather than their authentication by the Church, was what established a cult. Indeed, the Church itself was not always critical; although Eugenius II gave away the body of St Hilduin in 825, Gregory IV (827–44) solemnly translated another body of the same saint from a catacomb where it had originally been buried to a chapel in St Peter's.[17] Indeed, the popes were quite cavalier in their treatment of saints' bodies. That of St Marcellinus, an earlier pope, was sent to the Frankish lands by either Leo IV or Gregory IV, though the sources disagree as to which pope did so.[18]

The power of sanctity, however, was seen as extending beyond the actual physical remains of the saint to objects with which he or she had come into contact. Bede tells that the dust of the place where St Oswald was killed was put into water and was used to heal the sick, and that the water in which St

Cuthbert's body had been washed had a similar healing power. Alcuin followed Bede, and added that miracles had taken place at the site where Oswald had fallen.[19] Such relics represented the continuing power of the saint, who remained a present force after his or her death. The miracles performed, which demonstrated this, could be both benevolent or malevolent, for one function of the saint was to protect his own. This mixture of posthumous saintly actions features largely in Gregory of Tours' accounts of the actions of his own particular patron saint, Martin of Tours, whose miracles included both the establishment of a peace treaty and the reaching of a settlement between the sons of a queen who had prayed to him, and the death from jaundice of a man who had plundered Tours.[20] Repentance could set aside the saint's anger, for when a tax collector had extorted money from a house dedicated to Martin, he suddenly took ill in the courtyard of the church, but was cured when he called on the saint's name. Gregory was not the only writer to rate Martin very highly – Venantius Fortunatus in his *Life of St Radegund* referred to him in equally laudatory tones as 'the glorious Martin, Christ's senator and confidant'.[21] Martin's shrine remained a popular centre for centuries; in the *Works* of Rodulfus Glaber, the writer described an epidemic in the last decade of the tenth century, and commented that the church of St Martin was one of three which particularly attracted the faithful seeking relief.[22] There is little doubt that the church at Tours made a deliberate attempt to foster the cult, and there is evidence of communities actively encouraging similar devotion sometimes at a time of crisis – for example, the rise of the cult of St Cuthbert at Lindisfarne took place at a time when the episcopal status of the church there was being called in question.[23]

The saints were even seen as having control over their own bodies after death. After the death of St Hypotemius, an attempt was made to move his body from Angers by Frankish monks, but the monks who tried to steal it were unable to do so. By contrast, when the monks of Redon in Brittany tried to take it, their theft was seen as pleasing to God, because the body could then be moved. In the *Life of St Radegund,* it was only after prayer that a finger of the saint was made available to a monastery.[24] They could also ensure that their bodies were revealed, even by miraculous means, as in the case of St Victor in 602, or protect the building in which they were housed, as when the church of St Kilian at Würzburg was struck by lightning but the fire remained in the beams until the saint's body and the church treasures could be rescued.[25]

Martyrs were the saints *par excellence,* but after Christianity became the established religion of the Roman Empire and the persecutions came to an end, the ready supply of martyrs dried up, and only those who served as missionaries in pagan lands ran the risk of dying for their faith. Even there, as was shown in the last chapter, martyrdoms were rare, because polytheistic paganism had a less exclusive outlook than Christianity. In such circumstances, other forms of heroic virtue were recognised as indicating the holiness of an individual, and one sees the growth of an idea of 'spiritual martyrdom' which fell short of physical death. The austerities of hermits and monks cultivated forms of suffering which might be seen as a step on the road to martyrdom. The recognition of certain characteristics as saintly marked an initial stage in the development of a cult, but a good life was not in itself sufficient – supernatural recognition of sanctity required the testimony of posthumous miracles, or evidence that the individual had had divinely inspired visions or possessed prophetic gifts. In his *Life of St Columba,* Adomnan refers to the saint as 'our blessed patron', and later describes him as a 'pilgrim for Christ', but the text is divided into three sections, relating his subject's prophetic revelations, his miracles, and angelic visitations to him.[26] Although this Life is outside the mainstream of European hagiographical writing, it does reflect some of the essential criteria which were used to determine sanctity.

In the High Middle Ages, the right to pronounce on the sanctity or otherwise of an individual passed to the Papacy, but in the first millennium of the Church's history, sanctity was recognised and cults were developed more locally. These were positively encouraged by the churches where the remains of the saint were buried, because the power which emanated from the relics was a means of attracting worshippers and their offerings. More subtly, the saint could serve as a guardian for anyone who extended patronage to the church. The Merovingian king Guntramn built the church of St Marcel at Chalons to house the saint's body, and thereafter was buried there himself.[27] His successor Dagobert I, who died in 638, gave large endowments to the monastery of St Denis, because he desired the saint's 'precious patronage'. The combination of saintly power and royal associations was to characterise the abbey thereafter. Even before the end of the Merovingian dynasty, the Carolingian mayor of the palace, Charles Martel, had himself buried there, perhaps as a tacit and symbolic claim to quasi-royal status, and after Charles's son Pippin was formally anointed as king, he too chose the abbey for his burial.[28]

The cult of relics was not merely a phenomenon of the early period of the medieval Church, nor was it confined to the uneducated. In the twelfth century, Guibert of Nogent laid particular stress on incorporeal relics of Christ, such as fragments from the Cross or the Crown of Thorns, which had been collected by the founder of his abbey – as we saw above, corporeal relics of Christ were impossible because of the doctrine of the Ascension. Later, John of Salisbury, one of the most intellectually sophisticated men of his age, thanked the abbot of Celle for sending him relics of St Aigulf, and later reported a miracle of healing performed on a man by drinking water in which a phial containing a relic of Becket's blood had been washed.[29] When Louis VII of France set out on crusade to the East, he went to St Denis to honour his patron saint, and the pope and the abbot produced the saint's reliquary to be kissed by him.[30] In the following century the French monarchy displayed this form of piety even more conspicuously in Louis IX's building of the Sainte-Chapelle in Paris to house relics of the Passion, which he had obtained in Constantinople.[31] The Church authorities were aware, however, of the dangers which might result from excessive devotion to relics, and the Fourth Lateran Council tried to curb some abuses, forbidding future sales of them and commanding that they should not be displayed outside a reliquary. Newly discovered relics were not to be venerated without papal authority, clearly an attempt to curb enterprising fraudmongers.[32]

Pilgrimages

The cult of relics involved bringing holy objects to particular places to sanctify them, but it was possible for individuals to go themselves to the holy places of the faith in search of spiritual fulfilment. Rome was one such, which attracted pilgrims who wished to die there in an atmosphere of holiness. Bede tells of two kings of Wessex in the seventh century, Caedwalla and Ine, who went to die near the tombs of the apostles, and at a later date the *Lives* of St Wenceslas of Bohemia suggest that he too at the end of his life had wished to renounce the world and go to Rome – one indeed suggested that he wished to receive a monastic habit there.[33] In the eleventh century the Anglo-Danish king Cnut and the Scottish king Macbeth were both recorded as making pilgrimages to Rome, and at a lower social level, a guild at Exeter offered financial support to pilgrims making this journey.[34] Other pilgrims travelled even further, for even after the fall of Palestine to Islam, the emotional appeal of the Holy Land survived in the Western Church. Even those who could not travel there might send funds; in May 984 Gerbert (the future Pope Sylvester II) sought financial help for the church at Jerusalem, and Glaber recorded that Duke Richard II of Normandy sent £100 of gold there. He also told how the church there appealed to Christians throughout the world after the Holy Sepulchre had been destroyed by the Emir of Cairo.[35] The advent of the millennium attracted many pilgrims to the Holy Sepulchre, some of whom had good cause to seek pardon for their sins. Fulk Nerra, the count of Anjou, went to Jerusalem three times, and the chronicler commented that after one of these visits he moderated his customary ferocity. Sweyn Godwinson, who was exiled from England, went to Jerusalem and actually died on the return journey. According to one writer he did so in expiation of the murder of his cousin Beorn.[36] From the early ninth century another major centre of pilgrimage developed at Compostela in north-west Spain, after the discovery of a tomb reputed to be that of St James. Between the mid-tenth and the early twelfth centuries it attracted increasing numbers of pilgrims from beyond the Pyrenees, and became one of the most important international holy places in the West.[37]

Asceticism

When one is trying to identify what were regarded as the essential characteristics of sanctity in the Dark Ages, probably the most common was the asceticism of the saint. The pursuit of this may be seen as a conscious attempt to create a kind of synthetic martyrdom, because the martyr was regarded as the ultimate witness to the faith. Venantius Fortunatus, writing about St Radegund some time after her death in 587, told how she carried a basin full of burning coals, 'so that she might be a martyr though it was not an age of persecution'. Excessive fasting and the wearing of hair shirts were accepted practices for the ultra-pious.[38] The nature of sanctity can be clearly identified from hagiographic literature, which must be distinguished from biography. Above all it depicted the characteristics of holiness which were shared by the saints, a point explicitly emphasised by Gregory of Tours:

> It is better to speak of the 'Life of the Fathers' rather than the 'Lives of the Fathers', the more so since there is a diversity of merits and virtues among them, but the one life of the body sustains them all in this world.[39]

This attitude explains why many of the stories in the *Lives* are identical and transferable from one saint to another; they reflected the shared sanctity of their subjects. Hagiography was a major literary genre, and it has been estimated that over 600 *Lives* survive from the period up to the ninth century.[40] Furthermore, many of the recorded miracles were intended not only for general edification but also for instruction in particular moral virtues. In the *Lives* of St Glodesind, St Burgundofara and St Austerberta, miracles were shown protecting girls who wished to remain celibate when their parents hoped for their marriages. Nor were they concerned only with preserving their own virginity; St Waldetrude, who was married, persuaded her husband to abandon sexual relations and become a monk, and St Sadalberga's husband allowed her to become a nun, and assisted her in establishing a convent.[41]

The origins of this asceticism can be traced to the retreat to the Egyptian desert to pursue a life of prayer and contemplation. This renunciation of the world is not exclusively Christian, and had immediate Jewish precedents in communities such as that which produced the Dead Sea Scrolls. Christian asceticism seems to have originated from various streams of piety, individuals who fled to escape persecution before the recognition of Christianity by Constantine, and others afterwards who sought a more individual religion when this recognition had led to the spread of more formal and perhaps at times more superficial Christianity. Although the background must be sought in the eastern Mediterranean, the practice of withdrawal spread to the West. Works of edification, relating the lives of the Desert Fathers, were being translated from Coptic and Greek into Latin by the late fourth century, and these had a profound influence on the development of spirituality.

The most important of these works was the *Conferences* of the Scythian monk John Cassian, which provided guidance on the life of prayer. In some cases the ascetic was a hermit, but he often attracted followers who formed a community around him, which was influenced by the ideals of community of goods which are recorded in the Acts of the Apostles.

The origins of Western monasticism

In early monasticism, one can see the persistence of contrasting ideals of solitary and communal life. Asceticism and renunciation were common features, but it was always a problem for the would-be solitary that he attracted followers who wished to emulate him. Ascetics could group together, and one of the earliest of such groups in the West was that established at Poitiers by the bishop there, St Hilary, about the middle of the fourth century. While he himself came to be regarded as a saint of importance, he was eclipsed by one of the men who was attracted there, St Martin, who was to be one of the most influential figures on early Christianity in Gaul, both as a bishop and as a monastic founder. Martin deliberately moved his community outside his episcopal city to Marmoutier, a barren place, and pursued a life of strict, although not eccentric, asceticism. Only rough clothing was worn, and all normally abstained from wine. The community, and particularly its senior members, was devoted to prayer, and the only art followed was that of the copyist, presumably in order to furnish the monks with pious literature.[42]

In southern Gaul too monastic houses were being established from the early fifth century, by John Cassian at Marseilles, and by Honoratus at Lérins, off the Riviera coast. At Lérins, Honoratus tried to accommodate a balance between solitary and communal life, providing a central house under an abbot, but also hermitages where those who aspired to a solitary life could withdraw. The different types of religious life were identified and distinguished in the first chapter of the greatest of all the monastic rules, that of St Benedict, which begins by distinguishing four kinds of monks, of which the first two were Cenobites, living in a monastery, and Anchorites, living on their own. Benedict approved of both of these, but condemned the other two groups, the 'Sarabaites', whom he described as following no rule, and the 'Gyrovags', who wandered around, again without a rule.[43] These two latter groups made no significant contribution to later developments, and may therefore be passed over briefly, apart from being noted as an indication that in the formative years of monasticism, the pursuit of holiness (or according to St Benedict pseudo-holiness) took various forms, some of which proved dead ends. Precisely who these were is uncertain, but the distinctions drawn in the Rule demonstrate that early monasticism took many varied forms. Although the Rule of St Benedict ultimately came to be accepted as the norm for ideal monasticism, in the early stages there was far more diversity, with the heads of individual houses taking an eclectic approach to earlier rules when formulating their own. And although the two categories of Cenobites and Anchorites represented a mode of life in which individuals remained in the same place, there were monks of undoubted piety who did travel around. Alcuin tells how Willibrord, as a monk at Ripon, heard that learning was flourishing in Ireland, and went there to study, remaining for twelve years. Willibald's *Life of Boniface* tells how the saint was permitted to move from Exeter to Nursling, which was better equipped for learning, and later how the monks of Nursling provided him with money to leave the house to embark on his missionary activity on the Continent.[44] One even finds men being called back from a monastic life into the world to serve the wider Church. The most notable example of this was Pope Gregory I, who had abandoned the world to become a monk but was called back to it and served as a papal envoy to Byzantium. Even as pope, however, he saw the monastic life as the best way by which an individual could prepare himself for heaven and protested when the Emperor Maurice issued a decree that state officials should not become monks, declaring that this would be unjustifiable in face of an imminent Last Judgement.[45]

Even although austerity was seen as a sign of sanctity, attempts were made by the church authorities to keep this within reasonable limits. Gregory of Tours tells of a Lombard, Vulfolaic, who attempted to live on a pillar in imitation of St Simeon the Stylite of Antioch, but the local bishops, who were key figures in maintaining ecclesiastical order, commanded him to come down, arguing that the climate near Trier was not suited to this form of piety. They later demolished the pillar, so that he should be compelled to live a communal life. Solitaries undoubtedly ran the risk of physical and psychological illness; the hermit Anatolius of Bordeaux, after eight years of taking little food and indulging in perpetual vigils and prayers, took panic and claimed that he was being tortured internally. He was removed to Tours, where his condition improved – Gregory attributed this to the power of St Martin but one may suspect a more moderate lifestyle also helped! – but he relapsed after his return home.[46] Some saints were able to discipline themselves into moderation. Bede relates that Cuthbert abstained from intoxicating drink, but not equally from food, as this might render him less able to work, for he was of robust frame and of unimpaired strength. Even he, however, did desire solitude, retiring to a hermitage on the Farne Islands. This last act was particularly commended by Alcuin in his poem on the bishops, kings and saints of York. Alcuin's own master Aelberht also retired into solitude for the last two years and four months of his life.[47] As Alcuin was more involved in the world than Bede, his idealisation of the eremitical life is all the more striking as a reflection of contemporary spiritual values. This desire for solitude can be echoed elsewhere. Colman of Lindisfarne retired to Inishboffin after the triumph of the Roman party at the Synod of Whitby, and Wilfrid on his deathbed referred to Caelin who had been a leader in observing the rule, but wished to give himself to solitary contemplation.[48] The solitary life was not without its dangers, and while Gregory of Tours esteemed those who withdrew into the 'desert', it was recognised that those who did so might fall into the sin of spiritual pride from which some had to be recalled by disciplinary measures.[49]

In fact the early development of monasticism was somewhat haphazard, depending very largely on the influence of individuals. Sometimes the reputation of a solitary attracted followers, and he then accepted them as monks into a communal life. This could pose problems for the individual concerned in reconciling his own desire for solitude with a sense of responsibility for his disciples; St Patroclus resolved this by remaining at his cell in a deserted area, but constructing a monastery under an abbot five miles away. St Martius on the other hand accepted participation in communal life.[50] Some abbots were stricter than others; Gregory of Tours makes it clear that each had his own particular approach, some attracting followers by their austerity and others by their gentleness. This is well exemplified in the contrast between the austere Lupicinus and his gentler brother Romanus, who established themselves in the Jura, although the followers whom they attracted were not always able to accept the disciplinary measures and restrictions on diet which were imposed.[51]

This dependence of individual houses on the leadership of an individual left them vulnerable to decline. Although a strong and charismatic figure could provide inspiration, there was no guarantee that a successor could emulate him, and after the first flush of enthusiasm had worn off, the rule might be relaxed under a negligent abbot. Attempts might be made to restore discipline. One abbot, Brachio, who had himself founded two monasteries, was called on to re-establish discipline in another house at Menat; although it is not known who took the initiative in this, it may possibly have been the bishop or perhaps even a well-disposed layman.[52] The lay power early recognised that the patronage which they gave to monasteries might be repaid not only in material forms, but also more intangibly in giving their authority spiritual sanction. This is reflected in the history of the abbey of St Denis which was noted earlier.[53] Lay influence might, however, also be deleterious to the pursuit of monastic ideals, as patrons might well exploit the rights granted to monasteries in their own interest. Bede complained to Archbishop Egbert of York in 734 about men who obtained grants from the king on the pretext that they were founding monasteries, but settled down on them themselves as lay abbots, even with families. In the Frankish Empire in the mid-ninth century, the foundation charter of Wildeshausen from Count Waldbert, who became abbot himself, specified that one of his heirs should be *rector et gubernator* of the abbey. It had been a mark of the genuine piety of the Northumbrian founder Benedict Biscop that he had adjured his monks that he was not to be succeeded by a relative.[54]

The Rule of St Benedict

In the course of these centuries, one of the most important developments was the tendency to standardise monastic practices, and within this process the Rule of St Benedict emerged to unique prominence among monastic rules. The origins of the Rule have been vigorously debated since the mid-twentieth century, with suggestions being made that it derived from another and longer document, the Rule of the Master, but the most recent study of the subject has argued very forcibly that it should be restored to its traditional eminence.[55] The most convincing textual arguments for the priority of Benedict's Rule lie in the study of the liturgies prescribed in the two rules and in the methods by which the two writers dated the equinox, but there would also seem to be an inherent probability that the shorter rule would be the earlier one – one can think of few cases in history where any regulations are abbreviated rather than expanded when being revised! Irrespective of the dates of the two rules, however, it was Benedict's rather than the Master's which was to influence later monastic life. The existence of both of them, however, and the survival of many others associated with particular founders and their houses, reflects the wide range of monastic practices in the sixth and early seventh centuries, and the fact that individual abbots formulated the customs for their own establishments, and derived these eclectically from other houses. As yet, there was no such thing as a monastic order – each house was an autonomous entity.

Benedict himself lived in the late fifth and early sixth centuries, and the little that is known of his life comes from the *Dialogues* of Pope Gregory I, who commented on the discretion of his rule and the lucidity of its language, characteristics which certainly are shown in the Rule attributed to him. He had begun his career as a hermit, and acquired a reputation for holiness. Although he was invited to become the abbot of a monastery near Subiaco, he fell out with the monks, and left them after they had tried to poison him. In the ensuing years he founded a number of small houses, and eventually established the monastery with which his name became inextricably linked, that of Monte Cassino, where he lived for the rest of his life. Had it not been for his written legacy of the Rule, he would simply have been one of a number of holy abbots, and would have made little long-term impact on the history of monasticism. But his ordinances for his own community made him one of the most influential figures in the whole history of the medieval Church, for there can be no debate about the eventual dominance of the Rule of St Benedict in later monastic customs.

Its appeal lay in its unique combination of spiritual wisdom and practical common sense, which could provide guidance at all levels of the spiritual life. Its brevity also gave its regulations a greater element of flexibility, because it could easily be modified to meet changing circumstances. It was designed originally for the needs of an independent house, under the rule of the abbot, who was advised to vary his approach to his monks according to the character of each individual, using persuasion or rebuke as seemed most appropriate in each individual case. Authority remained with the abbot, but the Rule reminded him that he in turn would be answerable to God. Central to the observance of the monastery was the obligation of saying the offices, and the details of these were clearly laid out, with penalties being laid down for those who arrived late. The Rule made provision for the children of the monastery, some of whom might have been offered by their parents when they were still under age, for the sick and for the aged; the dietary regulations, essentially vegetarian, could be modified 'with loving consideration' for those who were physically unable to cope with the full strictness of the Rule. At its most demanding the Rule was austere, but it never ran to extremes, for Benedict's fundamental approach to legislating for his house was pragmatic and practical. Although initially it was only one rule among many, its proven excellence eventually led to it being adopted far more widely.

It took time before this occurred. Initially, it was used along with other materials by various monastic legislators when they drafted ordinances for their houses, and the seventh century was an age in which there were many *regulae mixtae* or mixed rules. In England, Wilfrid organised his monastery at Ripon on Benedictine lines, but although the Northumbrian monastic founder Biscop was sufficiently devoted to the saint to assume his name, his houses at Jarrow and Wearmouth followed an eclectic rule – on his deathbed he claimed to have derived the ordinances for them from no fewer than seventeen monasteries.[56] England, however, did play a prominent part in furthering the spread of the Rule of St Benedict as the ideal form of monastic observance, because the Anglo-Saxon missionaries to the Continent, Willibrord and Boniface, favoured it, although it was not in any way seen as a sacrosanct document. The *Life of St Sturm* stated that Boniface had approved the Rule of St Benedict at Fulda, but told how Sturm and other monks had gone to Rome to investigate the customs of various houses, and the *Life of St Leoba* added that this journey had also taken in the monastery of Monte Cassino.[57]

It was only the changing political circumstances of the late eighth and early ninth centuries which created conditions propitious for the Rule to be more widely adopted. The English missionaries to the Continent had greatly benefited from the patronage of the rising power of the Carolingian family, which by 800 under Charlemagne had brought much of Western Europe under its control. Although within half a century tensions within the imperial family were to lead to renewed political fragmentation, within this period attempts were made to consolidate monastic life on a Benedictine pattern. This was not always successful. Even in the ancient house of St Martin at Tours there were periods when the inmates were secular canons rather than monks, and although a modified Benedictine rule was restored under Alcuin (796–812), the house was again one of canons by 816.[58]

But changes were on the way. A monk Witiza, who in his early days had attempted to pursue a more rigorous lifestyle according to the rules of Basil and of Pachomius, decided to adopt the Rule, as well as the name, of Benedict when he founded a new monastery at Aniane under Charlemagne's protection. From then onwards, he was a vigorous advocate of the Rule. Charlemagne's son, Louis the Pious, called him to court and gave him authority over the monasteries of Francia between the Loire and the Meuse, to impose reform on the Benedictine model. Two synods at Aachen, in 816 and 817, issued decrees which were incorporated into an imperial edict, and imperial authority was employed to secure their enforcement.[59] But although the monastic traditions of the Frankish lands looked back to Monte Cassino – Paschasius Radbertus in his *Life of St Adalard* described it as the place where the fount and origin of all religion was supposed to be, and in his *Life of Wala* praised the 'most holy rule' as the pattern for monastic government[60] – the Rule could not be regarded as the sole form of monastic life. The very fact that central authority was imposing it meant that it was being adapted from its original intention of providing a pattern of life for an autonomous house under the jurisdiction of its own abbot. More significantly, there were modifications to the Rule itself, particularly in the development of the monastic liturgy, for although this had always been central to observance, it had been balanced by other obligations of manual work and study. Manual work now became the task of employed servants, although study survived as another aspect of monastic life.

Political disorder, decay and monastic reform

For monasticism to flourish, however, stable political conditions were necessary, and these were not present in the second half of the ninth century. Western Christendom was exposed to the violence of the Vikings in the North and the Saracens in the South, and abbeys which lay in the path of the invaders were both desirable targets because of their wealth and easy victims because they were not defended. The British Isles, Gaul and Italy were particularly vulnerable to attacks from the sea, for although Central Europe was under assault from the Magyars, the damage which they inflicted was less drastic. Some houses were destroyed, and others migrated, often carrying their relics with them, such as the monks of Lindisfarne who fled with the body of St Cuthbert and remained peripatetic for several years before settling at Chester-le-Street. In Italy the Saracens sacked Monte Cassino in 883. In many cases, regular observance disappeared, and much church property was seized by lay magnates. It is perhaps noteworthy that when Asser described how Alfred of Wessex granted him the monasteries of Banwell and Congresbury in the late ninth century he wrote more in terms of a transfer of property than in language which suggested a grant of spiritual powers.[61] Alfred did, however, make some attempts to restore observance in England, founding a house of monks at Athelney with the scholar

John the Old Saxon as abbot, and one of nuns at Shaftesbury with his own daughter as abbess.[62] It was not, however, to be until the following century that the English monasteries were to make a recovery, and that took place under the influence of new developments on the Continent.

In an age of disorder, monasteries required the support of an influential lay patron, and it was such patronage that marked a new beginning in the early tenth century. Brutal though many of the laity were, they were not always immune from feelings of guilt for their violent actions, and support for monasticism (still clearly esteemed as a pious ideal) was one way in which they might hope to atone for their evil deeds. Duke William I of Aquitaine in 909 established a monastery at Cluny in Burgundy, perhaps as penance for a murder which he had committed. (The fact that he had no direct heir may have made it easier for him to grant the necessary territorial endowment.) His endowment charter expressed the hope that although he himself could not despise all the things of the world, he might receive the reward of the just by supporting those who did. There were two marked characteristics of the foundation: the duke restored to the monks of Cluny the right to elect their own abbot, and he placed the foundation under the protection of the apostles Peter and Paul. (Although in practical terms this involved legal subordination to the Papacy and the making of certain payments to Rome, the founder's motive was almost certainly to secure spiritual patronage from the saints rather than temporal support, as the popes of the period were more concerned with Roman dynastic politics than with the condition of the Western Church as a whole.)

In a sense the later eminence of Cluny was fortuitous, and depended on the men who were chosen to rule it. In the early tenth century it was simply one of a number of reformed monasteries, but its fame developed under a series of very distinguished abbots, notably Odo (926–42), whose fervour attracted esteem and admiration, and the long-lived Odilo and Hugh, who between them spanned the entire eleventh century (994–1109), and who when asked to participate in the reform of other houses pursued a policy of making them dependent on the monastery of Cluny.[63] The fame of Odo's sanctity had attracted pious men, both clerical and lay, into the community,[64] but he did not necessarily impose the customs of Cluny on houses under his influence. The great Benedictine house of Fleury was reformed by Odo, but preserved many of its own traditions.[65] Odo's achievements might well have come to nothing, however, if it had not been for the chance continuation of saintly and charismatic leadership in later generations. Fulbert of Chartres referred to Odilo as a 'holy archangel of monks' and wrote to him as his 'inexpressibly dear father and lord'. This spiritual appeal was reflected in the case of an anonymous bishop who renounced his office to enter the house, raising the problem, which had to be referred to the pope, of whether he should still have power to conduct ordinations.[66] But goodness as such was not enough to consolidate reform – it was reinforced by the tendency to impose the authority of Cluny on the houses which it had reformed. This led to the appearance of something which can be described as approaching a religious order, which was very different administratively and organisationally from the earlier self-contained abbeys which had nothing in common but the Rule.

Cluny had not been unique in the early tenth century. In Flanders a similar reform can be seen at Brogne, which extended its influence in the Low Countries, and in Lorraine the house of Gorze also became head of a federation of reformed abbeys, which was to extend its influence into the German Empire.[67] In all these cases lay support strengthened the hands of the reformers, and the same was true of tenth-century England, where the kings of the house of Wessex gave their support to prelates such as Dunstan of Canterbury and Aethelwold of Winchester. This reform was closely linked with Carolingian Gaul: Aethelwold sent a monk to Fleury to learn the Rule of St Benedict, so that he could teach it to his brethren at home, and it is worth noting that tenth-century English texts of the Rule derive almost exclusively from this tradition. Gallican influences can also be traced in a major liturgical text of the reform, *The Benedictional of St Aethelwold,* although this also drew on Gregorian and perhaps some native English material.[68] Similar eclecticism can be seen in the customs which were drawn together in the most important document produced by the English reform movement, the *Regularis Concordia,* or Agreement on the Rule. While it notes that some customs were borrowed from houses at Fleury and Ghent, and attention was paid to a decree of the Council of Aachen of 817, it also expressed a wish to preserve the 'goodly religious customs of this land'. It also in its liturgy for the night of the Resurrection borrowed a service from Gorze, probably through the intermediate influence of Ghent.[69]

The most marked characteristic of the English reform was the support which it received from the lay power. Wulfstan of Winchester noted the benefactions made by Eadred to the Old Minster at Winchester and to the monastery at Abingdon, and later stresses the friendship which existed between Edgar and Bishop Aethelwold. And although there was something of an anti-monastic reaction immediately after Edgar's death, the young king Aethelred II attended the dedication of the Old Minster at Winchester after its rebuilding, along with all the leading men of the kingdom.[70] The close ties between the royal house and the reformers are clearly seen also in the text of the *Regularis Concordia,* which declared that royal power should be besought to safeguard holy places and increase the goods of the Church, and where special prayers were stipulated for the king and queen.[71]

The traditions of tenth-century monasticism, particularly as they were developed at Cluny, laid far greater stress on the corporate worship of the community, which became increasingly elaborate, than the earlier traditions of the Rule of St Benedict. In the course of this the earlier traditions of manual work were increasingly squeezed out of the daily life of the houses, but this was not new. Later there was to be a reaction against this, and a desire to restore the older balance,[72] but in its early days it set a pattern of worship which spread widely, as other houses came under Cluniac influence. The extent of this influence, however, has been debated. Undoubtedly monks from Cluny were called in to assist in monastic reform in other houses, and some of these were absorbed under its rule, having only a prior as the immediate ruler and the monks there professing obedience not to an abbot of their own but to the abbot of Cluny. But in other cases, as already noted, the role of Cluny was more restricted, and the extent of its achievement must not be exaggerated. Sometimes reform attempts had little success. Abbot Mayeul of Cluny was called upon to intervene at Fleury in 986, when a man secured possession of the abbey with the support of the lay nobility, though against the wishes of most of the monks, but the case was not resolved until after the death of the intruder and the election of a successor acceptable to both parties. Mayeul's approach was less radical than some other monks desired, for although he condemned the offender, he did not excommunicate him, but other abbots of the diocese of Rheims did so.[73]

Such episodes demonstrate the vulnerability of the monks to the pressures of the lay nobility. This is hardly surprising, not least because founders of houses expected special privileges, which could be transmitted to their descendants. But reformers might try to break such ties gradually. Two letters of Pope Sylvester II recognised the rights of magnates to exercise the right of 'advocate' of a monastic house for life, but stipulated that the monks were to have the right to elect a new abbot when the present one died. But the pope himself moved carefully, and sometimes had to leave an element of authority in the hands of the king, as at Lorsch, although at Arezzo he was able to claim full control, including even the responsibility for the consecration of the abbot.[74] In this period, the lay power played an ambivalent role in dealings with monks. Support for them could be a means of acquiring spiritual merit, and patrons could hope to be remembered in the prayers of the community, but they also could use monastic goodwill as a method by which they could enhance their own position, and at times could impose an abbot on a house against the wishes of the monks. Around 1004 Fulbert of Chartres lamented that the local count had done this, and that his opponents among the monks had had to flee the house of Saint-Père.[75]

In the first half of the eleventh century some laity continued to support monastic reform. Orderic Vitalis stressed the role of the Dukes of Normandy as patrons on their own account, who both restored existing monasteries and founded new ones, and as an inspiration to the piety of their nobles. He was perhaps exaggerating with the charity of hindsight when he wrote that magnates would have thought themselves beneath contempt if they had not supported clerks and monks on their estates,[76] but it is worth remembering that by the time he was writing the spokesmen of the Gregorian reform movement were liable to consider the laity more as enemies than as friends of the Church. The evidence of foundations bears out some of Orderic's praise. Duke Richard II brought William of St-Bénigne to

Fécamp around 1001, and the reform which he implemented there spread throughout Normandy. He was an active reformer on the fringes of the Cluniac movement, having been attracted by the reputation of the then abbot there, St Mayeul, although he never became a Cluniac monk himself. The Norman house of St Évroul also looked to Cluny for guidance, and received it, but it too remained an independent house.[77]

The fortunes of this house exemplify some of the problems of monasticism in this period, and the competing pressures to which interested parties might subject it. Robert of Grandmesnil had served as a squire and a knight to William of Normandy before entering the house, which had been founded by his family. His rapid promotion to the post of prior probably reflects family interests, although if Orderic is correct he put pressure on his relations to safeguard their souls through charity. When he fell out with Abbot Thierry, the duke had to intervene and order the archbishop of Rouen to settle the dispute, and one suspects that if Robert had been from a less influential family, such a problem could have been resolved more easily. When he himself succeeded to the abbacy, he was driven out during a period of unrest, and appealed to Rome, from where he returned with letters ordering his restoration and accompanied by a papal legate, an action which roused the duke to a violent rage. While the duke declared that he would receive legates who were dealing with matters connected with the Christian faith, 'if any monk from his duchy dared to bring a plea against him, he would ignore his cloth and hang him by his cowl from the top of the highest oak-tree in the wood nearby'.[78]

In such circumstances, the duke held the whip-hand, and Robert had to take refuge in the abbey of St Denis, from which he launched an anathema against the duke's candidate, Osbern, before returning to Rome to appeal to the new pope, Alexander II. The latter evidently felt that it would be pointless to try to secure Robert's return, but instead gave him the use of a church in Rome. Later, the Norman ruler of Calabria, Robert Guiscard, gave him a church and endowments to build another monastery, where he appears to have established himself. It is significant of the competing claims to authority that when Osbern appealed to the pope for absolution, he pleaded that he had accepted the abbacy in good faith, and was torn between the two sides. Absolution was granted, and Robert accepted it, effectively renouncing his own claims. A postscript to the story, however, reflects the continuing importance of family influence – a nephew succeeded him in the Calabrian monastery.[79]

There can be no doubt that the interests of monasticism could be furthered by a powerful and benevolent lay patron. After his conquest of England, William of Normandy called on a monk, Lanfranc, to take charge of the see of Canterbury, in a period when attitudes to lay influence on the Church were undergoing a drastic change. Lanfranc was fundamentally a man of the old order, who accepted this relationship of dependence on the king, but he was one of the last of his kind. This was not due simply to the emergence of reform movements which looked to the Papacy, but also to changes in monasticism itself, where the traditions of learning and worship which had dominated it for some two centuries were being challenged by a return to more austere forms of piety. These in turn represented a style of Church reform which differed from the political and legal claims put forward by the popes, and were less concerned with the position of the Church in the world than with the inculcation of personal devotion and a search for spiritual fulfilment. For the future, ecclesiastical idealism was to be channelled along parallel tracks of hierarchical authority and pious aspirations.

Earlier monasticism had done much to set the agenda for both of these. The moral ideals of monastic life, poverty, obedience and chastity, had lain behind much ecclesiastical reform between the sixth and the eleventh centuries. Monks had played an active part in the conversion of pagan lands, and their houses had been leading focal points of religious and intellectual life. Celibacy had been developed as an ideal for the secular clergy from the time of the late Roman Empire, but the practice was more honoured in the breach than in the observance. The influence of the monastic life, however, kept it before men's eyes, although in fact it would take long to be achieved as the norm. Monks were seen as the most powerful intercessors with God by men who wished to endow ecclesiastical institutions for the good of their souls, and men with a monastic background were called to many high offices in the Church, including the Papacy itself, and were to contribute to the growth of the reform movement. But although monks from Cluny were prominent in this, the reforms were based on much wider foundations than a single great house. In some ways the monasteries might be less than totally sympathetic to a pope-centred reform, because they often possessed close ties with their founders' kindred, who were still seen as their patrons. Their estates too left them liable to criticism, particularly as the newer, more austere orders emerged. This, however, was still in the future, as the Church moved into the latter years of the eleventh century.

|3|

The rise of the Papacy

Rome, Byzantium and the West

Because of the prominent role played by the Papacy in the activity of the
Western Church in the central Middle Ages, there is a danger of thinking that
this had always been the case and letting it dominate the history of the
Church as a whole. Although the popes developed an ideology for their primacy, there was a wide gap between this and their actual power.[1] It took
time, however, before such claims were translated into reality, and not until
the ecclesiastical revolution of the eleventh century can one see the Papacy
effectively assuming the position which it retained until the Reformation.
During early centuries some individual popes did play a significant part in
the wider life of the Church, but this was due to their own characters rather
than to any institutional power, and at other times their influence was far
more circumscribed. The term 'Holy Roman Church' (*sancta Romana ecclesia*), which recurs regularly in writings about authority in the Church
throughout the Middle Ages, was used with a number of different connotations in varying circumstances and at different periods. It might mean quite
literally the Church and clergy in Rome, the authority of the pope as bishop
of Rome, the collective authority of the pope and the cardinals, the bureaucracy of the Western Church headed by the pope, or even the Western
Church as a whole. Furthermore the pope himself had a number of different
roles, which again varied with the passage of time. First and foremost he was
bishop of Rome, with spiritual authority there, but in the absence of any
other focal point for government, he found himself also undertaking various
secular tasks. Later, as the Papacy acquired lands in Italy he developed also
into an Italian territorial prince, with the same problems as his lay neighbours. From early times he was seen as a prelate of higher status than other
bishops in the West, but this moral authority was increasingly enshrined in
administrative structures, and the pope became the fountain of justice in
ecclesiastical cases and the source of spiritual graces to the faithful.

Its greatest strength in the early medieval centuries was that the pope was regarded as the successor of St Peter. Even before the end of the Roman Empire in the West, Rome had emerged as its greatest ecclesiastical centre. The term 'Apostolic See' (*sedes apostolica*) appears in the late fourth century, and in 422 Boniface I claimed primacy in the Church. Later Leo I claimed that this authority derived from Christ's commission to St Peter.[2] As the Church had developed, five centres had stood out as pre-eminent, Jerusalem, Antioch, Alexandria, Constantinople and Rome, but the first four of these all lay within the Eastern Empire. These five churches, the 'Pentarchy', remained important until the seventh century, when the rise of Islam destroyed the first three as effective centres, leaving Rome and Constantinople in possession of the field, but also ultimately contending for dominance. As was shown in the previous chapter, holiness was closely bound up with tangible remains and sanctified places, and Rome was the holiest city in the West, where many early martyrs had died, including two of the greatest, Peter and Paul. From there too, relics could be obtained to sanctify altars throughout Christendom. The Irish missionary monk Columbanus declared in 613 that the glory of Rome depended on the relics of Peter and Paul, and declared that Rome was head of the churches of the world, apart from the special privilege of the Lord's Resurrection. The pope's power flowed from St Peter, although in doctrinal matters he must be guided by the general consensus of the Church.[3] This emotional appeal of Rome persisted, and in the ninth century Gerald of Aurillac was said to have made a point of visiting Rome every second year, to gaze spiritually on the two lights of the world, SS Peter and Paul.[4] The respect given to Peter is reflected in the prominence accorded to him in the Old Saxon *Heliand* epic of the same century.[5] The popes themselves may have stressed their loyalty to him – the official papal history, the *Liber Pontificalis*, notes that Leo IV's gifts to the saint's church reflected his veneration.[6] The association of the Papacy with Peter was generally accepted, and Bishop Claudius of Turin, who in the early ninth century claimed that the saint's authority was personal and ceased with his death, was an isolated dissident.[7]

But as the spiritual power of the Papacy grew, its political and material influence was also developing. By the time that the last Western emperor was deposed in 476, Italy had become a battleground between the survivors of the old order and barbarian invaders, and after that date one can see attempts by the Byzantine rulers to recover power in the West and particularly in Italy. In this period the Papacy inherited an intangible aura from the memory of the Roman Empire, and represented a strong element of continuity from imperial times. In the first century after 476 well over half the popes of the period came from either Rome itself or its near hinterland. A substantial number were drawn from influential families in the city – indeed, one such produced at least three popes in a century and a quarter, Felix III (483–92), Agapitus I (535–6) and Gregory I (590–604) – and there is little doubt that this contributed to their authority. Even those who were not pure

Romans might well be Roman-born. This was true of Gelasius I (492–6), who was of African descent, Boniface II (530–2), of Germanic origin, and Pelagius II (579–90), who was of Gothic stock. The most dynamic of these early popes was Gregory I, who not only was responsible for sending a mission to England, but who also took an interest in the politics of the Frankish kingdoms, and wrote in 595 commending the political influence of Queen Brunhild.[8] He was also a spiritual writer of distinction, who was still remembered some two generations after his death as a saintly man and an eloquent teacher.[9]

The early fortunes of the Papacy were closely bound up with the changing political scene in Italy. It still preserved ties with the continuing Empire in Byzantium, which laid theoretical claim to power in the West and sometimes indeed was able to translate theory into practice in parts of Italy, even to the extent of influencing papal elections. The imperial restoration in Italy under Justinian was short-lived, when the Lombard invasion drastically curtailed the Byzantine lands in Italy from the 560s. Only in Ravenna was Byzantine power securely based, and attempts were made in the late seventh and early eighth centuries to make the see there independent of Rome, although ultimately these were abandoned. Long before this, however, relations between the Papacy and the emperor were uneasy, alternating between friendliness and hostility. The last imperial visit to Rome took place in 663, and according to the *Liber Pontificalis,* this saw the removal of many precious goods from the city.[10] Equally, a number of popes visited Constantinople and were honourably received there.[11] Intellectually too the Papacy was closely linked with the Byzantine world, and after the end of the Western Empire was still drawn into the theological disputes which divided churchmen in the East. In the years immediately after 476 the most important disputes were over Monophysitism, and in the seventh century the crucial issue was that of Monotheletism, the doctrine that Christ had two natures (as defined by the Council of Chalcedon) but only one will. On the whole the popes of the period opposed this doctrine, although one, Honorius I (625–38) gave some support to it, and was later anathematised by the third Council of Constantinople in 680–1. In much of the West these theological issues were of little concern, and did not affect the relationship between the Papacy and the other churches there. It was not until the Iconoclast controversy in the eighth century that a matter of ecclesiastical practice drew the other churches of the West into disputes between the popes and the Eastern Church.

These were the churches which ultimately came under papal administrative authority, but the rise of a Rome-centred government was gradual and influenced by demands from the localities. Indeed, it may well have been dissident clergy, who had fallen foul of their fellows in their own countries, who laid the foundation of a more centralised papal power by appealing to Rome. Gregory of Tours tells of how his predecessor Bricius was driven out from his see and returned with papal permission, although it must be stressed that there is no evidence of papal authority being employed to enforce his return. Appeals were also made by two men who had been suspended by a local episcopal council.[12] Such approaches to the Papacy from Gaul, where there had been continuous and indigenous Christianity from the time of the Roman Empire, are a more striking indication of the respect in which it was held than those from lands such as Anglo-Saxon England, which was more closely linked with Rome through the mission sent by Pope Gregory I to Kent. Undoubtedly direct papal activity in England enhanced its authority there, and the German lands which were brought Christianity by missionaries from England inherited this tradition. In England itself, however, loyalty was formally directed more to St Peter than to the pope during the debates of the Synod of Whitby, although in practice this strengthened papal influence. The agreement at this meeting that St Peter was the supreme saint in heaven seems to have been crucial in swinging King Oswy's support behind the Roman party, and this had administrative repercussions soon after when the pope sent Theodore of Tarsus to England as archbishop of Canterbury. (Incidentally, it demonstrates both the continuing connections of the Papacy with the Byzantine world that he chose a man from the eastern Mediterranean as archbishop, and the suspicion in which it was held that he sent a Westerner, the African abbot Hadrian, with him.) Shortly afterwards Wilfrid, who had been the principal advocate for Roman customs at Whitby, was to appeal to Rome for support when he was driven from his see. It is hardly surprising that his biographer, Eddius, emphasised the power of Roman jurisdiction, and that his opponents were less well disposed to it.

Adherence to Roman customs, however, extended beyond those regions which were bound to the Papacy through its missionary activity. On one practical question which saw divisions within the Western Church, that of determining the date of Easter, one can see diversity of opinion within Ireland, which is often erroneously seen as lying outside the sphere of Roman influence. In fact the southern part of the island adopted the Roman Easter as early as the 630s, while the north, along with the Scottish lands and Northumbria, did not. Only after the Synod of Whitby did Northumbria come into line, followed at a later date by the Church at Iona and in the north. It is by no means clear how far disputed issues were referred from Ireland to Rome in practice, although from an early date it seems to have been the principle that they should be. If outlying churches followed different customs from those employed in Rome, this was more probably due to difficulties of communication than to any desire for autonomy. Indeed, a lack of awareness of what exactly was happening in Italy may have enabled them to maintain a loyalty focussed on St Peter at times when the bishopric of Rome was torn by political tensions. The physical presence of the saint's relics in Rome was critical in attracting devotion there, and it would be almost literally true to say that they were responsible for saving his see from the harm which his successors' actions might inflict on it.

Throughout Christendom, the local diocese was the basis of ecclesiastical organisation, and in many cases it was ruled over by a local man. The background of those men who occupied the see of Rome suggests that for long periods the same rule applied there, and some struggles which led to the election of antipopes reflect attempts by powerful local families to gain control of it. It was a tempting prize for the ambitious, because the Papacy had gradually acquired widespread landed estates, principally in southern Italy, which gave it considerable wealth. This could be used for the benefit of the local community: Gelasius I at the end of the fifth century and Gregory I at the end of the sixth were able to supply the city of Rome in times of famine.[13] Furthermore, with the decline of imperial administration, authority in secular matters passed to the bishop. How effectively this was exercised depended on various factors: the ability of the individual pope, the extent of pressure which he faced from Byzantium (in turn affected by the emperors' other interests) and the level of the threat from the Lombards. The pope could serve as a focus of local loyalty – when the emperor tried to arrest Sergius I (687–701) and take him as a prisoner to Constantinople, local military forces in Rome and Ravenna joined together against the imperial agent, who saved himself by taking refuge under the pope's bed.[14]

The Frankish connection

But the Papacy was always vulnerable to political dangers in Italy, and in the mid-eighth century the Byzantine emperors themselves were too preoccupied by other threats on their Anatolian frontier to devote time to Italy. At the same time, the popes were at odds with Byzantium over the question of reverence due to images, although in fact this did not prevent them from seeking military assistance against the continuing threat from the Lombards, as when Stephen II appealed, though without success, to the emperor against the threat from King Aistulf.[15] By this date the Papacy already had ties with Frankish Gaul, and missionaries spreading Christianity into Germany had looked to it for support. In 739 Gregory III told Boniface to continue teaching the 'holy, Catholic and apostolic traditions of the see of Rome' – the echo of the Nicene Creed was clearly deliberate – and named him as a papal representative vested with apostolic authority to a council being held on the banks of the Danube. It is therefore hardly surprising that the Papacy's search for a new ally led it north of the Alps. Gregory III had established contact with Charles Martel in 739 and 740, and when the Carolingian family finally superseded the Merovingians, it was the Papacy which formally authorised Pippin's succession as king in 751. This in turn was followed in 754 by Stephen II visiting Gaul, and obtaining support from his protégé against the Lombards.[16] The balance between theoretical and practical power was always delicate, for while the Papacy needed the military assistance which the Franks could provide to defend their position in Italy, the latter clearly recognised the moral superiority which the pope could exercise as the successor of St Peter. What was never clearly resolved, and was to remain a problem for centuries, was the extent to which the lay rulers were entitled to intervene in papal affairs. While both sides could derive reciprocal benefits from co-operation, the nature of these could never be precisely spelled out.

This alliance created a new political axis for the Papacy, and also had a profound effect on the affairs of the Italian peninsula. The principal losers were the Lombards, whose power was greatly diminished, and the Byzantine emperor, whose former lands in Italy passed to the Roman see when Pippin refused to return Ravenna and its adjacent lands to him.[17] The Papacy made a conscious effort to validate its take-over of the old imperial lands, and this probably was the context for the compilation of the so-called *Donation of Constantine,* perhaps the most famous forgery of the entire Middle Ages (a period of history in which the faking of documents was probably never surpassed). This purported to be a grant from the Emperor Constantine to Sylvester I of authority over 'the city of Rome and all provinces of Italy and the western regions'. The lands as originally defined embraced those which Pippin was said to have granted to Stephen II in 756, although at a later date papal propagandists interpreted the document as meaning rule over the entire West, and as such it lay at the heart of much political polemic for some seven hundred years, until its authenticity was demolished by the humanist scholar Lorenzo Valla.[18] The original purpose of the forgery is not clear, and there is no evidence that the pope used it to justify his title to Italian territorial power to the Franks, but it probably was employed to validate the new authority which he had taken over from the emperor.

The connections established between the Papacy and the Frankish royal house laid the foundation for a close tie between the pope and the emperor when Charlemagne was crowned on Christmas Day 800. The circumstances of this, however, were closely bound up with the more immediate political pressures of the preceding decades. The extension of the pope's territorial powers made control of the Holy See an attractive proposition to some of the local nobility. In 767 Duke Toto of Nepi forced his brother Constantine on the see, and had him consecrated, although he had still been a layman at the time of the election, and it was over a year before he was captured, blinded and mutilated in a bloody counter-revolution, which was headed by the *primicerius* or chief secretary. But the Roman families were still at the mercy of Lombard and Frankish pressures, and the final overthrow of the former, when King Desiderius was defeated by Charlemagne in 774, and his kingdom was absorbed into the Frankish Empire, left the latter in control. Although Hadrian I was a highly born Roman, and an able pope, he had in practice to acknowledge that the Frankish ruler would call the tune. His successor, Leo III, who lacked the advantage of birth, had to rely on him even more strongly, when an aristocratic reaction tried to overthrow him, and he was forced to flee to Charlemagne, who was then in Saxony. Frankish support was sufficient to restore him to Rome, and his enemies were condemned. His action in conferring an imperial crown on Charlemagne symbolised the closeness of the alliance between the two men, and the essential dependence of the Papacy on the lay power.

Even more clearly, it marked the culmination of the Papacy's break with the Byzantine Empire. This had been foreshadowed in 772 when the papal chancery ceased to date its documents by the emperor's regnal year, and in 795 when Pope Leo III sent the protocol of his election to Charlemagne rather than to Byzantium. In fact the century had seen tension on ecclesiastical as well as on political matters. When in 726 the Byzantine emperor Leo III began to campaign against the veneration of images in churches and ordered their destruction, Gregory II opposed him, and for over sixty years there were deep divisions on the issue between East and West. In its opposition to the Byzantines, the Papacy had strong support from the lay powers in the West, possibly an indication of the comparative lack of intellectual sophistication there, but also a reflection of where its real power base was. It was not until the second Council of Nicaea in 787 that iconoclasm was condemned in the East, and unity was restored on the subject. A fundamental distrust developed between the Eastern and Western churches, which continued into the ninth century. Nicholas I attempted to recover jurisdictional authority in Illyricum, which had been lost in the early eighth century, and also clashed with the emperor over the deposition of the patriarch Ignatius in 858 and his replacement by the layman Photius. After mutual sentences of excommunication were exchanged between Photius and the popes, the latter eventually emerged victorious, when Photius was condemned at the fourth Council of Constantinople in 869–70. Papal concern with this crisis is reflected in the space allowed to it in the *Liber Pontificalis*. This schism did not raise serious doctrinal questions, but was primarily concerned with questions of authority, because Photius had strongly opposed the extension of western practices into Bulgaria. This council demonstrates the continuing association of the Eastern and the Western churches: it still recognised the importance of the Roman see, even though the pope's representatives were not allowed to preside at it, for when it laid down the order of precedence among the ancient patriarchates, it gave Rome the first place ahead of Constantinople.[19]

At the same time, however, a long-term doctrinal difference was emerging between East and West. The Nicene Creed, as approved by the Council of Constantinople in 381, was the definitive statement of the beliefs of the whole Church. In its original form it had declared that the Holy Spirit proceeded 'from the Father', but at some point, probably in the sixth or the seventh century in Spain, the word *Filioque* ('and the Son') was added to it. This addition was included in the form of the Creed used in Charlemagne's chapel. The Carolingians believed in standardisation – one thinks also of the imposition of the Rule of St Benedict under the influence of Benedict of

Aniane – and tried to spread the use of this form more widely in the West, and although Pope Leo III advised against it, they had widespread success. But the Western liturgy was not yet uniform, and as the Roman form of the mass at that date did not include the Creed, no such change was made at the papal court. Not until about 1030 was the new credal formula adopted in Rome, providing yet another point of divergence between East and West. By the middle of the eleventh century, the accumulated differences between Rome and Constantinople proved unbridgeable: not only was there fundamental mutual dislike and distrust, but there were no elements of common interest which might overcome these and draw them together. There were also more practical problems. Disputes over jurisdiction in southern Italy angered the patriarch Michael Cerularius, who closed down Latin churches in Constantinople and attacked the Western practice of using unleavened bread in the Eucharist. Attempts at conciliation were futile, because those taking part were unyielding, and in 1054 the papal legate excommunicated the patriarch and his supporters. This act led to a counter-anathema: from then on the two churches remained divided, apart from one or two very brief periods.

This survey of East–West relations, however, runs ahead of other aspects of papal history. From the time of the Frankish alliance in the eighth century until the popes successfully asserted their independence of imperial influence in the eleventh, the fortunes of the Papacy were closely bound up with those of various secular powers, which might affect it for good or ill. One legacy of Charlemagne was the exercise of imperial control over papal elections; Paschal I virtually apologised to Louis the Pious in 817 for having been chosen without his approval, claiming that the papal dignity had been forced on him by popular acclamation but against his will,[20] and when Sergius II was chosen in 844 without awaiting imperial confirmation, the emperor sent his son to Rome to prevent a recurrence of such events. Charles the Fat may have attempted to depose Stephen V in 885, because he had not been consulted, but the pope was able to convince the emperor that the election had had the support of the resident imperial envoy in Rome.[21] But the emperor's practical power was matched by ecclesiastical reverence for the office of pope; the Frankish bishops in 849 referred to the pope having primacy in the whole world, and in his *Life of Wala,* Paschasius Radbertus about the same time described him in such terms as 'supreme bishop', 'supreme pontiff', and 'the holy and supreme pontiff, vicar of the blessed Peter', descriptions which echo that of 'supreme prelate' in the *Liber Pontificalis*.[22] The foundation charter of the abbey of Vézelay in the mid-ninth century subordinated the house to 'the blessed apostles at Rome' and committed it to 'the holy bishops of that eternal city, those who in the place of the apostles have . . . held that see'.[23] Respect for the Holy See as an institution was not always accorded to individual holders of it – indeed the *Royal Frankish Annals* suggest that the affairs of the Roman people had been confused by the wickedness of several popes[24] – but there was a perception of its status which provided a foundation on which later popes would be able to build. Furthermore, legal issues affecting the Church were being referred to Rome from elsewhere in Christendom, establishing a series of precedents for the development of papal authority.

The extent of this varied with both the character of the individual who held the office and the strength of the lay rulers who might curtail it. Nicholas I quashed the decision of a synod at Aachen which had sanctioned the divorce of Lothair II of Lorraine from his wife and his marriage to his mistress, and deprived the archbishops Gunther of Köln and Theutgaud of Trier of their sees for supporting it. Although Lothair's brother, the Emperor Louis I, attempted to browbeat the pope he obtained no concessions, even when his troops ransacked Rome. Furthermore, a synod at Soissons declared that anyone who ignored the mandates of the apostolic see should be anathema. The varying responses of the two archbishops demonstrate doubts about the extent of papal powers – Theutgaud submitted, but Gunther defied the condemnation and continued to celebrate mass. He must still, however, have recognised the papal power of excommunication, because he made a later, though still unsuccessful, attempt to secure absolution in Rome.[25] The pope's success was probably due more to his strong personality than to recognised papal powers. Contemporary annalists seem to have condemned the archbishops' rebelliousness, but the St Bertin writer, possibly Hincmar of Rheims, was a good deal more hostile to a papal attempt to secure the reinstatement of the bishop of Soissons, who had been deprived by the bishops of the Gaulish Church.[26] At the same period, however, there is a record of two Breton bishops who were accused of simony being sent to judgement by the pope in Rome, 'which is the head of all churches that are under the whole of heaven'. The ties between the Papacy and the Empire were reflected in a number of visits which popes made north of the Alps, and when John VIII was in Gaul, a number of cases were referred to him for decision.[27]

Roman feuds and Italian politics

On balance the influence of the Carolingian emperors was probably beneficial to the Papacy, by freeing it from dependence on the Roman nobility. It is significant that the crumbling of imperial power at the end of the ninth century was followed in the first half of the tenth by one of the bleakest periods in papal history, when it fell prey to the feuds of Roman families and eventually fell under the malign influence of the house of Theophylact. Possibly the main cause of these disorders was the rivalry between those families which still looked to the Franks for military assistance, and those which favoured the house of Spoleto, which was becoming increasingly powerful in central Italy. A warning portent of things to come was the assassination of John VIII in 882, probably following his political failure against Moslem attacks in southern Italy, and possibly Hadrian III may also have died through foul play. There were clearly also personal vendettas, demonstrated most vividly in the fate of Formosus, an able and ascetic man of exemplary life, who was elected pope in 891, but who was already bishop of Porto. Traditionally canon law did not allow for the translation of a bishop from one see to another, and his earlier status was held against him after his death, although not before. After his death, the Spoletan party, which he had opposed, gained control of the Papacy in the person of Stephen VI, whose reign saw the grisly 'cadaver' synod, at which Formosus' body was disinterred, clothed in full vestments and placed on a throne where he was tried for perjury and for violating canon law on the translation of bishops. He was found guilty, the three fingers of his right hand with which had given blessings were hacked off, and his body was thrown into the Tiber. All his acts were declared void. Stephen himself was deposed and strangled a few months later. The events of the next few years, and the precise nature of the factions, are by no means certain, but certainly there was complete political instability – in under eight years between the death of Formosus in 896 and the accession of Sergius III in 904 the average length of tenure of the Roman see was under a year, and three of the popes held office for less than a month. During this period Formosus was rehabilitated and condemned again, depending on which faction held sway.

The emergence of the family of Theophylact, who first appears in the records in 901, did lead to order being restored in Rome, and he gave his support to Sergius III (904–11), a strong anti-Formosan, who began his reign by having two of his predecessors strangled. The price of order, however, was the degradation of the Papacy into dependence on the Roman nobility. Theophylact died in 920, but his formidable daughter Marozia succeeded to his position of influence until she was supplanted in 932 by Alberic, her son by her first marriage, who certainly resented and possibly feared the power of his mother's third husband. Alberic dominated the city and the affairs of the Papacy, assuming the title of senator of Rome, until his death in 954. Most of the popes of this period were protégés, not to say puppets, of the family, and the only one who may have tried to show some independence, John X (914–28), was probably deposed for resisting its influence and trying to balance it by building up the power of his own brother Peter. (It is a comment on the changing status of the Papacy, and of a perception that it was essentially different from other bishoprics, that no serious grievance was raised when John was elected after having been previously archbishop of Ravenna, less than twenty years after Formosus had been condemned for a similar action.) He was a vigorous pope, who played an active part in political and diplomatic moves to deal with the threat posed by Moslem raiders who had ensconced themselves in central Italy. John was personally involved in the war, even in the actual fighting in 915. Some months after his deposition he was murdered in prison and two short-lived dependants of Marozia succeeded him, before the Papacy passed to her illegitimate son – some sources suggest that his father may have been Sergius III, but this is not certain – who took the title of John XI. After Alberic's coup d'état in 932, John was imprisoned for a time, although he may later have been released and allowed to exercise only ecclesiastical functions until his death in 935 or 936.

Alberic dominated Roman affairs for a generation. His half-brother's four successors were all his nominees, one of whom was imprisoned and mutilated after conspiring against the powerful senator. Politically too, he was able to exclude Transalpine intervention in Italy. But although he kept the Papacy subordinate, he did take a benevolent interest in some ecclesiastical matters, calling in the much respected abbot of Cluny, St Odo, to reform monasteries in Rome.[28] Alberic's influence persisted even after his death, for his bastard son Octavian, who had succeeded to his father's temporal power, a year later obtained the Papacy as well, assuming the title of John XII. In moral terms he represented the lowest point of the tenth-century Papacy. Still in his late teens or early twenties, he had few spiritual interests, although he did give some support to reformed monasteries. His reputation was for being addicted to debauchery and hunting. He lacked his father's political ability (in practical terms a more serious disadvantage than his immorality), and under pressure from Italian enemies turned for assistance to the most powerful ruler of the West, the German king Otto I. The latter had sought the imperial crown in 951, but the pope, under Alberic's influence, had refused to receive him, so he welcomed the invitation and was duly crowned in 962.

The German emperors and the popes

Imperial intervention saved John from his temporal enemies for a time, but Otto's influence was resented, and the Romans soon split into pro- and anti-German factions. Before long the pope aligned himself with the latter, and when Otto returned to Rome he was forced to flee to the Campagna. A synod, presided over by the emperor, deposed the pope, and a respectable official (Leo VIII) was elected to replace him. A Roman reaction against the Germans brought John back, and Leo in turn was deposed, but when John died (allegedly while in bed with a married woman), they attempted to elect a respectable deacon (Benedict V) rather than recall the emperor's nominee. In the end Leo did recover the Papacy, Benedict was forced to abdicate and went into exile in Germany, where he died, much respected for the holiness of his life. These events suggest that the emperor had gained control of the Papacy from the Roman nobility, but the extent of imperial influence for the next eighty years was at best intermittent, depending on whether or not the emperors were able to intervene personally in Italy. During their absences, the feuds of the Roman noble families reasserted themselves; one particularly, the Crescenzi, who were related to the house of Theophylact but were at odds with the main line of the family, made a vigorous attempt to dominate elections. Benedict VI, who was supported by the imperial party, was overthrown by the Crescenzi candidate Boniface VII and strangled in prison. Boniface in turn was excommunicated after the election of Benedict VII, who may have been a compromise candidate acceptable to both the emperor and the Romans, but was able to make a comeback after his successor's death and the imposition of an unpopular imperial official, John XIV, who, like various of his predecessors in the century, came to a violent end.

Under Otto III the emperor had further success in reasserting his position. He had been called in by John XV, who had fallen foul of the Crescenzi, but the pope had died of fever before his arrival, and he was able to impose his cousin, Bruno of Carinthia (Gregory V). But the pope depended on imperial support, and when Otto returned to Germany he was driven out and superseded by a candidate with Crescenzi support, who held the Papacy for a year before the emperor restored Gregory, and had his rival blinded and mutilated. On Gregory's death, probably from malaria, Otto secured the election of one of the most brilliant men of his age, Gerbert of Aurillac, the archbishop of Ravenna, who took the title of Sylvester II, one which, looking back to the time of Constantine, symbolised an idea of papal–imperial cooperation. Sylvester's territorial authority in Rome depended largely on the emperor, after whose death in 1002 the Crescenzi again recovered influence, but he was able to exercise his spiritual functions and try to enforce reform until he himself died a year later. This can be seen in letters which he wrote to the Doge of Venice and the Patriarch of Grado, ordering them to hold a synod to deal with simony, clerical marriage and the pursuit of wealth by the clergy. His language was uncompromising; when the bishop of Asti refused to attend a papal synod, he was told: 'You prefer to putrefy midst the dung with your beasts of burden rather than to shine among the pillars of the Church', and he described the bishop of Laon to his face as Judas and refused to start a letter to him with any formal greeting. He justified his actions by exalting the glory of the Holy See and the power of St Peter to bind and to loose.[29] These views were not universally shared. Rodulfus Glaber, while accepting that the Roman see was 'rightly regarded as universal throughout all the world', nevertheless felt that the pope was breaking the tenor of canon law, by sending a cardinal to consecrate a monastery when the local archbishop had refused to do so. He accepted that the dignity of the Apostolic See entitled the pope to more honour than any other bishop, but did not recognise that he possessed greater rights of jurisdiction.[30] Fulbert of Chartres too was somewhat ambiguous in his attitude to the Papacy. In a letter to the pope between 1006 and 1008 he pays lip service to him as one 'to whom the whole care of the Church has been entrusted' and a decade and a half later he went to Rome on pilgrimage, but he also persuaded the bishop of Orleans not to go to Rome for consecration, as this would derogate from the honour of his archbishop.[31] Perhaps most revealing of all was a letter to Archbishop Arnulf of Tours, in which he said that if the pope had not sent him the *pallium,* the symbol of archiepiscopal authority, without lawful reason, there was no need for Arnulf to resign, but that if Arnulf had been slow in asking for it, it would have been prudent to wait until he had done so. Fulbert added as a general comment that some prerogatives of the Roman Church which should be honoured had been neglected.[32]

The conferment of the *pallium* was found earlier in England, and both the *Anglo-Saxon Chronicle* and Simeon of Durham refer to various archbishops of Canterbury and of York receiving it in the eighth and early ninth centuries. The chronicler does not mention its receipt at Canterbury, however, between the grant to Ceolnoth in 833 and that to Aelfric in 997. In 1022 Aethelnoth went in person to Rome to obtain it.[33] It is not, however, clear if the pope had temporarily ceased to confer it, or if, perhaps more probably, this was merely an omission on the chronicler's part. Certainly in the third quarter of the eleventh century it was to become a very serious issue, when Archbishop Stigand received his from a man who was subsequently condemned as an antipope, this act compounding doubts about his status after he had supplanted a lawfully appointed predecessor. One consequence of this was that the pope gave his blessing to Duke William of Normandy's invasion of 1066.

After the deaths of Otto III and Sylvester II, imperial influence declined and the Roman noble families were able to reassert their position, although emperors did visit Rome at least intermittently. Until 1012, the Crescenzi were again dominant, but in that year the counts of Tusculum, descended from the main line of the Theophylact family, regained authority in Rome, and also took possession of the Papacy. Benedict VIII (1012–24) and John XIX (1024–32) were brothers, neither of whom was ordained at the time of their election, and the latter was succeeded by his nephew, Benedict IX (1032–44, 1045, 1047–8), who lost the office three times and recovered it twice. The earlier two were able to establish friendly relations with the Empire, and after the defeat of his allies by the Byzantines at Cannae in 1019 the former went to seek assistance from Henry II, whom he had earlier crowned. Benedict's abilities were political rather than spiritual, although a synod which he held at Pavia in 1022 promulgated laws against clerical marriage. He was the first pope to make use of the Norman military adventurers who were active in southern Italy, an action which foreshadowed later political developments, and was opposed to the attempts of the Byzantines to recover power there. Benedict IX, however, was a pope more in the mould of John XII, and was overthrown in a revolt in 1044 which reflected family feuds as much as hostility to his own dissolute behaviour. Significantly, the bishop of Sabina, who was appointed to replace him, was a protégé of the Crescenzi, but he retained the see as Sylvester III for under three months, before being himself overthrown in a counter-revolution which brought Benedict back. The latter, however, abdicated in

1045 in favour of his godfather, who took the title of Gregory VI. The circumstances of the election are unclear, but it seems certain that substantial sums of money changed hands. Despite this, he was initially well received, and was acclaimed by members of the reforming party within the Church, including the hermit leader Peter Damiani.

The genesis of papal reform

It was probably coincidental that in 1046 the Emperor Henry III travelled south into Italy, perhaps primarily with the intention of receiving imperial coronation. But there is no doubt that he was a devout ruler, who was also deeply concerned with the fortunes of the Church, and who was deeply opposed to simony. When he reached Sutri, near Rome, in December, a synod there saw either Gregory's deposition or his resignation, Sylvester's condemnation and Benedict's flight. Gregory went into exile in Germany, where he died, but one of his companions there was the young subdeacon Hildebrand, who was soon to become one of the most dynamic figures in the reform movement. The assembly at Sutri was a crucial turning-point in the history of the Western Church, for the popes who followed those who had been deposed, reforming German clerics named by the emperor, were to establish a system which within a generation was to turn the relations of the secular and the spiritual power upside down. The Papacy, having been one of the institutions in the Church most vulnerable to local power politics, and their concomitant corruption, was to secure its independence and become the driving moral force behind a momentous programme of reform.

The reform began with the men who succeeded to the Papacy. The next four popes were all Germans nominated by the emperor, two indeed being his kinsmen, and although they reigned for less than eleven years altogether, they gave the Papacy an entirely new sense of direction, and gathered together as advisers men firmly committed to raising ecclesiastical standards. The greatest of the four, Leo IX (1049–54), not only took action against simony and clerical marriage at his first synod in Rome in 1049 but took the message of reform to the rest of Christendom later in the same year, holding synods at Rheims and Mainz. Even more important was the fact that the Roman nobility had lost the firm grip on the Holy See which they had exercised for most of the previous century and a half. Even after direct imperial influence waned on the death of Henry III in 1056 and the succession to the Empire of his 5-year-old son, the reformers had sufficient power to retain control when the abbot of Monte Cassino, Frederick of Lorraine, was elected pope as Stephen IX in 1057. The imperial court was not consulted about this election, so in a sense he represented the separation of the reform movement from imperial influence, not least because his brother Godfrey, duke of Lorraine and by marriage count of Tuscany, had been an enemy of Henry III. However, the ideals which he pursued were the same as those followed by the imperial nominees who preceded him. The men closest to him were all active reformers: Peter Damiani, whom he made cardinal bishop of Ostia, Humbert of Silva Candida, his chancellor, and Hildebrand, who had returned from Germany after the death of Gregory VI and been made treasurer of the Roman Church by Leo IX. On Stephen's death, the Roman nobility attempted to regain control of the Papacy by securing the election of John of Velletri, from the family of the counts of Tusculum, as Benedict X, but the reformers refused to recognise his title, elected a rival candidate and with the support of Godfrey of Lorraine drove him out of Rome.

The reformers' candidate, Nicholas II, continued the attack on simony and also was responsible for an election decree which conferred the responsibility for choosing the new pope on the cardinal bishops, who were to consult among themselves and then with the cardinal clerks, after which they would associate the remainder of the clergy and the people with them. 'Honour and dignity' were conceded to the emperor, but what this involved was not clearly defined. There may not have been an intention to exclude the emperor entirely, but his role was far reduced from what it had been in the time of Henry III, when the initial discussions had taken place at the imperial court.[34] Nicholas also brought about a diplomatic revolution in papal policy, by coming to terms with the Normans of southern Italy, whom he invested with territories there and in Sicily, in return for a promise of military assistance.

The Empire did not abandon its influence easily, and may indeed have had some encouragement from the Roman nobility. It challenged the position of Nicholas's successor, Alexander II, by supporting an antipope, whose troops gained control of Rome, and it was only after a shift of power in Germany that Alexander definitely secured his authority, and renewed the campaign for church reform. It was, however, after 1073, when Hildebrand, who had been a prominent adviser of the popes from Leo IX onwards, was himself elected pope as Gregory VII, that the Papacy threw down the challenge to imperial influence.

Throughout the third quarter of the eleventh century, it is easy to see the development of reform at Rome. It is, however, important to bear in mind that many of the ideals which the reformers advocated, notably the bans on clerical marriage and on simony, were already being encouraged elsewhere. Even some of the popes who were eventually deposed had shown some sympathy for the new values which were being advocated. It is worth bearing in mind that Hildebrand not only remained loyal to his first master, Gregory VI, until his death, but that by taking the title of Gregory VII himself, he proclaimed this almost a quarter of a century later. John of Velletri, the later antipope Benedict X, had been considered as a candidate for the Papacy in 1057, and was esteemed in reforming circles, although he was related to the counts of Tusculum. Not all the struggles of this period should be seen as simply between pro- and anti-reform parties in the Church, for they can be better understood as contests for power and influence between groups whose interests cut across the issue of reform. (Even at the Papacy's lowest point in the tenth century, its lay master, Alberic, had encouraged monastic reform in Rome.) This is more understandable if one remembers that the Papacy was always faced with the problem of reconciling its diverse roles of local bishop (with both spiritual and temporal functions), custodian of the tombs of the martyrs, and inheritor of the authority given by Christ to St Peter. The perceptions which Christendom had of these depended on where individuals lived. To a Roman the pope was his local bishop, and because of his geographical proximity he would see him warts and all, while a Christian living beyond the Alps would be more inclined to accord reverence to his spiritual role. The emperors, with political interests in Italy, might be sympathetic to some new ideals in the Church, but they were also concerned with both temporal matters and with securing imperial coronation, which only the pope could confer, and it would be naive to think that they were not self-interested when they intervened to settle disputes at Rome.

What can be said, however, is that between 1046 and 1073 the values and ideals of ecclesiastical reform were increasingly incorporated in the papal agenda, and that this restored, and later enhanced, the moral authority which had been lost in the tenth century. The next stage in the development of the Papacy was to be the translation of the esteem felt for the see of St Peter into a powerful monarchical authority.

|4|

The Church in the localities

Bishops and dioceses

As we saw in the last chapter, one of the functions of the pope was that of bishop of Rome. As such he had a certain pre-eminence, but in the Church as a whole, other bishops could exercise similar functions in their own dioceses. Although effectively independent of any central authority, they might meet for consultations in local councils, normally summoned by the lay ruler, and pronounce collectively on matters of Church policy. In Dark Age Europe, and particularly after the barbarian invasions, when unified authority in the West had broken down, the local bishop represented continuity and order to his community, which was primarily an urban one – bishops were associated essentially with cities. The diocese was the basic unit of church organisation – it was to be a long time before a parish structure was developed at the more local level – and he himself was the crucial person in transmitting the faith. It was he who had the power to ordain priests and thereby secure the administration of the sacraments. This power of order was basic, but he normally acquired also a power of jurisdiction over his flock. In those parts of Western Europe where Christianity persisted from Roman times without a break, as in Frankish Gaul, local traditions were strong, and influential families which could trace their descent back to imperial times might well gain control over the office of bishop – many of the kindred of the chronicler Gregory of Tours were also bishops there, and their prominence in the Gaulish church went back before the barbarian conquests. It is clear, however, that the barbarian rulers came to terms with them, recognising that they had a useful part to play as influential local figures, not merely because of their spiritual role but also possibly because they could reconcile the existing Romanised population to their new masters. The large number of small Italian dioceses throughout the Middle Ages reflected the circumstances in which they were established in Roman times.

Not all areas which were Christianised, however, possessed towns, notably those regions beyond the imperial frontiers to which Christianity penetrated in the late Roman and sub-Roman periods. In Ireland, early dioceses can probably be equated with local petty kingdoms, but local churches were founded unsystematically, and the extent of episcopal authority, particularly compared with that of the abbot of the local great *monasterium*, has been a matter of considerable debate. This term, however, is an ambiguous one – it is significant that the two words 'monastery' and 'minster', which have distinct connotations, both derive from it – and certainly in some areas of Christendom, including Anglo-Saxon England, the occupants of such establishments were not always monks, who had withdrawn from the world, but priests who exercised a measure of local pastoral care, which was in the High Middle Ages taken over by the smaller parish unit. The laity were served by visiting clergy from these communities, who visited the surrounding countryside and preached to the people, possibly at places identified by standing crosses. Bede suggested that they might conduct baptisms, which was recognised as a priestly duty at the Council of Clofesho in 747.[1] Indeed, it seems likely that the same establishments may in some cases have included both men whose devotion took the form of pious contemplation and others who undertook a more pastoral role, the two contrasted forms of religious observance which were to recur throughout the later history of the Church. In Anglo-Saxon England the bulk of clerics resided in larger centres of population, from which they extended their activity to surrounding rural areas.[2]

It is important in any study of the Church at this period not to interpret words such as *monasterium* and *parochia* in their later sense, because this could be misleading. In the early period, the term *parochia* itself referred to an area much wider than that which it came to denote from the High Middle Ages onwards, and which possibly corresponded to secular administrative areas. In Scotland, indeed, the term *parochia* was still being equated with the territorial limits of the diocese of Glasgow as late as the mid-twelfth century, even though smaller local churches were being founded at this period. At an even later date it was employed to denote a mother church for an area with special baptismal rights. Increasingly parish limits were more stabilised from this date, and may well have been prompted by the parallel development of the new structures of feudal tenure in lay society, although there were later adjustments (both unions and divisions), usually in response to changes in the distribution of population. Significantly, however, there was administrative resistance to change because of the vested interests of existing parishes.[3] Throughout Europe, however, there was no uniform pattern, and one suspects that in the early period, in the context of a missionary Church, practices varied according to immediate needs, and that it was only as it became more securely established that clearer administrative structures were set up. As this occurred the more centralised churches may have secured rights as centres of baptism and burial, which were only later devolved back to the local parish churches.

Before Christianity was given official recognition in the late Roman period, local communities had chosen their own leaders, and this practice continued to a later date, although, as discussed below, kings and aristocrats came to play an increasingly influential part in the choice of bishops. There were, however, disagreements over the nature of the office. Was a bishop to be seen as a prominent leader, who should appear as a man of dignity, or was an austere and humble saint to be preferred? Sulpicius Severus approved the humility of St Martin, and was embarrassed by another bishop who sat on his throne like an emperor's tribunal, but he reported that some men had opposed his consecration because his person was contemptible, his hair unkempt and his dress shabby.[4] In Anglo-Saxon Northumbria, Bede praised the humility of St Aidan as bishop of Lindisfarne.[5] But in an age in which the possession and display of the symbols of power was a means by which an individual's importance could be measured, bishops had to be seen as powerful figures. The Gaulish episcopate acquired many rights and privileges during the years of the invasions, and it was their ceremony which Wilfrid emulated when, at his consecration, he was borne into the oratory on a throne by nine bishops.[6] With the passage of time, however, such pomp came to be regarded as unseemly. In the ninth century, Louis the Pious commanded bishops and clerics to give up girdles adorned with golden belts and jewelled daggers, regarding it as monstrous that a representative of the Church should aspire to the accoutrements of worldly glory.[7]

The bishops' prominence in their communities was liable to draw them into secular affairs, so it is hardly surprising that lay rulers were concerned at their choice. Gregory of Tours tells that in the early sixth century St Nicetius was consecrated as bishop of Trier with the consent of the people and by the decree of the king. In the middle of the century a dispute over the succession to the see of Clermont demonstrates even more clearly where real power lay. A locally elected candidate tried to assume full powers before he was fully inducted into office, but a council of bishops, meeting under royal auspices, chose an alternative, who was favourably received by the people. It was the latter who secured the post.[8] Two points about this episode are worth noting; the local community's views were still considered, even when their original preference had been set aside, but the king was able to influence them, and was able to rely on a council of bishops to assist him. Indeed, the bishops' importance in the social and political structure of Merovingian Gaul is reflected in the way in which the chronicler Fredegar groups them, almost automatically, with the lay magnates as the kings' principal advisers.[9]

Bishops and the lay power

Such lay influence reflected the reality of power in the West, which diverged from the theoretical assertion of ecclesiastical independence in the general councils of the Church. The second Council of Nicaea (787) laid down that the election of a bishop, priest or deacon brought about by a lay ruler should be void, and the fourth Council of Constantinople (869–70) condemned the nomination of bishops through the intrigues of the civil power. The accepted procedure envisaged at the earlier of these councils was that they should be chosen by their fellow bishops in a province, with the proceedings being confirmed by a metropolitan.[10] These provisions probably reflect a more developed hierarchy in the East than was found in the contemporary Western Church, although some aspects of this approach may also have applied in the West. The Clermont case, cited earlier, suggests a procedure for consulting existing bishops, even at a time when popular assent was still regarded as necessary. One cannot assume uniformity of practice throughout the whole Church, and it is perhaps necessary to distinguish between those lands with a continuous tradition of Christianity and those which had been recently converted. In England and Germany, the Papacy played an important part in appointing bishops in the period of the early missions, but as the Church became firmly established the interest of the lay power in appointing bishops increased. In England as early as 666 Wine was alleged to have bought the see of London from the king of Mercia, but in the following year the pope nominated Theodore of Tarsus as archbishop of Canterbury, perhaps taking advantage of the fact that an archbishop elect, sent for ordination by the kings of Kent and Northumbria, had died in Rome. Royal influence was very clear in the choice of the first archbishop of York, Egbert (735), who was of royal blood and whose brother Eadberht succeeded to the Northumbrian throne in 738. Although Alcuin states that Egbert's successor was elected by popular acclaim, it would be surprising if he had been chosen without royal approval.[11] Royal influence was clearly demonstrated in the mid-eighth century, when King Offa of Mercia had the principal see of his immediate kingdom, that of Lichfield, raised to the status of an archbishopric, a position which it failed to retain when Mercia went into decline. In Spain, where King Reccared had played a decisive part in turning his kingdom from Arianism to Catholic Christianity, he and his successors summoned a series of church councils, or in some cases attracted criticism for failing to do so.[12] King Sisebut (612–21) imposed a bishop on the see of Barcelona, and rebuked a bishop of Tarragona for being too interested in the theatre, while by the end of the seventh century Erwig established a system by which the king chose and the metropolitan of Toledo approved candidates for episcopal vacancies.[13]

In the last resort, the Church needed the protection of the lay rulers, and in return it had to concede substantial influence to them. A well-disposed king could strengthen it, for lay influence was not always as malign as the church reformers of the eleventh century were to suggest, indeed asserting their views so successfully that these have coloured retrospectively much historical thought on the earlier period. Einhard paid tribute to the piety of Charlemagne, and Asser did the same for Alfred of Wessex.[14] The fact that

kings were consecrated gave them a quasi-clerical status, which strengthened their moral authority in dealing with Church affairs. At the same time,
the lay power did sometimes incur ecclesiastical opprobrium, as when
Paschasius Radbertus denounced uncanonical appointments to bishoprics
without elections.[15]

The character and extent of lay influence in ecclesiastical matters varied
with the powers which individuals could exercise, and when imperial
authority broke down in the ninth century, more local rulers assumed it. In
the late tenth century the earlier career of Gerbert, the future Sylvester II,
underwent many changes of fortune in an age of political upheavals.
Archbishop Adalbero of Rheims recommended him to the empress for a
bishopric, although unsuccessfully, and when the archbishop died, some
people envisaged him as a possible candidate for that see, but the troubles
after Hugh Capet's election as king of France saw it going to an illegitimate
Carolingian, Arnulf, who later supported a rival claimant to the French
throne. A synod of bishops deposed Arnulf, and Gerbert obtained the see,
but his rival sought papal intervention, and Gerbert was described as an
intruder and a schismatic. Only imperial support from Otto III enabled
Gerbert to make a fresh start to his career, when he was created archbishop
of Ravenna, to move a year later to the Papacy.[16] Complaints were sometimes made about royal appointees; about 1012–14 Fulbert of Chartres
protested that the church of Bourges did not wish to have the royal nominee, abbot Gauzlin of Fleury, as its archbishop, and in 1021 he suggested
that the count of Troyes had been corrupted by money in imposing a bishop
of Meaux, who had seized the episcopal palace without the consent of the
king and the bishops of the province. Later, he suggested that the king and
the archbishop of Sens should take action against the bishop.[17] This latter
episode clearly acknowledges that theoretically the king had some say in
episcopal appointments, although other churchmen also participated. It is
also clear, however, that the local nobility might possess greater actual
power in their area. Fulbert certainly saw the king as a potential ally against
such local magnates rather than as a tyrant, not only describing him as 'his
very kind lord and king' but also appealing to him for help; 'we are bearing
these injuries and not taking vengeance for your sake, waiting and praying
for you to do us justice'.[18] The king, however, was not the only layman who
could be seen as a protector of the Church; Glaber wrote warmly of the
Norman dukes from William I (928–42) to Richard III (1026–7) as men
who imposed order on their lands, protected pilgrims, and made generous
gifts to it.[19]

The price of royal protection could easily become royal dominance. After
Fulbert's death, the king forced a bishop on the canons of Chartres, who
had wished to elect their own dean, and their protests were of no avail.
Glaber attacked clerical simony, and in a revealing sentence declared that
kings had been corrupted by bribes, and preferred to appoint to the rule of
churches those from whom they could expect more gifts.[20] Royal wishes

were not always fulfilled, because the king might possess less actual power than the local great family, and Odo of Blois chose a nominee for the see of Sens other than the king's choice, 'so that the royal power should not be fully exercised in the area'. At Lyons in 1030, the local count tried to impose his son on the see, after the bishop of Aosta, a nephew of the former archbishop, had tried to seize it, but eventually the Emperor Henry III imposed the archdeacon of Langres on it. The pope was also drawn into the struggle, and actually offered the see to Abbot Odilo of Cluny, who declined it. Although he was unable to impose his own candidate, the fact that he was asked to intervene demonstrates that even at a date when the individual holding the Papacy was of low reputation, the prestige attaching to the see still encouraged the faithful to appeal to him.[21] Even after appointment, a prelate was still assumed to depend on the lay power, and Adam of Bremen paid tribute to Archbishop Lievizo: 'content with what he had, rarely went to court to acquire more'. It is noteworthy that Adam regarded this as creditable, for he expected archbishops to be wise to the ways of the world, and was scathing about Archbishop Herman: 'he was a man as harmless as a dove, but possessed too little of the wisdom of the serpent'.[22]

In theory, an episcopal appointment was for life, and bishops originally were supposed to be wedded to their sees and not moved from one to another. This had, of course, lain behind some of the disputes affecting the late ninth-century Papacy.[23] But political instability in the decades preceding this papal crisis had seen the erosion of this rule – an archbishop of Bordeaux was translated to Bourges in 876 because of insecurity caused by 'the pagans', presumably Vikings. This action had been approved by a synod, although it incurred the disapproval of the greatest Frankish churchman of his day, Archbishop Hincmar of Rheims. A decade later the pope decreed, at the king's request, that bishops whose dioceses had been devastated by the pagans might be granted other vacant sees.[24] These cases show a measure of papal intervention in Frankish affairs, although this was by no means always acceptable and was sometimes resisted. In 865 the St Bertin annalist accused the pope of high-handedness in trying to reinstate the bishop of Soissons, who had been canonically deposed by the bishops of five West Frankish provinces, and in 876 the Frankish bishops refused to accept the primacy of the archbishop of Sens, as outlined in a papal letter.[25]

Bishops and archbishops

The desire of the bishops to preserve their diocesan autonomy from an immediate superior, either clerical or lay, had a curious consequence in that they were more inclined to accept the authority of a distant pope, possibly because he was less well placed to interfere in their routine activities. In the years around 850 an immensely influential forgery, known to historians as the Pseudo-Isidorian Decretals, was compiled somewhere in the archdiocese of Rheims. This was a very learned and carefully integrated mixture of genuine and false material, containing alleged papal decretals and canons of church councils. Its purpose was to defend the episcopal church against interference by archbishops, church councils and laymen alike. By claiming that the lesser clergy could appeal directly to Rome, these decrees eroded the authority of the archbishops. At the time the popes were unable to turn these ideas into practical control, although Nicholas I welcomed them, but they provided a foundation on which later popes asserted a much more extensive authority.[26]

Political disorder and uncertainty in the centuries following meant that in practice issues of authority remained unresolved, and it is clear from various passages in the letters of Gerbert (Sylvester II) that as late as 1000 the supervision which an archbishop could exercise over his suffragans had to be one of persuasion rather than of command. A few years later, Glaber still envisaged bishops as masters in their own dioceses: 'Each bishop is the bridegroom of his own see, and equally embodies the Saviour, and so none should interfere insolently in the diocese of another bishopric.'[27] But Glaber was aware that bishops could be translated, and in the Lyons case of 1030 noted how an individual might aspire to promotion from bishop to archbishop. While the church was becoming more hierarchical, much *de facto* authority still rested in the locality.

One reason for this may well have been that in the early eleventh century the boundaries between the archiepiscopal provinces had not yet been clearly defined; in this it reflected the lack of clarity in divisions between the lands of lay rulers. As a result, bishops might well recognise the authority of archbishops other than their own. Although Fulbert of Chartres wrote regularly to his own archbishop, Leotheric of Sens, he corresponded with other archbishops as well, although in some cases these letters may have been written to personal friends rather than to ecclesiastical superiors. But it is more significant that he was also willing to act in response to a command of another archbishop, that of Tours, to take action against Count Fulk Nerra of Anjou. Admittedly he did not immediately comply with the order to excommunicate the count, but instead admonished him for carrying off ecclesiastical property, but the action must still be seen as a response to the command for action. A similar willingness to seek assistance outside a limited geographical area occurred at Chartres after Fulbert's death. After the imposition of a royal nominee on the see, the canons protested not only to their own provincial, the archbishop of Sens, but wrote also to the archbishop of Tours, to the bishop of Beauvais and to the abbot of Cluny, both from the province of Rheims.[28] The Church might be weak in practice, but churchmen did feel it incumbent on them to try and defend their rights by all means possible, and these were not limited by the bounds of ecclesiastical provinces.

Local divisions – proprietary churches

Lay authority over the church can be observed also at a lower level than that of the diocese. Most notably this can be seen in the existence of the so-called proprietary church, when the laymen who provided the endowments necessary to maintain a benefice retained an interest in the complex of legal rights attached to it. They were able to do so, because they had furnished the resources and provided protection to the churches. This practice became the norm throughout the lands occupied by the Germanic people and reflects the dominance of aristocratic families over all aspects of society.[29] Attempts were made to abolish such proprietary churches, which in some places even included bishoprics, but at this period without success.[30] The existence of this system was one factor behind the attempts of the reformers in the eleventh century to get rid of the system of lay investiture (see Glossary), and also explains why this problem was so difficult to resolve, because the laity could hardly be expected to abandon existing powers without a struggle. Even when the laity could no longer technically confer the church on an individual, they were often still able to retain rights of patronage, which enabled them to nominate a candidate to the bishop for institution.

The influence of the laity over local churches went back a long way, and developed in various ways in different parts of Christendom. There was, however, a common feature behind it, namely that the spread of Christianity, as was noted in chapter 1, was brought about from the top. In areas where it had already taken root under the Roman Empire, diocesan bishops had made conscious efforts to spread it from the towns to the countryside, and in lands which were converted from paganism the authority of the lay power supported the efforts of the Church. The first legislation for rural parishes headed by a priest was approved by the Council of Vaison in 529; before then the term *parochia* was applied to the diocese, and it was the clergy of the bishop's church, the episcopal *familia,* which served the local churches.[31] As population grew, and new settlements were established, small churches were set up in large numbers with the support of the local territorial lords, who still retained some influence over them. Relations between these churches and more centralised ecclesiastical establishments cannot be precisely determined, and as was noted earlier in some areas it is likely that the latter had a privileged role, and that the faithful had special obligations to them. In times of disorder, however, it might be difficult for the older centres to retain their influence, and it was in these circumstances that responsibility for baptisms and burials was devolved to the local churches.

One should guard against the belief that the influence of these local lords was automatically a disaster. If they were personally pious and exercised their patronage to the Church's advantage, they could strengthen its position in a particular locality, but if their main concern was the retention of proprietorial rights, particularly over the material possessions of the

Church, their power could impoverish it. The expansion of the Church into regions previously unconverted, or which had previously been unpopulated, made it necessary to establish new centres of Christian life – if new settlements were too remote from existing parish churches for their inhabitants to have easy access to the services of the Church, an alternative was provided, and in such circumstances lay influence probably contributed to its spread. One consequence of it, however, was that the power of the older super-parishes was eroded.[32] The geographical spread of the Church, however, did not only lead to the establishment of proprietary churches. It also made it necessary to develop new administrative structures between the diocese and the parish – the archdeacon, who had originally been a servant of the bishop in his cathedral city, acquired jurisdictional powers over a portion of the diocese, and most dioceses ended up containing several archdeaconries. Lower still, parishes came to be grouped in rural deaneries, from the ninth century in western France, but not until the eleventh century in Germany.[33] Ecclesiastical organisation developed on an *ad hoc* basis, and was not imposed from the top, although one may reasonably presume that these new structures developed through a process of imitation, as bishops saw how their fellows were exercising their diocesan authority. There were structural diversities among towns as they developed – sometimes a town remained as a single parish and at other times there were separate churches in almost every street. At Köln the division of the city into parishes went back to the tenth century, while twelfth-century London possessed over a hundred parishes, a number of which were not even under the jurisdiction of the local bishop but were immediately subject to the archbishop of Canterbury.[34]

But rights of patronage could easily be developed into rights of exploitation, as the proprietors retained the profits from payments of tithes, a compulsory obligation, made by the inhabitants.[35] There was always the possibility that they might use ecclesiastical resources to provide endowments for their younger sons, so as not to encroach on the family's territorial resources. In such circumstances there may have been some lay pressure for the implementation of a rule of clerical celibacy, to prevent churches from becoming simply the possession of a priestly family, although in many parts of Christendom this type of hereditary church was not uncommon. It was not necessarily the evil practice that the reformers of the eleventh and twelfth centuries tried to suggest, because some distinguished churchmen came from clerical families. (A good example of this was the Englishman Ailred, descended from the hereditary priests of Hexham, who became abbot of Rievaulx in the twelfth century.) But there was always a danger that a church might be inherited by a man unsuited to the post, who held it purely for its material resources. On the other hand, when strictly proprietorial rights were ended, the families which held them often obtained rights of patronage, which led them to remain as parochial benefactors, even to the end of the Middle Ages.[36]

The Peace Movement

It is perhaps easier to see how the laity could dominate the Church than to judge how far ecclesiastical teaching affected the conduct of the laity. But one should not overlook that because political authority was often inadequate to enforce order, the Church served as a focus for popular aspirations for a more peaceful world. This was seen most conspicuously around 1000 in the so-called Peace Movement, in which church leaders joined with the devout laity to try and impose order by means of a binding oath and the provision of penalties for lawbreakers. This movement had its origins in Aquitaine, but spread widely through the French lands. It was noted by Glaber, although in fact he postdates its origins – the earliest council which approved peace legislation was that of Charroux in 989. The councils which tried to enforce peace were emotional and revivalist in tone, and indeed encouraged piety in other directions as well as in maintaining peace – strong encouragement was given to pilgrimages to Jerusalem at the time of the millennium of the Passion. The church authorities, however, lacked the ability to overcome existing feuds and vested interests, and Glaber lamented that clerical and temporal leaders alike fell into avarice and had recourse to robbery.[37] Even if peace could not be imposed, attempts were still made to restrict violence, notably in the so-called 'Truce of God', which tried to prevent it from the evening of Wednesday to the following Monday. This was a conscious attempt to avoid days which were deemed particularly holy, Thursday as that of the Last Supper, Friday as that of the Crucifixion, and Sunday as that of the Resurrection.[38]

The movement was a complex one, in which pious sentiments and social need interacted with the attempts of bishops to extend their own power when royal authority was lacking. Miraculous acts to punish offenders were associated with the power of the relics which were invoked by the clergy. It is clear, however, that it was able to draw on popular enthusiasm, which was encouraged by preachers, and even by some members of the higher clergy. In the 1030s, the archbishop of Bourges required all males of his diocese over the age of 15 to bind themselves by oath to maintain the Peace, and indeed mobilised them against individual members of the local nobility. They had some initial military success against them but were themselves eventually defeated by force.[39] The Peace Movement was an episode in social as well as in ecclesiastical history, and the attitudes of those who described it reflect differing perceptions of how order could be established, whether reliance should be placed purely on supernatural means or if physical force was a legitimate weapon against oppression and disorder. At times, the Church was willing to adopt a populist line, but it was itself too bound up with the economic and social structure of society to support this consistently. In the end the development of more powerful monarchies would do more to establish order than the efforts of churchmen.

Throughout this period the organisation of local churches was closely bound up with the lay power at various levels. There was no consistent pattern in this relationship, for it depended essentially on the individuals concerned at any particular time and place. Undoubtedly there were pious laymen who gave support to ideals of church reform, although such support was not wholly altruistic. At best they would be hoping for a reward in the hereafter, and frequently they could derive more immediate material benefits from ecclesiastical goodwill, whether this took the form of a bishop supporting a king, or a parochial benefice being employed to support a cadet member of a powerful local family. And if a pious layman could indulge in such exploitation, the Church was obviously more vulnerable to threats from those secular lords who cared little for it. As was noted earlier, the Church reformers of the eleventh century, who saw such lay influence as harmful and struggled to break it, had a crucial victory in determining the perceptions of later generations on the whole question of relations between the spiritual and the secular powers. No doubt in some cases their attitude was justified, but it should be remembered that there were also times when the Church's interests were furthered by lay action, which the ecclesiastical authorities themselves welcomed.

|5|

Belief and worship

Beliefs and practices

One of the characteristics of the Church in the years between its initial emergence and its formal recognition in the early fourth century had been its
attempts to define the precise terms of its doctrine. After it could safely come
into the open, a series of great councils formulated many of the articles of
belief which the Church and its successor churches from the sixteenth century have held subsequently. Doctrinal issues continued to raise passions in
the Eastern Church, but from the time of the barbarian invasions down to
about the eleventh century, theological controversies in the West were rare,
because although there was a tradition of learning, and indeed were some
men of outstanding intellect within the Church, such as the Spaniard
Isidore, the Englishman Bede and the Irishman Eriugena, they were isolated
figures in the way that they towered above lesser men. Their intellectualism,
moreover, did not lead them to challenge the official teachings of the
Church, still less to inspire any heretical movements. There was no formal
procedure of theological training nor permanently established centres of
learning, such as were to be created at a later date. No general council met
in the West until the First Lateran of 1123, and the last before that date (and
the last recognised by both East and West) had been the Fourth of
Constantinople of 869. As one major role of councils was the definition of
doctrine, the absence of any such meetings is indicative of theological quies-
cence at this time. And although there might be isolated intellectual heretics,
or even small groups which adhered to dissident doctrines, nothing developed at the popular level which could be described as a widespread heretical movement. The limited number of men with intellectual interests meant
that for the majority of believers, the precise nature of their faith was of little concern. They were willing to accept what the Church taught, and
devoted their talents to the greater glory of God. (One need only look at the
works of early Christian art, such as the Ardagh and Derrynaflan chalices,

or the Lindisfarne and Echternach Gospels, to see the level of artistry which was attained in providing articles to meet the needs of the Church.) If disagreements arose within the Church, it was more over matters of practice than over issues of belief – this can be seen in the controversy over the date of Easter, to which Bede devoted perhaps more attention than it really merited, because it was an issue in his native Northumbria. It is worth stressing that some parts of the Irish world had already accepted the Roman dating of Easter when the question was debated at Whitby.

An even more critical controversy was that over the reverencing of images, prompted by the Iconoclastic movement in the Eastern Church in the eighth century. Here the Western Church gave strong support to the use of images, perhaps because in the less intellectually sophisticated West the authorities considered that the great majority of believers required some visible focus for their worship. At the end of the sixth century Gregory the Great had affirmed the educational value of images in churches, while stressing that this teaching function must be distinguished from worship; he affirmed that pictures enabled the illiterate to follow the stories from Scripture and learn whom they should follow.[1] This was his justification for the use of images, and Gregory's eighth-century successors made it clear that they accepted it. The stress in the *Liber Pontificalis* on the images set up by the popes of this period may well represent conscious Western opposition to Eastern Iconoclasm.[2] Western support for the Iconoclasts was rare, although in the early ninth century bishop Claudius of Turin may have been affected by it, for he ordered the removal of images from churches in his diocese and disapproved of the veneration of the Cross. His views provoked a reaction in favour of images, not only in Italy but also in Gaul. Claudius did not confine his opposition simply to images, for he was also critical of other aspects of 'tangible' religion, such as relics and pilgrimages.[3] Italy, more closely connected with the Byzantine world than its Transalpine neighbours were, may well have retained a greater degree of intellectual sophistication, and it is noteworthy that a charge of unorthodoxy on an issue of Christology in 887 was brought against an Italian bishop, Liutward of Vercelli, rather than a northern one.[4]

The only doctrinal heresy which provided any serious threat to mainstream orthodoxy at this time was Arianism, which was an inheritance from the ancient world. Its significance should not be exaggerated, however, because even when it was at its most influential, shortly after the barbarian invasions, its threat was not total, because Arian rulers such as Theodoric the Ostrogoth were willing to extend favours to their Catholic subjects –Theodoric presented two silver candlesticks to St Peter's – and they in turn might appeal for his intervention, as in the struggle for the Papacy between Symmachus and Laurence around 500.[5] Indeed, in Theodoric's city of Ravenna, the separate baptisteries of the Orthodox and the Arians still survive, so it is clear that there was some measure of co-existence. In fact the mosaics in the latter depend on those in the former.[6] Pope Hormisdas was alleged to have sent envoys to Constantinople on Theodoric's advice, and his successor John I served on an embassy sent by the Ostrogoth king to the Byzantine emperor.[7] The most important barbarian kingdoms which upheld Arianism were those in Visigothic Spain, which did not accept orthodoxy until late in the sixth century, and in the parts of Italy under Lombard rule, which abandoned Arianism in the second half of the seventh century. By contrast, the adherence of the Franks under Clovis to Catholic Christianity at the end of the fifth century weakened the influence of the Arians, and may have played an influential part in securing the barbarian West for Catholic Christianity. It took time, however, before Arianism succumbed to orthodox pressure, and for a while it was still seen as dangerous. Gregory of Tours was apprehensive about it, mentioning a number of Arian persecutions of the orthodox in the *History of the Franks,* and recording miracles attesting the truth of Catholic Christianity against Arianism in the *Glory of the Martyrs.*[8] Frankish awareness of Arianism as a heresy continued to a later date; Fredegar noted as significant the conversion of the Spanish Visigothic king Reccared, and the enforced baptism of those Goths who had not yet been converted, and when Columbanus went to Italy, he is recorded as having written a learned work against them.[9]

Doctrinal deviance

Thereafter, doctrinal disputes were sporadic in the West until after 1000. There were only two episodes of any real significance that left an impression on contemporary writers. The earlier of these was the movement known as Adoptionism, which broke out in Spain in the late eighth century. Theologically this was related to earlier Nestorianism, and emphasised the humanity of Christ, affirming that he was an adopted son of God. It may also have had a political dimension in that it was connected with the attempts of the see of Toledo to assert its dominance in the Spanish Church, which did not see itself as so subordinate to Rome as did the Church in England and in Gaul.[10] The movement created something of a stir within the Carolingian Empire, for the *Royal Frankish Annals* record the recantations of one of the main upholders of Adoptionist doctrine, Felix, bishop of Urgel, in 792 and 794, and Alcuin, perhaps the leading intellectual figure at Charlemagne's court, wrote two works against the heresy.[11]

Adoptionism may have looked back to the ancient world, but the other significant episode, the condemnation of Gottschalk, may reflect the revival of learning and philosophy, and the study of ancient texts within the empire of Charlemagne. Gottschalk was a well-educated man, who had picked up strong predestinarian ideas, probably in Italy where the works of St Augustine were perhaps read more widely than in Transalpine Europe. There may indeed have been some regional variation in attitudes, because a papal view expressed in 859 differed little from the doctrines for which Gottschalk was condemned in 848 or 849, and again in 861. The opposition to him came above all from prelates who had a pastoral concern, including such great men as Hraban Maur and Hincmar of Rheims, who felt that if an individual's eternal destiny were already fixed, their flocks would have no incentive to lead a more Christian life. (This tendency for pastors to lay a greater stress on conduct and drift towards Pelagianism was to recur at other periods.) But it reflects the lower level of intellectual sophistication in northern Europe that this condemnation was an isolated event and did not have widespread repercussions. The intellectual response to Gottschalk was relatively limited and there was no widespread controversy, although a number of treatises were written on predestination. They were not, however, widely circulated, being written as dossiers for kings, bishops and councils. It should be noted, however, that one of the outstanding thinkers of the age, the Irishman Eriugena, wrote a treatise on predestination, in which he defended free will and was critical of Gottschalk's point of view. This was too anti-predestinarian to be accepted, and was itself condemned at two local synods, which were clearly trying to maintain a balance between rival points of view.[12] The absence of any prolonged controversy on this matter, however, indicates the lack of systematic theological debate at this period, and perhaps also the limited extent to which ideas circulated. Although recent studies have demonstrated the existence of intellectual debate, which aroused alarm in some quarters, it is clear that this never developed sufficiently to undermine the authority of the Church. Theology was concerned with confirming the doctrines of the faith, in some cases explaining them to new converts from paganism, and did not allow scope to those who might wish to explore the philosophical implications of belief, when orthodoxy itself was often only weakly defined. Where doubts did exist, they were kept within the confines of the clerical order, and did not spread into the lay world, where individuals did not indulge in rational speculation on theological matters. This is not to say that some laity were unconcerned with the deep issues of human existence, but they were willing to turn to the clergy as experts who could resolve their problems.

Other episodes of apparent dissent recorded in the chronicles were less important. The Annals of Fulda tell of a woman in the diocese of Constance who prophesied the end of the world, and who had sufficient charisma to strike fear into many people, including even churchmen. After admitting that she had been coached by a priest for the sake of gain, she was condemned by a synod at Mainz in 847. The nature of her prophecies, however, suggests that fear of an imminent apocalypse was sufficiently common for her to attain a measure of credibility among the people.[13] On the other hand, the apostasy of a deacon, Bodo, to Judaism, and his active proselytising on behalf of the latter religion in Spain, attracted public notice without any significant support. Hostility to Judaism was, of course, the norm, and it is significant that Reginardus, count of Sens, whom Fulbert of Chartres described as a heretic and a persecutor of the Church, was also suspected of Jewish leanings.[14]

Penitential discipline

Essentially, the teachings of the Church seem to have been accepted, and for most people religion was a matter of observing the approved rituals, without any particular concern about the precise substance of the faith. Occasionally, visible aspects of Church practice, such as the date of Easter in seventh-century Northumbria, attracted attention, but these could be resolved. Conduct counted for more than belief, and if individuals fell foul of the authorities it would probably be the result of social, and particularly sexual, indiscipline. To judge from the number of offences listed in the books of penances, almost any form of sexual relationship was regarded as undesirable. In the *Penitential* of Cummean (seventh century) there were thirty-three clauses dealing with fornication, and a substantial number of the twenty-one dealing with offences of boys also referred to sexual matters. Twenty-eight clauses dealt with sins of pride, eighteen with avarice, and only sixteen with anger.[15] The *Penitential* of Theodore contains twenty-two clauses on fornication, though one may doubt if some of the forms of deviance described were particularly common, and thirty on possible marriage irregularities.[16] Penances were imposed for sexual intercourse on Sundays and at various seasons of the year. Distinctions were even drawn between different forms of kissing; in the Roman *Penitential* 'simple' kissing incurred a penance of seven fasts, but 'lascivious' kissing one of eight. Similar distinctions were drawn in the *Penitential* of Cummean.[17] The clergy were, at least in theory, subjected to even more austere discipline in such matters; a bishop guilty of fornication was assigned twelve years of penance, and the desire to commit it, even if no actual act took place, received a penance of one year.[18] In view of these attitudes, it is perhaps hardly surprising that some heretical movements carried them to their logical conclusion and regarded the flesh and the devil as identical. The profession of faith made by Gerbert, when he became archbishop of Rheims in 991, but mainly deriving from pseudo-Isidore (*c*.850), was primarily concerned with steering a middle course in Christology between Nestorian and Monophysite doctrines. It also, however, contained a declaration that he did not prohibit marriage nor condemn second marriages. He also affirmed that he did not forbid meat-eating.[19] It is improbable that at this date dualist doctrines, which shunned the flesh in every respect, had yet penetrated to the West, although they were already taking root in the Balkans. But orthodox disciplinary ideas may well have prepared the soil in which they later took root.

By comparison with the penances imposed for sexual misconduct, those for failure to guard the elements in the mass properly were startlingly light compared with those which were found at a later date. This suggests that although by the ninth century there was a vigorous debate between Paschasius Radbertus and Ratramnus of Corbie whether the presence of Christ in the Eucharist should be understood as literal or figurative, and although reverence was always shown to the host, the elements were not regarded with the same awe as they were at a later date. In the Welsh preface of Gildas (sixth century), an individual who let the host fall to the ground was merely punished with the loss of supper, and in the *Penitential* of Cummean, failure to guard the host properly so that a mouse ate it incurred only forty days of penance, or twenty if a part was lost in church. In the *Penitential* of Theodore, the accidental mislaying of the host led to three weeks of penance, and one of three periods of forty days if it were lost by neglect. The so-called *Roman Penitential,* which survives in the writings of an early ninth-century bishop of Cambrai, deals with the dropping of the host in the section described as 'Of petty cases', and again provides relatively light penances.[20] The only early penitential which made a provision that implied respect for the elements was that of Bobbio (700–25), which stipulated that a priest who spilled the wine had to suck it up, and if an altar cloth was stained the priest had to drink the water with which it had been washed.[21] By contrast the *Monastic Constitutions* of Archbishop Lanfranc of Canterbury laid down that if the elements were allowed to fall to the ground, the area had to be scraped and cleaned, presumably to avoid the risk of trampling on the Lord's body. All involved in the accident were to be severely punished with flogging and a penance, while all other priests present were to offer themselves for punishment, seven of them being chosen at the discretion of the chapter.[22]

The development of Eucharistic thought

These changing attitudes must be seen against the development of Eucharistic thought. This had developed from patristic times, and in the Carolingian period new theological questions were being raised as to what precisely constituted a sacrament. But at this time matters were still open to debate, such as that between Radbertus and Ratramnus. This, however, was conducted without the condemnation of one or other of the parties as a heretic, which contrasts with the condemnation of Gottschalk in the near contemporary debate on predestination. The growth of logical studies from the late tenth century led to stress being placed on the antithesis between image and reality, and this was applied to the nature of the elements in the Eucharist. By the mid-eleventh century formulations of belief, of increasing subtlety, were expressed in 1054, 1059 and 1079.[23] As Lanfranc had been involved in the proceedings against the Eucharist views of Berengar of Tours, who had been critical of the belief in transubstantiation, he may have been particularly severe on those who took inadequate care of the elements. At a later date an accident to the elements might be turned to pious use –

John of Salisbury recorded that after the spilling of consecrated wine at the Council of Rheims (1148), the portion of the carpet on which it had fallen was cut out and kept as a relic. A penance was imposed on those responsible, but the nature of this was unspecified.[24] Even after the formal definition of the doctrine of transubstantiation at the fourth Lateran Council, the penalties laid down were less severe than Lanfranc's. A cleric who negligently left the Eucharist lying around rather than safely locked away was to be suspended for three months, but a more serious punishment was to be imposed 'if anything unspeakable happened'.[25]

The development of the liturgy

The doctrine of the Church was enshrined in its liturgy, but despite the centrality of the mass in worship, in the early centuries this was by no means uniform. In the centuries following the grant of toleration by Constantine, different rites developed in various places, although from this period there was a decline in the practice of improvisation which had been marked in Christianity's underground centuries. In 416 Innocent I urged that all the Western churches should follow Roman liturgical practices, but this was no more than an aspiration. Liturgies remained eclectic; early liturgical manuscripts from Merovingian Gaul, of which a considerable number survive, show wide variations, deriving not only from local traditions but also from those of Spain and Rome. Frankish councils in 517 and 554 tried to impose provincial uniformity, but although the form of the mass was unified, even within the region there was still some diversity in the associated prayers.[26] It reflects the local independence of the Frankish Church that it was the Council of Vaison which introduced two basic elements in the mass, the *Kyrie* and the *Sanctus,* into Gaul in 529. The *Agnus Dei* was introduced in Rome by Sergius I in 701, but the *Credo* took a long time to become fully established. It had been sung in Spain in the fifth century and was taken into the Frankish rite in the Carolingian period, but it did not enter the Roman rite until the eleventh century.[27] This apparently minor variation of practice had profound consequences for the Church as a whole, because this text of the Creed contained the *filioque* clause, and it was its appearance in the Roman rite that precipitated the split with the Church in Byzantium. Even in Rome itself there was more than one tradition of Latin chant, where the order called the 'Old Roman' survived till the High Middle Ages, and in the ninth century there was still a Greek community which chanted the psalms in the Byzantine manner.[28]

Attempts were made to unify rites in the Carolingian period, an age of greater political unification in which the lay rulers, notably Charlemagne, tried to strengthen their own power by attempting to introduce a common form of worship in their lands. But while Gallican and Roman liturgical traditions were blended into what is now generally regarded as Gregorian chant, particularly under the influence of Bishop Chrodegang of Metz, and attempts were made to enforce it, substantial variations in worship survived throughout the ninth century. Although Leo IV (847–55) threatened an abbot with excommunication if he did not follow the Gregorian rite, and Hadrian II (867–72) confirmed the Gregorian antiphonary, it was to be substantially later before most local liturgies were superseded by a common liturgical order.[29] Indeed, at an early period there does not even seem to have been any feeling that uniformity of rites was necessary over the Church as a whole. Gregory the Great instructed Augustine of Canterbury to gather the best from all churches, 'placing it like a bundle in the minds of the English', but in fact Roman customs gradually became dominant, although the practice of Roman chant at any particular time varied with the extent of Roman influence on the English Church.[30] The most important common feature of the Western rite was the unchallenged position of Latin, where only the *Kyrie* preserved a Greek text in the recurrent element or 'ordinary' of the mass (as opposed to the 'proper', which comprised the elements appropriate to particular feasts), whereas the Byzantine rite tended to use more than one language.[31] This had repercussions in missionary activity, particularly in parts of central Europe which were open to influences from both East and West. In ninth-century Bohemia, where the more successful early missionaries came from Byzantium, the *Lives* of the earliest missionaries Cyril and Methodius (significantly written themselves in Old Church Slavonic) relate how they were summoned to Rome, where the popes' attitude to the vernacular was inconsistent. Hadrian II was prepared to accept a Slav liturgy, and John VIII acquiesced in it after initial opposition. Stephen V's opposition to the vernacular, however, led Methodius's followers to leave Moravia for Bulgaria, where they employed the Byzantine rite but in the Slav language.[32] Church Slavonic did, however, survive into the eleventh century in Bohemia, including the composition of a liturgy of St Wenceslas. After the schism between East and West in 1054 it came increasingly under pressure, and Gregory VII refused recognition to the Slavonic liturgy in a bull of 1080. His reason for this reflects an increasing desire to assert clerical rights in the Church, for he declared that if Scripture was made clear to all, it might be vulgarised and subjected to disrespect.[33] By 1100 the Slavic church had disappeared from Bohemia. Vernacular worship was not restored there till the fourteenth century, when Charles IV was granted a special dispensation by the pope for it – even then, monks had to be called in from Croatia to recreate it.[34] Bohemia was always vulnerable to pressures from the German Empire, and the decline of the Slav liturgy may have been accelerated by the Magyar invasions which drove a wedge between the northern and the southern Slavs.

It was not just in central Europe that Gregory VII tried to impose liturgical uniformity. In Spain the Mozarabic liturgy had developed more freely in its non-biblical sections than the Roman one, and although most of the additions to the text date from the seventh and eighth centuries, some others continued to be made until the early eleventh.[35] Roman influence was evident in Catalonia and Aragon before it extended to the other Spanish kingdoms, and its spread reflects the extension of papal authority in each of them. In 1074 Gregory wrote to the king of Castile and León that these kingdoms should follow the Roman rather than the Toledan rite, on the grounds that the Roman Church had been founded by Peter and Paul and consecrated in the blood of Christ. In 1081 Gregory expressed his pleasure that the Roman order had been celebrated there, although in fact it was not until four years later, at the Council of Burgos, that it was decided to impose the Roman rite in place of the traditional Toledan liturgy. Some of the clergy resisted the change and had a measure of lay support.[36] The theological implications of liturgical variations were still a matter for concern in the early twelfth century, when Paschal II was asked about the validity of ordinations and marriages conducted by the Mozarabic rite, and it reflects traditional diversity that he ruled in favour of both.[37]

Within the context of the liturgy, however, one can see local variations, notably in the addition of tropes, or verses commenting on the main text, and some of these circulated from one country to another. In the tenth century *Winchester Troper* from England, some sections derived from the monastery of St Gall. Adam of Bremen noted that Archbishop Hermann brought a certain Guido (not the famous Guido of Arezzo, but from the name presumably an Italian) to his see to teach music and that he reformed the chant of the church. A later archbishop, Adalbert, sought to increase the impressiveness of worship by the elaboration of the offices. 'He sought for everything that was grand, everything that was resplendent, everything that was glorious whether in things divine or human. And on this account he is said to have delighted in the smoke of spices and the glittering of lights and the resounding of deep sonorous voices.'[38] Music may indeed have been seen as prefiguring the courts of heaven, and certainly in the ninth century Paschasius Radbertus used the image of music as a form of heavenly harmony.[39] In the Benedictine Rule, the liturgy was known as the *Opus Dei* or the Work of God, and this developed with the passage of time and with changes in the character of monasticism itself. In early Benedictinism, relatively few monks were priests – indeed it was not until the ninth century that there was a requirement for abbots to be in priestly orders – and the celebration of the Eucharist was restricted to Sundays and major feasts. As more monks were ordained, perhaps because the monasteries were playing a significant missionary role, and it was necessary to have men who could administer the sacrament in newly converted lands, the Eucharist became more prominent in monastic services. The *Opus Dei* was developed to a high degree at Cluny, where the prime activity of the monks was liturgical and the services became increasingly elaborate. Various additions had already been made to the original Benedictine liturgy by the ninth century, and by about 1000 duties in choir occupied the greatest part of the monks' days. On major festivals about eight hours might be spent in choir.[40]

Spiritual ideals

A belief that the powers of evil were rampant, and needed to be opposed by all possible means, led to worship being regarded as a form of spiritual warfare. Many recruits into this spiritual army were involuntary, a large number of both monks and nuns being oblates, who had been offered to the religious life in childhood by their parents, and were brought up to the religious life – indeed there were debates about whether such individuals had to confirm such views when they reached the age of discretion.[41] Besides these, however, there was also a steady flow of pious laymen into the cloister in middle life. The motivation of such men probably varied from one to another, although it was fundamentally due to a sense of guilt at various kinds of sin, either personal or collective. One may suspect that the identification of the flesh with the devil may explain why the Norman noble Ralph, of the house of Giroie, who became a monk at Marmoutier and later at St Évroul, prayed (successfully) for an incurable leprosy, so that his body might be delivered from its sins, while his nephew Robert of Grandmesnil, who forced his wealthy relations to profit their souls by distributing their goods for the needs of the faithful, may have reacted more against avarice than against lust. In the case of Richard of Heudicourt, fear of death after being wounded in battle determined him to fight under the monastic rule by the practice of virtue.[42] The writer's use of the image of warfare for the spiritual life emphasises the idea of struggle against the forces of evil. The thought of the next world, and the desire to make adequate preparation for entering it, was the most profound influence on those who voluntarily entered monasticism.

It is only occasionally that one has light thrown on the outlook and beliefs of the ordinary laity, not least because the available sources were written by churchmen. One must, however, distinguish between what was taught and what was believed by the mass of the people, because in newly Christianised lands conversion was not a matter of individual persuasion but one of formal change imposed from above by the local rulers. For many people, one suspects that they saw the new religion simply as a different and probably more potent form of magic, and this certainly is reflected in the stress placed on relics and miracles in the religious beliefs of the time.[43] In such cases old attitudes might still survive, and men might indeed resent the implications of a new religion which proclaimed that their ancestors might be damned, as this represented a break with the solidarity of tribal traditions.[44] A different problem existed in areas where Christianity had been established since Roman times, although again it reflected religion as an inheritance rather than something to which the laity came by individual conviction. This was symbolised most clearly by the replacement of earlier forms of pre-baptismal instruction by the practice of infant baptism.

Probably the spiritual concerns of most of the laity, like those of the men who entered the religious life, focussed most sharply on the relationship of the present life to the hereafter, as evidenced by Bede's famous story (and in this context it is irrelevant whether it is literally true or a literary topos) of the Northumbrian noble who compared man's life with a bird flying into the hall on a dark night, and then disappearing again into the unknown. The question of judgement was bound up with death, and even those who remained in the lay world were concerned with their future destiny. Prayers for the sick and rituals for the anointing of the dying were brought together in eighth-century liturgical works, and the period saw increasing stress being laid on rites for deathbed penitence, and the development of services to commemorate the soul and aid it in the afterlife. Though these derived from various sources, the unity brought about by the Carolingian Empire saw an increasing synthesis of distinct traditions.[45] Burial, the final stage in the individual's rite of passage, was also brought under the Church's control, although it is by no means certain that one can assume that interments with grave goods necessarily date from the pagan period – in the early period at any rate the Church did not outlaw the practice. There does, however, seem to have been a decline in the amount of material that was deposited in inhumation burials. In Anglo-Saxon England unfurnished inhumation became the norm by the eighth century, and this was paralleled in Northern Gaul by about 700. In some parts of Germany the deposit of grave goods persisted until well into the eighth century. By contrast, although unsurprisingly, southern Gaul, Italy and Spain, where the invasions may have disrupted existing Christianity less, followed late Roman practice from an early date, with few or no grave goods. Most cremation burials probably date from pagan times, although the repeated condemnation of these in Christian writings may suggest that this practice may have survived for a time after the conversion.[46]

How issues of sin and redemption were understood probably lies beyond what the historian can ascertain, although one has some pointers to the beliefs taught in literary and artistic sources, which show that Christian ideas were interpreted in the light of contemporary social attitudes. The great Anglo-Saxon religious poem, *The Dream of the Rood,* derives both from the heroic mould of secular literature, with Christ being depicted as the hero who freed mankind, with the cross as a banner of victory, and from a contemporary and international liturgical innovation, the introduction of the Feast of the Exaltation of the Holy Cross by Sergius I (687–701).[47] In the Saxon gospel epic, the *Heliand,* Jesus is described by the term *drohin,* meaning a personal lord to whom loyalty was owed, and his gathering of the disciples is depicted in terms of a chieftain gathering his war-band – indeed Jesus is designated in highly contemporary secular terms as a 'generous mead-giver'.[48] Iconography stressing the victory of Christ at the Last Judgement can be supported by literary evidence. The Irish hymn known as 'St Patrick's Breastplate' looks to the day of judgement when a triumphant Christ will ride up the heavenly way, in imagery appropriate to that of a victorious king. The early Church's expectation of an imminent Second

Coming may well explain this eschatological imagery, even though by this period it was now more prepared to see this as a distant rather than an immediate prospect. Sanctity too was depicted in heroic terms which would have been comprehensible to lay society in the *Life* of the Mercian saint Guthlac (d. 716), who resisted the assaults of demons while living in a marsh comparable to the haunts of Grendel and of the dragon in *Beowulf*.[49] In such situations, the Christianity of the people may have been essentially a more powerful form of magic than that of traditional pagan religion.

Images of the Passion

Although many crosses were set up in the conversion period to mark centres of religious observance, these often were ornamented with imagery which was more decorative than instructive, and initially at any rate they were crosses rather than crucifixes. One wonders if this may have reflected the tradition which was manifested most strongly in the Iconoclast movement in the East, where the depiction of Christ was condemned. Crucifixes are found, but they were not accorded the same prominence as they were given later. Indeed, in many cases where the crucifixion is depicted in art, it may well have been as part of a narrative sequence rather than as a means of focussing the attention of the worshipper on the suffering Christ. On the Ruthwell Cross from Dumfriesshire, probably dating from the second quarter of the eighth century, the crucifixion is depicted in a panel at the foot of the cross, while the largest figurative panel depicts Christ in majesty, with his feet on two beasts – on the near-contemporary cross at Bewcastle, the majesty figure is again dominant and a similar motif appears on an ivory plaque, possibly of English origin, but now in Belgium. The Douce Psalter, from the tenth century, contains the same image.[50] It has been suggested that the crucifixion at Ruthwell is in the lowest panel so that it would be accessible as a spiritual focus to worshippers praying at the foot of the cross, but this remains unproven.[51] In an age of conversion, such iconography was a form of spiritual teaching, but when the converts were from a society where heroic values were highly esteemed, it was perhaps deemed necessary to depict Christ as victorious rather than as a suffering victim. Even empty crosses could be shown with the figure of Christ separated from them. In an apse mosaic from S. Stefano Rotondo in Rome, from the mid-seventh century, a bust of Christ surmounts the cross, which is flanked by two saints.[52] In the more sophisticated society of Italy, there may have been less wish to show Christ as a triumphant victor than there was for the more barbarous northerners, but the emphasis is more on the overcoming of death than on the suffering which preceded it.

The crucifixion, of course, was a recurrent theme in sacred art, although in the earlier part of our period it was more often engraved on an ivory or on a cross than carved on stone in the round. Increasingly the suffering of the crucified figure was stressed by the artists in a more naturalistic form, although there was also a tradition in which the figure of Christ was shown more as a triumphant Lord than as a Saviour who suffered in his humanity. Earlier art works showed the arms in an outstretched position, carrying little of the weight of the body, although often with a drooping head. But some ivory panels from as early as around 820 do show the body being held up by the weight of the arms. A crystal from 867 and a cross carved on the imperial crown (973/983) both depict the body falling forward and being carried by the arms.[53] Such imagery was not universal, however, and even in the late eleventh century, a crucifix from Helmstedt shows the arms in a horizontal position even though the head is drooping.[54] The new styles were probably adopted at different dates in various parts of Christendom, and it is perhaps significant that it was in Germany, which lay close to those areas of Christendom where the greatest innovations in religious life were taking place in the tenth century, that the crucifix made for Archbishop Gero of Köln depicted a suffering and human Saviour. Probably the emphasis on a victorious Christ in the art of Ottonian Germany was connected with the desire to depict the majesty of power, which applied to a divinely ordained emperor as well as to Christ.[55] Elsewhere the more triumphant image persisted, although it is not clear for how long, because the dates of the works cannot be certainly determined – two crucifixion plaques, one from Penrith in Cumbria and the other from Clonmacnoise, which display a triumphant Christ, have been variously dated between the tenth and the twelfth century.[56] Early eleventh-century gospel books saw both images of the crucifixion; some, in a tradition originating at Trier, show the suffering and compassionate Lord, while others, such as one from Regensburg, still depict the victorious Christ.[57] In Denmark the change from the triumphant to the suffering image came at a late date.[58]

Much early Christian art was narrative and didactic rather than emotional, and in the Mediterranean world, under the influence of Byzantium, the dominant theme was that of the majesty of God, and often looked forward to the Last Judgement. In the Roman Church of S. Lorenzo fuori le Mura, Christ is shown as enthroned in an arch mosaic from the late sixth century.[59] The figure of Christ in Majesty surrounded by the symbols of the evangelists also appears on the sarcophagus at Jouarre of the Frank Agilbert, who had been bishop of the West Saxons.[60] The ubiquity of such imagery must have served to emphasise the might of a victorious God rather than to appeal to the emotions of the individual.

The appearance of unorthodoxy

Beyond the limits of orthodox beliefs, one still sees the survival of semi-pagan folk customs and traditions, which were to persist for centuries, sometimes vaguely Christianised and at other times beyond the limits of acceptability, such as witch cults. Towards the end of the period, the problem of heresy re-emerged in a new form. This may be connected with an increasing level of lay religion, and the willingness of participants to try to clarify what they personally believed. More significantly, the ecclesiastical authorities began to pay attention to such beliefs, and to see deviance from orthodoxy as a problem. This in turn reflected more clearly defined limits of orthodoxy. In some cases pious churchmen may simply have been suspicious of men who were attracted to classical culture – Rodulfus Glaber referred to a man from Ravenna who was condemned by his local bishop for asserting that the sayings of the poets should be preferred to the Scriptures, and suggested that his attitude was shared by others in Italy, Sardinia and Spain. He also applauded when Hervé, the treasurer of St Martin at Tours, turned away from the liberal arts, 'because most learned from such studies only pride'.[61] This was perhaps a more critical view of the classics than that held at an earlier date by other monks, whose activities as copyists helped to preserve many works of classical literature. Even men of theological distinction, such as Paschasius Radbertus, were acquainted with some ancient literature – although much of his language derived from the Scriptures, he also quoted from various classical writers, notably Terence.[62]

Another case of alleged heresy may reflect little more than popular discontent at some aspects of church life. About 1000, a man named Leutard, from the diocese of Chalons-sur-Marne, who was accused of iconoclasm, of denying the obligation to pay tithes, and of other unnamed heresies, apparently attracted a number of followers. After the bishop restored these to orthodox faith he committed suicide.[63] Heresy persisted in the diocese, and about 1015 the bishop called a council to deal with it. In the neighbouring diocese of Cambrai-Arras, the bishop proceeded against a group of suspected heretics of alleged Italian origin about 1025, but the precise nature of their beliefs is uncertain. They disbelieved in the need for the organised Church, and wished to abandon the world, earn their living by labour, injure no one and show charity to all of their own faith. In such cases baptism would be unnecessary, because the evil life of the priest administering it could interfere with the recipient's salvation, and because an infant could not understand the need for it, and might relapse into vice later in life. It has been argued that they were early Cathars (see Glossary), but they do not appear to have held some of the latter's characteristic views, notably vegetarianism and the renunciation of marriage. They appear to have regarded themselves as a sect, but are perhaps best understood as a group of pious enthusiasts, some of whose views differed only narrowly from those of the orthodox. They did not, however, develop into a heretical movement.[64] They may cast a shadow forward to later heresies, reflecting how individuals might carry the Church's teachings beyond acceptable limits, but they were not in any way typical of the religion of the time.

THE AGE OF UNIFICATION
(1050–1270)

|6|

Gregorian reform – the clerical order

Gregorian reform

The movement for reform in the Western Church which is commonly called after Pope Gregory VII was in fact already under way before he ascended the papal throne. Nevertheless its name is appropriate, for it was during his pontificate and under his initiative that the whole ideal of reform took a new and much more militant course. Furthermore, one of the main consequences of this movement was that enhancement of papal power to which the 'papal monarchy' of the central Middle Ages owed its essential character. Reform, particularly that of the individual, is an ideal fundamental to Christianity but from the late eleventh century existing ideals were blended with newer ones and not only brought about actual changes in church life but also formulated a set of ideals for it which became established as the right order of Christian life. Significant though many of the changes were in themselves, it would not be too much to say that the reformers' greatest victory was to establish for several centuries the acceptable form of what the Church and its relations with the lay world should be. Above all, this took the form of the Church claiming an autonomy from the lay world which it had not possessed at an earlier date.

Nevertheless the historian should be cautious about how the concept of reform is interpreted, and it would be foolish to see it as a sudden revolution. There had been earlier movements which asserted new spiritual ideals, and these had co-existed with practices which the most spiritually dynamic figures of the age may have condemned but which were not necessarily regarded as undesirable, let alone as evil, by everyone. It is unquestionable that some aspects of the tenth- and early eleventh-century Church were open to criticism, but this does not mean that it should be condemned in its entirety. Nor indeed did all reformers follow a common programme, and the developments in the Church at this time must be seen as piecemeal and often spontaneous, rather than as a result of a deliberate programme. Only retrospectively can one see how they attained their eventual form.

At the same time, it must be borne in mind that these struggles for power and influence generated a massive theoretical debate, which reflected two significant developments, the emergence of a more conscious monarchical authority among the lay rulers of Christendom, and the increasing intellectual unity of the West. A consequence of this was the realisation of the antagonists that advantages were to be gained from seeking some moral justification for their actions. Both sides saw themselves as the guardians of a divine order in the world, and portrayed the other as being in revolt against God. The character of political debate rapidly became more analytical and sophisticated, from pamphlets marked more by their skill in rhetoric to others which deployed biblical and canonist arguments in support of their case.[1] This intellectual framework made an important contribution to the increasing centralisation of the Western Church from the eleventh century onwards.

The origins of the reform Papacy

While one must pay close attention to gradual changes of ecclesiastical practice and even more of ecclesiastical attitudes, the changing balance of influence between the lay and the clerical rulers of the Church can be seen most dramatically in two contrasting events just over thirty years apart: the dominance of the Emperor Henry III, when he deposed rival popes at the Synod of Sutri in 1046 (this being followed by the election of a series of German popes who encouraged reform of the church without challenging imperial influence), and the humiliation of his son, Henry IV, who had to do penance to Gregory VII at Canossa in 1077, before being released from papal excommunication. This reversal of power was due to a blend of accidental circumstances and various deliberate acts of policy. Perhaps the most important chance factor was the death of Henry III in 1056 and the succession of his son as a minor. In the years after Sutri, the emperor had secured the election of several successive German popes, but in 1057, at the time of the first vacancy after his death, the leading reformist churchmen in Rome chose the abbot of Monte Cassino as pope, without consulting the imperial court. This move was probably not a deliberate snub to the young emperor and the court – a delegation was subsequently sent to Germany to secure imperial approval – but rather an attempt to exclude the great Roman families from recovering their influence over the Roman see. The absence of a powerful emperor who might intervene south of the Alps, however, enabled a group of strong-minded churchmen, imbued with a range of reform ideals, to gain influence at the centre of the Church. Men such as Cardinal Humbert, Peter Damiani, and the Archdeacon Hildebrand were by no means agreed on all that needed to be done, but there were considerable areas of common ground among them.

The earliest phase of the reform movement focussed on two particular themes, simony and clerical marriage. In neither of these matters was there any particular cause for conflict between the secular and the spiritual powers. Indeed, on the question of clerical marriage, laymen may well have welcomed the attempts to enforce celibacy, because this could enable them to extend their ecclesiastical patronage to cadets of their families, in the knowledge that the benefices concerned were not heritable, and could be employed again in later generations to make provision for their relatives. It is perhaps noteworthy that although clerical concubinage was regularly condemned, the marriage of churchmen was regarded with far more hostility. Hostility to simony was also long-standing, and it was agreed that to take money for the gifts of the spirit was a grave sin; on the other hand it was by no means always clear for what precisely money had been paid, and it may be that towards the mid-eleventh century, criticism was extended towards payments which related to the material rather than the spiritual rights of the Church. Various early eleventh-century writers commented critically on simony; Glaber declared that those who had been appointed through simony were zealous in their avarice, because that had been how they had obtained office, and Wipo stated that although Conrad II had initially accepted money for the bishopric of Basel he was later penitent for this.[2] In the mid-eleventh century a vigorous attack on simony was launched by the first of the German popes, Leo IX, who took action against it not only in Italy but also in synods which he held at Rheims and at Mainz, even to the extent of removing bishops who were guilty of it. He also took steps against clerical marriage. After his death men such as Humbert and Peter Damiani continued propaganda against simony, even to the extent of arguing that the ordinations of simoniac bishops were invalid.[3]

Between the Synod of Sutri and Gregory VII's accession, the event which has probably attracted the most attention was a Roman synod of 1059, at which Nicholas II issued a decree giving the cardinal bishops the power to elect the new pope. The cardinal clerks were then to join in the election, with the rest of the clergy and the people giving their assent. This set aside the traditional right that inhabitants of a diocese had to choose their bishop, and the decree may have been partly intended to validate Nicholas's title, as he had been elected outside Rome, without popular acclaim, by a group of cardinal bishops. Imperial rights were left vague, but there is little doubt that the absence of an adult emperor at the time contributed to the acceptance of this measure, which also asserted the rights of the clergy against those of the Roman nobility. These had played a part in the choice of Nicholas's predecessor Benedict X, who was later driven out and deposed. (His status remained dubious, for the next pope to take the name was designated Benedict XI.) The importance of the measure should not be exaggerated, because it certainly did not end disorder at papal elections, but it did mark a step in the rise of papal autonomy from lay interference. This counted for more than the enactment of a precise election procedure. In fact, when Hildebrand was chosen pope in 1073, taking the title of Gregory VII, the procedures which had been stipulated in 1059 were not followed. Various bulls which he issued between his election and his consecration give an account of how the crowd had dragged him to 'the place of apostolic rule'.[4] This fact was not overlooked by the pope's enemies – Henry IV alluded to the election decree in 1076, and when an imperial synod at Brixen in 1080 tried to depose the pope one justification for its action was that it had been overlooked.[5]

Simony

After his election as pope, Gregory seems to have stepped up the campaign against simony. Even before his consecration he denounced the election of a simoniac, Godfrey, as archbishop of Milan, describing him as an execrable heretic and urging the recipients of his letters to resist him to the best of their ability.[6] But Milan was already a centre of spiritual unrest; from the 1050s a radical movement, which came to be known as the Patarenes, had attacked married clergy and the practice of simony. Much of their support derived from the poorer classes in the city, although the leaders were drawn from some of the wealthier members of society. Opposition to them, however, was not based purely on the defence of the practices being attacked, but also involved a claim of Milanese independence from papal influence, asserting the traditions of St Ambrose against those of St Peter. The first leader of the Patarenes, the clerk Ariald, was murdered in 1066 but his successor, the layman Erlembald, established ties with Hildebrand and made a plan for a canonical election to be held on the archbishop's death. The latter, however, attempted to anticipate this by resigning in favour of his subdeacon, Godfrey, and having him invested by the emperor. Anti-Roman sentiment led the Lombard bishops to consecrate Godfrey, while Erlembald tried to secure the election of his own candidate. Eventually, in fact, the emperor's actions alienated him from the Milanese clergy, who by the end of the century were to become strong partisans of the Papacy.[7]

In Milan, political factors complicated the issue, but there is no doubt that Gregory was determined to attack simony on principle wherever it occurred. References to the problem occur frequently in his letters, and at times his actions even had imperial support. He asked Henry to intervene against the simoniac bishop of Bamberg, instructing him to ensure the election of a pastor to the see in accordance with divine law. On other occasions, however, Henry was seen as supporting simoniacs, and in a letter of 1076 the pope made it clear that this was the reason for his excommunication. Clergy suspected of the offence were attacked or replaced in places as far apart as Brittany, Flanders and Narbonne.[8] At the same time, however, the pope took steps to ensure that the ordinations of clergy by simoniacs would remain valid if the recipients were not guilty of the offence and were unaware of the status of the officiating bishop. In this he took a more moderate approach than some more hard-line reformers, such as Cardinal Humbert, who had asserted that a bishop who had received simoniacal consecration was incapable of conducting ordinations.[9] It took time, however, before measures against it were effective. It was clearly seen as a major problem at the First and Second Lateran Councils (1123, 1139) – the first canons of both referred to the offence – but by the Third (1179) simony itself had disappeared from the list of named offences which were condemned, although its enactments included bans on demanding money for sacraments and for receiving men as monks in return for payment.[10]

Clerical distinctiveness – bloodshed

The condemnation of simony was coupled with attempts to emphasise the distinctive status of the clergy. This was most marked in the increasing emphasis on the ideal of celibacy, but the movement was not limited to this. The developing perception of clerical status was to be clearly demonstrated in the mid-twelfth-century *Libellus de diversis ordinibus,* which declared that monks, canons and clerks should fast and abstain more than ordinary Christians.[11] The clergy not only had to be different, but had to be seen to be different – a council at London in 1102 not only deprived various abbots who had been guilty of simony but also laid down regulations for clerical attire and for the enforcement of the tonsure.[12] Attempts were also made to separate the clergy from activities which involved bloodshed, whereas at an earlier date, even popes had led armies into battle. Indeed, even in the mid-eleventh century bishops might be involved in war. The *Anglo-Saxon Chronicle* noted the death in battle in 1056 of Bishop Leofgar of Hereford (who had kept his moustache till he became a bishop) and a number of his priests. In the Bayeux Tapestry, Odo of Bayeux is depicted in full armour and wielding a club, to 'encourage' his young soldiers, although Orderic Vitalis declared that the duty of the clergy who were present at Hastings was to support the fight with their prayers.[13] Gregory VII, however, laid down penalties for clerks who carried arms and were guilty of homicides. This did not initially prevent churchmen from being involved in military leadership, provided that they avoided actual combat. In the First Crusade, where the army was under the command of Bishop Adhemar of Le Puy, he gave instructions on the adequate feeding of the horses before the battle of Antioch.[14] This attitude to clerical shedding of blood became increasingly restrictive; by the Fourth Lateran Council of 1215, clerks were not only forbidden to take command of mercenaries, but were also debarred from participation in legal proceedings (including the ordeal) which might give rise to bloodshed.[15] Such actions also incurred critical comment; Guibert of Nogent felt that it was inappropriate for the bishop of Laon to couch a lance in warlike manner, even in jest.[16]

There were practical problems in avoiding bloodshed, because the Church's material existence was bound up with the feudal structure of society. Churchmen who held lands by feudal tenure might find themselves obliged to lead contingents from their estates to war, although they might avoid actual participation in fighting. It is clear that in twelfth-century León bishops did not merely send contingents to the royal army, but also served in person, although changing attitudes can be seen when this practice was condemned at the Council of Palencia in 1129. However, when Abbot Samson of Bury led a contingent of knights to Windsor during the English civil disorders of Richard I's reign, he is unlikely to have borne arms himself, as he excommunicated all makers of war and was described as shining in counsel rather than in prowess.[17] During the Hundred Years War, however, the archbishop of Sens was taken prisoner and the bishop of Chalons was killed at the battle of Poitiers, and two years later the bishop of Troyes played an active part in military resistance to the English.[18] But the ecclesiastical authorities probably distanced themselves from churchmen who behaved as soldiers. Jean de Venette suggested that when a canon of Amiens was beheaded for supporting the king of Navarre against the king of France, without the church courts intervening to claim him, they had been indifferent to his fate, because he had behaved more as a soldier than as a churchman.[19]

Nor indeed was war the only context in which churchmen ran the risk of being involved in bloodshed, as they might act as royal judges. Archbishop Hubert Walter was recorded as ordering the hanging of a certain William the Bearded for stirring up the citizens of London against the king.[20] The English judicial bench continued to contain churchmen till the late thirteenth century, who may well have participated in capital sentences. In this sphere, however, attitudes changed; in the fifteenth century men who had taken part in such proceedings even as laymen had qualms about whether they were eligible for orders and sought dispensations to receive them.[21] Already in the thirteenth century, French church councils, at Valence (1248), Albi (1254) and Vienne (1289), had tried to detach the clergy from involvement in public affairs, and particularly in lay courts.[22] One may suspect that avoidance of bloodshed was one factor behind such measures.

The converse to the ban on clergy being involved in the shedding of blood was that their own persons were increasingly regarded as exempted from the imposition of physical punishment. It took time, however, before churchmen succeeded in securing this protection. In late eleventh-century England it was a matter of controversy whether the bishop of Durham, who had been involved in revolt against William Rufus, should be tried as a bishop or as a feudal vassal. Reformers' reservations about old-style churchmen are reflected in Orderic Vitalis's attitude to Odo of Bayeux, whom he described as worldly. He did suggest, however, that the English magnates had discouraged the king from executing him for treason, specifically because he was a priest. Similarly, although Guibert of Nogent detested

Bishop Gaudry of Laon, he condemned the latter's brutal murder in 1112.[23] On the other hand the fate of Bertulf, provost of St Donatian at Bruges, who was involved in the murder of Count Charles of Flanders in 1127, was apparently regarded as justifiable by Galbert of Bruges, who wrote an account of it. Bertulf was hanged naked in the market-place of Ypres, with his breeches being removed before execution to display his pudenda to the crowd as a further act of humiliation.[24] But by the mid-twelfth century the right of the church courts to claim the persons of criminous clerks was one of the major issues in dispute between Henry II of England and Archbishop Becket, and in the late thirteenth century the provincial council of Vienne of 1289 stipulated penalties for laity who arrested and detained clerks, and ordered that clerks arrested for open crime should be handed over to the episcopal court as soon as possible.[25]

Clerical distinctiveness – celibacy

The abandonment of weapons may have been easier for churchmen than the acceptance of an ideal of celibacy. There were certainly places in the early eleventh century where clerical marriage was assumed as the norm, even if it was regarded with some disapproval. The *Northumbrian Priests' Law* from the 1020s laid down 'If a priest leaves a woman and takes another, let him be anathema'. The framer of the law clearly could not bring himself to use the word 'wife', although in practice he clearly accepted that the priest should be married.[26] Orderic Vitalis, writing of Normandy in the eleventh century, commented on the fact that bishops as well as priests 'freely shared the beds of concubines and openly boasted of their numerous progeny'. He saw the Council of Rheims of 1049 as a turning-point, when priests were forbidden to bear arms or take wives. His comment on the council, however, was that priests were more reluctant to live chaste lives than to abandon their weapons. Both practices, however, persisted, and Guibert of Nogent described two archdeacons of the church of Laon respectively as 'more of a soldier than a priest' and 'more than averagely incontinent with women'.[27]

Celibacy was seen as a form of personal purity essential for men who handled the holy elements of the body of Christ, and the increasing stress laid on it must be associated with the affirmation of a doctrine of transubstantiation in the Eucharist. Indeed, this enhanced the awe with which the most pious men regarded the priesthood, and some, such as the future St Gilbert of Sempringham, were reluctant to accept ordination through a sense of their own unworthiness.[28] Before long, at least theoretically, celibacy became the most distinctive mark of clerical status. It is not surprising that it was emphasised more strictly among the regular clergy than among seculars because it had its origin in monasticism, but the command in an Icelandic Penitential of the thirteenth century that a monk or regular canon discovered in the sin of incontinence should incur the same penance as one guilty of homicide does carry the defence of the ideal to extremes.[29]

It took time, however, before celibacy could be enforced in practice, and there was widespread opposition to papal decrees of 1073 and 1075 against clerical marriage.[30] In 1075 the pope wrote to the archbishops of Mainz and Magdeburg, and to the bishop of Constance, banning those who had committed fornication from the ministry of the altar. A diocesan council at Constance, however, rejected the celibacy decrees, provoking a furious counter-blast from Gregory, who denounced the bishop for insolence and disobedience, for 'allowing those who had joined themselves to women to continue in their shame'. The fact that he also wrote to the clergy and laity of Germany forbidding obedience to bishops who failed to implement the celibacy decrees suggests that the opposition was not confined to one diocese.[31] Further letters of 1079 banned people from hearing the offices of priests who were guilty of fornication, and in 1080 he reproved the bishop of Thérouanne for tolerating it.[32]

The affirmation of a decree was a very different matter from putting it into force. In practical terms it was impossible to deprive married priests of their wives, because they would either abandon their clerical status or substitute illicit sexual relations for their previous legal ones. The clergy were clearly unwilling to abandon family life, and Archbishop John of Rouen was stoned out of a synod when he forbade priests to keep concubines.[33] In Normandy, however, Duke William supported the reformers, and at the Council of Lillebonne (1080) 'by the king's foresight and the advice of the barons sound provision was made for the prosperity of God's church and the whole kingdom'. This included a ban on clergy down to the order of subdeacon having wives.[34] Well-disposed lay rulers could give an impetus to change, and reform-minded higher clergy realised that some form of compromise was required if this was to be achieved. Gregory VII evidently hoped for more from some laymen than from bishops, because in 1075 he wrote to Rudolf of Swabia and Berthold of Carinthia commanding them not to recognise clerks who had been appointed simoniacally, or who were charged with fornication, irrespective of what the bishops might do or say.[35] Probably the first area where attempts were made to impose celibacy was in communities, which could be more closely monitored than local churches. Archbishop Lanfranc of Canterbury wrote to John of Rouen that if a canon were to keep his prebend, he should not be allowed to keep his wife, but at the Council of Winchester in 1076 he laid down that while priests should be forbidden to marry in future, those who had wives should not be required to put them away. Lanfranc's successor, Anselm, tried to lay down celibacy for all men receiving orders from the subdiaconate upwards, and forbade priests' sons from inheriting their father's churches. But these measures had little effect, and in 1107 the pope permitted the archbishop to grant dispensations at his discretion, because a married clergy was common in England.[36] There were similar problems at Bremen, where Archbishop

Adalbert tried to enforce the decree of the Council of Mainz against clerical marriage and exhorted the clergy to be free from 'the pestiferous bonds of women', but accepted that not all of them could attain such perfection. These were instructed to preserve the marriage tie with modesty in accordance with the saying, 'If you are not chaste, at least be cautious'.[37]

If even reform-minded prelates had problems in imposing the new practices, the situation was more difficult when members of the higher clergy were themselves married, even if this was informal and discreet, as in the cases of Bishop Roger of Salisbury, Henry I's great administrator, and his nephew, Nigel of Ely. Such men could hardly attempt to enforce on their subordinates a rule which they themselves did not observe, so it is hardly surprising that clerical marriage persisted. As late as 1160, in a transaction which verges on the simoniacal, a priest, Daniel, granted the church of St Edmund to the canons of St Paul's, London, on condition that his son Ismael hold it for life in return for an annual payment of 12d. One of the chapter's witnesses to the charter was Henry, described as son of the bishop (though it does not say which bishop).[38]

Nevertheless, measures against married priests were reiterated in Church councils from the late eleventh century in increasingly strict terms. A decree of the Council of Clermont in 1095 forbidding the ordination of sons of priests unless they had first made a monastic profession was clearly intended to prevent benefices becoming hereditary.[39] Paschal II's Council of Troyes (1107) enjoined continence on priests and perhaps also on deacons, laying down that those who were married should be deprived of office. (The same sanctions were also applied against simony.[40]) At the First Lateran Council (1123), priests, deacons and subdeacons were forbidden to live with concubines and wives, and at the Second Lateran Council (1139) men in these orders (including bishops) who had taken wives were to be separated from their partners and compelled to do penance. No one was to hear the masses of priests whom they knew to be married and the marriages themselves were to be regarded as invalid, because they were against canon law. Measures were also taken to prevent hereditary succession to churches, for sons of priests were to be removed from the ministry of the altar, unless they were living under a rule in a house of monks or canons, a reinforcement of the decree of Clermont. The language of the Third Lateran Council's decree (1179) almost certainly reflects changing attitudes, for it simply provided penalties for clerks who kept mistresses, the assumption being that such women could not be regarded as wives.[41] But at the local level opposition persisted. At a provincial synod in Rouen in the early 1120s, a canon forbidding cohabitation with women led to priests complaining of the conflict between body and soul. It may not be accidental that a later council in 1128 attempted to apply the celibacy rule only to priests. In the 1150s, Archbishop Theobald of Canterbury wrote to the bishop of Worcester, ordering that a man who had married when he was already a subdeacon, and who had later received priest's orders, should be debarred from the priesthood, unless the woman was prepared to take a vow of continence.[42]

Popular responses

The new rules could effectively be enforced only when they were generally accepted, and one factor in discouraging such acceptance may have been people's fear that they might be deprived of the Church's services if the sacraments of married priests were deemed invalid. This may have provoked the extreme reaction in the diocese of Cambrai, where the people allegedly burned a man to death for making such an assertion.[43] Elsewhere the new rules were more easily accepted, and Guibert of Nogent, writing about the Gregorian period a generation later, suggests that there were popular demands to deprive married priests.[44] On the other hand, the further communities were from the centres of ecclesiastical reform, the less likely was clerical marriage to be questioned – the reiteration of decrees on the subject in León at various councils between 1114 and 1155 suggests that the authorities could not enforce them, while in England there is evidence for clerical marriage even among the cathedral clergy at Hereford around 1200, and into the thirteenth century in rural areas.[45] As late as 1205, Innocent III ordered the bishop of Winchester to remove priests who were ministering in churches in succession to their fathers, and, very significantly, commanded him to take the initiative in institutions if the patrons refused to nominate suitable persons to benefices.[46] This suggests that the acquiescence of the laity in hereditary succession to benefices was one factor which made the imposition of celibacy difficult. Even towards the end of the Middle Ages, there seems to have been acceptance of *de facto* clerical marriage in remote areas. In Ireland, there is evidence throughout the fifteenth century of men seeking dispensations for ordination despite being sons of priests, and in the 1460s a traveller in the Basque country noted that the priests there and in parts of Spain were apparently regarded as lawfully married.[47]

Probably in many areas *de facto* clerical marriage persisted despite the attempts of the authorities to suppress it, and although there were undoubtedly cases of lax morality there were also cases when churchmen may well have had stable family relationships. Both situations are reflected in the register of Archbishop Rigaud of Rouen in the third quarter of the thirteenth century. Walter, the priest of Bray-sur-Baudemont, was far from exemplary, being suspected of usury and witchcraft, as well as admitting sexual relations with at least four different women, including two prostitutes. But a priest who admitted keeping a woman for twenty years, and Stephen, the parish priest of Commeny, who was disciplined for sinning again with a concubine by whom he had had children (in the plural), may well have been living in his own eyes, although not in those of the law, as a married man.

One has a similar picture in the case of a canon of St-Mellon, who was not only forbidden to continue living incontinently but was also instructed not to continue maintaining his daughter and her mother in his own home, 'which he has long done with scandal'.[48] A similar situation can be seen in fourteenth-century Barcelona, where two churchmen admitted to long-standing relationships with their mistresses, and to having children by them. The authorities may well have been trying to implement the law more strictly at this time, because a considerable number of cases of clerical concubinage were heard between June and December 1346.[49]

In such circumstances, it is hardly surprising that the rule of celibacy was criticised. Arnold of Villanova, physician to Boniface VIII, had doubts about it, and at the Council of Vienne (1311–12) it was suggested that the Western Church might adopt the Greek practice of allowing clerical marriage. Pierre Dubois criticised the Church Fathers who had enjoined perpetual continence (noting that they were frequently old and decrepit), and made it clear that he believed many churchmen did not observe their vows. Indeed, he even saw a possible value in one form of clerical marriage, suggesting that Western girls might be married to the Eastern clergy and convert their husbands to the Roman tradition.[50] And although the Council of Basel in 1433 instructed provincial synods to deal with clerical concubinage, and two years later suspended churchmen who persisted in it, admitting that some authorities took bribes from offenders to allow them 'to wallow in their filth', voices were raised to argue against it. When the Council elected the widowed Amadeus of Savoy as its pope, it was suggested that it might be preferable to have lawfully married priests, 'since many would be saved in a married priesthood who are damned in one that is celibate'.[51] The Fifth Lateran Council took the traditional line, laying down punishments for clerical concubinage at its ninth plenary session in 1514.[52] In the end, the resolution of this issue was to reflect the division in the Western Church in the sixteenth century, when the reformed churches legalised clerical marriage, while the Catholics maintained traditional prohibitions.

Overall, the reformers probably achieved a limited measure of success. The cruder forms of simony were removed, although there were still a number of customary payments made, which might be construed as offering money for spiritual services. Fees were paid to bishops annually for the consecration of chrism, and candidates for admission to monasteries might be required to bring an endowment with them.[53] The distinctive character of the clergy was further enhanced in the Church's teaching on confession. Down to the second half of the eleventh century, while confession to a priest was recommended, confession to a layman was considered adequate. In 1080 Gregory VII insisted that true confession had to be made to a priest, and a contemporary tract clarified official attitudes by stating that while lay confession (in the absence of a priest) could make a penitent worthy of pardon, this was not a sacrament, and only confession to a priest provided for the remission of sins.[54] The period also saw a decline in the number of married clergy, and gradually popular feeling became less willing to acquiesce in the practice. Possibly one reason for the reformers not achieving more was that another aspect of their programme began to bulk increasingly large, that of lay investiture, a question which had far wider repercussions on the position of the Church in society.

|7|

Gregorian reform – Popes and the lay world

Lay investiture

The 'purification' of the clergy did not necessarily impinge on the relations between the spiritual and the lay powers, although some aspects of the reform programme, such as the veto on clerical marriage and the consequent elimination of the possibility of hereditary benefices, had implications for these because it affected issues of patronage, which was regarded as a right of property. Furthermore, the role of the higher clergy in royal government made it a matter of concern to kings that acceptable individuals should be appointed to bishoprics and the abbacies of major monasteries. Indeed, kings themselves were seen as possessing spiritual authority. Wipo, the author of *Deeds of Conrad II,* not only himself described the emperor as the Vicar of Christ, but referred to the archbishop of Mainz regarding him in the same light.[1] Even towards the end of the eleventh century some at least of the higher clergy still accepted this. Adam of Bremen said of Archbishop Adalbert, who died in 1072, that he prided himself on having only two masters, the pope and the king, to whose dominion all the powers of the world and of the Church were rightly subject.[2] For him, these two loyalties were not incompatible, hardly a surprising fact as he had been present at the Synod of Sutri, when the emperor had deposed three contending popes, thereby successfully asserting a right to control at least some of the activities of the Papacy itself. Adalbert's position as guardian of the young Henry IV, furthermore, had enabled him to secure from the king the grant of the abbey of Lorsch in 1065. Adam's accounts of the election of earlier archbishops regarded it as normal that they should receive the *pallium* from the pope and the pastoral staff from the lay ruler.[3] In Normandy, Orderic Vitalis apparently accepted it as a matter of course that the duke invested an abbot with the pastoral staff in 1066, even although he himself was writing long after the practice had been condemned.[4]

In an age when the distinctiveness of clerical status was being asserted, however, it is hardly surprising that the reforming party in the Church challenged such imperial claims and asserted that appointments to high positions in it should be exempt from lay interference. Although in the first two years of his pontificate Gregory VII concentrated his reforming zeal on questions of simony and clerical marriage, even on occasions appealing for help to the lay power against possibly recalcitrant bishops, in 1075 he turned his attention to that of episcopal elections, promptly becoming involved in the struggle over the succession to the see of Milan.[5] Henry IV, having successfully defeated a Saxon revolt, was ambitious to extend his power south of the Alps, and certainly was willing to support an anti-Roman faction in the city. He nominated a new archbishop, thereby provoking a sharp reaction from the pope. Gregory's earlier reforming measures had already aroused hostility in Germany, and a synod of bishops at Worms in January 1076 retaliated by a complaint that the pope's own election had been irregular. When the emperor invited the Romans to depose the pope, Gregory responded by excommunicating him. This established a precedent which later popes were to follow – in the following century John of Salisbury noted that Alexander III's excommunication of Frederick Barbarossa was following Gregory VII's example.[6]

The investiture struggle

The ensuing struggle involved both political and ecclesiastical issues, in which the interests of the various participants cannot always be clearly distinguished. Henry was vulnerable to a renewal of princely opposition led by the Saxons, and the German bishops were divided. By the autumn of 1076, however, the emperor was pressurised into a compromise, swearing obedience to Gregory and withdrawing the attempt to depose him. If he did not obtain absolution within a year, the princes would withdraw obedience from him. At the expense of personal humiliation, involving a petition to Gregory for absolution (which he obtained after a three-day delay at Canossa in January 1077), he regained the political initiative and wrong-footed his enemies in Germany, without making any significant practical concessions to the pope.[7] There were still pro-imperial clergy, notably in Lombardy, but when Henry's German opponents elected Rudolf of Swabia as king in March 1077, Gregory was unable to give him whole-hearted support, even although the rebels had support from the papal legates and pursued a Gregorian policy. The emperor was militarily the stronger, soon reducing Rudolf's authority to a very limited area. As his power grew, he became increasingly intransigent in his dealings with Gregory. Furthermore, some of the more moderate German bishops were becoming critical of the pope's attitude, possibly believing, as Henry's biographer did later, that while they would not deny the pope's right to act against the emperor, Gregory had been deluded by Henry's enemies.[8] Furthermore, Henry still had political support in Lombardy. In March 1080 it was Gregory who took the first step to a renewed breach, by declaring the emperor deposed, but in June Henry retaliated by calling an assembly which not only declared that Gregory had been wrongly elected but also chose as an antipope the archbishop of Ravenna, who took the title Clement III. Rudolf of Swabia's death in battle in the autumn tipped the military balance further in Henry's favour, and although Gregory found new allies in southern Italy among the Norman settlers there, he was eventually forced out of Rome, to die in exile at Salerno in May 1085.[9] The impression given by his letters, particularly perhaps in his last years, is of a man on whom the strain of conflict had told severely, and who was retreating into a somewhat sickening self-righteousness, in which he saw his own views as the only acceptable ones and his enemies as the agents of the devil. In a general letter to the faithful from the second half of 1084 he denounced the way in which lay rulers 'had taken counsel together with a vast throng against Christ, the Son of Almighty God, and against his apostle Peter, to destroy the Christian religion and spread their depraved heresy'. His own concern had been to restore the Church to its true glory but 'because this entirely displeased the ancient enemy he has armed his members against us in order to turn everything upside down'.[10] By this time many cardinals and officials of the papal court had deserted to the antipope, whose position was all the stronger because he was not simply an imperial puppet. He was prepared to legislate against simony and clerical marriage, and made attempts to secure recognition as pope from various rulers of northern Europe.

However much the Papacy as an institution might assert its autonomy of lay power, and its spiritual role in the Church, individual popes in an age of conflict and possible schism always faced the need to secure recognition from the lay rulers of Christendom. However much they might wish to lay down a principle of ecclesiastical independence, political exigencies meant that they had to be pragmatists. The emperor was not the only lay ruler who wished to assert authority over the Church in his territories, and the pope could not afford to antagonise potential allies. Although the question of lay investiture was important, and became increasingly so, the popes were prepared to turn a blind eye to lay influence if a prince were sympathetic to other aspects of the reform programme, such as ending simony and attempting to suppress clerical marriage. In England, William I's invasion had been supported by Alexander II, probably because Archbishop Stigand of Canterbury was in schism from Rome, having received his *pallium* from Benedict X, whose election and consecration had been irregular. William was determined to maintain traditional royal rights, and his nominee to Canterbury, Lanfranc, was willing to support him. Despite this, Orderic Vitalis described the duke as 'a tireless defender of holy Mother Church'.[11] Gregory's view was less enthusiastic; he praised William with faint damns, declaring that he was to be more honoured than other rulers, even though he was not as scrupulous as the pope might wish. His virtues, however, were

recognised; he did not sell churches, he established peace among his subjects, refused to join the pope's enemies, and was believed to have acted
against clerical marriage.[12] Around 1082–3, however, the pope, in a letter to
the archbishop of Lyons, did condemn the king's action in arresting Odo of
Bayeux as showing inadequate respect to the priesthood.[13] But William
made his control over the English Church clear. He laid down that a pope
was not to be recognised without his consent, papal letters were not to be
received until the king had first seen them, local church councils were not to
pass laws without his agreement, nor was the Church to proceed against any
of his barons without royal instructions.[14] It was not difficult for the king to
assert such powers, because the English episcopate did not question them
until the following reign, when Archbishop Anselm took a stronger
reformist line against William Rufus. At the Council of Rockingham, when
he informed the king that he intended to go to Rome to receive his *pallium*,
the king and the episcopate combined to oppose him. The bishops argued
that obedience to the king was preferable to any owed to the pope, because
the latter could neither offer protection against royal anger nor harm the
archbishop if the king were well-disposed to him.[15] It is hardly surprising
that the higher clergy accepted traditional practices, because their outlook
reflected the circumstances in which they had grown up, and they might not
even have been aware of the development of papal policy, even if they were
sympathetic to some aspects of it. Only with the passage of the generations
did clerical opinion throughout Christendom fall into line with the new
ideals, and even when these were accepted on principle, *de facto* royal
power was still recognised.

In France too some compromise was reached. One factor which affected
papal attitudes here was that the kings did not press their claims on lay
investiture as strongly as the emperors. For one thing they had less influence
over bishoprics in their territories than the emperors had in theirs, because
much effective authority lay in the hands of local noble families. Although
one sees attempts to extend royal authority over the episcopate – it was one
means by which monarchical power was increased – these generally had the
support of the Church, which saw royal influence as a lesser evil than that
of the feudal nobility. Gregory established an extra channel of papal authority in France by appointing one of his most enthusiastic supporters, Hugh of
Die, as a permanent legate there in 1075, and later by giving him primatial
authority as archbishop of Lyons.[16] Gregory made considerable use of
legates, and his letters demonstrate that he regarded disobedience to them as
tantamount to disobedience to the Holy See.[17]

Papal reform policies did not remain static, and increasingly the investiture question came to the fore. But the antipope Clement still had considerable political power in Italy and after Gregory's death there was confusion
in the reformist camp. Almost a year elapsed before Abbot Desiderius of
Monte Cassino (Victor III) was elected to succeed him, and it was nearly a
further year, during which for a time he resigned the papal insignia, before

he was eventually consecrated. He died in little over four months, and the new vacancy lasted for half a year, with the new pope, Urban II, being elected outside Rome. It was a time of tension, in which the more fanatical Gregorians attacked Victor so fiercely for his earlier attempts to mediate between the contending parties that he excommunicated some of them, including Hugh of Die. Urban successfully maintained a balance within the reform camp, adhering in principle to Gregory's policies but being flexible in applying them. But it was not until 1093 that the antipope Clement was eventually driven out of Rome, and even then Urban was never secure there. The lack of a territorial power base always left him vulnerable, and his influence in Christendom was weakened by the schism. In Italy, he obtained Norman support at the cost of political concessions, and elsewhere his most powerful support came from the French king Philip I, who never supported the antipope. Even here, there was a potential clash, when Philip persisted in an adulterous liaison which led to his excommunication, and a retaliatory threat to withdraw his obedience. But significantly, neither side pressed issues too far, and France did not desert Urban.

Indeed, France saw one of the most famous actions of Urban's pontificate, the Council of Clermont in November 1095, at which the pope preached a crusade to deliver Jerusalem from Moslem domination. (It reflects the relations between France and the Papacy that most of the participants in the resulting expedition to the East were either from Norman Sicily or from the lands of the French king.) But this was not the only action of the council, where Urban not only renewed Gregory's reform legislation on lay investiture but also forbade bishops and priests to do homage to the laity.[18] This represented a hardening of ecclesiastical opposition to the lay power, and indeed in many ways one which failed to accommodate a political and social system in which the Church played a significant secular role. Nevertheless the assertion of such views affected the development of the political debate, and it was impossible for any compromise to be reached with Henry IV, not least because the pope had little contact with the German clergy. Many of these favoured aspects of reform, but felt that it was necessary to come to terms with the emperor.[19]

The schism was still in being when Urban died in 1099, but when he was followed to the grave by Clement a little over a year later, the situation altered. Although the antipope's adherents attempted to prolong the division in the church by electing two short-lived successors, neither enjoyed significant support. Most important, neither had backing from Henry IV, who summoned a meeting to Mainz on the news of Clement's death to consider how to restore unity in the Church.[20] Urban's successor, Paschal II, was not willing to compromise, however, and intensified the attack on churchmen doing homage to laymen at a council in Rome in 1102. His hostility was not confined to the emperor, for when Henry I of England tried to seek a confirmation of traditional royal rights, the pope retorted by denouncing lay investiture and clerical homage as an abomination.[21] One effect of this was that Archbishop Anselm, who had been recalled from exile by the new English king, refused to do homage to him (although he had earlier done it to William Rufus), and was again forced into exile.

Paschal's ideological affirmations of reform policy were mitigated by pragmatic concern for effective Church government. Pragmatism involved compromise and this could be achieved only if the pope made some concessions. Some churchmen were willing to yield on appearances, if the substance of reform could be secured, and as early as 1097 the canonist writer Ivo of Chartres was prepared to distinguish between a bishopric as a spiritual entity and its territorial possessions. In England a provisional compromise was reached in 1105 and finally agreed two years later, by which the king agreed to abandon any claim to invest bishops with the symbols of spiritual office, the ring and the pastoral staff, but was permitted to take homage from a newly elected bishop for his lands. As episcopal elections were to take place at the royal court, the king could still effectively control many aspects of church life. The York chronicler, Hugh the Chantor, commented that the king lost 'a little perhaps of his royal dignity, but nothing of his power to enthrone anyone he pleased'. Later he referred to Henry granting the see to two successive archbishops of York, and relates how a bishop said to Archbishop Thurstan, 'Let God's counsel be, but see that you abide absolutely by the king's'.[22] Orderic Vitalis stated bluntly that in 1111 Henry summoned the dean of Le Mans to England and appointed him archbishop of Rouen.[23] Undoubtedly the king could advance his own men to spiritual office; his great administrator, Roger, was consecrated to the see of Salisbury shortly after the settlement, although as a married man he hardly matched the reformers' ideals. Eadmer noted that the king also asked for the early consecration of the bishop elect of London, Richard of Belmeis, as he 'was a man very able to secular matters'.[24] A similar compromise was reached in France, where the king renounced his rights of both investiture and homage, but retained the right to grant lands to bishops and receive an oath of fealty for them.[25]

It is a measure of the importance of personal tensions in the struggle and the fear of losing face that the lay power with which a settlement was hardest to reach was the Empire, at least as long as Henry IV lived. His ecclesiastical policy still had some support, and on his death his biographer lamented that 'the monasteries have lost their patron, the cloisters their father'.[26] In his last year he had to face a revolt from his son, who won the support of the old Gregorians in Germany, although his own policy on investiture does not appear to have differed from his father's. Even while Henry IV was alive, his son, with the apparent acquiescence or even positive support of the German episcopate, invested a number of bishops in the traditional manner. The old emperor made some attempts to reach a reconciliation with the pope (probably to detach him from his son), seeking the mediation of the abbot of Cluny and of Philip I of France, but without success; in one letter he claimed that the papal legate refused him absolution unless he first confessed that he had persecuted the Church unjustly in imposing an antipope.[27] At the Synod of Guastalla in October 1106, some two months after the old emperor's death, the pope conceded that the original penalty of excommunication on clerks who had received lay investiture should be modified to the loss of their ecclesiastical rank, but the gap between him and the young Henry V was great enough for him to abandon an intention to visit Germany.[28] Nevertheless, there are indications that Paschal was prepared to take a more pragmatic approach, and perhaps accept the possibility of a compromise along the lines agreed in England. At a number of his councils, at Troyes (1107), Benevento (1108) and the Lateran (1110), penalties were imposed for lay investiture, but no mention was made of the question of homage.[29] The question of investiture involved the spiritual status of the clergy, and the right of the lay power to confer spiritual office was denied; homage, however, concerned material matters.

Politics and ecclesiology could not be separated, and Henry V, after restoring lost imperial power in Germany, was concerned also with recovering it in Italy and obtaining imperial coronation. It was with this last objective in mind that he led an army into Italy in 1110, and in the following February an apparently radical agreement was reached by which the emperor would abandon investiture with the ring and the staff, and that non-regalian possessions of the Church would become its outright property. The Church in return would surrender the *regalia*, rights and property pertaining to the Empire. The problem was that what the term *regalia* comprised was by no means agreed, and it was certainly not the pope's intention to abandon all the Church's material possessions – indeed Henry swore that he would restore the papal states as described in the old imperial donations.[30] But this agreement could not be implemented, and the emperor attempted to resolve the issue by force; he took the pope and the cardinals prisoner, and extorted a privilege that he had the right to confer investiture with the ring and staff before a bishop was consecrated. Unsurprisingly, this privilege was revoked once the pope recovered his freedom. Relations between him and the emperor remained uneasy, and the fundamental issues unresolved, for the remainder of his reign and in the one-year pontificate of his successor Gelasius II. One reason for this was Henry's need to devote attention to Germany, where his power had been challenged by a Saxon revolt, and although he did revisit Italy, he could devote only limited attention to it. The Papacy likewise was weakened through the factional struggles of Roman nobles from the Frangipani and Pierleoni families which were attempting to control it, and Gelasius had to escape to France, where he died.

Compromise and its aftermath

Gelasius' successor, Calixtus II, was able to achieve a compromise with the Empire. Although he had earlier been a hard-line reformer – he had excommunicated Henry and threatened to withdraw his allegiance from Paschal in the troubles of 1111–12 – his accession to the Papacy was followed by the opening of negotiations on investiture, and after the failure of one set of discussions in 1119 a settlement was reached at Worms in 1122 on similar lines to that which had already been attained in England. Concessions were made on the issues of principle, the emperor renouncing the right to invest a bishop with the symbols of spiritual office, and the pope conceding that the emperor could invest a bishop with those of his temporal power. Elections to bishoprics and abbacies were to be held in the king's presence, so he was able to exert substantial influence over the Church by ensuring that his own men held key offices in it.[31] Although the stricter reformers criticised the settlement, Calixtus was able to overcome their opposition at a general council which he convened to the Lateran in the following year.

While this agreement may be seen as a settlement of the struggle which had been continuing since the 1070s, it would be a mistake to overrate its importance. Certainly new principles were laid down for the relationship between the spiritual and the temporal powers, and the clergy's distinctive status was upheld by excluding the lay ruler from the conferment of the symbols of spiritual office. The abandonment of this indeed marks an important stage in the declericalisation of royal power, because although the ceremonies of coronation, above all that of anointing, had set monarchs apart from their subjects as quasi-spiritual persons, this was no longer seen as empowering them to exercise special powers over their ecclesiastical subjects. In the medieval world, ideas and ideals were embodied in key symbols, and the acceptance by the emperor and by kings that they could no longer confer the ring and the pastoral staff on prelates would have been well understood as having a far deeper significance. The Church had raised the banner of ecclesiastical independence, and contemporary writers accepted this as an ideal; Orderic Vitalis glossed the text *'Tu es Petrus'* in terms which emphasised papal power, described Henry IV's expulsion of Gregory in a hostile but understated comment – 'the emperor intruded Guibert of Ravenna and greatly disturbed the Roman Church' – and was critical of Paschal II's concessions to Henry V in 1111.[32] Even more striking was the comment of Otto of Freising a generation later; although he was essentially an imperialist, and denounced Gregory VII's excommunication of Henry IV as unprecedented, he was equally hostile to the election of the imperialist antipope when he wrote that 'Guibert, archbishop of Ravenna, called Clement (or rather Dement!) was elected bishop of the city with the consent of the king'.[33] This attitude was a far cry from the acceptance in the eleventh century of the actions of the Synod of Sutri.

Although the church reformers secured control of the high moral ground, it is hard to see fundamental changes in the real site of power in the Church. There were undoubtedly times when a lay ruler's political weakness gave churchmen greater freedom – it has been demonstrated that the English episcopate of the 1160s largely comprised men who had been appointed through ecclesiastical channels rather than under lay influence during the period of civil war between Stephen and Matilda,[34] and the tensions in the Empire after Henry V's death without an heir in 1125 meant that claimants to the succession found it desirable to cultivate the support of influential prelates. Lothar of Saxony owed his election to the papal legate, the archbishop of Mainz, and in the early years of his reign royal control of episcopal elections was allowed to slacken. Tensions between rival families in Germany continued until the election of Frederick Barbarossa as emperor in 1152, but as the Papacy itself suffered a schism from 1130 it was possible for even papal writers to describe Lothar by the more traditional designations of the emperor, as patron and defender of the Roman Church.[35] At the same time, however, papal intervention increased in the internal affairs of the German Church, as churchmen there, like their contemporaries elsewhere in Christendom, looked to the Papacy to resolve election disputes or contested points of canon law. Nevertheless, it was only in particular circumstances that royal power was curtailed; for much of the time, the Church, faced with the demands of two contending masters, found it more discreet to comply with the wishes of the one who was physically closer, and had more effective coercive powers. This remained a fact of political life for churchmen throughout the entire Middle Ages.

The pope's authority was vulnerable also because of his varying roles, which were not always easy to reconcile. Although his spiritual preeminence was increasingly accepted, this could not be separated from his temporal powers. He exercised political authority in Rome and in the States of the Church but sometimes this was more theoretical than actual. Tensions among the great Roman families gave rise to trouble as they tried to exploit the pope's power in their own interests and competed to hold the office. Within the college of cardinals too, there may well have been differences of opinion on how far the Church should continue the struggle for reform, whether it would be preferable to adhere to the strict Gregorian traditions or to compromise along the lines of the agreement reached at Worms, and concentrate on a more personal style of church reform as exemplified by the ideals of some of the new religious orders. There is, however, little explicit record of the views held by individual cardinals, and some arguments for the existence of ideological differences among them are based on purely circumstantial evidence. The need for military support during the struggle with the emperors had involved the popes in an uneasy relationship with the Norman rulers of Naples, who were sometimes hostile and sometimes friendly, and in the twelfth century this was further affected by emperors' attempts to reassert their power in Italy. It would therefore be simplistic to seek a single cause for the outbreak of the 1130 schism, because it is better understood in terms of rivalries among various pressure groups, and not all adherents of the contending factions fall into neatly defined parties.

The schism of 1130

The relative importance of these various issues, and indeed of the personal factors involved, has provoked considerable debate in recent scholarship.[36] The schism of 1130 had been foreshadowed by a disorderly election in 1124, when the candidate backed by the Frangipani, and supported by the influential and dynamic chancellor of the Church, Cardinal Haimeric, succeeded in overthrowing the original choice of the cardinals, who had favoured the nominee of the Pierleoni. In 1130, however, the same factions existed, but neither could secure a clear victory over the other. There is, however, no doubt that there were considerable irregularities in the election, and that an attempt to compromise by appointing an electoral college of cardinals to conduct it was abandoned by the supporters of Haimeric, who unilaterally chose Cardinal Gregory of St Angelo, who took the title of Innocent II. He undoubtedly had the support of most of the cardinal bishops, but the other faction, which chose Cardinal Pierleone (Anacletus II), probably had a narrow overall majority. However much the power of election had been limited to the cardinals by the election decree of 1059, it was still disputed how far the views of the cardinal priests and cardinal deacons could count against the bishops.

A good case could be advanced to support the validity of Anacletus' election, but the rallying to Innocent of the greater part of Christendom was eventually decisive. Orderic Vitalis' first mention of the schism noted that Innocent had support in the western parts of Christendom, while Sicily and Apulia followed Anacletus, but later in his history he mentions only Innocent, and stresses the importance of the Cluniacs giving him their backing.[37] Two factors particularly tipped the scale in Innocent's favour; Haimeric brought the papal chancery into his service and he secured the good will of a number of influential churchmen, most important of whom was St Bernard of Clairvaux, whose support was powerful and uncompromising. Anacletus was variously designated as Antichrist and as the beast of the Apocalypse, and Innocent's election was regarded as more sound, because his supporters prevailed in both numbers and excellence. Shifts of loyalty to Anacletus by bishops at Angoulême and Tours, when they were disappointed in getting favour from Innocent, called forth Bernard's most scathing rhetoric. But one letter, addressed to the emperor, shows an ugly anti-Semitism against Anacletus, whose father had been a converted Jew. Displaying an amnesia about St Peter's racial origins, Bernard declared that it was 'to the injury of Christ that a man of Jewish race has seized for himself the see of Peter'.[38] The propaganda campaign on Innocent's behalf was backed up by military force, although the emperor's expedition to Italy in 1133 achieved more for him in the form of imperial coronation than it did for the pope, who was forced to retreat before the forces of Roger of Sicily. Effectively, however, Anacletus' death in 1138 confirmed Innocent's victory, for although the antipope's supporters elected a successor, he resigned within two months, through the mediation of Bernard, and at the Second Lateran Council, called by Innocent to celebrate the end of the schism, action was taken against the rebels, and reform decrees were reissued. Politically, however, Innocent was less secure, being compelled in his later years to make concessions to Roger of Sicily, and facing a popular revolt in Rome itself.

The late twelfth century

There is no doubt that the Papacy's status was enhanced theoretically by the outcome of the struggle over investitures, and both its dignity and its practical authority were further emphasised by the development of canon law and the increasing tendency for disputed cases to be referred to Rome for decision. But if one looks at the Church throughout Christendom, it is equally clear that lay rulers still exercised a great deal of power over churchmen through ensuring that the key ecclesiastical offices within their lands were in the hands of sympathetic bishops. Furthermore, they were regarded as the natural protectors of the Church. David I of Scotland was a noted patron of monasticism – indeed his successor who called him 'a sair sanct for the croun' clearly felt that his generosity exceeded his sense[39] – and Galbert of Bruges described Count Charles of Flanders, who was murdered in 1127, as 'father and protector of the churches of God' and as 'a good prince, devout and strong, Catholic, the supporter of the poor, the protector, after God, of the churches of God'.[40] This may well have been the way in which kings regarded themselves, and when Henry II of England in the Constitutions of Clarendon (1164) reasserted the customs of his grandfather's time, he should not be seen simply as a reactionary, but rather as a ruler who still held to an earlier tradition of royal influence, which could be exercised for the benefit of the Church. In one clause of the Constitutions (significantly one accepted by the Papacy) the king saw himself and the Church as natural allies against the territorial nobility.[41] Furthermore, royal rights were acknowledged – John of Salisbury, despite having suffered at the king's hands for supporting Becket, constantly affirmed that he had no wish to damage royal interests, a clear indication that he was prepared to recognise Henry's traditional rights.[42]

In practical terms the Church made certain gains. The development of a more structured canon law, particularly after the compilation of Gratian's *Decretum,* assisted in channelling appeals to Rome, and the summoning of papal councils, accompanied by a claim that the lay power could not debar bishops from attending them, provided a new means of centralisation. Practice, however, frequently diverged from theory, depending on a king's capacity to enforce his claims. One who lacked power could be forced into concessions – in 1169 the king of Hungary granted a formal privilege to his archbishop that he would not depose or translate bishops without papal advice, and allowed the Church to control episcopal lands during the vacancy of a bishopric.[43] But in many cases residual power remained with the lay rulers as the men on the spot, and nowhere was this more evident than in appointments to major benefices. It is not always clear how kings intervened, but it is reasonable to infer from the earlier careers of men who became bishops that they owed their promotion to royal favour. In the kingdom of León there is evidence of the electors submitting their choice to the king and of elections being held in the royal presence, and at least one-third of the bishops appointed there in the twelfth century had a background as royal servants. It is probably not just a coincidence that Diego Gelmírez, who secured the elevation of his see of Compostela into an archbishopric in 1120, had not only served the crown before his appointment as a bishop but later, in 1127, was given control of the royal chancery. Royal influence also operated in a number of appointments to cathedral chapters.[44] John of Salisbury noted that the king of Sicily named in advance the candidate whom he wished to have elected (and that these were often suitable men) but that because the Papacy initially forbade the consecration of these nominees, few sees had bishops. However, when a settlement was reached, most of the bishops were confirmed by the pope after examination. In 1156 the contending parties to the church of Köln brought their case before the Emperor Frederick Barbarossa, who chose the archbishop before sending him to Rome for papal consecration. Such imperially nominated bishops were well regarded by their contemporaries; Bishop Hartmann of Brixen, an imperial adviser, was described as pre-eminent among German bishops for the sanctity and austerity of his life, and Bishop Eberhard of Bamberg as zealous for the honour of the Empire as well as being distinguished for his piety and purity of life.[45]

In England, the Battle Abbey chronicler saw the lay power as totally in control in 1125, when the king assigned an abbot to the house, although in 1139 the papal legate and certain barons of the realm assisted the king and queen in choosing a successor. It is hardly surprising therefore that Henry II, looking back to his grandfather's time in the Constitutions of Clarendon, asserted royal influence, laying down (in a clause which the Papacy did not accept) that elections to bishoprics and demesne abbeys should be held in the king's chapel and with royal assent.[46] One might have expected that after Becket's murder the Church could have recovered some independence, but this was not the case, and it is significant that four royal administrators, who had supported the king during his struggle with the archbishop, were among the men appointed to vacant bishoprics in 1173. In one case at any rate, royal pressure was blatant, with the king sending a writ to the monks of Winchester in these terms: 'I order you to hold a free election, but nevertheless I forbid you to elect anyone except Richard my clerk, the archdeacon of Poitiers.' Even former partisans of Becket seem to have accepted the election, which at least went through formal canonist procedures, with the election being held in the episcopal see and being approved by a gathering of bishops before both decisions were confirmed by the king.[47] The king's wishes prevailed in monastic elections as well, when he recommended the prior of Canterbury for election as abbot of Battle, and having him chosen because the monks knew nothing of other candidates. Jocelin of Brakelond's account of the election of Abbot Samson of Bury St Edmunds in 1182 suggests that there was a practical compromise; the election was held at court, with the monks submitting a list of names, from which the king made a number of deletions, before leaving them the final choice. Before the monks went to court, however, they did not know whether or not they would be allowed a free election.[48] Even the most powerful popes acknowledged that kings possessed some rights in ecclesiastical appointments. After the Canterbury election dispute in John's reign, in which Innocent III secured a resounding victory with the king's submission and a promise that he would not in future assert the claims of a protégé as he had done, the pope still admitted that the canonical electors had to obtain royal permission to hold an election, and while John promised to consent to such elections, the reservation to this promise, 'except for a lawful cause', represented a small chink in the armour of papal supremacy. As the text of the submission was rehearsed in a papal letter, one must assume that Innocent accepted this.[49]

In the final analysis the change in the balance of authority between the Church and the lay power was more marked in theory than in practice. There were still conflicts over the rights and wrongs of the question, but both popes and kings were practical men who only occasionally regarded the assertion of their claims as of greater importance than the more routine questions of effective management. Although both the Emperor Frederick Barbarossa and Alexander III made lofty claims to justify the power which they exercised, it is probably true to say that the bitter conflict between them arose more out of political rivalries in Italy, and out of the imperial challenge to the temporal authority of the Papacy, than out of the theoretical issues of authority which had made compromise so difficult in the struggles of the late eleventh and early twelfth centuries. The diversity of roles which the popes had to play, as ecclesiastical ruler and as territorial prince, left them with problems which could not always be disentangled.

The Crusades

Indeed, in one area the popes made a determined effort to harness the activity of the Christian laity to the Church's ends, namely in the Crusades to the East. These not only reflected political struggles between Christendom and Islam, but also demonstrate various developments within the Western Church. The willingness of the Western laity to participate in the campaigns, often at very considerable expense to themselves, reflects the religious sensibilities of the aristocracy, whose militarism could be directed into pious channels. Furthermore, the focus of the Crusaders on the liberation of Jerusalem emphasises the importance of the tangible in contemporary religious thought, as indeed does the Crusaders' collection of relics. Crusading to the earthly Jerusalem developed symbolic overtones by the early twelfth century, when Paschal II exhorted Robert of Flanders to reach the heavenly Jerusalem by fighting for the reformers against the emperor. At a lower political level, many charters granted by Crusaders before their departure for the East referred to Jerusalem as the goal of their expedition, and regarded their actions as a form of penitence for their sins, particularly if they or their ancestors had imposed unjust burdens on the Church. Others found the Crusade a spiritual experience and when they returned to the West decided to withdraw from the world.[50]

Although the rescue of the holy city provided an emotional incentive to the nobility of the West, it had originally been an appeal from the Byzantine Empire for assistance against the Turks after the latter's victory at the battle of Manzikert in 1071 which provided the opportunity for intervention in the East. Gregory VII proposed in 1074 to lead an army there, and an imperialist writer advised Henry IV to do the same, so as to acquire glory. Both men probably hoped that victory over the Turks would enhance their moral standing in the West. It cannot have been easy for the Byzantines to make this appeal, as it was less than two decades previously that the schism had taken place between the Eastern and the Western churches. Both the fact that they did so, and the Papacy's response, demonstrate that despite this division there was still a perception that the unity of Christendom was deeper than its dissensions. In 1074 Gregory VII called for volunteers to join him in trying to help the Eastern Empire and expressed his desire to help Christians who were being slaughtered by the heathen.[51] The pope was also concerned, however, with enhancing his own powers. Even earlier, Gregory had written to men who were hoping to campaign against the Moors in Spain, and significantly had stressed that recaptured lands were to be held from the Papacy. Urban II at Clermont took a similar attitude to lands recovered for Christendom in Palestine, and Paschal II evidently assumed such authority when he granted a privilege to the patriarch of Jerusalem confirming his power over lands which had been recovered from the infidel.[52] Gregory had been more diplomatic, however, in dealings with Moslem rulers where reconquest was not a possibility, and where there were Christians under their rule. In a letter to the king of Mauretania, he not only confirmed that he had ordained a bishop at the king's request and noted that the latter had released some Christian captives, but also acknowledged, probably as a piece of diplomatic tact, that Christians and Moslems worshipped the same God, although in different ways.[53] Christian intolerance hardened later, and the lay historian of the First Crusade, while admiring the fighting abilities of the Turks, described them as 'enemies of God and Holy Christendom' who could be slaughtered without qualms. He described a mosque as a 'house of the devil', although it could be taken over and consecrated as a church. Christian casualties, by contrast, were described as martyrs, who were destined to go direct to heaven.[54]

Urban II had been negotiating with the Byzantine emperor for some years over relations between the churches of Rome and Constantinople and over military assistance, before he proclaimed the Crusade at the Council of Clermont in 1095, perhaps in response to a renewed appeal which had reached him in the previous year. His motives in this may have been mixed; he probably intended to secure the high moral ground in his struggle with the emperor, and it is noteworthy that Orderic Vitalis contrasts Urban, described as 'a mighty leader against the Moslems', with the antipope, and Fulcher of Chartres' account of the Crusade refers to Henry IV as 'the so-called emperor' and attacks the antipope.[55] The quarrel between the pope and the emperor affected the composition of the crusading expedition, which comprised men from the obedience of the lawful pope, from Italy (including a substantial Norman contingent) and from the lands of the French Crown. As these men formed the nucleus of the ruling class in the crusading kingdom of Jerusalem, set up after the capture of the city in 1099, it committed the French nobility far more deeply to crusading than their German counterparts; although there were German participants in the First Crusade, none of the leaders came from the Empire. This French dominance also explains why chroniclers in their lands showed so deep an interest in events in the East. Although Orderic Vitalis was primarily concerned with the Anglo-Norman realm, his history includes a lengthy account of the First Crusade, derived from Baudry of Dol, and accounts of later fighting with both the Turks and the Byzantines. He also describes struggles between Christians and Moslems in Spain.[56] This reflects how the reformed Papacy harnessed to its own ends a developing sense of unity within Western Christendom.

The Crusades created a further problem, however, in relations between the West and the Byzantine Empire. Urban II at Clermont referred to the Eastern Christians as brethren, implying that they were part of the Christian world which needed to be cleansed from invasion,[57] and probably wished to promote unity between them and the Western Church. During the Crusade, however, he pursued a conciliatory policy towards the Eastern Church over appointments to ecclesiastical office in the lands recovered from Islam. The mass of Western feeling was probably more hostile to the Greeks than Urban's, although one may note that many of the visions of saints which the Western Crusaders claimed to see during their campaign were those of Eastern saints such as George and Demetrius, while surprisingly few were of St Peter. A desire to emphasise the primacy of his own see may indeed explain why Paschal II enjoined particular devotion to the apostle in a letter to the Latins who settled in the Holy Land after 1099.[58] Papal interests in the East remained a potential source of tension, however, although in practical terms it was not until the Fourth Crusade of 1204 was diverted into an attack on Constantinople that these were translated into militant anti-Byzantine action.

This, however, was merely the culmination of tensions during the earlier campaigns which intensified existing divisions between East and West. Political and religious issues could not be separated, so it is hardly surprising that the Emperor Alexius found the disorderly force of adventurers who claimed to be coming to his aid uneasy allies, and moved them on from Constantinople as soon as possible. The first force under Peter the Hermit was destroyed by the Turks in Asia Minor, and the later arrivals also had to face tension with the imperial forces.[59] Distrust of the Byzantines must have been reported back to the West – Orderic Vitalis shows deep distrust of the Eastern emperor, and alleged collaboration between the Byzantines and the Turks. He also tells a garbled story of tensions which arose when the Crusaders attempted to enforce the Western rite in Antioch, and although this is inaccurate, it mirrors the developing mutual hostility. The leaders of the crusading army wrote after the fall of Antioch that they had subdued the Turks but had been unable to overcome the heretic Greeks and Armenians, and before long Fulcher of Chartres was writing about the trickery of the Greeks. The installation of a Latin patriarch at Antioch in 1100 marked the abandonment of Urban II's policy of co-operation with the Greeks.[60] Time exacerbated these tensions, not least because the existence of the crusading states posed problems for Byzantium, and the theme of Greek deceit was a recurrent motif in Odo of Deuil's account of the Second Crusade. He even described the Emperor Manuel as non-Christian and asserted that the Greeks purified their altars if a priest had celebrated on them according to the Roman rite and rebaptised Westerners who married Greeks.[61] The English chronicler, William of Newburgh, also alleged that the emperor was guilty of treachery towards the Crusaders, although he admitted that the latter had provoked his action through their own behaviour.[62] Whether or not Odo's allegations were true, they were evidently believed in the West, because provision was made at the Fourth Lateran Council (1215) for measures against Greeks who showed contempt for the Latin priesthood and Latin baptism, with specific reference being made to the washing of the altars and to rebaptism. The Greeks were exhorted to conform like sons of their mother, the holy Roman Church. This may, however, simply reflect increased East–West hostility after the establishment of the Latin Empire of Constantinople after the Fourth Crusade. Whether or not such practices occurred in the crusading lands, there is a record of rebaptism in the Slav lands, probably in the early 1140s, so it is clear that the allegation is more than a figment of hostile Western imagination.[63]

The defence of Christendom against Islam remained an important question in people's minds, although some attitudes to it were highly simplistic. Hugh of Poitiers was bewildered by the failure of the Second Crusade, feeling that it was incomprehensible that God had let down those fighting in his cause, when he wrote 'By God's mysterious judgement, a greater part of the army was destroyed'. By contrast, some writers describing the failure of an expedition to the East in 1101, which had been intended to reinforce the

Christian states in Palestine, explained it simply as a judgement of God upon sin.[64] Continuing papal concern can be seen in two decrees of the First Lateran Council, one granting remission of sins to those who went to Jerusalem to defend Christian people against the infidel and the other imposing penalties on those who failed to meet their crusading vows. While there was no specific provision about crusading in the decrees of the Second Lateran Council, service in Jerusalem or in Spain (another frontier with Islam) in the service of God was provided as a suitable penance for persistent arsonists.[65] Neither of these councils was held at a time when there were formal expeditions to the East, but it should be remembered that there were proposals for these which never were implemented. One such is recorded in the *Letters* of John of Salisbury in 1169 and 1170, and it reflects the importance of Jerusalem in the West that one of the acts which Henry II had to perform as a penance for the murder of Thomas Becket was to give money to support two hundred knights in the kingdom of Jerusalem.[66]

Crusading remained an admired ideal, and it is significant that the fall of Jerusalem to Saladin in 1187 prompted a new crusade. The Papacy remained closely involved with the movement; Innocent III urged the French and English kings to make peace in 1203, because their war was harming the Church, and the Saracens had picked up courage while the French were fighting fellow Christians, and in 1214 he reiterated that this war was preventing aid to the Holy Land 'which we most ardently desire for the salvation of Christian people'. John of England's willingness to take a crusading vow was almost certainly no more than a tactical device to win papal support, but Innocent had little option but to accept it at face value, and reprove the king's enemies, whom he described as worse than Saracens for trying to depose a king, who, it was hoped, would succour the Holy Land.[67] Even in the thirteenth century, Louis IX of France was a determined Crusader, and his biographer Joinville declared that he should be regarded as a martyr because of the sufferings he had endured as such.[68] But although Louis' crusading was undoubtedly a manifestation of his piety, popular enthusiasm for such campaigns to the East seems to have waned, not least perhaps because the Papacy itself was turning the idea of the Holy War to other ends, in struggles against its enemies in the West.

| 8 |

Regular ideals in a changing world

Ideals and organisation

The ideals of monasticism had made a major contribution to the reform movement in the Church, notably in stressing an obligation on the clergy to be celibate. Urban II indeed had been prior of Cluny before being called into papal service by Gregory VII, who may himself have spent some time in a Cluniac monastery. But the monastic ideal of withdrawal from the world to pursue pious contemplation and fight evil through the weapons of prayer was an uneasy partner for the political activism of the reformed Papacy. There were also men who sought the ideal of a purer Church through developing such a life of prayer, and others who developed a new kind of regular observance by combining obedience to a rule with evangelism to the laity.

It was not only the Church which was changing. Western Europe was experiencing substantial economic growth, towns and trade were developing, and lay society was becoming more articulate. Increasing affluence raised the question of how society should regard the acquisition of wealth, in face of New Testament teaching in the parable of the rich fool and Jesus' challenge to the rich young ruler. As people heard the preaching of the Gospel they found that they might have to question not only their own lifestyle but also the increasing acquisition of property by the Church. Lay criticism of the Church order will be considered later,[1] but within the Church itself there were men who sought to idealise poverty as the way to salvation.

Regular observance did not face simply a challenge of new ideals. Its older structures of organisation, which had sufficed in the tenth and eleventh centuries, no longer fully met the requirements of monastic life. One characteristic of the period was the growth of more structured administration in both lay and ecclesiastical society, and the new orders were themselves to develop comparable machinery of government, which was intended both to preserve the ideals of the founders and to strengthen an order's effectiveness in pursuing its mission. In a sense, it was the twelfth century which invented the idea of the organised religious order. Originally each monastery had been an independent entity,[2] although increasing reliance on the Rule of St Benedict had served to establish a pattern of common practices over a wide area. The tendency to call in monks from particularly respected houses, such as Cluny, to reform houses which were in decline, and their adherence to the customs of the reforming house, represented a half-way house to the structured order. The general umbrella of the Rule provided scope for considerable variations, as for example at Vallombrosa, the founder of which died in 1073, where the monks were also dedicated to strict enclosure and perpetual silence, which attracted the praise of Gregory VII.[3]

At an earlier date, Cluny represented an ideal of observance – indeed Gregory VII praised it for its fervour, declaring that there had never been an abbot there who was not a saint.[4] But by the end of the eleventh century it could no longer sustain its position in the forefront of religious reform. It had become too much a part of the ecclesiastical establishment, and as its austerity waned, it no longer displayed the spiritual dynamism of earlier years. There was a desire to return to what was seen as the purity of older values, but this could take various forms. Some men sought to go back to the austerity of the desert, and an eremitical lifestyle, others sought to combine a corporate life with more outward-looking missionary activity, and others again sought to restore a more literal observance of the Rule of Benedict, purged of later accretions.[5] The various changes in regular observance from the late eleventh century onwards were not always mutually compatible, but one or other of them influenced later developments in varying degrees. The desire to return to the wilderness, which appeared most conspicuously among groups of hermits, did not simply lead to individual manifestations of piety but, paradoxically, contributed to the growth of later orders with a more rigid administrative structure, the two greatest of these being the Carthusians and the Cistercians. In the case of the former, the pattern of life was to be a compromise between the conventual and the eremitic, whereas the latter adopted a more fully conventual life. But even before the establishment of the monastery at the Grande Chartreuse one sees a combination of the conventual and the eremitic at Camaldoli, where the monks living a corporate life at the foot of the hill provided an early training for men who subsequently settled in individual hermitages as solitaries. Not all men found this ideal suitable, but it is noteworthy that the founder of Vallombrosa, whose house was wholly conventual, had originally tried his vocation there.[6]

The Carthusians owed their origin, at least indirectly, to the investiture contest, for their founder, Bruno, the chancellor of the archbishop of Rheims, who had joined the imperialist party, decided to withdraw from the world. After a spell in southern Italy, he established a monastery near Grenoble, which by the mid-twelfth century developed its own customs. There was no monastic *horarium,* and each monk had his own cell, but the community met for mass on Sundays and feast days. The monks pursued lives of personal poverty, and preserved this despite the wishes of would-be benefactors. They returned a gift of silver vessels made to them by the Count of Nevers, but he still found a means of assisting them, sending them hides and parchment instead, for Bruno's intellectual background encouraged the monks to accumulate a rich library by borrowing and copying books. The count remained supportive, and even became a monk there a year before his death. The community attracted the admiration of Guibert of Nogent, who wrote: 'These monks are so filled with zeal for the life of meditation which they have adopted that they never give it up or grow lukewarm, however long their arduous mode of living may last.'[7] This zeal persisted – of all the great monastic orders, it alone can claim that it has never needed to be reformed.

The Cistercians, on the other hand, originated in an exodus of monks from an existing house, and initially focussed on the literal observance of the Rule of St Benedict, although this was gradually modified. It developed its own characteristics, such as the use of *conversi,* or lay brothers, to provide a labour force, while the more educated monks fulfilled the routine of services in choir. These had been found earlier at Vallombrosa, at Cluny and among the Carthusians, but the Cistercians developed the practice more fully. Like so many religious movements, it began in the dissatisfaction of an individual, Robert of Molesme, with his own spiritual life. He had abandoned his position as an abbot at Tonnerre to join a group of hermits in Burgundy, which developed into a community at Molesme following the Benedictine rule. But with the passage of time, the new community itself felt that it was not preserving its rigorous ideal, and Robert and a number of monks set up a new monastery at Cîteaux.[8] Robert himself was ordered back to Molesme by the pope, but his two successors were able to establish the house, where the monks lived a life of hard manual labour. Its future dominance could not have been foreseen in the early years, but 1112 marked a turning-point with the arrival of the young Bernard and a group of thirty men, including several of his brothers, whom he had persuaded to abandon an aristocratic way of life for that of a monk.[9] His subsequent reputation may have led historians to overestimate the order's weakness before his arrival – after all, Cîteaux established new monasteries too soon after his profession for him to have emerged to prominence, at La Ferté in 1113 and at Pontigny in the next year – but he undoubtedly made his mark early, and when a further house was established at Clairvaux in 1115, Bernard was made abbot there, remaining so till his death in 1153.

St Bernard of Clairvaux

Bernard was undoubtedly the most outstanding figure in the early twelfth-century Church, and indeed one of the greatest churchmen of the entire

Middle Ages. His career touched on all the great issues of his day, and his spiritual writings remained an inspiration to succeeding generations. This influence is all the more remarkable because he held no position higher than that of abbot of Clairvaux, certainly a senior position in an emerging religious order, but not one which gave him legalised authority over more than the monks of Clairvaux and its daughter houses. He certainly believed that he was God's prophet to his age – in a letter to the French king he wrote, 'Bernard, styled abbot of Clairvaux, sends health from the King of kings and Lord of lords'[10] – but while this is not unusual among religious reformers, it is clear from the heed that was given to him, that his contemporaries regarded him in the same light. Otto of Freising referred to his preaching of the Second Crusade by saying, 'The abbot . . . was looked upon by all the people of France and Germany as a prophet and apostle'.[11] He was brilliantly paradoxical, a man whose ideal was one of austerity, withdrawal and contemplation but who intervened – his enemies might say 'interfered' – in all wider aspects of church life, a man who could attack his opponents in terms of undiluted vitriol but who still could win their respect and even remain in charity with them at the end, a man who could write brilliantly but who attacked the new intellectualism of the age.

He was perhaps a man torn between incompatible ideals, one of monastic contemplation and the other of employing his multifarious talents for a wider apostolate within the Church, when both pope and emperor sought his support in this. He may well have been at his happiest with his monks, for his first biographer, William of St Thierry, commented that they were willing to confide in him, and in his letters to them when he was away he lamented that he was forced to move in affairs that troubled the peace of his soul. His preference for the ideal of the cloister can be seen in him declining election to the archbishopric of Rheims, and affirming that it would be cruel to part him from his monks.[12] But Bernard could never do anything half-heartedly, and whatever he did he would carry through without reservations.

Bernard's aristocratic background perhaps explains his self-confidence, and gave him an assurance to speak out without respect for social status, even of the greatest. This is nowhere better demonstrated than in his intervention in the disputed archiepiscopal election at York in the 1140s, where he denounced not only Archbishop William but also his most influential supporter, Bishop Henry of Winchester, the brother of King Stephen and formerly papal legate in England, whom he variously described as 'that deceiver of Winchester, the prevaricator of the judgements of Rome' and as 'that old whore of Winchester', writing that 'that Philistine in a spirit of turbulence does not blush to set up that idol Dagon next to the very ark of the Lord'. Even the pope was not beyond reproof. When Innocent II went back on a promise of forgiveness which he had given to Cardinal Peter of Pisa, a former supporter of Anacletus II, who had returned to the pope's side through Bernard's mediation, the latter took it as a personal affront and called on him to reinstate the cardinal.[13] However, his spiritual idealism may sometimes have made him almost naive in dealings with his fellows. William of St Thierry suggested that he thought that his monks, like himself, would be proof against the temptations which affected ordinary mortals, and that he could be amazed when in confession they revealed themselves to be mere men.[14] But this was combined with a personal charisma which won their affection; when he warned men that their actions were leading to damnation and told them of the sorrow that this caused him, they were moved to repentance and even to discipleship. Yet, like Virgil's image of the mission of Rome, if he 'warred down the proud', he would also spare the humble and show consideration for their feelings. He apologised to the bishop of Worms for failing to answer a letter, and claimed that it had always been his habit to answer all letters from people of whatever background, he pleaded to an abbot to receive back a fugitive monk, or at least give him leave to make a fresh start elsewhere, and sought alms for the house of Molesme, unknown to the monks there, so that the prospective beneficiary would not be embarrassed by a request nor the monks by a refusal.[15] His concern for the individual was also demonstrated by his advice to the pope not to promote a young Carthusian monk to a bishopric in Lombardy, as his health was poor, but to give him a more suitable see where the people could benefit from his rule.[16]

What is more surprising is that he was prepared to encourage three young men to enter an order other than his own, as he felt that they lacked the physical strength to cope with the rigours of Cistercian life. He even sent them with a recommendation to a Benedictine abbot.[17] This provides a perspective on some of his dealings with other orders, although there is little doubt that he saw the Cistercian way as the best, and that he was prepared to support monks who left other orders to embrace it, and even defend their actions to the abbot of the house which they had left. On the other hand, if a monk left Clairvaux to live in a more relaxed house, he incurred the full wrathful weight of Bernard's rhetoric.[18] The touchstone for Bernard, however, was whether or not the individual concerned observed the Rule of St Benedict. In his *Apologia,* written about 1125, he claimed that he had never encouraged, and indeed sometimes rebuffed, men who transferred from Cluny to Cîteaux, and asserted that he was prepared to praise all orders which led good and virtuous lives.[19] While he criticised what he regarded as abuses at Cluny, notably excesses of diet and dress,[20] he asserted that monks who transferred from one order to another should be judged as individuals. His relations with Cluny were coloured by his personal affection for Abbot Peter the Venerable, whom he described as 'his most reverend father and dear friend', a description which was echoed by a meeting of Cistercian abbots. In a letter to Pope Eugenius III, himself a Cistercian by background, he rejoiced in his friendship with Peter, and paid tribute to the way in which he had reformed his house and tightened up its discipline.[21]

Perhaps even more remarkable than Bernard's friendship with Peter, whose achievement in restoring Cluny after some problems with an unsatisfactory abbot was well recognised, was his affection for Abbot Suger of St Denis. Suger had combined service to Louis VI, whose *Life* he wrote, with the rule of his monastery, where he devoted much attention to ornamenting the sanctuary as a means of elevating the spirit of the viewer – 'meditation has induced me to reflect, transferring that which is material to that which is immaterial', so that 'by the grace of God, I can be transported from this inferior to that higher world in an anagogical manner'. He did not believe in extreme austerity, and took steps to improve the monks' diet and the care of the sick. He changed the choir stalls from stone and metal to wood, because the coldness of the former had caused hardship to those attending worship.[22] Such material considerations would not have concerned Bernard, whose personal austerity of life left him emaciated and suffering from permanent gastric trouble. Furthermore, Suger's edification of the building was totally contrary to his condemnation of excess ornamentation in churches. He accepted that bishops might need to employ this to arouse lay piety, but he asserted that monks should have abandoned it, and was particularly critical of the carved grotesques which might ornament the cloister, and distract readers from their study.[23] One might have expected Suger to be anathema to Bernard, yet he commended his success on restoring the level of observance at St Denis, and in a letter to him on his deathbed described him as 'his dear and intimate friend Suger', expressed a wish to be with him to receive his last blessing, and affirmed that what bound them together was greater than death.[24]

Bernard's prominence in the Church would have been impossible at an earlier date, but the twelfth century saw increasing ecclesiastical centralisation in the aftermath of the struggles over investiture. Although the monastic ideal of contemplation represented a different set of values from those of Gregorian reform, the latter emphasised the exercise of authority from above, and this may have coloured the organisational developments of the Cistercians. Also, as the countries of Western Europe were drawn increasingly together into a single cultural entity, the development of scholarship and of a community of learned men enabled him to use his skill with words to influence the ideals of the Christian life. Indeed the unity of twelfth-century Christendom is nowhere better demonstrated than by the widespread geographical destinations of Bernard's letters. It is not surprising that many were directed to France, Italy and Germany, the heartland of Western Christendom, but he also wrote to a Scottish king, Irish and Swedish archbishops, a papal legate and a duke in Bohemia, churchmen and royalty in Spain and Portugal, a queen of Jerusalem and the patriarchs of Jerusalem and Antioch.[25] His charismatic influence was vital in attracting men into the Cistercian order, and increasingly his reputation led to his advice being sought on a wide range of matters. An early reference to him, from about 1130, before he attained his full prominence in Christendom, described him as 'full of wisdom'.[26]

The development of the Cistercians into an order was gradual, and reflected the problem of sustaining the reforms which had been carried out. The precise stages of development are conjectural, but the broad lines are clear. When La Ferté was established, abbot Stephen Harding of Cîteaux insisted that it should follow customs identical to those of the mother house, which retained spiritual, but not material, supervision over it. A system developed by which the abbots of the senior daughter houses attended a chapter meeting at Cîteaux, where they could check on faults of discipline, while the abbots of houses which had made foundations were responsible for the regular visitation of their daughter establishments. With the passage of time a general chapter of the order developed, which became its sovereign body. The rule was eventually embodied in the document known as the *Carta Caritatis*. The early supervision of monastic houses by the bishop, as in the Benedictine Rule, disappeared, probably because control within the order was essential to preserve uniformity of practice as it spread throughout Christendom. Yet in some senses, the Cistercians were not a fully developed order; they had no single head, and the visitation system operated in accordance with the chances of foundation, irrespective of where the daughter houses were. But the exercise of oversight was not strictly hierarchical, for each house remained an independent unit.[27] Of the daughter houses of Cîteaux, it is not surprising that Clairvaux had the largest family of daughter houses (68 out of the 343 which had been established by the time of Bernard's death in 1153). Most of these had been founded deliberately, but in some cases monks set up their own house (as for example those who left St Mary's, York, to establish Fountains) and then sought directions from Bernard on the Cistercian way of life. One chronicler indeed described the merging of the small order of Savigny with the Cistercians as its adoption of the customs of Clairvaux, rather than of Cîteaux. Not all who sought Bernard's advice, however, became Cistercians, although they consulted him because they admired his holiness. In the case of St Gilbert of Sempringham the sticking-point was the supervision of nuns, which the Cistercians were unwilling to undertake.[28]

Prominent though Bernard was, one man's influence could not have brought about such a massive expansion of monasticism if it had not had popular support. This support may indeed have been counter-productive for the monastic ideal, because benefactions and the acquisition of wealth inevitably eroded austerity. While some houses were undoubtedly founded by groups who split off from existing communities, they required patrons to give them land on which they could establish themselves; even if this was originally waste, the monks cultivated it, and this in turn brought wealth and with it criticism. Many patrons conferred their favours on a wide range of orders. David I of Scotland, for example, supported Tironensian and Cistercian monks, and Augustinian canons, while his steward, with royal encouragement, founded a Premonstratensian house.[29] Patrons could pose problems for the orders as well as assisting them; in the *Dialogue on*

Spiritual Friendship by the Cistercian abbot Ailred of Rievaulx, one partic-
ipant was depicted as complaining that the abbot let 'Pharaoh's Agents'
have him to themselves, while the monks could rarely enjoy his conversa-
tion. To this Ailred replied that it was necessary to humour those from
whom one might hope for favours or whose ill-will was to be feared, but
that when they were gone, the resulting solitude was more delightful. Ailred
was a man of sensitivity and humanity as well as of practical wisdom, seeing one duty of the abbot being to adapt his approach to the individual tem-
perament of each of his monks.[30]

On the whole, regular canons were more involved in pastoral works than
monks – among other things the canons were responsible for many of the
hospitals founded at this time – but it is impossible to draw a clear line
between them. Many canons separated themselves from the world and were
not involved in pastoral activity, whereas monks might well preach to the
laity, although this was contrary to the Rule. Bernard was the greatest
preacher of his age, and some of his successors became involved in missions
to deal with the threat of Catharism in the Languedoc. The Cistercians were
not unique in their involvement in popular preaching – a far less spiritual
monastic head than Bernard, the Benedictine abbot Samson of Bury St
Edmunds, not only preached to the people in the speech of his native
Norfolk but was critical of men who abandoned pastoral cares to turn
anchorite.[31]

The regular canons

The canons shared many monastic characteristics, such as communal life,
the renunciation of private property, and the observance of a timetable of
services. They followed one of the so-called Rules of St Augustine, an adap-
tation of a treatise which the saint had written for his sister in the late fourth
century, when she had entered a religious community. This provided a flexible basis for observance, because there were considerable areas of communal life which were not defined, and different houses made individual
modifications to it.[32] On the Continent there was a clear tendency for hermitages to develop into communities, which frequently adopted this rule, as
rising numbers of members made it necessary for them to have a more fully
structured organisation. In England, patrons were more prominent in establishing houses, but there too there was an incentive to transform a hermitage
into a house of canons as this was less costly than one of monks, as the numbers in many of them were small. This enabled patrons of comparatively
limited resources as well as members of the higher nobility to support them
and obtain both spiritual benefits and a certain social *cachet* from their
actions.[33]

Developments among the regular canons were influenced by contemporary monasticism. St Norbert, the founder of the Premonstratensians, had

earlier been a hermit and a preacher, whose followers had adopted the Rule of St Augustine. After his election as archbishop of Magdeburg, where he established the chapter as a body of canons of his order, his successor at Prémontré drew up a rule which stressed a more contemplative and less pastoral life.[34] It was probably due to St Norbert's appointment to Magdeburg that some other German bishoprics also established Premonstratensian chapters. The revised rule drew on the *Carta Caritatis* for the order's administrative structure, borrowing such Cistercian characteristics as a general chapter and a system of periodic visitations, as well as employing lay brothers for various manual tasks. The abbot of Prémontré, however, had a higher standing in his order than the abbot of Cîteaux in his.[35]

There were inevitably tensions among the various new orders, particularly when the more zealous members of each claimed that they were following the only road to salvation. But others appreciated the spiritual value of diversity in observance. In the mid-twelfth century an unknown regular canon from Liège wrote a work called the *Libellus de diversis ordinibus,* in which he analysed the different kinds of monks and canons, according to the strictness of their observance, seeking models for the behaviour of each in both the Old Testament and the life of Christ, and trying to demonstrate what was good in each calling.[36] His ideal for conduct and discipline was expressed in the word *mensura* (moderation), incidentally one used also in the Rule of St Benedict, and accepted that both manual and non-manual work could be blessed. Those who were critical of others could be falling into the sin of pride, and a balance should be struck between the observance of old practices and the introduction of new ones.[37] But not all people welcomed diversity, and by the beginning of the thirteenth century, the Papacy at any rate felt that the proliferation of new orders was getting out of hand. Two decrees of the Fourth Lateran Council tried to impose tighter control. One stipulated that monks who did not hold general chapters should henceforth do so triennially, for each kingdom or province, and the other imposed a ban on the foundation of new orders. Cistercian influence clearly lay behind this tighter administrative structure, because it was laid down that abbots of the order were to attend such meetings to give them the benefit of their experience.[38] There was, however, a marked distinction between the proposed triennial councils and the Cistercian pattern of government, because the former were related to a more territorial structure for the Church.

The zenith of traditional monasticism was probably reached in the first half of the twelfth century, and after the death of Bernard it was never to carry quite the same weight, although regular churchmen were still seen, at least potentially, as a powerful moral influence. In 1168 John of Salisbury wrote to the bishop of Poitiers during Henry II's struggle with Thomas Becket, and marvelled that none of the religious were warning the king of the dangerous path which he was following.[39] But influence in the higher levels of the Church was increasingly passing to the secular clergy, and from the twelfth century onwards a new breed of men, university-educated clergy, whose training was philosophical and intellectual rather than contemplative and devotional, became increasingly prominent. Significantly, training in canon law became a valuable qualification for high ecclesiastical office.

The friars

At the same time, the development of towns and trade, and the emergence of a more educated, and more questioning, laity, was posing new pastoral problems for the Church. These factors lay behind the thirteenth-century establishment of the orders of friars in which pastoral care and involvement with the laity were more prominent than withdrawal and contemplation. The two greatest of these orders, the Franciscans and the Dominicans, each owed their character to their founders and to the challenges which they personally faced. Francis of Assisi came from a prosperous merchant family, whereas the Spaniard Dominic was an Augustinian canon. It is not accidental that it was in the regions of highest economic development, in the Mediterranean world, that the friars not only had their roots, but also their greatest influence. They drew their patronage from townspeople, where orders such as the Cistercians, with a higher proportion of their houses north of the Alps, relied most for support on a feudal aristocracy.

The more that poverty and austerity were preached as the ideal of Christian life, the more men felt that these diverged from the affluence of contemporary society, which was shared by many in the hierarchy of the Church. Pious lay people, who were concerned for the salvation of their souls, felt ill at ease with the wealth which they had acquired, and sought to atone for it by charitable deeds and the adoption of a humble lifestyle. At the very least, churchmen might feel that this was a reproach to them, if not an overt act of rebellion, and in an age when the distinctive status of the clergy was increasingly emphasised, the devout layman had to move very cautiously to avoid antagonising them. This was not easy, as groups such as the Waldenses and Humiliati discovered.[40] One reason for this was that groups which adopted an austere mode of living were concerned with justifying their behaviour, and in an age of growing literacy sought this in the Scriptures. Articulate and devout men wished to deepen their faith by going back to its sources, but needed to do so in a language which they could understand. In the years before 1200, vernacular versions of the Bible were becoming available to the laity. In an age when the Church itself was facing the implications of a more speculative theology in the emerging universities, where its beliefs were being defined more precisely, there was always a danger of speculation lapsing into unorthodoxy, and that as doctrines were clarified those who could not accept them would be left outside. If this was a problem even in clerical circles, the danger was clearly greater when lay-

men, unskilled in the language and methods of philosophy, started to pon-
der the Scriptures, and perhaps fall into heresy and rebellion. Furthermore,
orthodox Christianity was facing its most serious challenge for centuries as
the rival ideas of Catharism were already spreading in the Languedoc.
Indeed, it was an encounter with this heresy which spurred Dominic to set
up his Order of Preachers to tackle the threat which it posed by educating
the laity in the orthodox teachings of the Church.

The nature of this emerging dissent will be examined later; for the
moment it should be noted that the new orders of friars represented practical methods of countering the danger, within the acceptable and recognised
framework of a religious order. Dominic's approach was to counter intellectual divergences from orthodoxy, and from the start he and his followers
were involved in teaching and preaching. Francis was initially more concerned with the pursuit of an idealised Christian life than with the problems
of the Church, and it was less his own wishes than the response of the ecclesiastical authorities to his actions that created the order which now bears his
name. Both orders derived something from the pious attitudes of the twelfth
century, and one could indeed claim that the Cistercians foreshadowed both
the preaching tradition of the Dominicans and the ideal of imitating Christ
which was the hallmark of the Franciscans. Both too operated within a tradition of loyalty to the Church and its authorities, however radical their
actions appeared, and it was this initial obedience to the Papacy which
saved the Franciscans at any rate from the fate of some groups which shared
their ideal of poverty, but which fell foul of the hierarchy. Furthermore,
while Francis rejected materialism in his way of life, he did not condemn the
material world as evil in itself (in striking contrast with Cathar teaching),
seeing Creation as the act of God and therefore as good. While esteeming
asceticism as a form of piety, he was prepared to set limits to it, declaring
that each man should eat enough food for his own requirements, striking a
mean between superfluity of food and excess of abstinence.[41] His personal
humility was the basis of his appeal to his followers, for he was no administrator, and was willing to surrender his position as superior of the order as
it developed, promising obedience to his successor.[42]

These orders only just beat the ban imposed by the Fourth Lateran
Council on new foundations. Francis had renounced the ways of the world
about 1205, following a life of penance and begging for his food, and before
long he attracted followers, most of them pious laymen, drawn from his
own class of well-to-do families in Assisi. By 1208 he adopted an ideal of
absolute poverty for himself and his disciples in accordance with a literal
interpretation of the Gospel. Those who wished to join the brotherhood had
to sell all their possessions and distribute the proceeds to the poor. Poverty
was seen as a mystical virtue, because it imitated the earthly life of Christ.
Furthermore, and it was in this that Francis diverged from the practices of
the monastic orders, this poverty was not to be simply an individual act of
renunciation but also a corporate condition of life. For Francis such

renunciation also had a practical advantage, because it meant that his followers would not become embroiled in quarrels through defending their rights.[43] The group became involved in preaching to the people, an action which could have raised serious problems in an age when the Church authorities were highly sensitive to the dangers of unorthodoxy. But in 1209 an encounter between Francis and Pope Innocent III led to the band of brothers being formally recognised. The friars' preaching was to concentrate on moral matters and avoid theology, and before they left Rome all members of the group received the tonsure, giving them clerical status. The years following this papal recognition saw the expansion of the group into an order as men were drawn into it by the moral appeal of its lifestyle.

The friars' early preaching was directed towards the personal repentance of the hearers, and the restoration of peace in the towns and villages which they visited. Francis also had an ambition to carry Christianity into the world of Islam, and made a number of abortive attempts to evangelise both the Saracens and the Moors, but although in 1219 on a visit to Egypt he was able to preach before the Sultan and be kindly received, his actual mission had no success. But expansion brought problems in its train. The basic rule might suffice for a small band of itinerant evangelists travelling around Italy, but as numbers grew and the brothers expanded their activity in conscious missions throughout Christendom, a fuller administrative structure became essential. The founder's original ideal proved too successful for its own preservation. The speed with which the order spread, and attracted recruits, rapidly turned it into an international force in the life of the Church.

Dominic was already a churchman when his encounter with Cathar heresy set his career on a new course. The development of his spirituality is less well known than that of Francis, but he too had a charismatic influence on those who knew him. Like Francis, he followed an ideal of personal humility, but his missionary approach was more combative than the Italian's, perhaps because Spaniards, accustomed to a frontier with Islam, were conditioned by the militant ideals of the *Reconquista*. While accompanying his bishop on diplomatic missions in 1203 and 1206, Dominic encountered both Cathar heretics in the Toulouse and Cistercians at Montpellier, who had been unsuccessful in the struggle against heresy. It may well have been Dominic's bishop, Diego of Osma, who argued that the best way of combatting heresy was to pursue a humble lifestyle, what was known as the *vita apostolica*. This was a commonplace notion in twelfth-century piety, but it was also comparable to the practices of the Cathar *perfecti*, who had contrasted their own humility with the pomp of the Church hierarchy. But Dominican humility was not the uneducated holiness of the Franciscans – from the start, the group recruited educated men, who had the skills to preach and convert the people. The local bishops in southern France gave them support, notably Fulk of Toulouse, who supported Dominic's attempt to get his group of preachers recognised as an order.[44]

Initially this was unsuccessful, because the petition for recognition coincided with the meeting of the Fourth Lateran Council, where the foundation of new orders was forbidden, but the group adopted the simple solution of adopting the Rule of St Augustine, which Dominic was already following. In 1217 Dominic sent his followers out from their base at Toulouse, possibly because they were endangered by the threat of war, this mission having the support of Pope Honorius III, who instructed the clergy to assist them in their preaching. From the start they concentrated their attention on centres of learning, particularly Paris and Bologna, the leading places in Western Europe for theological and canonist studies respectively. The first general chapter of the order was held at Bologna, and there it was agreed that subsequent meetings should alternate between the two great university cities, a clear reflection of the order's academic orientation. When a mission was sent to England in 1221, it is noteworthy that Oxford was their intended destination. Dominic himself died in that year, and his successor was Jordan of Saxony, who was already a Bachelor of Theology at Paris when he had been drawn into the mendicant order. Under his rule, recruitment in the next decade was focussed consciously on the universities.

Less than a year before his death, Dominic made a determined effort to organise his followers, appointing provincial priors to govern in five areas, and planning the foundation of a number of further provinces. This provincial structure was the order's basis for the rest of the century.[45] Following Dominic's death, the order developed a hierarchy of chapters, conventual, representing each house, provincial, and general, with the master general of the order being elected by the prior and one representative of each province.[46] But while Dominic set out a highly effective pattern of government, Francis had no desire to produce a constitution. Indeed, he led by example rather than by exercising any legal authority. His first rule of 1221 was spiritual rather than legislative, and suffered from imprecision, and it was not until 1223 that a more effective one received papal approval. It was still, however, revolutionary, in that the new friar entered the order rather than an individual house, and professed his obedience to the overall head rather than to a local superior. The implication of this was that the general of the order possessed a level of power far greater than any abbot in a traditional monastic order.[47]

In his later years, Francis exercised a high level of moral authority within the order, but was unable to undertake any role as its commander in chief. Indeed, he resigned as head of the order, professing obedience to his successors. He withdrew into solitary and intense spiritual contemplation, which culminated in him receiving the stigmata, the marks of the wounds of Christ, in 1224. Despite the reverence in which he was held, by the time of his death in 1226, the order was changing out of all recognition from his own ideals. The tensions which resulted from the twin ideals of poverty and humility on the one hand and of mission and service to the world on the other, which had existed from the start, created complications for the order

for the next century. Francis himself respected learning, declaring that theologians should be honoured as dispensers of the Spirit, but he also feared
that brothers of the order who tried to edify their fellows might thereby
reject the higher vocation of holy simplicity.[48] This issue of learning became
one of the major bones of contention later in the century between those
Franciscans who wished to maintain the strictest poverty and humility, and
those who were prepared to compromise on the issue. Learning also
involved the possession of books, and this was incompatible with absolute
poverty. The recruitment of priests into the order made it essential for them
to have the necessary property for them to say their offices.[49]

Even during his life, Francis had been popularly hailed as a saint, and it
took less than two years after his death for a bull of canonization to be
issued. His reputation made Assisi a centre of pilgrimage, and it is not surprising that the Franciscans were anxious to commemorate him. But the
interment of the body and the building of the great basilica to house it represented precisely those aspects of church life which Francis had rejected,
the use of money and the obtaining of privileges. Furthermore, on his
deathbed, he had again in his *Testament* affirmed his belief in poverty and
humility and declared that those who held office in the order were bound to
observe its rule literally. The natural course of action for the friars was to
turn to the pope, for both personal and disciplinary reasons. Gregory IX
had had a long association with them, as protector of the order under
Innocent III, while for Francis obedience to the Papacy had been a guiding
light. In such circumstances papal pronouncements could carry extra weight
with the order, and indeed its fortunes for the next century were closely
bound up with papal attitudes. The popes in general supported those friars
who wished to relax the strict letter of the rule, but were prepared to accept
their scruples and provide a mechanism by which they could at least adhere
to the letter of the rule while relaxing its underlying principles. The bull
Quo elongati of 1230 solved the problem of ownership by declaring that the
friars could have the use of property, such as houses and books, while its
actual ownership was vested in a 'spiritual friend' who could act as trustee.
This was carried further by Innocent IV in the privilege *Ordinem vestrum* of
1245, by which the Apostolic See assumed the right of ownership of the
goods of the order.

Increasingly the more zealous supporters of absolute poverty were marginalised within the order, although the influence of the friars within the
Church as a whole grew as their power was eroded, and as some of them
drifted into heresy, their outlook will be considered later.[50] But the practices
of the two great orders became assimilated to each other – the Franciscans
adopted some aspects of Dominican organisation, and accepted the value of
recruiting educated men into their numbers, while the Dominicans moved
from the owning of possessions to an ideal of poverty. This was more moderate than that of the Franciscans, as is reflected in the views of Aquinas in
the mid-thirteenth century, that perfection did not essentially lie in poverty,

which was merely a way leading to salvation.[51] There is, however, no doubt that a belief in the spiritual merits of material poverty was very influential in the thirteenth-century Church, and it is noteworthy that whereas in the twelfth century groups of hermits which came together often became regular canons, two similar groups which developed in the thirteenth pursued a mendicant ideal, namely the Carmelites and the Austin friars. All these orders played a significant part in the intellectual and evangelical activities of the Church, at times incurring jealousy from the secular parish clergy for encroaching on their pastoral work. Nevertheless these orders probably represented the most dynamic force in church life in this period.

|9|

Heresy and orthodoxy

The rise of heresy

The twelfth century saw for the first time since the late Roman Empire the existence of heresies which provoked a powerful response from the Church authorities. It has been pointed out that heresy can be defined only with reference to orthodoxy,[1] so in some senses the emergence of heretical ideas must be related to the increasingly clear definitions of orthodoxy which are found at this time. This is certainly true as far as academic dissent is concerned; every time that a doctrine was defined as orthodox, the act of definition could leave dissentients on the wrong side of the boundary, and liable to ecclesiastical sanctions if they did not conform. This, however, does not necessarily cover more popular heresies, which took two distinct forms; on the one hand there were individuals who did not necessarily diverge far from orthodoxy in their beliefs, but who were unwilling to accept the legal authority of the Church to control their actions – this was the case with the earlier Waldensians – and on the other there were adherents of a Catharism, a dualist doctrine which rejected the material world as inherently evil. This had earlier taken root in the Byzantine world and in the Balkans, and began to penetrate the West in the mid-twelfth century. Precisely when this occurred is not clear, for some views held by early heretics, which might have been influenced by Cathar teachings, could have been no more than the logical development of ideals of orthodox piety, vegetarianism representing an idealisation of austerity in diet, and objections to sexual relations being a transference to the lay world of an ideal acceptable in monasticism.

A few cases of heresy in the early eleventh century have already been noted, but there is a significant gap in recorded cases of popular unorthodox belief for the best part of a century afterwards. The years of the Gregorian reform movement and the subsequent struggle between the pope and the emperor, and the early period of the Crusades, do not appear to have seen any heretical movements, although there were one or two isolated prosecutions such as those of Tanchelm of Antwerp and Henry of Le Mans. Both of these began as zealous, perhaps over-zealous, reformers, but later put forward extreme ideas, which gave rise to social disorder and scandalised the church establishment. The evidence for their careers is sparse, and may well be distorted in sources emanating from their opponents, so it is hard to judge how extreme their actual ideas were.[2] Possibly heresy went unrecorded simply because both lay and ecclesiastical authorities were preoccupied with other matters, but it is also worth noting that none of the decrees of the First and Second Lateran Councils, in 1123 and 1139 respectively, refer to heresy; while the absence of repressive measures cannot prove that there was none, it certainly suggests that unorthodoxy was not regarded as a serious threat. Even in the mid-twelfth century the problems which the Papacy was facing in its struggle with the Emperor Frederick Barbarossa may have curtailed action at a time when Cathar doctrines were being voiced more openly in the West. Even so, the Church was slow to take extreme measures. Although the Cathars were anathematised in 1179 at the Third Lateran Council, the decree against them affirmed that the Church's discipline should not involve the shedding of blood.[3] This was followed up by the decree *Ad abolendam* of Lucius III in 1184, in which he condemned the recent spread of heresy, and declared that the Church's power should be aroused to put an end to it. This marked a turning-point in ecclesiastical attitudes to heresy, because hitherto the problem had been left to the discretion of individual bishops, but now it was seen as a matter concerning the whole Church. The condemnation was directed primarily against the Cathars, as specific reference was made to individuals described as *consolati* and *perfecti,* terms which they undoubtedly used. Both clerks and laymen guilty of heresy were to be handed over to the secular arm for punishment, the former after deprivation. The lay powers were enjoined to support the Church, and the ecclesiastical authorities were empowered to investigate suspect heretical meetings.[4] But the weapon used was both blunt and ineffective, as enforcement still depended on the co-operation of the local bishop and the lay power. It failed, too, to discriminate between genuine heretics and a number of evangelical groups, including the Humiliati, who were also affected by it.[5]

By 1215, however, the authorities were markedly more concerned with maintaining orthodoxy. The decrees of the Fourth Lateran Council opened with a credal affirmation, in which at least two points were directed against Catharism, the statement that baptised sinners can be restored by penitence and that married persons as well as virgins can find favour with God and attain eternal blessedness. The decrees also renewed the command to hand heretics over to the lay power for punishment, laid down sanctions against temporal lords who failed to clear their lands of 'heretical filth', and established a procedure for identifying suspects, prior to them being questioned. The importance attached to such measures, reflecting the alarm felt by the authorities, is demonstrated by the fact that indulgences granted to Crusaders were extended to those who fought against heresy.[6]

The Waldensians

Heresy is a phenomenon which occurs only in an age of religious sensitivity, and it is hardly surprising that the twelfth century, an age of spiritual turmoil, saw an increasingly literate laity asking questions for itself. It is not perhaps accidental that some heretics of the period denied the value of infant baptism, because they saw that if the sacrament was received by an adult it would represent a personal statement of conversion to a new life.[7] Because both orthodox and heretical piety were rooted in the spirituality of the age, the boundary between them was at times so narrow as to be almost indistinguishable. This was particularly true of the origins of the Waldensians, for the conversion of Valdes of Lyons to a life of poverty about 1176 bore a close resemblance to that of Francis a generation later. There were differences – Valdes was married, and after his abandonment of his fortune as a merchant made provision for his wife and endowed his daughters to enter a nunnery. A generation earlier he might have entered a Cistercian house, but instead he pursued a life of poverty and charity. He wished to interpret the Gospels literally, and sought to obtain translations of them into the vernacular. His desire to preach, however, brought him into conflict with the authorities locally, so he sought recognition from the pope. Valdes was no rebel, and Alexander III was not wholly unsympathetic. He approved the vow of voluntary poverty taken by him and his followers, but forbade preaching unless they had the approval of the local clergy, something which was unlikely to be forthcoming. There was nothing unorthodox in his own confession of faith, which was indeed couched in terms which explicitly distinguished his views from those of the Cathars.[8] The growing distinctiveness of clerical status and the desire of churchmen to maintain it was probably one factor in their resistance to lay groups which wished to preach to the people, and it is noteworthy that Innocent III later insisted that Francis and his followers should receive the tonsure when he recognised their group as an order.[9] In southern France and northern Italy there was a further problem, which may partially explain why the Waldensians eventually found themselves on the wrong side of the division between heresy and orthodoxy, namely the danger that pro-poverty groups might be infiltrated by the far more radical doctrines of Catharism. Also, and perhaps more serious, was the fact that although Valdes himself was willing to accept the authority of the Church, some of his followers were less compliant, continued to preach, and were excommunicated.

It is a measure of the moral success of orthodox reform in the twelfth century and of the impact it made on an increasingly articulate lay world that its values were so widely accepted. Similar attitudes to those of the Waldensians can be found among the Humiliati of northern Italy, who rejected usury and the accumulation of wealth, and made their living by simple manual work. But they too sought a right to preach and were unsuccessful. In 1184 they and other sects were condemned, although the

Humiliati of Milan were reinstated two years later. The main activity of
such groups that incurred condemnation was preaching, which was clearly
seen as encroaching on the role of the clergy.[10] The fate of such groups
depended on the attitude of particular popes, and it is noteworthy that
Innocent III took a markedly more tolerant view than some of his predecessors of groups pursuing an ideal of poverty if they were still committed to
theologically orthodox views. He ordered that measures against the
Humiliati should cease, while he investigated their request for recognition.
He even conceded them a limited right to preach, provided they avoided theological questions, and continued to support them despite episcopal opposition. They repaid his trust by working actively against heresy.[11] Innocent
also of course gave his blessing to Francis, and was prepared to pardon
repentant Waldensians who were willing to obey the Holy See. In 1208 he
wrote to the archbishop of Tarragona, relating the submission of Durand of
Huesca, a former Waldensian who had pledged himself and his followers to
work against heresy. He had to warn Durand a year later that complaints
were still being made against him, and exhorted him to obedience, but his
trust and moderation were probably repaid, for a *Summa contra hereticos*
from the 1230s commented that some reconciled Waldensians had continued in piety to this date.[12]

Not all Waldensians, however, accepted reconciliation to the Church. By
the thirteenth century they had developed into a distinctive sect, which indeed
survived as an underground movement beyond the end of the Middle Ages.
But like so many sects, it proved vulnerable to divisions. These may have
been partly prompted by personal rivalries among the leaders, and partly by
problems of communication as the movement spread from its origins in
Lyons across the Alps to Lombardy. Valdes himself was essentially moderate, and may well have hoped for reconciliation with the Church, but more
radical groups appeared elsewhere. One, detected at Metz in 1199, was
highly critical of the clergy, and the Lombard Waldensians became increasingly exclusive in their attitudes, insisting that they were the sole path to salvation. By 1205 a definite split occurred, with the Lombards holding the
neo-Donatist view that the sacraments of an unworthy priest were invalid,
while the Lyonists followed the orthodox doctrine that any duly ordained
priest had powers of consecration. The groups remained in touch with each
other, recognising that they had much in common, and in 1218 a meeting
was held at Bergamo to try to reach agreement. While some compromises
were reached, the Lyonists accepting the Lombard demand to appoint ministers for life, and abandoning Valdes' original insistence on manual labour,
two issues could not be resolved. One was the question of the powers of
priests to consecrate, while the other reflected traditions of personal loyalty,
with the ultramontanes insisting that Valdes was in heaven while the Italians
held that this question could not be answered.[13] Thereafter the movement
remained divided, although some contacts were preserved among different
groups. It spread widely north of the Alps, in Germany and Austria, and

small communities took root in the Alpine valleys. The more extreme wing probably became dominant, and in the early fourteenth century the inquisitor Bernard Gui, who clearly distinguished the views of different heretical groups, saw their main offence as contempt for the authority of the Church. Links were maintained among them by travelling preachers, but the development of local divergent practices in worship suggests that these must have been tenuous.[14] Periodic persecutions failed to wipe them out completely.

The Cathars

As early as the late twelfth century, orthodox writers distinguished between the two main streams of heresy, the Waldensian and the Cathar. One such, Peter de Vaux-de-Cernay, commented that the Waldensians were bad enough, but were much less wicked than other heretics and indeed agreed with orthodox Christianity on many matters.[15] Catharism originated in the Eastern Empire, notably in the Balkans, where it was known as Bogomilism, and was undoubtedly the most radical heresy which affected the medieval Church in the West, because it abandoned the mainstream Judaeo-Christian (and indeed also Moslem) belief in a single god, replacing it with a dualist theology that there were two conflicting powers in the universe, one good and one evil. The former was identified with the spiritual world and the latter with the material, including all forms of sexual relationship, and any resulting products of it. The world, the flesh and the devil were identified by believers in a very literal sense, although not all their views were quite so unanimous, even on major doctrinal issues. There was, for example, disagreement as to whether Satan, the evil power, had once been subordinate to God (modified dualism) or if the principle of evil was totally independent (absolute dualism). Full members of the sect, the *perfecti*, were rigidly ascetic, pursuing a strictly vegan diet (apart from fish, which were believed to be the product of water) and renouncing marriage. They were supported by adherents, who did not follow the same practices, but who might hope on their deathbed to be 'perfected' by a ritual called the *consolamentum*. Only those who had themselves been consoled could administer this, and if they lapsed from their strict principles their administrations were deemed invalid. This insistence on the administering 'perfect' being in a state of grace raised problems for believers, and on occasions led to individuals with doubts being reordained or reconsoled.

These doctrines penetrated into the West by various routes, but the dates at which this occurred are not always clear. Reports of heresy trials in the Rhineland in the 1140s suggest an Eastern origin for the offenders, but it is possible that some Frenchmen who settled in Constantinople around the time of the First Crusade may have brought back heretical doctrines and also been responsible for translating Greek material into Latin. It was not, however, until the mid-twelfth century that these doctrines became widespread in the

West.[16] Both absolute and modified doctrines were brought to the West, the former generally from a Greek and the latter from a Slav background, and the distribution of Cathar beliefs reflects which missionaries operated in particular areas. A Greek missionary, Nicetas, established absolute doctrines in the Languedoc and at Desenzano in Italy, but most of the Italian Cathar churches followed the modified form.[17] There are renewed references to heresy in the Rhineland and to the condemnation of a group of fugitives in England in the 1160s, and to further cases in the 1180s, and Catharism certainly survived in Germany till the early thirteenth century. The centre of gravity of heretical activity, however, had by that time moved further south.[18]

One of the most striking characteristics of mid-twelfth-century Catharism in southern France was that it was open rather than secretive, because it had social support from members of the local landed class. It may have secured this because many of the heretics' ascetic practices did not greatly differ from those of orthodox piety, and when families split between orthodox and heretical members, they were mutually tolerant. Furthermore the Cathars used the Latin Vulgate as their biblical text and, in the early stages at any rate, a Latin liturgy. Only later did the southern French group adopt a vernacular liturgy and an Occitan translation of the New Testament.[19] In 1165 the Cathars met the church authorities in open debate at Lombers, and although the local bishop condemned them he was unable to enforce any sanctions against them and could only warn the local knights not to support the heretics any longer. As yet, even when sanctions could be imposed they were not particularly severe by later standards – proceedings at Toulouse in 1178 were supported by both the French and the English kings, but the most serious penalty imposed was a confiscation of property, flogging through the streets, and taking an oath to go to Jerusalem for three years. Other offenders were excommunicated, but incurred no additional punishment.[20] Men continued to support heresy openly until after 1200; after all, it was an encounter with it in this area that prompted Dominic both to embark on his career of anti-heretical preaching and to emulate some of the poverty of the Cathar *perfecti* so as to deprive them of their moral appeal.[21] In northern Italy too, the heretics secured popular support, possibly because of the political disruption during the struggles between the pope and the emperor, but also because in some towns such as Orvieto and Verona it was openly acceptable for a time. It is unlikely, however, that heresy there was as widespread as in southern France. Certainly when it was condemned at the Third Lateran Council in 1179, no mention was made of Italy, and the heretics were stated to be particularly numerous in Gascony, Albi and Toulouse.[22]

The anti-Cathar crusades and the Inquisition

It was in the early thirteenth century that the church authorities intensified their repressive measures, with the determination of Innocent III to destroy heresy. In 1204 and 1205 he appealed to Philip II of France to eliminate heretics from his kingdom. The papal legate, Peter of Castelnau, pressed Count Raymond VI of Toulouse to take political action against them, and excommunicated him when he failed to do so. When the legate debated with a group of *perfecti* near Carcassonne in 1207, the audience did not commit itself either way, a measure of the protection the Cathars enjoyed. But Peter was murdered in 1208, and Innocent proclaimed a crusade against the heretics. This attracted support from the French king, who was anxious to extend his influence in the south, and from various northern lords, who hoped to make material gains from it. Although Raymond submitted and joined the crusade, there were other southern lords who were known to protect the Cathars, and the army marched against the lands of the Trencavel family in Béziers and Carcassonne, where heretics were numerous. In the former town at any rate, many inhabitants were massacred irrespective of their religious beliefs, although elsewhere the conquerors seem to have been more selective and concentrated on burning *perfecti*, if they could find and identify them. Because fugitives from these areas fled to Raymond's lands it was impossible for him to satisfy the demands of the legates, and war was renewed in 1211, culminating in the victory of the northerners under the elder Simon de Montfort at the battle of Muret in 1213.[23]

The crusade inflicted severe damage on southern French Catharism, although it did not succeed in eliminating the Cathar diocesan structure, nor did the sect immediately lose its lay sympathisers. Religious and political questions were inextricably bound together, and the southern aristocracy were willing to support the house of Toulouse against the Montfortians. The northerners' brutality may have made it harder for the orthodox missionaries to reconvert the people, and Raymond VII of Toulouse, for political rather than doctrinal reasons, was equivocal in supporting repression. Gradually, however, Cathar influence declined. In the 1230s it was destroyed in Toulouse itself, although it survived in the countryside till the following decade. The establishment of inquisitorial procedures gradually led to more efficient repression, and political factors assisted religious suppression. The fall of the Cathar castle of Montségur in 1244, with the capture of more than two hundred *perfecti*, was followed by intensified persecution, and when the line of the Counts of Toulouse died out, the lands passed to Alphonse of Poitiers, the brother of Louis IX.[24] French Catharism was increasingly marginalised, and although its devotees in remote areas still attracted attention from the Inquisition, few of these were literate, and none were influential. It therefore ceased to be a major problem to the church authorities.[25] In some parts of France heresy does not seem to have been a serious problem – the register of Archbishop Eudes of Rouen contains only one case, unfortunately without details, in 1253, and the canons of the provincial council of Vienne in 1289 suggest that although heresy existed in that area, it was not seen as serious, and no particular heresy was identified. Offenders were to be excommunicated, and in each parish investigations were to be conducted by the oaths of the priest and two or three trustworthy laymen.[26]

The destruction of the Cathars in southern France meant that fugitives were dispersed, particularly to Italy. Here a more unstable political scene made persecution intermittent, and when the popes were involved in political struggles against the emperors, heretics could hope for at least tacit protection from communes or tyrants opposed to the Papacy. Although Frederick II's *Liber Augustalis* provided for the punishment of heretics (and from the language employed particularly the Cathar *perfecti,* who were to be burned), and declared that rulers should use the secular sword to protect the Church against its enemies, he was inactive in taking measures against heresy and his illegitimate son Manfred gave them support.[27] After Frederick's death in 1250 the church authorities were able to intensify persecution, although it was well on in the century before some groups were suppressed. The collapse of old imperialist loyalties in northern Italy with the invasion of Charles of Anjou in support of the Papacy led to the arrival of the Inquisition in the area. A group of 178 *perfecti* from Sirmione on Lake Garda were burnt at Verona in 1278, but there were still Cathar trials at Bologna between 1291 and 1309.[28] But by the fourteenth century, Catharism had ceased to be a serious threat to the Church.

The orthodox assault on Catharism combined persuasion and repression. Although in the earlier period the main characteristic of the sect had been its evangelical way of life and many Cathars were comparatively ill-educated, recent studies of it have suggested that some at any rate had a measure of intellectual training, and may well have had collections of authorities on which they could rely in debate. Some of the *perfecti* could read Latin, and may have been trained in philosophy.[29] One writer, about 1213, claimed that the Italian Cathars sent students to Paris to learn logic and theology, so as to strengthen their own error and overthrow the Catholic faith.[30] The internal evidence of one major text, the *Book of Two Principles* (probably dating from 1240–50), shows some awareness of contemporary philosophical writing, although this was not particularly deep, and a substantial knowledge of the Vulgate in both the canonical and apocryphal books. The writer was an absolute dualist, and not only used logical arguments to rebut orthodox views, but also employed arguments from contemporary Catholic polemicists to attack the doctrines of the modified dualist party.[31] Persuasion evidently brought some heretics back into the Church, and such converts could prove their sincerity by becoming zealous fighters for orthodoxy. Rainerius Sacconi admitted having been a heretic for seventeen years and a 'heresiarch' before he was converted by Peter of Verona and entered the Dominicans. In 1250 he wrote a *summa* against the Cathars and the Waldensians, and between 1254 and 1259 he was inquisitor for Lombardy. His writings are one of the best sources for the different groups within the Cathar movement, and in his *summa* he identified sixteen Cathar churches in Lombardy.[32] Other writers of anti-Cathar polemic also

note the diversity of their opinions, and indeed one suggested that these disagreements created a scandal which drove some of their supporters back to
orthodoxy.[33]

Physical coercion, however, was the principal means by which heretics
were brought back into the fold. Traditionally, responsibility for maintaining orthodoxy had rested with the local bishop, but in the twelfth century
the episcopate had been unable to suppress unorthodox thought. In an age
of increasing papal power, it is hardly surprising that the pope decided to
take a hand, and in 1231 Gregory IX issued a bull providing that those
found guilty of heresy should be handed over to the secular power for due
punishment. This probably implied a death sentence, as this was something
which the laity but not the clergy could inflict. In the same year the Emperor
Frederick II laid down that death by burning should be the penalty for
heresy. At the same time, the pope commissioned men to act as inquisitors
to search for heretics, and within a few years the procedures had become
widely established throughout Europe. The new orders of friars, particularly although not exclusively the Dominicans, were entrusted with carrying
out these investigations.

The term 'Inquisition' has emotive connotations, and although there is no
doubt that inquisitorial procedures and the actions of some bloodthirsty
inquisitors, including the use of torture to extort confessions, justify some of
the opprobrium attached to it, it must be remembered that it was initially a
body which was primarily concerned with imposing penances on offenders
and with recalling them to the faith, and with destroying the support which
they had from the laity. Heretics who recanted would not suffer the death
penalty. On balance its sentences were less brutal than those imposed by lay
powers – it was the latter which burned two hundred *perfecti* after the fall
of the Cathar stronghold of Montségur in 1244 and it is not clear how far
the inquisitors were involved. The majority of those convicted by it suffered
lesser penalties. The *perfecti* were perhaps unlikely to recant, and were subjected to rigorous measures, but the Waldensians, and even Cathar *credentes*, might escape with penances. In the early stages torture was not part
of the procedure, and was authorised only in 1252. Nevertheless the inquisitors had the odds stacked in their favour, because those whom they accused
were clearly assumed guilty unless they could prove their innocence. They
were not told the names of witnesses against them, nor could they call witnesses on their own behalf. In areas where the inquisitors were most active
and most brutal, heresy was effectively suppressed, as in the measures taken
in the Rhineland by Conrad of Marburg. His actions were resented, and he
himself was murdered in 1233, but Catharism certainly disappeared from
the area.[34] The Inquisition, admittedly, always had some opposition from
the local lay powers, for the simple reason that it was seen as encroaching
on their rights. This perhaps explains some of its difficulties in Italy –
although the friars were strong there, and indeed were even able to secure
the conversion of some heretics, of whom the most notable, Sacconi, himself

became a friar and an inquisitor, they also had to face the determination of the city republics to preserve their own rights of jurisdiction.[35]

Piety and millenarianism – orthodox and heretical

The social milieu of the twelfth century was conducive to the rise of religious individualism, which always ran the risk of falling foul of the ecclesiastical authorities. These conditions for the growth of popular piety survived into the thirteenth century, and there were occasions when the activity of individuals sparked off a spiritual revival, which the Church could harness to its own ends. This was true of the activities of a lay preacher calling himself Brother Benedict who appeared at Parma in 1233, later moving south to Spoleto and Apulia, where he was last recorded in 1236. He inspired widespread popular enthusiasm, which was later taken up in the north by both the Franciscans and the Dominicans, who organised preachings, processions and the singing of hymns. This became known as 'The Alleluia' or 'The Great Devotion', and shows how spiritual enthusiasm could be aroused among the people.[36] The friars harnessed the movement to the pacification of feuds in the towns, and their preaching was perfectly orthodox.

There was, however, always a danger that spiritual idealism could overstep the point where the frontiers of orthodoxy and heresy were ill-defined. The most conspicuous example of this was the appeal of the more radical Franciscans, who wished to adhere to the founder's ideal of absolute poverty and refused to accept those mitigations of it which the Papacy authorised after his death. Their ideal of imitating the life of Christ and the apostles also came to be linked with an expectation of the early Second Coming, a theme of spiritual teaching which owed much to the writings of the Calabrian Cistercian abbot Joachim of Fiore, who had died in 1202. He had postulated an eschatological theory of history, interpreting it in terms of three ages, each associated with one person of the Trinity, and forecasting the coming of a time in which the organised Church of the Second Age would be superseded by the Third Age of the Spirit, in which individuals would be directly inspired by it, without requiring the mediatory role of the Church. This would come after a period of tribulation, during which Antichrist would appear for a time. The forerunners of the Third Age would be a new order of monks, who would be inspired by a spiritual understanding of it. Increasingly the radical Franciscans identified themselves with this new order, and Francis with its herald, the angel of the sixth seal in the Apocalypse. Joachite teaching also spread among the laity; by the mid-century it was being affirmed that 1260 was to be the year of cosmic destiny, and this saw an outbreak of Flagellant processions, as the devout sought to carry their imitation of Christ into an identification with his suffering. But when the year passed away without the Second Coming, the expected date for it was moved forward, and an underlying current of apocalyptic thought persisted for the rest of the Middle Ages, surfacing particularly in periods of social and political upheaval.[37]

The circulation of such ideas provided a heady mixture, which was hardly congenial to the ecclesiastical establishment. The Franciscan order faced a crisis in the 1250s, when a young friar at Paris, Gerard of Borgo San Donnino, wrote a work which pushed Joachim's ideas to a logical conclusion beyond the original author's views, claiming that the Old and New Testaments were abrogated with the advent of the Third Age, and that all authority now was contained in Joachim's works.[38] Not only were Gerard's works condemned, but the minister-general of the order, John of Parma, who had tried to emphasise the principle of poverty, was suspected of heretical associations and compelled to resign. He was succeeded by the distinguished young theologian Bonaventura, who attempted to strike a balance between the two wings of the order. But when it came to the most critical issues his outlook was much closer to the Conventual or relaxed wing than to the rigorist Spirituals. He still supported the ideals of individual and corporate poverty, but he was an organiser and a scholar, who was prepared to dilute the poverty of the order to support learning. Austerity was to be preferred to asceticism, and, perhaps more critically, wisdom to humility. Bonaventura's ideals survived his death and lay behind the bull *Exiit qui seminat* of Nicholas III of 1279. This distinguished between holding a legal right to goods, which the friars would not have but which was retained by the pope, and actual use (*usus facti*), which accepted that every friar had a right to food, clothes and books for the pursuit of wisdom. They had at the same time, however, to pursue a simple life.[39] The bull consolidated the compromise system established earlier in the century, but it alienated the Spiritual wing of the order. It also was vulnerable in that it depended on the pope's continued willingness to act as trustee for the order, and rumours had been circulating as early as 1274 that he might not and would insist that the Franciscans accept property.[40] In the fourteenth century, this came to pass.

Even before the earlier alarm, there was resistance among friars who rated the obligation of poverty more highly than that of obedience. Three areas, the March of Ancona, Provence and Tuscany, were particularly affected by this, and in the first two regions they had to face persecution. The most articulate leader of the pro-poverty group, Peter John Olivi, was willing to remain within the law and accept the bull *Exiit*, but some of his followers were less cautious and were disciplined in 1292. In fact compromise between the rival wings of the order was impracticable, with both groups claiming to be the true heirs of Francis. The only real solution to the problem was one which neither side wanted, the division of the order. Celestine V was the most improbable pope of the century, the leader of a remote community of hermit monks, who was chosen to break a deadlocked election, and in practical terms was a disaster for the Papacy. But perhaps his vision would have solved the question, when he supported the radicals, whom he permitted to break from the main order and call themselves 'The Poor Hermits of Pope Celestine'. After his abdication, however, Boniface VIII withdrew the concessions made to them and they were forced to flee. Tensions continued, and although attempts were made to preserve the unity of the order, a number of the Spirituals drifted into rebellion against the pope, and into heresy. Although Olivi remained within the fold of the Church during his lifetime, his works were condemned posthumously and the Conventuals later dug up his bones and defaced his tomb. It is noteworthy that in the handbook of heresies by the fourteenth-century inquisitor Bernard Gui, the Franciscan radicals, whom he called 'Beguins', occupied the largest amount of space.[41]

Joachite influences affected other areas of church life also, most notably the sect which called itself the Apostolic Brethren. This was founded in 1260 by Gerard Segarelli, who followed a lifestyle similar to that of the early Franciscans. They were perhaps more intolerant, for some of them attacked the rich. Their initial offence was disobedience to the Church, but after Segarelli was burned in 1300, his successor Dolcino was an eschatological prophet in the Joachite tradition. He was executed in 1307. They created concern in northern Italy, and Gui's *Manuel* devotes some space to them, but elsewhere their influence was not widespread.[42]

Mystical movements

Belief in direct inspiration by the Holy Spirit, of course, was the essence of the mystical approach to God. In an age of pious aspiration, both men and women sought such immediate spiritual experiences, but by its very nature a do-it-yourself religion left a dilemma for the ecclesiastical establishment. On the one hand, anything which strengthened piety was welcome, but on the other there were dangers that the normal sacramental order of the Church would be disregarded, and that the clergy who administered it would become irrelevant. If individuals could find spiritual fulfilment without the services of the Church, furthermore, they might claim direct divine illumination and propagate ideas which ran counter to the Church's teaching. Furthermore, as mysticism spread down the social scale, it developed a vernacular character, with the result that the ideas expressed might lack the doctrinal precision which could guarantee orthodoxy or be clearly seen as heresy. Furthermore, the inherent nature of mystical experience, as something that lay beyond the normal categories of reason in its awareness of the infinite, was in a sense incommunicable by the use of finite language. The resulting danger was that the often paradoxical images employed by the devout could easily be misunderstood – references to the ravishing of the soul by God could be interpreted in terms of sexual abandon. In such circumstances, it is not altogether surprising that accusations of libertinism and antinomianism were brought against mystical groups by those who took their utterances literally.

Although mystical perceptions could by their very nature be experienced only by individuals, like-minded pious people came together in groups to pursue their devotional life. Some such secured ecclesiastical patronage, notably those of women called beguines. They were essentially an urban phenomenon, and were drawn particularly from those who could not afford to enter a nunnery. The most prominent figure in the early years was Mary of Oignies, who attracted a number of devout women to her at the beginning of the thirteenth century and won the support of a future cardinal, James of Vitry. Indeed he may have tried to secure their recognition as an order, but was unable to do so because the Fourth Lateran Council had forbidden new foundations, although he did secure permission for them to live a communal life. Not all women identified as beguines, however, necessarily adopted such a lifestyle. After this the practice spread widely through northern Europe – for example, documents from Strasburg identify 122 individuals as beguines before 1318. They believed in a life of poverty and supported themselves by manual labour, and some churchmen saw them as a potential buttress against the spread of heresy – indeed Mary of Oignies supported the crusade against the Cathars. It is not accidental that many beguine houses came under the spiritual guidance of the friars, particularly of the Dominicans, although one can also see at the same time the foundation of houses of Dominican nuns, who were more closely linked to the order. Although the beguines generally were completely orthodox, being described in a Rouen register of 1269 as 'the daughters of God', some individuals may have deviated into heresy, and by the end of the thirteenth century, their opponents began to spread accusations of this against them.[43]

An alleged case of heretical mysticism, affecting a beguine from Hainault, Marguerite Porete, took place in the first decade of the fourteenth century. One of her books had already been condemned as heretical and burnt by the bishop of Cambrai, when she was accused of spreading heresy by means of another book, the *Mirror of Simple Souls*. After refusing to answer interrogation, she was found guilty of relapse and burnt in 1310. In fact the survival of this work suggests that it was not essentially heretical – indeed it circulated as an aid to devotion among monks and nuns in later centuries – although some of its language might be interpreted in a misleading or even an unorthodox sense.[44] Marguerite may have been the victim of a heresy scare at the time, for the Council of Vienne in 1311–12 asserted that the beguines, particularly in Germany, were preaching erroneous doctrines and forbade their way of life (although safeguarding the rights of faithful women to live in their hospices).[45] It was alleged that there was a sect of the Free Spirit, which was guilty of antinomian teachings, which were then set out. In fact there is no proof that such a sect existed in any organised sense, and inquisitorial proceedings may have formulated a more systematic set of beliefs than were held by the accused individuals. The responses of interrogated suspects are sometimes very close to the beliefs alleged in the bull of condemnation.[46] Some individuals may have been guilty of the offences laid to their charge, for the history of some modern sects shows that individuals who claim spiritual powers can compel rigid obedience from their followers, but proof of this is lacking, and accusations of sexual orgies are a perennial form of hostile allegation against any more or less secret group.

It is hard to judge how far an undercurrent of heresy survived into the fourteenth century, or how widespread it was. Catharism was effectively eliminated, and Waldensianism survived only in isolated areas and among small secret groups. It may have contributed to the ethos of some later heretical movements, and survived until the Reformation, when it was absorbed into developing Protestantism.[47] Joachite apocalyptic coloured some popular belief, and on occasions may have overstepped the limits of orthodoxy, but again did not attract any widespread popular movement. Even Flagellant groups saw their actions as a form of orthodox devotion, particularly in a time of crisis, as in the anticipated (and eventually anticlimactic) apocalyptic year of 1260 and again in the mid-fourteenth century at the time of the Black Death.[48] This emphasises the narrowness of the margin between orthodoxy and heresy, which persisted to a later date. The main significance of such movements was less in the ideas which they propounded than in the underlying attitudes of individuals, and particularly of the laity, to the Church establishment. Traditionally the roles of the clergy and of the laity were clearly differentiated, and the emergence of a more educated and more articulate lay society posed a challenge to the constraints which this imposed. Older ideals of withdrawal from the world were no longer seen as the only path to salvation.

| 10 |

Logic, theology and law

The development of systematic theology

One implication of the closer ties which the Gregorian reform movement established throughout Christendom was a greater awareness of the need to stress the Church's doctrinal unity. Theological studies are prompted by a desire of the learned for faith to be supported by understanding, and from the eleventh century there had been an increasing awareness of how classical philosophy provided techniques of analysis which could be employed in discussing matters of faith. Indeed this revival of dialectic, and the determination to subject questions to rational analysis, made the late eleventh and early twelfth centuries a period of crucial importance in the development of European thought. At the same time, there is always a tension in theology between reason and revelation – can divine truths be understood by rational means, or do they depend purely on faith? The first great theological crisis which affected the Western Church as a whole in this period was that over the nature of the Eucharist and the views expressed by Berengar of Tours.[1] Although men had used logic before in their arguments, this controversy developed some of the technical vocabulary which was to be basic to the life of the later medieval universities.[2] This analytical method was applied to the main authoritative texts of the faith, the Bible and the writings of the Church Fathers, the greatest of whom, and probably the most revered, was St Augustine. Quite apart from his dominance as a theologian, Augustine had also claimed that the seven liberal arts (grammar, rhetoric and dialectic comprising the *trivium,* and geometry, astronomy, arithmetic and music the *quadrivium*) were vital training for the highest of studies, that of the Scriptures. Indeed, the outstanding characteristic of medieval theology from the twelfth century onwards was its use of logical analysis to refine the beliefs and teachings of the Church.

Traditionally education had centred on the monasteries and on monks, but in the twelfth century the centre of gravity in theological study moved to the cathedral schools and to the secular clergy. The most profound theologian of the years around 1100 was a man with a monastic background, the former prior of Bec, Anselm, who had been appointed archbishop of Canterbury. Anselm was profoundly influenced by Augustine and his ideal of the discovery of God through a progression of mental activities from cogitation, through meditation, to contemplation.[3] His thought was couched in terms of meditation, and it was this which led to his famous ontological argument for the existence of God. He depended on rigorous logic, but was not concerned with the kind of dialectical argument which set up alternative contradictory views and tried to resolve them. Other monastic writers had a similar approach. Rupert of Deutz, writing in the early twelfth century, said that he used philosophical language not because God was subject to the vanity of philosophers, but to express his ideas better and more briefly. He was concerned with contemplating rather than demonstrating God.[4]

On the whole, monastic theologians concentrated on the Scriptures and on the devotional lessons which they taught, and it is hardly surprising that controversies arose between them and those who were more concerned with justifying their arguments logically. Such disputes were aggravated by the characters of the participants, this being demonstrated most clearly in that between Bernard and Abelard, which made its mark on the awareness of men outside the world of academic debate.[5] The first was not only the spiritual Colossus of his age but also a literary genius of great intellectual power, who, however, eschewed dialectic and the methods of the modern school, preferring the traditional method of accumulating citations from the Church Fathers. He set limits to the scope of reason, writing in his *De Consideratione* that he does not attempt to explain, and to the question 'What is God?' replies that He alone knows.[6] It would be wrong, however, to see him as totally opposed to learning, for about 1142 he defended his advice to the Englishman Robert Pullen to spend some time in Paris, 'for the sake of the sound doctrine which is known to be taught there'.[7] The second was an abrasive and arrogant philosopher, a teacher who inspired devotion and intellectual excitement among his pupils, but who left bitterness among those whom he had routed in argument. Nevertheless, although he was determined to explain the truth where others had simply asserted it, he still wrote, 'I do not wish to be a philosopher if it means conflicting with Paul, nor to be an Aristotle if it cuts me off from Christ'.[8]

In the final analysis, the bitterness of the dispute between Bernard and Abelard sprang from the fact that each was totally convinced of the rightness of his cause. Nevertheless there were men who could sympathise with both sides in some of the debates, recognising that the disputants were honest in their search for truth. It is perhaps not accidental, however, that the controversy over which John of Salisbury took an eirenic view was Bernard's dispute with the less provocative Gilbert de la Porrée rather than that with Abelard, accepting that Bernard was guided by the love of God but also paying tribute to Gilbert's intellectual distinction, and concluding his remarks on him, 'I am sure that he no longer disagrees with the abbot and the other saints, for they both see face to face the truth they spent their lives in seeking'.[9] He was also willing to distinguish between the essentials and inessentials of doctrine and declared that there were matters on which men might disagree without endangering their salvation.[10]

It was, however, the conviction that right belief was essential to salvation that lay behind the determination of controversialists to win their arguments. (It reflected the same principle as the persecution of heretics to compel them to return to the faith, where harsh methods were adopted with the best intentions.) The development of a new philosophical approach to religion was probably due primarily to the transmission of a new range of ancient philosophical texts to the West, but it is not clear precisely when, nor by what routes, these arrived. Until the development of the early universities, there was even uncertainty as to the scope of logic, but even before then, the accessibility of these texts and hence the raw material for philosophical debate was piecemeal. One can say that until after 1000 and possibly 1100, the main source of texts on the subject was the work of Boethius, but that around 1130 the 'New Logic' became available in the West. This may have been affected by the intellectual interests of some Greek-speaking Westerners involved in diplomatic contacts with Byzantium during the crusading period. The accessibility of works which they brought back may well have given an impetus to the new analytical theology in the West. New translations of Aristotle's writings on logic became available to Western scholars, and are quoted from the time of Abelard onwards, although he himself, while aware of the new learning, was still strongly influenced by Boethius.[11] By the twelfth century, men were aware that they were intellectually in a new age, this being well exemplified in the famous remark of Bernard of Chartres that his generation were dwarfs perched on the shoulders of giants, to which he added the telling comment that it could see further because it was carried aloft by them.[12]

The development of learning in the twelfth century was often fortuitous. It depended primarily on the activity of individual masters who attracted pupils, for the secular clerks who were now playing an increasingly prominent part in intellectual debate were not bound to one place as monks were but travelled around, in pursuit first of learning and then of its rewards in the form of employment. In the early years of the twelfth century Laon was a major centre under Anselm (not to be confused with his Canterbury namesake, who may have been his master), but the schools of Paris increasingly eclipsed all others. An individual master, however, might hope to establish a school of his own – Abelard said (with characteristic immodesty) that after he had roused the jealousy of his fellow students and incurred the hostility of his teacher William of Champeaux, the leading master at Paris, through his own superior ability, he set up a school, first at Melun and then at Corbeil.[13] The fame of a master attracted pupils, either voluntarily or because they were sent by their families – two ministers of Henry I of

England sent their nephews to Laon to study under Anselm, and two of these at any rate had successful careers, ending their lives as bishops of Lincoln and Ely.[14] These exemplify the practical rewards which flowed from academic study, but probably the patronage which they received from influential relations contributed as much to their careers as their studies. At the same time the skills acquired from such study were clearly esteemed by influential figures in both Church and government.

The ability of distinguished masters to attract pupils is demonstrated by John of Salisbury's autobiographical account of his own philosophical training at Paris. He sat at the feet of Abelard, and after his departure studied with other men, Alberic and Robert of Melun, the former of whom he described as full of questions and the latter of replies. The proliferation of teachers available is reflected in the string of names which he gives of other masters who influenced him over some twelve years, including Gilbert de la Porrée and Robert Pullen, who was later to be the first English cardinal and papal chancellor.[15] These masters came to Paris from various countries, a reflection of the fame which it had acquired as an international centre of learning. Pullen's future career again demonstrates how this common core of studies gave an individual an opportunity to build a career within an increasingly centralised church.

The rise of the universities

In the early twelfth century the fortunes of some schools had depended on the fame of one individual teacher, but at Paris success was self-generating. By the late twelfth century it had emerged as the leading centre of theological study in the West, and a similar development can be seen at Bologna, which achieved comparable standing in legal studies. Oxford too emerged from obscurity as a centre of learning in the twelfth century (for no very obvious reason among a number of English schools which had existed around 1100), and a few others such as Padua and Cambridge were established in the early thirteenth by dissident masters from existing universities. Toulouse was founded in 1229 as a centre of orthodoxy in the heretical lands of southern France, this indeed being a clear indication of the function of the medieval universities, which were seen as buttresses of orthodoxy rather than as centres of free intellectual speculation. Foundations such as Toulouse marked a new development because they were formally created, rather than growing spontaneously as had the earlier universities; they provided a model for foundations in succeeding centuries. Paris, however, provided the model for development elsewhere, most clearly in the way in which studies were institutionalised, with a curriculum which focussed essentially on logic as a prerequisite to more advanced studies. At the same time the masters established a guild to protect themselves from the hostility of the citizens and the encroachment of the ecclesiastical authorities, and became a self-governing corporation. During the thirteenth century a system was developed by which degrees were awarded, reflecting the stage of studies which an individual had attained. A comparable system was developed at Bologna, although there students were able to elect their own masters, and had more influence than their fellows at Paris. But the essential feature of the universities was that they were international bodies – their degrees were recognised elsewhere, and a man who had attained the level of mastership had the right to teach everywhere (*ius ubique docendi*). This clearly indicates the intellectual unification of Western Christendom in this period.

The course in arts, which was predominantly based on philosophy, was the foundation for further studies in higher faculties such as theology, law and medicine, and increasingly training in one of the first two of these became a prerequisite for attaining high office in the Church. It does, however, reflect its administrative and disciplinary character that its highest offices fell more often to men with a legal than with a theological background. This marks a shift in the determination of Christian orthodoxy – whereas in the past the bishops had been the guardians of the faith and the teachers of the faithful, and most theology came from a monastic background, from the twelfth century onwards doctrinal debates were carried on by scholars in the universities; it is noteworthy that the greatest theologians from the twelfth century onwards were all academics, who had refined their thought in the logical disciplines of the schools, and who tended to be analytical rather than devotional in approach. Even among the secular masters there were variations in approach, and some were more pastoral than speculative. The confrontational approach of Abelard, juxtaposing contradictory authorities, yes and no, *Sic et Non,* was only one means of approach. The techniques employed for study developed out of the traditional approach of commentaries on a biblical text, with discussions of its literal and symbolic meanings, and these gave an opportunity for the logical examination of problems. Anthologies were made of opinions (*Sententiae*) held on particular matters, which served as textbooks on which students commented, the most important of which, the four *Books of Sentences* by Peter Lombard, completed around 1150, became the standard introduction to theology for the rest of the Middle Ages. Literally hundreds of later writers wrote commentaries on it, because every young theologian had to lecture on it as well as on the Bible. It derived from both earlier streams of theology, that of Anselm and the writers of the Augustinian Abbey of St Victor at Paris, and the *Sic et Non* tradition of Abelard.[16] It was not an original theological work, but it was the starting-point for later theological writing.

The development of canon law

If the *Book of Sentences* represents a watershed in academic theology, it had been anticipated in legal studies about a decade earlier by another fundamental work, the *Decretum* of Gratian, a man traditionally believed to be a monk of Bologna, although this is in fact uncertain. Bologna had been a centre for studying Roman law for a generation, and this may have encouraged men to apply more systematic techniques to the law of the Church. The struggles of the Gregorian reform crisis had led to increasing study of canon law, not least because it provided powerful weapons for the popes in their dealings with the lay power. The most important of the pre-Gregorian canonists was Burchard of Worms, whose own *Decretum,* a collection of 1,785 canons, was completed about 1020 and was widely circulated throughout Europe by the mid-eleventh century, probably because its arrangement of material was more systematic than that in earlier collections and therefore of greater practical use. In the late eleventh century Bishop Ivo of Chartres produced probably three collections of canon law, one of which contained 3,760 canons. It was a briefer one, with just over a thousand canons, however, which was widely adopted as a guide to the law of the Church.[17] But because canon law had developed from a wide range of sources, there were contradictory decrees and decisions in individual cases, which it was desirable to reconcile. This was what Gratian did, in a work of which the proper title is the Concordance of Discordant Canons (*Concordantia Discordantium Canonum*). The logical structure of the arrangement of material drawn from the pronouncements of church councils, the writings of the Fathers, and papal letters made the work not only the textbook of canon law for the Western Church but also the first volume of the *Corpus Iuris Canonici*.[18] Legal scholars wrote commentaries on it, while in the practical implementation of the law it was regarded as basic. When it failed to resolve the issues, individuals could appeal to the pope, whose decisions in particular cases, formulated in decretal letters, clarified the law for the future. Periodically at later dates, popes collected these decretals and issued them as supplementary books of canon law, with the decisions being organised in accordance with the structure of Gratian's *Decretum.*

Thirteenth-century controversies

By the end of the twelfth century, the philosophical revolution had brought about profound changes in the intellectual approach of the Western Church to both its doctrine and its law. Both were to be modified in succeeding centuries, but while the principles of canon law developed more or less smoothly, theological speculation had a far more turbulent future, as scholars faced the question of how far questions of theology could be analysed in the light of earlier pagan learning. The truths of theology were seen as far more crucial, as the enforcement of right belief was regarded as essential for the Church's prime consideration, the salvation of the individual. The fate of those who denied them was liable to be far more drastic than that of those who resisted only the Church's legal powers.

During the thirteenth century European thought absorbed a vast quantity of new material. First and foremost came a much greater knowledge of the works of Aristotle, and a substantial body of commentary on it. Whereas Aristotle is now regarded primarily as a metaphysical and ethical philosopher, it should be borne in mind that until the Scientific Revolution of the sixteenth century it was his scientific works which were regarded as an essential repository of truth. These works posed a problem for the theologians of the Middle Ages, because they derived from a culture which did not believe in a doctrine of creation comparable to that contained in the Old Testament and transmitted from Judaism to Christianity. Much of the Aristotelian material which reached the West came from Arabic and Jewish sources, through the highly cultured society of southern Spain. Islam and Judaism had much in common with Christianity, not least their reliance on a revealed truth contained in a holy book, and indeed Moslem philosophers had had to face similar intellectual questions to those which the Christian commentators of the thirteenth century did. The critical issue for them was how religious beliefs could be reconciled with the arguments of a more materialist philosophy. The relationship between faith and reason, between the tradition of Augustine and the philosophy of Aristotle, was a crucial issue in thirteenth-century thought. Within the University of Paris a split developed between the philosophers of the arts faculty and the theologians, with attempts being made to forbid the reading of Aristotle in the lower faculty, presumably because there was a danger that speculations there might impinge on theology. But sanctions against prohibited works were intermittent and ill-applied. A ban was imposed on Aristotelian writings by the provincial church council of Sens in 1210, and this was renewed in 1215 and again in 1231 in Gregory IX's bull *Parens scientiarum*, which allowed the university to regulate its own constitution. At the same time, however, steps were taken to expurgate the dubious works, so that the rest might be studied. In fact, attempted prohibitions had little effect, not least because they had applied only to Paris and some of the works were read elsewhere. Indeed, from the middle of the century Aristotle was being described as 'the Philosopher', and regarded as intellectually authoritative. One result of this was that attempts were made to find a means of accommodating traditional Augustinian theology to the newer writings.

At the same time, another revolution was taking place in university life. In the twelfth century, teaching had been controlled by the secular masters, but the emergence of the orders of friars was followed by their virtual takeover of the schools. The Dominicans were concerned with intellectual matters from the start, and although Francis had been critical of book learning and his followers had preached penance rather than teaching, the years after his death saw his order becoming as active academically as the other. The outstanding intellectual figure in the order was St Bonaventura, who taught theology in Paris from about 1248 to 1257 when he became minister general of his order and was translated from the world of the intellect to that of action.

His theology remained fundamentally Augustinian, and it was more the terminology of his work than its substance which was Aristotelian. The great Dominicans were prepared to go further in the direction of Aristotle. The earliest was the German Albert, who taught at Paris in the 1240s and later at Köln. His written output was immense, and he was prepared to accept philosophy as a discipline which was autonomous within its own sphere. He did not, however, regard Aristotle as infallible, because he had been a pagan, and indeed some of his own teaching was influenced by Neoplatonism.[19]

It was a second Dominican, St Thomas Aquinas, one of the greatest theologians in the Church at any period, who was the outstanding figure in formulating a synthesis between Aristotelianism and Christian thought. He studied under Albert at Köln from 1252, and then proceeded to Paris where he remained until 1259, when he returned to Italy for nine years, partly spent at the papal court. He returned to Paris in 1268, remaining there until 1272. He was much respected by his contemporaries, notably pope Urban IV, who not only asked him to write a work *Against the Errors of the Greeks,* but also employed him to write hymns in honour of the sacrament of the Eucharist for the newly instituted feast of Corpus Christi. One can distinguish between his attitude to interpreting the visible universe, where his theory of knowledge was Aristotelian, and those areas of knowledge which lay beyond natural reason. While he saw human activities as having a value of their own, they were subordinated to the supernatural vocation of the Christian. Indeed, certain purely theological matters, such as the nature of the Trinity, lay beyond the realm of proof, or even of explanation. He may well have had some mystical experience, because shortly before his death he abandoned academic theology and said that what he had written was trash compared with a more direct and certain vision which he had enjoyed.[20] In his philosophical writings he employed an extensive knowledge of Aristotle, making use of new Latin translations of the Greek philosopher by William of Moerbeke – indeed, he encouraged the latter to make improved translations of Aristotle's works as he himself did not know Greek. These underlay his philosophical system but he rejected Aristotelian ideas which were incompatible with the doctrine of the Church. His first great work, the *Summa contra Gentiles,* begun in 1258, provided a synthesis of theology and philosophy based on Aristotelian foundations, but his masterpiece was his incomplete *Summa Theologiae,* which probably was begun in the 1260s. It perhaps reflects the nature of medieval academic study that this work, running to over two million words, was intended as a textbook for beginners in theology, to replace the *Sentences* of Peter Lombard!

Although there were theological differences between different masters at Paris – this can be clearly seen in distinctions between Bonaventura and Aquinas – these existed within accepted criteria of orthodoxy, because the matters in debate were not seen as essential articles of belief. But there were also philosophers within the faculty of arts who were prepared to adopt Aristotelian views which were incompatible with Christian teaching and which came under attack from the theologians. The extent to which these doctrines were purely Aristotelian has been debated, and in some cases they may have been coloured by the even more materialist philosophy of the Spanish Arabic philosopher Ibn Rushd, or Averroës. Technically these philosophers were not involved in teaching theology, but their metaphysical concerns affected theological questions, such as the eternity of the world and the mortality of the soul. The most distinguished of these Aristotelians was Siger of Brabant, who appeared in the arts faculty about 1260, and some of whose views provoked an attack by Bonaventura in 1266 and 1267. In 1269 Aquinas attacked another view held in Siger's work, that of the unicity of the intellect, or the existence of a single intelligence among all men.[21] More critically, in 1270, the bishop of Paris, Étienne Tempier, condemned thirteen propositions put forward by the philosophers, although no one was prosecuted individually. In fact Siger seems to have tried to keep within the pale of orthodoxy, and the thinness of the boundary between this and heresy is clearly demonstrated by the fact that some of Aquinas's views were also called in question. Not everyone doubted Siger's orthodoxy – Dante placed him in paradise alongside various doctors of the Church, describing him as one who syllogized truths which were hateful.[22]

There was a further, and much more extensive, assault on views which were regarded as unorthodox in 1277. Significantly, this action was initiated by a papal letter to Tempier, instructing him to investigate who had been teaching errors and to transmit information on this to him. The pope at the time, John XXI, was himself a former scholar of Paris, and a logician of some distinction, and thus well suited to intervene in matters of theological debate. Indeed, the investigation of dubious propositions extended more widely than Paris, because not only did Tempier condemn 219 propositions, with Siger being mentioned by name as one of the holders of unorthodox views, but a few days later the archbishop of Canterbury visited the University of Oxford, and issued a similar measure there. The pope subsequently issued further letters to implement these condemnations. Both the papal involvement and the obvious co-ordination of action by the two prelates emphasise how the debated views were a matter of concern in Christendom as a whole, and the extent to which Parisian theology was taken as a critical norm for belief throughout the West.

Yet when one considers the details of the condemned propositions, it becomes evident that the measures were not simply a reaffirmation of orthodoxy but also reflect a conservative reaction directed against some of the more innovative theologians as well as the pure philosophers. How exactly the list was compiled is unclear, but it looks rather as though Tempier invited masters to submit information on doubtful propositions, and amalgamated these, somewhat uncritically, into a blanket condemnation. The nature of the condemned propositions suggests that some of the traditionalists had taken the opportunity to demonstrate their disapproval of a wide range of ideas – indeed some of the propositions were not even theological. Some condemned the treatise on courtly love by Andreas Capellanus, and others looked back to the philosophical debates of the twelfth century. More significantly, some of them were found in the writings of Aquinas, or followed logically from his teachings.[23] There was, however, an underlying unity in the attack, which had long-term consequences for theology. It was directed against the support of faith by rational demonstration, and in the long run this was to drive a wedge between reason and revelation. Later scholars were no less acute, but they took a different approach to theological questions, basing their teachings more on faith than on reason.

| 11 |

Authority and government

Papal plenitude of power

The settlement of the dispute over investitures by the Concordat of Worms left the Papacy in a much more authoritative position in its dealings with the lay power than it had been half a century earlier. As was shown earlier,[1] kings still preserved considerable powers in their own lands, particularly on such matters as the appointment of the higher clergy, but the twelfth and thirteenth centuries saw considerable centralisation in Church government, the growth of more formal channels of communication between the Papacy and the local churches, and developments in its hierarchical structure, which strengthened the position of archbishops at the expense of the diocesan epis-copate. Even more important was the increasing perception of the pope as the supreme ruler of the Church on earth, this being clearly demonstrated by the use of the descriptive term 'the vicar of Christ', which came into regular usage as a papal designation about the middle of the twelfth century, and which was particularly emphasised by Innocent III (1198–1216). More specifically, in legal terms, canonist writers developed the use of the term 'universal ordinary', with the consequence that anyone could appeal to the pope, without reference to any intermediary, in virtue of his plenitude of power.[2] Another factor which strengthened the Papacy was the decree of the Third Lateran Council of 1179 to guard against schisms in papal elections, which inevitably weakened the power of an individual pope. This decree, by declaring that the college of cardinals required a two-thirds majority of those present to make an election, was to prevent any serious schism for almost two hundred years – few people took seriously an imperially induced schism in 1327 – although in the thirteenth century a new problem arose from deadlocked conclaves which led to long vacancies.

Papal dominance over local churches was further enhanced by the popes gaining control over the procedure of canonisation. Traditionally the recog-nition that an individual's spiritual virtues merited recognition as a saint was due to popular acclaim in his or her own area. This was perhaps encouraged by the local ruling families, from which many early saints came, and formal recognition was granted by the local bishop and synod. Nevertheless a tradition developed that the pope should be consulted, and by the early twelfth century such consultation was coming to be regarded as customary. Papal verdicts could discriminate between local and general recognition of an individual's sanctity – Alexander III promised to investigate the case for the canonisation of a Tuscan hermit, William of Malavalle, but authorised an office for his cult locally in the diocese of Grosseto before any verdict on this. It was not, however, until the end of the twelfth century that papal approval came to be regarded as essential for accepting an individual as a saint, although it was clearly deemed desirable.[3] In 1171, John of Salisbury was doubtful about whether Becket could be regarded as a saint and martyr, although he claimed that miracles had taken place at his tomb, and sought guidance from the bishop of Poitiers as to whether it was safe to include him among the martyrs in celebrating mass and in other public prayers. Shortly afterwards, he wrote to the archbishop of Sens, expressing wonder that the pope had not yet commanded Becket's inclusion in the catalogue of martyrs.[4] A generation later, in 1202, the Papacy took a positive initiative in canonising Gilbert of Sempringham, relating that an inquest had been held into his life and miracles, and declaring that he was now enrolled among the saints.[5]

The history of the Papacy, however, must consider its different roles, and the cross-currents of political and ecclesiastical issues, which could not always be disentangled. The pope could not escape involvement in the secular politics of Italy, and particularly of Rome, and political tensions were echoed within the college of cardinals. The schism within the Papacy after the vacancy of 1159 reflects some of these complexities. The city of Rome was itself vulnerable – problems from the rivalries of noble families were aggravated by the establishment of a commune in 1143, and relations with the Papacy were exacerbated by its welcome to the radical Arnold of Brescia, who was severely critical of the Church hierarchy and taught that the Church should return to the simplicity of the Apostles. At the same time, the old Roman families wished to reassert their influence over the Papacy, the Roman character of which had declined as it asserted its authority over wider aspects of Church life – since the death of Innocent II in 1143, there had been only one Roman pope (Anastasius IV, 1153–4), and indeed since 1154 the pope had been an Englishman (Hadrian IV). The Roman people were volatile, 'factious in their dealings with one another and jealous of their neighbours; they know neither how to be ruled nor to rule; to their superiors they are disloyal and to their subjects unbearable ...'[6] They wanted a papal presence in the city, perhaps as much for material reasons as it attracted business there, but wanted it on their own terms. In 1159, the candidate supported by the majority of the cardinals, the Siennese cardinal Roland (Alexander III), who had been a close adviser of his predecessor, faced Roman opposition, whereas his opponent Octavian, who came from the Roman Campagna, had family connections with the city.[7] Alexander was forced to leave Rome, but it is significant that when he was able to return in 1161, and more permanently in 1165, he was formally welcomed with a ritual reception, which symbolised popular consent to his rule.[8]

The situation was further complicated by the political activities of the emperor Frederick Barbarossa, who was attempting to reassert old imperial claims to authority in Lombardy. Although Hadrian IV had initially been well-disposed to the emperor, whom he crowned in 1155, the pope found himself forced to come to terms with the Norman rulers of Sicily, and this was seen as an abandonment of good relations with Frederick. At the same time, the rhetoric of the emperor's principal adviser, Rainald of Dassel, which emphasised imperial dignity, ran counter to papal ideology. Even before 1159, a new political alliance had been established between the Papacy, the Normans and the Lombards, which put serious strains on good relations with the emperor. In the election of that year, the alignment of rival factions among the cardinals into pro-imperial and anti-imperial groups was a further factor in the outbreak of the schism. Although there is no reason to believe that Barbarossa tried to secure Octavian's election, he certainly welcomed it, and in a council at Pavia in 1160, attended largely by bishops with imperial sympathies, recognised his title as Victor IV.[9] Norman military support was of major importance to Alexander's position in Italy during his struggle with Barbarossa, although as far as his authority in Christendom was concerned, recognition by both France and England in July 1160 was crucial. Barbarossa put diplomatic pressure on the French king to withdraw his support, and also hoped, albeit in vain, to exploit the quarrel between Henry II and Thomas Becket to detach the English king from Alexander. The pope may also have benefited from his longevity, and from the deaths of imperially supported antipopes, because Victor's successors had more limited support than he had. It was, however, the emperor's defeat by the Lombard League which eventually led to negotiations between the two parties and the ending of the schism.

While the Papacy's moral reputation stood high at this point, not least because Alexander consolidated his authority by summoning a general council of the Church to the Lateran in 1179, the settlement left the emperor with considerable practical authority, both in terms of imperial rights in Italy and in the extensive influence which he could exercise over the German Church. In fact Barbarossa's later years saw him achieve a major political coup in the peninsula, when his son Henry married the heiress to the Norman kingdom of Sicily. In 1194, Henry, a powerful and ambitious ruler, enforced his claim on the kingdom, but his death three years later, leaving a 2-year-old son as his heir, provided yet another turning-point in the political relations of the Empire and the Papacy.

The Papacy and canon law

In the lands where the Papacy was recognised during the schism, its influence increased steadily. Probably its jurisdictional authority, strengthened by the rise of a more systematic canon law, and by the willingness of all Christians to bring appeals to it on issues over which legal doubt had arisen, did more than anything else to enhance its authority, and it is noteworthy that the pontificate of Alexander III saw a vast upsurge in the number of decretal letters issued for the guidance of Christendom. Although modern scholarship no longer believes that Alexander was identical with the distinguished Bolognese canonist Master Roland – the pope's training had been in theology rather than in law – there is no doubt that he was more active than his predecessors in publishing such letters.[10] Access to Rome was a crucial issue, about which lay rulers were apprehensive. This is seen in Henry II's Constitutions of Clarendon, which tried to establish a system of appeals within the national hierarchy of the Church, with cases being taken to Rome only as a last resort. The king's action not only aroused opposition from the episcopate, headed by Becket, but a letter from John of Salisbury to the bishop of Exeter show that it aroused particular criticism. Another letter makes it clear that Henry's attempt to limit appeals to Rome and free access to the pope were critical issues at a conference in 1167.[11] It is significant that after Becket's death, appeals were renewed in substantial numbers; indeed, in this period a disproportionately high number of the appeals made to the pope originated in England, probably because the king had had to abase himself in order to be restored to the fold of the Church and make a visible surrender on a critical issue as a token of his penitence.

The hearing of such appeals established further ties between the central organisation of the Church and its various provinces. Some cases were settled at the papal court, but others were referred back to their country of origin to be heard by judges-delegate, usually bishops or abbots of major monasteries. Because judgements were given in the name of the Papacy, this procedure encroached on traditional episcopal rights. Papal intervention in the affairs of the local churches was not limited to legal decisions, however, and it is clear that the number of letters emanating from the Papacy on a wide range of issues increased very substantially from around 1130. In the twelfth century figures can be estimated only crudely from their chance survival – these suggest that the number approximately doubled under Innocent II, and more than doubled again by the time of Alexander III – but the preservation of the papal registers from the time of Innocent III onwards gives a clearer picture of the vigorous bureaucracy on which the popes relied to maintain its influence throughout Christendom. This administrative expansion continued until at least the fourteenth century.[12]

Legates and archbishops

The expansion of papal authority did not depend purely on the faithful coming to Rome, or wherever the pope might be at a particular time. It was also supported by the activity of legates whom the popes sent to individual nations of Christendom, either to deal with particular problems or with a more general remit to further ecclesiastical reform. In the late eleventh century legates might have additional powers – Bishop Hugh of Die, Gregory VII's legate in France from 1075, also acted as papal collector. Such permanent legates seem to have been given virtually viceregal powers, and may have been more powerful than those with short-term responsibilities – certainly in 1078 Gregory sent a furious letter to the bishop of Langres, when he and such a legate had passed a sentence of excommunication without consulting Hugh of Die.[13] But such representatives possessed the full authority of the Church, for Gregory commanded that his legate should be received as though the pope, or rather St Peter, were present.[14] He also kept a close eye on their activity, and in 1073 reproved the bishop of Ostia, his legate to Spain, for not reporting fully to him, and noting that there had been complaints against his conduct.[15] This kind of legate disappeared in the twelfth century, and the office developed in two distinct directions. Immediate problems might lead the pope to send out envoys with the responsibility for dealing with specific issues (*legatus a latere*), while routine legatine powers could be granted to a member of the local hierarchy (*legatus natus*). This could reduce the danger of clashes between the Church and the secular power, because the latter could usually play an active part in the appointment of local prelates. Contemporary perceptions of authority were not, however, always accurate. Eadmer's comment on the arrival of a legate in 1101, that it was unheard of in Britain for anyone to exercise authority as the pope's representative, except the archbishop of Canterbury,[16] overlooked the fact that only a generation earlier the arrival of papal legates had been the prelude to the deposition of Stigand and the appointment of Lanfranc to Canterbury. By the mid-twelfth century, legates were often cardinals, and their activities could give rise to criticism, particularly if they were involved in financial matters. John of Salisbury indeed described two legates to Germany as wolves in sheep's clothing.[17] By the late twelfth century a *legatus a latere* possessed greater powers than a *legatus natus*. Innocent III upheld the claim of the abbey of Bury St Edmunds to be exempt from visitation by the archbishop of Canterbury, but not from one by a legate who had come direct from the pope.[18]

Problems might arise in individual countries if one prelate was appointed as a permanent legate, because it could affect his relations with other bishops. Eadmer's comment on the rights of the archbishop of Canterbury reflects the views of that particular see, which are also reflected in both the letters and the actions of Lanfranc. As archbishop he asserted, 'it is agreed that this whole island called Britain is within the undivided jurisdiction of our one church'.[19] Letters which he wrote to Queen Margaret of Scotland and to the Irish kings of Dublin and Munster, and to the bishop of Munster, show that he was trying to turn this claim into practice.[20] He and his successors may even have had some success, because between 1074 and 1140 six Irish bishops (four of Dublin, one of Waterford and one of Limerick) are recorded as professing obedience to Canterbury.[21] This may not have meant much in practice, and one suspects that the bishops' actions may mirror political divisions within Ireland which made nominal obedience to Canterbury less of a burden than accepting the authority of the see of Armagh. Even within England, Canterbury's authority did not go unchallenged, most notably by the archbishops of York who made vigorous efforts to assert their independence from their southern neighbour. In theory they were able to do so, but in practice the pope frequently granted legatine authority to the archbishop of Canterbury. York also lost the influence which it claimed over the Scottish Church, when Celestine III in 1192 declared the latter to be a special daughter of the Holy See, although in fact the country did not acquire its own archbishop until the fifteenth century. The Welsh Church was less successful, when it proposed unsuccessfully in 1202 that St David's should be given archiepiscopal status, although the archbishop was still to have been subordinate to Canterbury.[22]

The proposal that Canterbury should exercise such authority even when St David's became an archbishopric reflects a wider question of what precise powers an archbishop possessed. The twelfth century saw the development of a much more acute sense of hierarchy, and it was only gradually that the boundaries of ecclesiastical provinces became clearly defined, with the archbishop having jurisdictional authority over his suffragans. In the 1120s, Fulcher of Chartres differentiated between primates and metropolitans,[23] but in the middle of the century there were still cases of some archbishops claiming either precedence over their fellows or even a right to exercise authority over them. Gregory VII gave the archbishop of Lyons authority over the provinces of Sens, Tours and Rouen as well as his own in 1079,[24] and at the Council of Rheims in 1148 the then archbishop reasserted this right. Similarly the archbishops of Vienne and Trèves claimed authority over Bourges and Rheims respectively. In the same year the archbishop of Milan claimed that the archbishop of Genoa should be regarded as one of his suffragans.[25] The nature of the problem was clearly demonstrated in the case of Palermo about 1151. When an archbishop was consecrated there, the king of Sicily asked that he should be granted the *pallium*, a vestment symbolic of metropolitan authority, and assigned suffragans, which the see had not previously possessed, as the title of archbishop would otherwise be meaningless. The pope, however, declared that the *pallium* merely indicated the dignity of the see and did not imply authority. A few years later, however, a number of sees were placed under Palermo's rule.[26]

Even the extent of an archbishop's power over his suffragans was ill-defined. In Gregory VII's time, papal letters suggest that this may have been more investigative than judicial, for it is uncertain if archbishops were given authority to pronounce a definitive sentence. A bishop could certainly receive consecration from an archbishop other than his own, a circumstance which would have been seen as diminishing the latter's power.[27] In 1204 Innocent III, writing to the bishop of Ely on various questions of canon law, stated that while the bishop was subject to the archbishop, the latter could not compel one of the bishop's subjects to undertake the duties of a judge-delegate.[28] These developments reflect a hardening of the Church's administrative structure, and probably enhanced papal authority at the top of the pyramid, not least because the pope would be left with the final responsibility of clarifying any demarcation disputes among the archbishops. He also was the ultimate authority whose approval had to be obtained before a new see was established, even if there had been a local initiative to set one up. When Anselm and Henry I wished to found a new see at Ely, because that of Lincoln was too unwieldy, they not only secured the assent of the bishop of Lincoln, but also wrote to the pope, 'knowing that no new diocese could properly be created anywhere' without papal consent.[29]

It is hardly surprising that there were problems over the boundaries of ecclesiastical provinces, and over the relationships of bishops within them to a particular archbishop. In view of the Church's temporal wealth, the lay authorities were, as shown earlier,[30] greatly concerned that key positions in it were held by individuals on whom they could rely. Political boundaries, however, were often ill-defined, and the spheres of influence of particular rulers could change, whereas lines of ecclesiastical superiority reflected the divisions of an earlier age, which the combination of tradition and inertia made hard to alter. (Even at the present day, the fact that the principal prelate of the Church of England has his see at Canterbury is due to the political dominance of a Kentish king 1,400 years ago!) In this context, the Papacy possessed a theoretical pre-eminence over the Church in the West that was generally recognised, although some of its political implications were challenged by the claims of the emperor. Whether or not this could be translated into practical authority depended largely on the personality of the individual pope and the immediate political circumstances of the time.

Innocent III

Innocent III (1198–1216) was undoubtedly one of the most dynamic and able popes of the Middle Ages. Elected, possibly as a compromise candidate, at the age of 37, he had the advantage of comparative youth (certainly by comparison with his immediate predecessor Celestine III, who had been elected in his mid-80s and died at over 90). He had been trained in theology at Paris and probably also in canon law at Bologna, and named as a cardinal by his relative Clement III in 1190.[31] At his accession he had a major political advantage in that the death of the powerful emperor Henry VI some four months earlier plunged the Empire into a schism in Germany, where Henry's younger brother Philip, who assumed the Hohenstaufen claim to protect the interests of his young nephew Frederick, was challenged by Otto of Brunswick. Neither of these had an interest in the Sicilian kingdom, which Henry had obtained by marriage. Frederick was still an infant in the guardianship of his mother, Constance of Sicily, and when she died fourteen months after her husband, he came under the protection of the pope, who was legally overlord of the southern kingdom. Although Innocent still had problems in asserting his authority within the states of the Church, he was able to exploit the dispute over the Empire, as both claimants were concentrating their attention on Germany, to extract territorial concessions in central Italy. Effectively, Innocent was the founder of the papal states as they existed for the rest of the Middle Ages. In 1201 Otto of Brunswick recognised Innocent's power in the lands which he had 'recovered' since the death of Henry VI, and when the pope turned against Otto, giving his support to the young Frederick of Hohenstaufen, the latter in turn had to make comparable concessions.[32] The Papacy's territorial power attained a new level, and while in one sense this strengthened the institutions of the Church by giving it greater financial resources, it also drew the popes more deeply into the political conflicts of Italy and indeed of Europe as a whole.

Because Innocent's position in Italy was less affected by imperial politics than that of many of his predecessors, he could concentrate much of his activity on furthering his spiritual authority. He regarded the papal plenitude of power as essentially spiritual, and when he intervened against lay rulers, justified his action as a judgement on sin. However, his exercise of such authority was not always successful; when he attempted to put pressure on Philip II of France to reinstate his divorced wife, a purely nominal acknowledgement of her status by the king, without any real reconciliation, persuaded Innocent to withdraw an interdict which he had imposed on the royal demesne. Similarly, the imposition of an interdict on England, and the subsequent excommunication of John, who had resisted his appointment of a third candidate to the see of Canterbury, when the king and the chapter were in conflict over the choice of an archbishop, did not in itself bring the king to heel. Only when John was threatened by a baronial revolt did he submit, in a well-timed move which turned Innocent from an opponent into an ally, who stood by him in the crisis following his enforced concession of Magna Carta to the nobility.[33] The interdict, however, may have had more effect in the long term than initially as a weapon of papal power, for although kings and popes still disagreed over appointments, the secular power was willing to accept that in the last resort a papal decision would have to count, and that there were limits to the extent to which a king could resist it. This increasing influence of the Papacy over appointments to high positions in the Church was one of its greatest strengths in bringing Christendom under its control.

One area of Christian activity in which the Papacy had already played a prominent role was in furthering Crusades to the East.[34] His predecessor had already proclaimed a new Crusade, but Henry VI's death had been a setback to reinforcing the Christian states in Palestine. Innocent was no less concerned with the problem than his predecessors, and in his first year as pope proclaimed another Crusade, to be ready in the following March. Support from Christendom was not forthcoming, with the schism in the Empire and war between the kings of England and France, and it was not until 1202 that any army began to assemble. (Significantly, none of the crusading leaders were major territorial rulers.) The ensuing Crusade, however, was a disaster, being diverted to attack Zara on the Dalmatian coast as a payment to the Venetians for transporting the army. A new factor entered the situation when a dynastic struggle in Constantinople led one claimant to offer to bring the Byzantine church back into the Roman obedience in return for military support, but he was unable to secure willing entry to the city, and in 1204 the Crusaders captured and sacked it. Shortly afterwards Count Baldwin of Flanders was elected as the new emperor of the East.

There is no reason to believe that Innocent had planned such an outcome, but he was powerless to prevent it in face of the people who possessed the actual military power. In terms of advancing the interests of Christendom, or even indeed those of the Papacy, his crusading ambitions were a failure. A command to the Venetians to restore Zara to Hungary went unheeded, and although he condemned the attack on Constantinople, he was prepared to exploit Latin control of the city as a means of reuniting the Eastern Church to Rome on his own terms. He hoped initially that the campaign would continue to Palestine, but in 1205 his legate dispensed the Crusaders from their vow to proceed there. Innocent's wish for a further campaign did not abate, but more immediately his attention was diverted to actions against the Cathar heretics in southern France and to supporting the Spanish war against the Moors, where the Christian kingdoms won a major victory at Las Navas de Tolosa in 1212. But in his last years he again attempted to mount an operation to the East, which was endorsed by the Fourth Lateran Council. Indeed, he himself was preaching the Crusade when he died in the summer of 1216.

The Fourth Lateran Council, on the other hand, was one of the most important events of his pontificate. Unlike the three previous general councils called to the Lateran, it was not summoned to mark a papal victory over an antipope and the ending of a schism; it was intended to consolidate papal authority and deal with the Church's continuing problems. It reflects the importance of the crusading ideal that the recovery of the Holy Land was seen as one of the objectives which it was intended to address, along with carrying out more widespread reforms. In terms of ecclesiastical legislation, it was probably the most important assembly of the Middle Ages, issuing no fewer than seventy canons over a wide range of issues. It faced the questions of a changing world, and it is clear that unity of the faith was one of its main concerns. The opening canon of the council was a precise credal statement intended to clarify issues of doctrine which had been debated, and, most significantly, the doctrine of transubstantiation had the first place. The doctrine of the Trinity was clarified, and a clear programme of action was laid down against heresy. The primacy of the Roman see was affirmed, and the precedence among the other four ancient patriarchies clarified. Disciplinary rules were stipulated for clergy and laity alike, including imposing the obligation on all adults to confess annually to their parish priest and receive the Eucharist at Easter. The general tone of the decrees encapsulated the principles of Gregorian reform, emphasising the special character of clerical status, and differentiating the clergy from the laity. This not only involved a ban on the laity usurping clerical rights, but also forbade the clergy from extending their rights of jurisdiction to the prejudice of secular justice. It attempted to systematise the government of the regular clergy, by forbidding the compilation of new rules, and insisting that any new order must conform to one already in existence. Not all these decrees could be fully sustained, but they provided the framework of the Church's life in succeeding centuries.[35]

The thirteenth-century Papacy

Papal history in the first half of the thirteenth century was profoundly influenced by the events of Innocent III's pontificate, and perhaps most particularly by his political activities. His successors were faced with maintaining the territorial power which he had established in Italy, and had to do so in face of renewed imperial interest in the peninsula in the person of the young Frederick of Hohenstaufen. This did not arise until the 1220s, for Frederick was initially more concerned with his German lands, and was willing to leave the Papacy some freedom of action in Italy, but his failure to support a proposed crusade, encroachments on the papal states, and the assertion of his rights in Sicily, led to the re-emergence of tension. Honorius III pursued a policy of appeasement, but the first three years of the pontificate of his successor Gregory IX saw a tougher papal line. The emperor's failure to go on crusade led to his excommunication, which was maintained when he did eventually depart for the East. One of Frederick's deputies in Italy launched an attack on papal lands, which was sufficiently successful to demonstrate the pope's weakness. In fact the emperor was willing to come to terms in 1230, and there was thereafter a truce for nine years.[36] During this period tension alternated with peace, but there were underlying difficulties – the pope criticised Frederick's alleged oppression of the Sicilian church, and the emperor occupied various papal lands in central Italy. The Sicilian church featured most prominently in the articles of condemnation, when Gregory renewed Frederick's excommunication in 1239, but it was probably the emperor's territorial ambitions which were the main reason for the renewed struggle. Certainly in the following years, although both parties put forward vehement propaganda against the other, the main contest centred on political issues. Both parties made concessions to potential allies in an attempt to win support, but for all the emperor's power, he could not consolidate his advantage, and was never able to gain control of Rome. After Gregory's death and the seventeen-day pontificate of Celestine IV, there was an eighteen-month vacancy before the election of Innocent IV, who had to go into exile in France, where Frederick was condemned at the first Council of Lyons, and the Germans were invited to choose an alternative ruler. Frederick challenged the pope's power to do so, and Innocent retorted by claiming that the successors of St Peter possessed temporal as well as spiritual sovereignty. The choice of an anti-king by the German electors further undermined Frederick's powers and when he died in 1250 the pope was able to return to Rome. There he and his successors continued to struggle against Frederick's heirs, his legitimate son Conrad and his bastard Manfred, to gain control of the southern kingdom.

Provisions

The Papacy's triumph in the mid-thirteenth century was essentially political, and reflects the fact that from Innocent III's time onwards it was a significant political force in Italy. At the same time, however, it was also strengthening its administrative power over the Church. It built further on the judicial authority which had been developed from the desire of litigants to seek a decisive verdict from the supreme court of the Church, and more significantly, strengthened its influence over clerical appointments throughout Christendom by the development of the system of provisions. As long as clergy were appointed in accordance with the wishes of a local patron, they could not be independent of lay power. This was particularly significant in the case of high ecclesiastical posts such as bishoprics, which were often the reward to men for their service to kings in purely temporal matters. Even though the reformers proclaimed the desirability of the Church being free from such influence, the *de facto* power of the laity still survived. During the twelfth century, however, the Papacy began to make appointments to benefices on its own authority – the earliest recorded case known dates from 1137[37] – and during the thirteenth the number of such appointments swelled to huge proportions. The pope's judicial power provided a means for this, because when disputes over appointments were referred to him for decision, he was able to set aside the claims of rivals and name a candidate of his own; this was well demonstrated by the Canterbury election dispute during Innocent III's pontificate.

The system of provisions attracted criticism from those who had lost their powers of patronage – the St Albans chronicler Matthew Paris claimed that the pope incurred hatred from prelates and patrons whom he had deprived of their right of conferring benefices, and alleged that the motive for such provisions was papal greed. Similar objections were raised to the system in Spain, although individual members of the clergy could benefit from it.[38] But it is worth stressing that the system had certain positive advantages, and that the main factor behind its growth was demand from potential beneficiaries, among whom the most important groups were officials of the papal court and poor clerks, often graduates, who lacked a benevolent patron. These petitioned the pope for a benefice, and gradually the Papacy responded. Provision was a weapon employed by the Papacy in furthering reform and freeing the Church from lay control. It has been noted that in some German dioceses no complaints are known about papal nominees, while frequent objections were raised to candidates supported by aristocratic influence.[39] There are also, however, cases recorded when patrons might appeal to the pope if a bishop refused to admit a priest to a benefice, and such appeals served to strengthen papal influence on appointments.[40] The crucial moment in the development of provisions came in 1265, when Clement IV reserved for papal provision all benefices which were vacated when the existing holder died at the papal court; this was the first step in the extension of papal rights over benefices throughout Christendom which became increasingly important during the ensuing century.

In view of the large numbers of churchmen who petitioned the Papacy for a provision, it was inevitable that a bureaucratic system developed to assess rival claims according to set rules. Only in a limited number of cases, such as those of papal officials or the relatives of cardinals, were these rules set aside, and it is probably fair to say that on most occasions they were fairly applied. There was a bias in favour of graduates – indeed the benefices for which they were eligible seem to have been graded in accordance with the level to which they had carried their studies – and one effect of the system was to make the Church more of a meritocracy. The universities saw how to exploit it, and by the fourteenth century sent rolls of their graduates to the papal court to secure positions for them. The whole system, however, gave the Papacy a new potential authority as a universal patron, and in the years following tensions developed between local interests and the claims of a centralising papal court. In many cases, one suspects, people took a pragmatic approach, and it was only occasionally where there had been encroachment on particular influential interests that complaints were a serious problem. The greater the extent of centralisation, however, the more local patrons were liable to feel a sense of grievance.

THE AGE OF
DIVERGENCE
(1270–1515)

|12|

From victory to captivity

The decline of papal dominance

If one compares the Papacy's apparent success in defeating the Hohenstaufen in the mid-thirteenth century with its fortunes fifty years later, when Boniface VIII succumbed to the power of Philip IV of France, and the Papacy itself left Italy and settled at Avignon, the inevitable question springs to mind of why it suffered such a reversal of fortune. In fact the decline in papal power was limited rather than total, for it was essentially only the balance of political influence between the popes and the secular power which was seriously altered – the Papacy still maintained powerful administrative control over the Church, although in the fourteenth century its attempts to strengthen this incurred significant opposition from the increasingly powerful lay rulers of Western Europe. Its institutions of government not only continued to function but indeed expanded, and even when there was a vacancy in the papal office, routine administration went on uninterrupted. Its authority in questions of doctrine remained – indeed the period sees the first affirmation that in such matters the judgement of the pope should be regarded as infallible – and it continued to serve as a final court of appeal on issues of canon law, and the ultimate source of spiritual favours for the faithful.

The Papacy's decline in the second half of the thirteenth century was primarily a collapse of the temporal power, and a loss of clear-cut political direction. One factor behind this was undoubtedly the problem of finding an agreed candidate for the papal office under the terms of the decree of 1179 which required a two-thirds majority in the college of cardinals. Some papal elections were protracted – after the death of Clement IV in 1268, the Papacy was vacant for two and three-quarter years before the cardinals elected Gregory X, and after that of Nicholas IV in 1292 the papal throne remained unoccupied for two and a quarter years. These were only the two longest vacancies – if one looks at the period between 1267 and 1297 there were ten conclaves, in half of which the vacancy lasted for more than half a year, and in the thirty-year period there was no reigning pope for six and a half years, over 21 per cent of the time. In such circumstances it was hardly surprising that there was little continuity in papal policy.

The Papacy's political problems were further aggravated by the family interests of individual popes. Temporal power made it essential for a monarch to dominate his lands and hereditary lay monarchs were doing precisely this throughout Europe. But when the monarchy was elective, as the Papacy was, each pope effectively had to start from the beginning. He had to dominate the towns and communes which the papal states comprised, and essentially had to rely on his own resources. The popes of the second half of the thirteenth century had various origins – some came from Rome, or at least from elsewhere in the papal states, others were outsiders. Those who already possessed family connections with the domains of the Papacy had allies to hand in their relations, but the price of this was involvement in family rivalries and factional in-fighting. Nepotism could be a useful weapon in securing support, but posed problems of its own. Outsiders, on the other hand, might be neutral in traditional vendettas, but still had to find supporters, and had to be cautious in choosing them.

Furthermore, the legacy of the struggle with the Hohenstaufen left the Papacy with a new problem of its own creation. Frederick II had been the last emperor who might have established a realm comprehending both Germany and Italy, and his death in one sense marked the end of an epoch. But there were still heirs of the family, who could back their claim to lands in southern Italy by force, and between 1250 and 1268 they posed a problem to successive popes. This could be resolved only if the Papacy found an ally with sufficient military resources to be named as an alternative ruler of the kingdom of Sicily. After an abortive attempt by Henry III of England to secure the throne for his second son Edmund, which foundered on the resistance of the English magnates to meet the costs, Urban IV, himself French by origin, turned to Charles of Anjou, the brother of Louis IX of France. He arrived in Italy in 1265, and until his death twenty years later dominated the Italian political scene. Initially he provided the military success which the Papacy needed; Frederick's illegitimate son Manfred was defeated and killed at Benevento in 1266, and his legitimate grandson Conradin, while making a last effort to reclaim his inheritance, was captured after the battle of Tagliacozzo two years later, and executed in Naples. Charles had the opportunity to consolidate his influence in Italy during the long papal vacancy of 1268–71, and once he had secured firm control of his kingdom, was determined to extend his influence further in the Mediterranean world. The Papacy lacked the strength to resist his ambitions, and its political fortunes were inextricably linked with them, not least because it treated the campaigns as a holy war and offered crusading indulgences to its allies.[1]

One area where Charles had ambitions was the Byzantine Empire. In 1261, Constantinople had been reconquered by the Greek family of the

Palaeologi, and the Greek Church had recovered control there. The new imperial family had, however, to face the threat that the heirs of the Latin Empire would attempt to regain power, while the papal desire to assert its power over all the Church drew it into the web of international diplomacy. Even before defeating Conradin, Charles had married his daughter to the heir of the Latin emperor, and promised to raise troops for a campaign to the East. Between the late 1260s and the early 1280s, relations between Byzantium and the West were conducted on both a secular and an ecclesiastical plane. The emperor Michael Palaeologus was willing to bargain church reunion for papal support in discouraging Charles's ambitions, and Gregory X, a pope who wished Byzantine support for a crusade to protect the remaining Christian enclaves in Palestine, was happy to accept this. A general council at Lyons in 1274 proclaimed the reunion of the churches, with the Byzantines conceding both the primacy of Rome and the credal question of the procession of the Holy Spirit. Plans were made for a crusade, and the pope imposed restraints on Charles. But although Michael Palaeologus was willing to make concessions to the pope, anti-unionist sentiment in the East made it impossible for him to deliver what the Papacy wanted. A series of short pontificates (three in seventeen months between January 1276 and May 1277) destabilised papal policy, and although Nicholas III (1277–80) attempted to preserve the union and resisted Charles's ambitions, he took a tough line also in negotiations with the Byzantines. His successor Martin IV, however, gave Charles strong support, excommunicated Michael in 1281 and annulled the union two years later.

Charles had been planning a campaign to the East under the guise of a crusade, but events overtook his plans, in the form of a popular revolt against him in Sicily, the so-called 'Sicilian Vespers', in 1282. His enemies, both in Byzantium and in Aragon, whose king was married to a daughter of Manfred, may already have been smuggling arms into the island, but the rebellion was spontaneous, prompted by dislike of the king's French officials. If the Papacy had remained neutral, and allowed the Sicilians to accept papal overlordship, it might not have suffered, but Martin IV threw his backing behind Charles, excommunicating the Aragonese and Byzantines, lending money to Charles, and, some nine months after the Vespers, proclaiming a crusade against the enemies of the Angevins.[2] Until the pontificate of Boniface VIII, alliance with the Angevins remained the cornerstone of papal policy. The popes probably believed genuinely that control of southern Italy was essential to their influence in Christendom, but the price which they had to pay was to emphasise their political role at the expense of any spiritual or moral leadership which they might claim.

Western Europe at the end of the thirteenth century was no longer as amenable to papal influence as it had been even fifty years earlier, for its two most powerful kings were far more aggressive in asserting royal influence than their mid-century predecessors had been. The firm, but undoubtedly pious – he was, after all, later canonised – Louis IX of France and the

arbitrary, pious but fundamentally ineffective Henry III of England had successors who were far more ruthless in asserting monarchical power.
Although Louis' son Philip III failed in a campaign against Aragon, in a war
partly prompted by rivalries in Italy, his grandson Philip IV was both ruthless and cynical in his government, and Edward I of England was no less so.
Both were determined to assert their power over all their subjects, and a
conflict between them in the 1290s had profound repercussions for their
relations with the Church. With the outbreak of war, they needed to raise
taxes from their subjects, including the clergy. This was already a sensitive
issue – the provincial council of Vienne in 1289 had imposed sanctions on
those who interfered with the Church's possessions, movable and immov-
able, and also took measures against those who attempted to assert the
jurisdiction of lay courts over churchmen.[3] If even local church councils
were guarding against encroachments on the liberties of the Church, the
Papacy was even more likely to be sensitive to such matters.

Boniface VIII

The years of conflict in Italy had created a credibility gap between actual
papal power and theoretical claims to authority. Canonist writers had
emphasised the absolute nature of papal authority, and Innocent IV, himself
a canonist of distinction, had justified his interventions in temporal affairs
with reference to principles of divine law.[4] Such perceptions of authority
were normal in papal circles, and were certainly held by the last pope of the
century, Boniface VIII, again a man trained in canon law. Boniface had
come to the papal throne in unique fashion, after the abdication rather than
the death of his predecessor, a fact which left him vulnerable to criticism by
enemies who claimed that such a resignation was canonically invalid. Had
he been a less abrasive personality, and if his pontificate had passed without
controversy, the circumstances of his accession might have been overlooked,
and most contemporary opinion seems to have accepted the validity of his
title. But Boniface's whole approach to politics was dogmatic and domi-
neering, and in the end he failed because he lacked the force to back up his
theoretical assertions. The Florentine chronicler Dino Compagni described
him as a man of great boldness and high intelligence, who ruled the Church
as he saw fit and brought low whoever did not agree with him, although he
also noted that many were pleased at the pope's death, because he ruled cru-
elly and provoked wars.[5]

The first major assertion of papal power came on an issue in which
Boniface almost certainly had right on his side. The taxation of the clergy by
Philip IV and Edward I prompted the pope in February 1296 to issue the
bull *Clericis laicos,* proclaiming (somewhat provocatively) that antiquity
showed that laymen had been very hostile to the clergy, and that this was
proved by present experience, particularly in matters of imposing financial

burdens on them, without the permission of the Holy See. In consequence he imposed an automatic sentence of excommunication both on those who paid taxes and on rulers who levied them.[6] Such complaints were justified by the decrees of the Third and Fourth Lateran Councils, which had forbidden laymen to impose financial burdens on the clergy.[7] Boniface may have hoped that the kings would capitulate, but they did not, and Philip retaliated by imposing financial sanctions on the pope, forbidding the export of precious metals and bills of exchange by which money could be sent from France to the pope. As the Papacy drew substantial revenues from the French Church, this action demonstrated Boniface's vulnerability to counter-measures.

It was not only in Christendom as a whole that Boniface's ambitions outran his capacity to uphold them. The same was true of his political position in Italy, where he lacked any strong territorial power base. His attempt to establish this by advancing the interests of his family, the Caetani, merely led him into a struggle with the powerful Roman family of the Colonna, during which two cardinals from the latter denounced the pope as a tyrant and appealed to a general council to determine the legitimacy of his election. The pope preached a crusade against them, incurring the criticism of Dante, who described him as 'the Prince of the new Pharisees, waging war . . . not with Saracens or Jews, for every enemy of his was Christian'. Philip IV's willingness to back the demands of the Colonna cardinals prompted a papal climb-down, modifying *Clericis laicos* in a further bull, *Etsi de statu*, in which, while nominally reaffirming the earlier measure, he added that in a case of necessity, the king could set the decree aside, and impose taxation on the clergy – the declaration of necessity, significantly, was left to the conscience of the king.[8] The measure was clearly seen as a sufficient compromise for the old political alignment between the pope and France to be renewed, and a cousin of the French king brought a small army to Italy to assist the pope and the Angevins against the Aragonese. (In fact this intervention rebounded on Boniface, because a settlement was reached in 1302, without papal involvement, by which the Angevins surrendered Sicily to the Aragonese, while retaining their mainland territories.[9]) The canonisation of Louis IX was a further gesture towards peace.

In the meantime, a new crisis had arisen between Boniface and the French. In 1295, the pope had divided the diocese of Toulouse, creating a new see at Pamiers, to which he appointed Bernard Saisset, the abbot of St Anthony's in the same town. This was a controversial appointment, for the bishop had fallen foul of his local lord, the count of Foix, and had had to flee to Italy, where the pope excommunicated the count. Saisset was not reconciled to the count until 1300, but in the following year allegations against him were made to the king, he was arrested and charged with heresy and treason. The king's motives were probably political, a desire to strengthen royal power in an outlying region of the kingdom, and many of the charges against Saisset look like deliberate mud-slinging, but the treatment of the bishop raised crucial issues of clerical freedom from lay jurisdiction, which the pope could hardly overlook.[10] He not only retaliated by summoning all the French bishops to a council in Rome to consider the state of religion in France, but sent a stinging and patronising rebuke to the king; its opening words, *Ausculta fili* ('Listen, son'), set the tone.[11] A ferocious pamphlet war broke out, with Philip circulating crude forgeries to paint papal action as even more offensive and derogatory to royal power than it was, although the ambiguity of Boniface's actual utterances gave Philip ample opportunity to misrepresent the pope's position.

The fact that less than half of the French bishops (and none from northern France where the king's power was strongest) attended the council may well have prompted the pope to make another pronouncement on the subject of papal authority immediately afterwards. This was the famous bull *Unam sanctam,* probably the most intransigent affirmation of papal powers at any time in the Middle Ages. In fact, it did not refer to the immediate questions in dispute, and contained relatively little which was new. Most of it comprised excerpts from earlier writers and even its resounding conclusion, 'We declare, state, define and pronounce that it is altogether necessary for salvation for every human creature to be subject to the Roman pontiff', was taken from a work of Aquinas, *Against the Errors of the Schismatic Greeks,* and referred to the pope's spiritual rather than his temporal authority.[12] In a sense it was only carrying to a logical conclusion the attitude of the second Council of Lyons in 1274, which referred to the pope as 'the vicar of Jesus Christ, the successor of Peter, the ruler of the universal Church, the guide of the Lord's flock'.[13] The importance of *Unam sanctam*, however, lay less in its text than in its context. The French bishops' failure to respond to a papal summons could be seen as virtual recognition of the superiority of a royal command in the event of a clash between pope and king, and the affirmation of the Church's unity in the opening words asserted a claim that this must override any separatist national interests which could be seen in the demands which kings were making of their clerical subjects.

Philip IV retaliated against Boniface personally rather than against the Church's claims in general, launching his attack on two fronts, theoretical and physical. Boniface's reputation was attacked at a gathering of the French clergy in the summer of 1303, with accusations being made both about his personal conduct and about alleged heretical beliefs. These charges were at best a farrago of exaggerations, coloured by vivid propagandist imagination. But the accusation of heresy laid the pope open to canonist attack, for the *Decretum* allowed only one case when the pope was open to judgement, namely when he departed from the faith; canonist commentators justified this on the grounds that a heretical pope would automatically cease to be head of the Church.[14] These verbal attacks were probably intended to justify military action against Boniface, because by this time Philip's adviser Guillaume Nogaret had already left for Italy with a small military force. This linked up the pope's enemies in Italy, headed by the Colonna, and in September they seized Boniface at Anagni and probably assaulted him. There may have been some disagreement between the pope's enemies on their best course of action, to kill him on the spot, compel him to resign, or remove him to France for trial by a general council. This gave the citizens of the town an opportunity to counter-attack and free the pope, who returned to Rome, albeit as a broken man, and died a month later.

However much it is possible to distinguish theoretically between the claims of the papal office and the rights of an individual pope, in practice the two were inextricably interwoven. Dante loathed Boniface, and with good reason, for it had been the pope's political intervention in Florentine affairs that had led to the poet's banishment from his native city, and envisaged his fate among the simonists in hell, but at the same time he deplored the outrage of Anagni. 'I see the fleur-de-lys enter Anagni, and Christ made captive in his vicar. I see him mocked another time, I see the vinegar and the gall renewed, and him slain between living thieves.'[15] Even an admirer of Philip, Pierre Dubois, writing about 1306, described the pope as 'the Holy father, by divine grace, supreme pontiff of the universal Roman Church'.[16] The institutional fortunes of the Papacy could not be separated from the fate of Boniface, and the French king's determination to pursue his enemy beyond the grave left the pope's successors vulnerable to powerful moral blackmail, because any posthumous condemnation of the individual would reflect on the Papacy as an institution.

Boniface's successor, Benedict XI, was prepared to compromise, absolving the two rebel Colonna cardinals, though without restoring them to their titles, and releasing Philip and his family from any censures which they had incurred. The French king's continued demand for a general council to condemn Boniface's memory forced the pope to absolve all Frenchmen who had been involved in the Anagni outrage, apart from Nogaret, who was left as the scapegoat for it. Benedict, however, survived as pope for only eight and a half months, and the resulting conclave, split almost equally between those demanding vengeance on the French and those favouring peace with them, was deadlocked for eleven months. The choice of the archbishop of Bordeaux, Bertrand de Got, who took the title of Clement V, was probably prompted by a sense that he could bridge the rivalries of the two groups. He was well regarded at the French court but held his archbishopric in lands under the rule of the king of England; he was also one of the French bishops who had responded to Boniface VIII's summons to a council in 1302, but he had not thereby incurred Philip's displeasure. He was in France at the time of his election – he himself was not a cardinal – and was crowned there. However much he may have wished to return to Rome, he was detained in France by the need to liquidate the legacy of Boniface VIII. Philip kept up the pressure by demanding a general council to condemn Boniface, and although he eventually abandoned this, was eventually able to secure the annulment of all of the late pope's acts which were hostile to his interests, the absolution of Nogaret, and the canonisation of Celestine V. On this last, Clement secured one concession – Celestine was canonised as a confessor, not, as Philip wished, as a martyr at Boniface's hand.

The suppression of the Templars

Philip's blackmail of the pope secured one other major victory in the suppression of the Order of the Temple. This was one of the military orders established in the twelfth century, which bridged the ideals of chivalry and those of the church, with the knights being supposedly a celibate body vowed to protect the Christian states in Palestine. They had played an important role in the East, but after the fall of Acre, the last Christian stronghold in the East, in 1291, had lost their main role. Their wealth, however, made them an obvious prey to the French king. In attacking the order Philip showed the same ruthlessness which he had displayed against Boniface. In September 1307 he ordered his officials to prepare for the arrest of all its members in France, and a dawn swoop on 13 October rounded up all but a very small minority of the knights.[17] With the support of the papal inquisitor in France, torture was used to extort confessions, and only a few courageous knights were able to resist it; most of the accused, including the Grand Master and other leaders of the order, admitted charges of heresy, blasphemy, sodomy and other deviant sexual practices. By the end of the year, Philip's officials had taken over the administration of the Templars' estates.

Although Clement was vulnerable to royal pressure, he made some effort to resist the proceedings, attempting to take the dispute into his own hands, by ordering the arrest of the Templars in all Christian countries, and the takeover of their lands. Later, he suspended inquisitorial action, thereby provoking a further confrontation with the king, who embarked on a further propaganda campaign to justify his actions and threaten the pope. Philip used the services of the archbishop of Sens, the brother of one of his principal councillors, to act against the Templars of his own diocese, fifty-four of whom went to the stake in May 1310. After this, resistance within the order collapsed, and the pope had little option but to fall into line. At the Council of Vienne the order had some support, but Clement, possibly influenced by the threat to renew proceedings against Boniface VIII, dissolved it by administrative ordinance.

The move to Avignon

The problems posed by Philip's vendetta against Boniface and by the Templar affair had another long-term consequence. Conditions in Italy made it difficult for Clement to return there, and in 1309 he settled at

Avignon, at least on a temporary basis. This base was carefully chosen, for it lay within the lands of his vassals, the Angevin kings of Naples, and was not too far removed from Italy, while by remaining north of the Alps he could keep in touch with the issues raised by Philip. Although his original intention seems to have been to use it only as a temporary base, the Papacy was to remain there for almost seventy years. The fact that he was succeeded by a fellow Frenchman, albeit after a long conclave (over two and a quarter years), may have contributed to the decision to stay. In the end, seven successive Frenchmen were elected as popes, and all the higher echelons of the Church's central administration, particularly the college of cardinals, passed increasingly into French hands.

Avignon had practical advantages as a centre for the Church – geographically it was more centrally placed within Christendom than Rome, and was more accessible to the large numbers of people who sought favours at the papal court – and the area was probably less turbulent than Rome. But the Papacy was historically linked with Italy, and for considerable parts of the so-called 'captivity', the popes made efforts to establish suitable conditions to return there. Clement V toyed with the idea of coming to terms with the emperor Henry VII, and with trying to reconcile contesting Italian factions, but this proved unsuccessful in face of existing factional interests. After the emperor's death, later plans for return involved direct military activity in the pope's name. Indeed, the costs of the campaigns to prepare the way for this played a significant part in moulding the character of the mid-fourteenth-century Papacy. In two periods particularly, between 1319 and 1334, and from 1353 to 1363, considerable resources were employed to try to bring about this return. The first ended with the military defeat of the pope's supporters at Ferrara in 1333, and it is significant that in the years immediately succeeding this the Papacy committed itself to a more prolonged residence at Avignon by building a palace there. After Cardinal Gil Albornoz's campaigns in the later period, and his skilful conciliation of and concessions to local territorial lords, Urban V did actually return to Rome in 1367, only for disorderly conditions to drive him back to Avignon, and it was not until 1377 that Gregory XI brought the Papacy back to Rome, where he died in the following year.

The Avignon popes were severely criticised in their own time, and this view has coloured much subsequent historical writing. But many of the critics were writing from particular political standpoints and had their own axes to grind: in an age in which politics were increasingly affected by national sentiment, which monarchs exploited to their own ends, English writers undoubtedly were apprehensive that a French pope would be prejudiced in cases of Anglo-French political rivalry, while the Italians may well have felt that they were entitled to the physical control of the Papacy. Certainly at the beginning of the Avignon period, Dino Compagni declared that the lack of respect felt towards the Church was due to its subservience to the French king, who had frightened Clement V.[18] Even more vitriolic were the attacks launched by Petrarch in the middle of the century. Using the apocalyptic language of the Book of Revelation, and sometimes quoting it explicitly, he constantly described Avignon as Babylon, the city of moral corruption, contrasting its wealth with the poverty of the apostles and denouncing the complexity of its administration. He also denounced its venality, although this was not new – similar criticisms had been made in the savage twelfth-century scriptural parody, the *Gospel according to Marks of Silver*.[19]

Yet if one examines the character of the fourteenth-century Papacy, it was in many ways similar to that of the thirteenth, and developments in government were a logical continuation of what had gone before. It inherited some of the faults of the earlier period – like the Italian popes who had strengthened their position by advancing the interests of their relatives, these French popes also had recourse to nepotism, and Gregory XI indeed was the nephew of Clement VI.[20] The majority of the popes were trained in law, with both Clement V and John XXII being canonists of importance, who issued supplementary collections of canon law. They were men with experience of the secular world, four of the seven having served secular rulers in governmental matters. If Clement VI was seen as a man who enjoyed the status of a great lord, it is worth noting that a chronicler described him both as 'a kind man, and much loved' and as a distinguished preacher. The former characteristic is borne out by the fact that during the Black Death, he took the Jews under his protection to safeguard them against pogroms.[21] They were efficient managers of the Church's business rather than men of spiritual distinction – only one (Urban V) has been beatified and none canonised – but equally there were no blatant scandals attaching to them, such as were found among some of their fifteenth-century successors.

Administrative developments in the Avignon Papacy

Resentment at taxation was undoubtedly one reason why the Papacy was criticised. This certainly increased in the Avignon period, not least because of the cost of the wars fought in Italy to prepare the way for the pope's return to Rome. More particularly, alongside the more traditional taxes which were levied on the Church as a whole, the period saw the development of taxes on benefices which were filled by papal provision, those called services and annates, and which were paid at appointment. Services on major benefices were paid at the papal Curia by the beneficiaries of the provisions; annates, on lesser ones, were gathered in individual countries by papal collectors. These taxes were developed particularly during John XXII's pontificate, when the most influential administrator was Gasbert de Laval, the head of the papal *Camera*, or chamber, the financial organ of the government. The same pope codified the regulations for making provisions early in his reign, reserving to himself the right of making them in all cases relating to the deposition of an existing holder, rejected election, surrender to the pope, or following the papal translation of a holder to another benefice. Once a benefice was brought within the ambit of a papal provision it remained so, and the pope therefore had the opportunity to extend his influence over all major Church appointments. Although a rightful patron could appeal against a collation, if there was a legal irregularity,[22] in practice by the end of the Avignon period, free elections to bishoprics and abbacies were virtually abandoned. The more benefices that came under papal control, the more were subject to service payments, although if translations took place too rapidly there was always a danger that the balance of the money from one might still be outstanding at the time of the next one.[23]

Cameral records show that the Papacy often had problems in securing payments, because turbulent political conditions, and from the mid-century also endemic plague, made it hard for individual churches to meet their obligations. The curial authorities were prepared to recognise the genuineness of such cases – in 1363 the dean of Chartres had his assessment to the papal tenth reduced on grounds of war and pestilence, and the bishop of Metz had his obligation to pay a tax deferred. In 1365 and 1369 the abbot of Cluny benefited from the cancellation of tax arrears, and was released from a sentence of excommunication imposed on him for non-payment.[24] On the other hand, sanctions could be maintained on defaulters, presumably when it was felt that the payments could have been made.[25] Much might depend on the pope's needs at any particular time; in 1371, when the Papacy was having difficulties in asserting its authority in Italy, a rather desperate appeal was sent to the bishop of Worms, ordering him to send the money in his hands and in those of his sub-collectors as quickly as possible. Other letters of a similar tone were also sent out.[26]

The period also saw further centralisation of legal activity, most notably with John XXII's organisation in 1331 of the court which came to be known as the Rota, which heard ecclesiastical civil pleas, particularly those in connection with benefices. Whereas the expansion of the system of provisions and the extension of taxation resulted primarily from central initiatives, such cases normally originated in the localities, and the increasing activity of the central courts was prompted largely by demand. John's successor, Benedict XII, reorganised the Penitentiary, which heard cases concerned with spiritual irregularities and excommunications, in 1338. Excommunication was not purely a penalty for spiritual offenders, for it also provided a sanction which could be employed to defend papal officials; the chamberlain was prepared to inflict it on two canons of Lübeck who had imprisoned a papal messenger.[27] Because the Curia was the ultimate court of appeal in legal matters individuals might be drawn away from their own dioceses, and churchmen might even have to obtain leave of absence from their parishes if they had cases pending there. Some serious offences, such as wounding a priest, were reserved to the Curia for absolution.[28]

Challenges to papal power

In general, Europe's lay rulers were prepared to reach some compromise with the Papacy on practical administrative issues, and the popes in turn were willing to abandon the confrontational style of Boniface VIII. But some tension survived, which led to national attempts to limit papal power, and, quite apart from specific measures, the political disputes of the period gave rise to some controversial writing which challenged papal claims to absolute power. Probably the most serious dispute was that between John XXII and the Emperor Lewis of Bavaria, but it marks the Empire's declining role on the European scene that this did not have repercussions on papal fortunes comparable with those caused by the struggles between the two powers in earlier centuries, or indeed with the struggle between Boniface VIII and Philip IV. The crisis began with a double election to the Empire, which tempted John into an ill-judged attempt to assert his authority. Lewis, however, defeated his rival and began to renew imperial interests in Italy, in alliance with the pope's enemies. The papal excommunication of the emperor led him to appeal to a general council, accusing John of heresy because of his attitude to the Franciscan teaching on the poverty of Christ, which had split the order.[29] Among the dissident Franciscans was the leading philosopher of the day, William of Ockham, who turned his attention from metaphysics to politics, and wrote a substantial number of works supporting the emperor. These writings challenged the fundamental basis of papal power, and claimed that the plenitude of power could not dispense with the law of nature.[30] He asserted that a pope could be removed from office for heresy, for being criminal and incorrigible, and by voluntary resignation. While the first pretext depended on canonist affirmations of when a pope could be judged by the Church, it also probably referred to Franciscan allegations that John was a heretic, while the last looked back to the abdication of Celestine V. Ockham called for a general council to judge an allegedly heretical pope. Although these ideas did not have any immediate influence, they did affect the growth of conciliar thought during the Great Schism.

Lewis was also joined by the secularist political writer Marsilius of Padua, whose *Defensor Pacis* was condemned by the pope in 1327. This work had been completed in 1324, but it is not clear when it had been begun, nor what prompted the author to write it. Although its character is more polemical than reflective, it was not produced as a piece of political propaganda for any particular occasion. Most probably Marsilius began writing around the time of the pope's intervention in Lombardy just before 1320, as he had been willing to accept a papal reservation to him of a benefice in his native city as late as 1318.[31] The work drew on both theoretical political writings, by Aristotle and by the Franciscans, with which he had probably become acquainted while at the University of Paris during the reign of Philip IV, and on the author's observation of the practices of his native Padua, to construct a model of government which subordinated the Church to lay authority. Marsilius joined Lewis in his march on Rome in 1328, during which he installed an antipope (Nicholas V), but the schism lasted for only a short time. The antipope remained unrecognised by anyone except the emperor, who was unable to give him adequate support. After Lewis's retreat northwards, Nicholas could not maintain his position and soon submitted. The emperor continued to support the intellectual dissidents at his court, who repaid him with their writings, but these had little effect on the day-to-day workings of the Church. Imperial interest in Italy faded after this date, and later rulers confined their attention to the lands north of the Alps.

Practical challenges to papal authority damaged it more than these academic writings. The lay powers of Europe had seen papal impotence in face of Philip IV's challenge, and were prepared to assert their influence over the Church within their own territories. In most cases, no formal settlement was reached, but there was in practice a tacit understanding of the boundaries of practical power, and although one finds kings taking steps to curtail papal rights, some of these were in the nature of shadow boxing, because they already had substantial *de facto* authority. Papal assertions of rights of provision did not prevent kings from securing the appointment of their trusted servants to major ecclesiastical posts. The emperor Charles IV, in an autobiographical fragment, affirmed that he had made his chancellor bishop of Trent and his brother's chaplain bishop of Brixen.[32] In France an assembly at Vincennes in 1329 asserted the distinction of lay and spiritual jurisdiction, and although it issued no edict on the rights of the two sets of courts, it was a pointer to the assertion of secular against ecclesiastical power. Various papal mandates to kings to safeguard ecclesiastical liberties went virtually unheeded, and in 1372 a royal ordinance seriously limited the power of the church courts.[33] English hostility to the Papacy antedated the start of the Hundred Years War – a parliament at Carlisle in 1307 complained about the detrimental effects of provisions on the English Church – but there is little doubt that after the outbreak of Anglo-French hostilities in 1337, anti-papal sentiment became stronger. In fact the English kings were more willing to compromise than their leading subjects in parliament, which passed various measures curtailing both papal rights of provision and its jurisdictional powers, the statutes of Provisors (1351) and of Praemunire (1353). In fact a royal ordinance had already restricted papal rights of appointment, but this had not been fully implemented; probably the king was willing to hold this power in reserve and apply it merely when it was convenient to him, whereas some of his subjects, whose rights of patronage had been curtailed, were more aggressively hostile to a French pope.

This indeed was the pattern of much church life in the fourteenth century. The theoretical universality of papal power remained largely intact, but practical power spoke louder than theory. If the pope wished to exert his authority in the daily running of the Church throughout Christendom, he could do so only if his actions were acceptable to the local monarchs. It is noteworthy that when Urban V reaffirmed his right to take the goods of deceased clergy, this was not to apply in the French or English churches, those under the control of the two most powerful kings in the West.[34] Most kings in turn had no desire to act as violently against the Church as Philip IV had done – they would accept a considerable degree of papal authority over the Church if royal powers were not curtailed, and some exercise of rights of patronage was conceded. The popes could tax the clergy, if the king had his cut. They were indeed often willing to allow the pope to act as a political arbitrator in the affairs of Christendom – the popes tried, though with little success, to negotiate a settlement in the Anglo-French war. A balance of power had been reached in which the role of the Papacy, both as a territorial power and as administrative and spiritual head of the Church, was recognised. A wise pope, however, would not push his claims too hard, because he knew that the lay power could always retaliate, and he would be the probable loser. When the Papacy returned to Rome in 1377, with a relatively young pope in Gregory XI, few men could have foreseen that it was on the verge of its greatest crisis in the later Middle Ages.

|13|

Schism and councils

The college of cardinals

The papal court at Avignon shared many features with those of lay princes, but one essential difference between papal and lay monarchy was that the ruler succeeded not by hereditary succession, but by election. Since the election decree of 1179 a two-thirds majority of the college of cardinals was required to choose a new pope, and as has been shown the problem of obtaining this could lead to protracted vacancies. The cardinals increasingly saw themselves, and were seen by others, as the great princes of the Church; indeed, had they not cultivated this status they would have carried less weight when serving as papal legates to the various kings of Christendom. As the papal bureaucracy developed, they were often given responsibility in its various departments. Some even served as leaders of the papal armies, such as Bertrand du Poujet and Albornoz in Italy. The popes, if they were wise, would consult them, and were indeed expected to do so. There was, however, a distinction between being expected to seek advice from the cardinals and recognising an obligation to accept it, and questions were raised from the late thirteenth century about how much power the college possessed, particularly in relation to the pope himself; did it collectively have the right to curtail the exercise of papal power, or was it totally subordinate to an absolute pope? Its basic power was to elect a new pope, but could the cardinals impose conditions on candidates for the Papacy and thereby limit them to acting in accordance with their wishes? The popes resisted any such encroachment on their power, and two bulls tried to define the terms of conclaves. Gregory X's *Ubi periculum* forbade the cardinals from making pacts during elections, and Clement V's *Ne Romani* forbade the college during a vacancy from altering this rule.

Despite these bulls, an attempt was made in 1352, after Clement VI's death, to draw up an electoral pact to safeguard the college's rights. The number of cardinals was to be restricted, and two-thirds of the existing

college should consent to new nominations. Furthermore, half the revenues
of the Holy See were to be reserved to the college. Within seven months after
his election, however, Innocent VI revoked the pact, on the grounds that it
infringed canon law and the papal plenitude of power. That a pope could do
this without facing any effective challenge exemplifies the potential for
absolutism which the Papacy possessed. Yet a pope who failed to exercise
such absolute powers with common sense and moderation, or at least with
sufficient skill to ensure that he had a reasonable measure of support within
the college, ran the risk of losing control of the Church as a whole. It had
been the alienation of potential allies more than the extravagance of his theoretical claims that had been crucial in the downfall of Boniface VIII, and a
similar clash was to lead to division of the Western Church in 1378.

The Great Schism of 1378

Most popes tried to strengthen their power by nominating well-disposed
cardinals, and in the Avignon period most looked to their own families for
some such nominees. By 1378, when Gregory XI died in Rome, the predominantly French college was faced with noisy demands from the local
populace for the election of a Roman, or at least an Italian. The complaints
could be justified – after all, the pope was, first and foremost, bishop of
Rome, and the city had been deprived of an active papal presence, apart
from occasional intermissions, for the best part of three-quarters of a century. It was hardly surprising that the Romans feared that the choice of
another Frenchman would continue this. The rioting undoubtedly frightened the college, but it also suffered from internal divisions. Of the sixteen
cardinals present, eleven were French, four Italian and one Spanish. Had the
French held together they could have furnished the necessary two-thirds
majority, but they themselves were divided into seven Limousins, a group
from which the last four popes had been drawn, and four others, who
resented their dominance. The Limousins had sufficient strength to block
any other candidate but lacked the power to enforce their own way. The
cardinals were probably frightened by the fear of violence, because they first
pretended that they had chosen an elderly and infirm Roman, Cardinal
Tebaldeschi, before acknowledging that they had elected a man from outside the college, Archbishop Prignano of Bari, who took the title of Urban
VI. He was a Neapolitan rather than a Roman, so the college had clearly not
capitulated totally under mob pressure, but evidently he was more acceptable to the crowd than a Frenchman. Ten days later, at Easter, he was
enthroned as pope, and was generally regarded as such.[1]

There is little doubt that if Urban had subsequently proved acceptable to
the cardinals there would have been no schism. The pleas of duress put forward during the summer in the hope of invalidating the election were simply a desperate attempt to find a legitimate pretext for getting rid of a pope

who proved impossible. The problem which lay at the root of the schism was the absence of any lawful restraint which could be imposed on a pope, whose power was becoming increasingly absolute. Indeed, the more that papal power grew, the more essential it became that the right man should be chosen for the office, and in this case it soon became clear that the college had seriously misjudged their choice. He had been a curial official, who was respected for his austerity and conscientiousness, and had served at Avignon for some twenty years. The cardinals possibly hoped that he would be willing to return there and may also have expected that he would regard them with the respect which they felt was due to their office. Once elected, however, Urban emerged into a different light, and the problem for historians is to assess how far later claims of the contending parties, made to justify their actions, have distorted the actual picture. The pope began by proclaiming a desire to reform the Church, beginning with the cardinals, but whether or not this claim was true is uncertain. (He never made any attempts later to carry out effective reform in his own obedience, although it could be argued that this was pushed into the background by the schism.) If he was genuinely a reformer, he approached the issue in the wrong way. His language towards the college was intemperate and abusive, and in some matters hypocritical. To accuse the cardinals of being traitors for deserting their sees and living at the Curia displayed a willingness to forget what he himself had done before being elected pope, and to employ physical violence against one of the French cardinals showed a disastrous lack of self-control. After one such outburst, the cardinal of Geneva warned Urban that his failure to treat the cardinals properly diminished their authority, and that they would do their best to diminish his.[2] Nor were Urban's verbal assaults confined to the cardinals; his dealings with the representatives of the lay power were equally abrasive.

It is hardly surprising that the French cardinals found the atmosphere of Rome intolerable, and withdrew to Anagni, calling on their Italian colleagues to join them, in the hope of establishing a common front against Urban. The division into these groups indicates how a growing sense of national identity in Europe was coming to colour men's political views and actions. On 9 August the French group issued a declaration to Christendom in which they claimed that their actions, both during and after the election, had been coloured by fear and that therefore the election was void.[3] Although the pope's actions may have made his removal from office desirable, there was no legal method of proceeding against him. The only cause for which a pope could be judged in canon law was heresy, and Urban had done nothing to merit such an accusation. The only alternative method of removing him was to argue that the original election had been invalid, on the grounds that it had not been free, and therefore that he had never been the lawful pope. In fact it took some time before the Italians came to Anagni, and indeed before they eventually did so they made some attempts to negotiate with their French colleagues on Urban's behalf. Issues of principle were raised, and suggestions were made that a general council should meet to save Christendom from disaster, although this in turn raised another problem, namely how the council should be summoned, as traditionally the issue of such a summons was a papal prerogative.[4] (This question was to arise again later, when attempts were made to resolve the schism by the action of a council.)

Clearly the French cardinals were determined to remove Urban, and were merely seeking a pretext to do so. The initiative was their own, for although they may have written .o the French king, he does not appear to have given them any real encouragement. They outmanoeuvred their vacillating Italian colleagues, one of whom, the elderly Tebaldeschi, died early in September. Hints were dropped to each of the other three that they had been selected as a suitable candidate for the allegedly vacant papacy, so they joined with the French, abstained from voting, and left a clear field for Robert of Geneva, who was elected on 20 September, and took the title of Clement VII. A week later Urban retaliated by creating twenty-eight new cardinals of his own, so there were now not only two popes but also two colleges. With this the division in the Church reached the point of no return, as both parties took steps to secure allies, whose support would strengthen their position.

It reflects the *de facto* authority of the lay rulers of Christendom over the Church in their particular localities that such a search for support was necessary, and it is a measure of the political character of the Church that the resulting support among these princes divided along political lines. Indeed the length of the schism was affected by such considerations, and particularly by French attitudes. At the start, the national background of the rebel cardinals secured them the support of France and its allies in the Hundred Years War, while England rallied to the Roman pope. The attitude of Portugal demonstrates clearly how secular affairs affected the schism – originally Clementist, it turned Urbanist under English pressure. The Oxford philosopher John Wyclif, who had not yet adopted a radical point of view which doubted the legitimacy of all popes, even referred to the pope as 'our Urban'. The almost even split in Christendom made a solution to the schism all the more difficult, because it was virtually impossible for one claimant to resolve the issue in his favour by the simplest expedient, the way of force. Clement attempted this, but after an attack on Rome failed in 1379 he withdrew to Avignon, leaving Urban dominant in the papal state. The latter's actions, however, threw away his advantages. Even in Italy he antagonised potential allies in the rulers of Naples through trying to advance the interests of a nephew; Clement's supporters were able to gain a foothold for a time, and it was not until the succession of a more politically adroit pope in Boniface IX that the Roman line regained its influence. Urban also aroused opposition among the cardinals whom he himself created, and a plot against him led to the arrest and torture of a number of them. His talent for making enemies amounted almost to genius, and by the time of his death in 1389, he had lost much of his political power and emptied his treasury.

The conviction of both the popes and their supporters that they were the legitimate inheritors of papal power made it hard to resolve the crisis. The deaths of Urban (1389) and Clement (1394) might have given an opportunity for a settlement but neither college was prepared to transfer its allegiance to another pope. Although the division in Christendom was universally agreed to be a scandal, no one within the Church was willing to hazard his own standing by making a move towards a compromise. Suggestions were made that both claimants should resign simultaneously to clear the way to elect an uncontested pope, or that negotiations might be held between the rivals. The mutual mistrust of the contending parties and the fear that any voluntary concession might be construed as an admission of a flawed title, however, provided a barrier to any success in this way. The cardinals who had been created after the outbreak of the schism were equally reluctant to make concessions, for fear that their own titles might be invalidated. Under pressure from the French king, the conclave which elected Clement's successor, Benedict XIII, demanded an oath that everyone should work to eliminate the schism, even to the extent of abdication when the majority regarded this as proper, but once elected Benedict refused to comply. His continued prevarication even led to the French withdrawal of obedience in 1398, but a later political upheaval at the French court led to it being restored. The instability of France during the dispute between the Orleanist and Burgundian factions led to inconsistency in French policy, which affected the wider European scene. Had other rulers followed the initial French withdrawal, it might have been possible to put pressure on the popes, but other countries too faced political upheavals. The overthrow of the English king Richard II in 1399 and political troubles in the Empire meant that rulers sympathetic to the policy of withdrawal were replaced by adherents of the Roman line.[5] At the same time, however, people had an ambiguous attitude as to which pope had the stronger title, and may even have accepted the *de facto* division of the Church. The Italian merchant Buonaccorso Pitti referred to 'the Pope in Rome' and 'the Pope in Marseilles' and later became involved with the first of the conciliar popes.[6]

The beginnings of conciliarism

The schism involved both political and ecclesiological factors. The laity had a crucial role to play in church affairs, but the schism could not be settled until the Church resolved its own problems. Within the Church, the fundamental reason for the persistence of a schism which was generally regarded as a scandal was the same as the cause of its outbreak, the absence of any superior authority which had the right to correct a pope. Theoretical papal authority had, of course, been questioned earlier in the fourteenth century, and the suggestion had been voiced that a general council of the Church had the power to pass judgement on him.[7] This idea was revived early in the schism, perhaps significantly by two Germans in the University of Paris, men whose own rulers favoured the Roman line but who were living under the rule of a king who favoured the Avignon claimant, Conrad of Gelnhausen and Henry of Langenstein.[8] Torn between rival claims to their loyalty, it is hardly surprising that they might wish to embrace a course of action which could heal the divisions. The University itself was an international body, and there had been some resistance in it to the French king's adherence to Clement VII. The idea of a council was taken up by a prominent young doctor of theology, Pierre d'Ailly, in a satirical letter purporting to be from the devil to the prelates of the Church denouncing those who had called for a general council.[9]

Yet although conciliar action had been considered in university circles, it was a different matter to translate ideas into action. The fundamental theoretical objection that a general council could lawfully be summoned only by a pope created a major stumbling-block to convening any such meeting. If the pope would not call a council, who had the power to do so? Even the future champion of conciliarism, Jean Gerson, wrote in his *De Schismate* (1402), 'A general council cannot be lawfully summoned without the authorisation of the pope'.[10] Only with the passage of time, and faced by the intransigence of rival claimants, did he accept the idea that the radical nature of the problem required equally radical remedies. In the winter of 1406–7, he made his first move away from strict canonist practice, by declaring that positive law should not prevent the holding of a general council, and by raising the possibility of a new college being formed from those of the contending obediences to give an undisputed Vicar of Christ to the Church.[11]

In the end it was the cardinals who took the decisive step. Attempts to bring about talks between the rival claimants established contacts between the rival groups, and Benedict XIII did travel to Italy with the idea of meeting the fourth pope of the Roman line, Gregory XII, who had probably been chosen because he was believed to favour union. It may well have been the latter's action in creating a group of new cardinals in May 1408, in violation of his conclave oath, that led most of his old cardinals to desert him. Almost simultaneously, the French had renewed their withdrawal of obedience from Benedict, so it was easy for the majority of the two colleges to come together – at the end of June they pledged themselves to work for the union of the Church, and summoned a general council to meet at Pisa in the following spring.[12]

The Council of Pisa

The meeting of the council in March 1409 was a crucial breakthrough in resolving the schism, most markedly because those present included not only churchmen from both obediences, but also ambassadors from the kings of France and England, and from one of the claimants to the Empire, Wenzel of Bohemia. Some countries were unrepresented – the Spanish kingdoms still supported Benedict, and Ladislas of Naples and the rival claimant to the Empire, Ruprecht of the Palatinate, adhered to Gregory – but most of Christendom rallied behind the cardinals. Most significantly, both France and England backed the council, for although their political hostilities were temporarily quiescent, their rivalry was still the principal determining force in the diplomatic alignments of Western Europe. The council proceeded in as legal a manner as was compatible with its revolutionary character as an assembly convoked by other than papal authority. It appointed as its president the one cardinal whose creation antedated the schism, whose position could not therefore be challenged, and affirmed the authenticity of the assembly as a general council. They summoned the rival popes to attend and when they (unsurprisingly) failed to appear, took proceedings against them for keeping the Church in schism, and a decree of deposition was passed against them at the beginning of June. Three weeks later the archbishop of Milan was elected pope as Alexander V.[13]

In one sense the Council of Pisa was a failure, for it did not end the schism, and indeed left Christendom divided into three rather than two obediences. This failure lay in the fact that it did not secure the withdrawal of support from the claimants of the Roman and Avignonese lines when it created its own pope. Nevertheless its importance should not be underestimated, for it not only broke the log-jam between rival contenders by showing that action could be taken against them, but also, more crucially, secured the support of the greater part of Christendom. The rulers who had sent delegations to the council continued to support its choice of pope, and these included all the most influential princes of the West. This made it easier to summon another council later – indeed one may wonder if the Council of Constance could have achieved what it did if it had not seen where its predecessor at Pisa had failed. The Council of Pisa had essentially a limited objective, to restore unity in the Church, but it soon became clear that this reunification had to be supported by implementing certain reforms within it. In the years after 1409 there was an increasing demand for reform 'in head and in members' (*in capite et membris*). The 'head' included not only the pope and his personal powers, although the dangers posed by these had been highlighted by the behaviour of Urban VI, but also the level of authority exercised by the papal Curia. And while church life in the localities could be reformed without reference to the pope, the previous three centuries had seen a close connection between the Papacy and ecclesiastical reform generally, and it was assumed that the popes should play a part in any reform measures. The issue of reform was increasingly voiced from the later sessions at Pisa, but the members of the council were not particularly interested in them, and were happy to postpone the question by calling for a further council three years later to deal with it.

The issue of reform was highlighted further when Alexander V died and was succeeded by cardinal Cossa, who took the title of John XXIII. John had abilities – as a military leader he had done much to restore the Church's authority within the papal states – but his moral standards were low, and he could not be seen as a standard-bearer of reform, even if one allows for the fact that medieval abuse was seldom restrained and that the charges brought against him at the time of his deposition were probably exaggerated. He made some effort to strengthen his position by appointing a number of cardinals, and by summoning a council which met at Rome in 1413. This achieved little, apart from condemning the writings of Wyclif, because proposals for reform which were put forward against the pope's wishes were shelved, and nothing was done to end the continuing schism. The smallness of the attendance reflected a lack of interest in reform, compared with the much greater concern that was felt about the restoration of unity.

The interaction of secular and ecclesiastical politics was demonstrated by the emergence of a new figure who played a crucial role in the eventual restoration of unity. The schism in the Empire, which had begun with the deposition of Wenzel in 1400, was eventually resolved when the throne passed to his brother Sigismund, who was recognised as emperor in 1411. One need not doubt that he was genuinely interested in reunification, but he also may have thought that he could enhance his standing in Christendom if he were active in this. John's political difficulties in Italy played into Sigismund's hands, and when the pope sought assistance from him against Ladislas of Naples in 1413, the price John had to pay was to summon a council for the following year, to meet in the imperial free city of Constance. The fact that the council met north of the Alps meant that it was less susceptible to papal pressures, such as had limited the effectiveness of the Council of Rome. Significantly, John tried to wriggle out of his commitment to the new council when Ladislas died, but the cardinals not only held him to it, but insisted that he should go there in person. In practice this left him more vulnerable to the council's actions when it eventually got under way. The pope may have hoped that a new council would uphold his title and condemn his rivals, but it soon became clear that there were a number of people at Constance who thought that church unity would be easier to restore if John were also removed. This feeling may have been enhanced by an offer from Gregory XII's envoys that he would consider resigning if his rivals did the same.

The Council of Constance

John played a part in the early events at Constance, preaching a sermon at the opening session, but it soon became clear that the council fathers were trying to weaken his position. The decision to organise the council by nations (after the model of the universities) rather than having voting by a simple head count was intended to prevent the pope from dominating it through the greater number of Italian prelates who were more likely to be sympathetic to him. The crisis of the council came at the end of March and the beginning of April 1415. John made a tentative offer of resignation, on condition that his rivals did the same, but then became involved in intrigues with Sigismund's enemy, Frederick of Austria, and fled from Constance to Schaffhausen, following this with a command to the cardinals to join him there – if they had all complied this would effectively have dissolved the council. But some of them remained, Sigismund brought pressure on Frederick, and the most learned theologian at the council, Jean Gerson, preached a sermon on the text *Ambulate dum lucem habetis* ('Walk in the light while you have light'), in which he claimed that the Church assembled in the council had its authority directly from Christ, and that everyone, even the pope, was bound to obey it.[14] Two of the cardinals who had remained at Constance came before the council and affirmed that it had been duly summoned and was not to be dissolved by the pope's flight, that it should not be dissolved until the schism had been removed and that it should not be transferred without its own consent. The emperor gave his support, symbolically emphasising his role by attending the plenary session of 26 March wearing his imperial robes and crown. This solidarity of Sigismund and the remaining cardinals helped to stabilise the situation and enabled the council to draft a decree which affirmed the superiority of the council over the pope; after some debate, because of the contrasting wishes of the cardinals and the other council members, this decree, *Haec Sancta,* was formally enacted on 6 April, in very much the same terms as those in Gerson's sermon, asserting the pope's subordination to the council in matters relating to the faith, the ending of the schism and the general reformation of the Church in head and in members.[15] This cleared the way for legal proceedings against John, which culminated in the pope's deposition on 29 May.

The decree *Haec Sancta* was a revolutionary measure, which challenged all the theoretical concepts of papal supremacy which had been developed since the Gregorian reform movement. Yet it must be understood only in the immediate circumstances of its enactment, as an *ad hoc* measure to deal with the problem of John's intransigence. The men who enacted it were reluctant rather than enthusiastic radicals, who demonstrated their essential conservatism by their heresy prosecution of Jan Hus, and it was only the overwhelming wish to resolve the schism which persuaded them that there was no alternative but to establish some authority superior to the pope's. John's flight from Constance marked a turning-point in attitudes to him; until that time most people at Constance considered him to be the lawful pope. An Italian curial official, Cerretano, referred to him by his title in the early stages of the council, while describing his rivals Gregory XII and Benedict XIII by their personal names of Angelo Corario and Pedro de Luna.[16] After his arrest he was treated with less respect, and after his deposition he was summarily dismissed as 'lord Baldassare Cossa, formerly pope John XXIII'.[17] It is noteworthy that the writers who described the proceedings clearly had no qualms about the council's right to depose the pope, at least as an individual. There were more doubts among the council fathers on the wider issues of papal authority. The distinguished canonist Cardinal Zabarella refused to read the clause of *Haec Sancta* affirming that the pope was bound to obey the council in matters concerning the faith and the ending of the schism on the grounds that it was not correct *de jure*. Cerretano did not mention Gerson by name but a reference to his sermon showed some reservations, because it disparaged apostolic authority.[18] Traditional values still coloured men's views, and in the end paved the way for a papal recovery. Doubts as to the legitimacy of papal titles during the schism, however, persisted to the end of the century – in the registers of Alexander VI confirmations of grants referred to John XXIII and Boniface IX, 'as they were called in their obediences'. By contrast, the later antipope created by the Council of Basel was designated in rather more hostile terms as 'the late Amadeus, duke of Savoy, called Felix V in his obedience'.[19]

John's deposition was perhaps the easiest task facing the council fathers, not least because he was in their custody. The events at Pisa had shown, however, that while it was easy to declare that a pope was deposed, this would not resolve the schism unless effective support could be withdrawn from him. John did not retain such support, but Gregory and Benedict still did. Gregory in fact was better than the pledge he had given earlier in the year, abdicating voluntarily on 4 July, even though Benedict had not done the same. He was restored to the rank of cardinal, subject to the restriction that he would be ineligible for re-election, and remained as the council's legate to the March of Ancona until his death just over two years later. Benedict, however, continued to prevaricate. However, the lesson of Pisa had been learned, that there was no point in proceeding to a new election until it was absolutely certain that the Papacy was vacant. The crucial role in this was played by Sigismund, who entered into negotiations with Benedict's temporal protector, Ferdinand of Aragon, and in January 1416 the king ordered a withdrawal of obedience from him throughout his lands. The king's death delayed the departure of ambassadors from his country to the council until the following autumn, where they were later joined by envoys from Castile. (Only Scotland remained loyal to Benedict.) The arrival of Spanish envoys cleared the way for proceedings against him, and he was eventually declared deposed in July 1417. He never accepted the judgement, and retired to the castle of Peñiscola on the coast of Valencia from where he continued to fulminate sanctions at his enemies. He created four new cardinals and remained defiant till his death in 1423, when his 'college' itself split in a further schism between two claimants one of whom had little support and the other none – the division of the Church which had begun as tragedy in 1378 petered out in farce.

Benedict's deposition raised a new problem at the council, whether to carry out reforms or to elect a new pope immediately. Originally it been agreed that reforms would have priority, but after Benedict's removal pressure built up for an early election. Sigismund, who had favoured reforms, probably in the hope of finding some solution to the problems of Hussitism in Bohemia, was deserted by his supporters, and in October it was agreed that a new election should be held. The only concession made to the reformers was the approval of a decree, called *Frequens,* which laid down a timetable for future council meetings to carry on the business of reform. This stipulated that the first was to meet automatically five years after the end of the Council of Constance, the second seven years after that and thereafter others at intervals of a decade. With a backward look at 1378 and the problems which followed the schism, the decree also stated that in the event of any future schism, the council was to assemble automatically.[20] In many ways the implications of this decree were even more revolutionary than those of *Haec Sancta,* because it removed the need for any papal summons and gave the councils an autonomous existence.

The election of the new pope was conducted by a compromise method to accommodate both the claims of the cardinals and the organisation of the council by nations, in order to ensure that whoever was chosen could claim the genuine support of Christendom. The original four nations had been expanded to five following the arrival of the Spanish delegates (despite an attempt by the French, prompted by political hostility to the English and the Germans, to force them into one nation, as at the University of Paris). It was agreed that each nation should choose six delegates, and that a candidate had to secure a two-thirds majority in each of them as well as from the twenty-three participating cardinals. This procedure makes it clear that despite considerable political antagonisms among the nations at the council (and it is worth remembering that while it was in session the Anglo-French war had been renewed and the battle of Agincourt had been fought) there was genuine determination on all sides to ensure that unity should be restored to the Church. The initial ballot seems to have been intended to take soundings rather than to secure a result, because each elector was allowed more than one vote. The eventual winner, Cardinal Oddo Colonna, had less overall support in the college than three other candidates on the second ballot, but by drawing votes from all five nations, clearly had the most widespread appeal. The votes switched to him, and after he had gained the necessary majority in all the nations and support from fifteen of the cardinals, two more of the latter shifted their support to give him the necessary majority.[21] Elected on St Martin's day, he took the title of Martin V.

Martin V and the papal recovery

The Church was now reunified, but the issues which had caused the schism, notably the problem of papal authority, both in relation to the power of secular rulers and within the Church's own structure, were not finally resolved. The council had healed the immediate split, but had raised an even more serious challenge to the pope's monarchical power, which had been more or less taken for granted for the previous three centuries. In the fourteenth century the idea that the pope should be subject to the Church's collective authority represented in a general council had been little more than a theory supported by academics with a little support from princes who were politically opposed to individual popes, but because a council had restored unity to the Church after a generation of division, the theory acquired new respectability. Furthermore, Martin V could hardly challenge conciliar claims, because his own title was legitimate only if the council which had elected him had itself been lawful. At the same time, one could hardly expect a pope to abandon the traditional prerogatives of his office, so during his pontificate of just over thirteen years, he trod a very delicate political path.

On balance he was successful in restoring the Papacy's position, despite political difficulties in the papal states, which delayed his return to Rome until 1420. His approach to these was pragmatic, but by an astute use of nepotism, exploitation of rivalries among various feudal families, and compromises between his legates and existing officials, he regained substantial ground. Despite all the territorial disruption during the schism, Martin was able to strengthen his revenues from the papal states, which by 1426-7 were not only greater in absolute terms than those enjoyed by Gregory XI before the Great Schism but represented a much larger proportion of papal resources.[22] Governmentally he reunited the administrative machines of the various obediences into a single whole, often allowing existing officials to retain their posts until death even if they were surplus to practical needs. In dealing with the threat posed by the councils, he showed similar tactical skill, complying with the decree *Frequens* by calling a council to Pavia in 1423 and transferring it to Siena following an outbreak of plague, although he did not attend it in person. He had a set of reform proposals drawn up by a commission of cardinals before the council met, but these were not implemented, although in 1425 he issued a reform constitution, mainly concerned with the lifestyle of the curial officials. In general he outflanked the conciliarists by avoiding offence, and although he was reluctant to summon another meeting he accepted the decision of the Council of Siena to have another meeting at Basel in 1431. In dealing with the lay rulers of Christendom, he was equally willing to compromise, by agreeing a series of concordats on various questions such as appointments to benefices, although he did mount a sustained and ultimately unsuccessful campaign to secure the repeal of the English statutes of Provisors and Praemunire of the fourteenth century.

The Council of Basel

Martin's avoidance of confrontation was not matched by his successor Eugenius IV, who lacked his political astuteness. Admittedly he inherited political problems in Italy, and was faced with a council which initially had strong imperial support. The threat posed by the Hussite movement in Bohemia affected the interests of Sigismund,[23] who saw in the council a body which could give him the opportunity to recover his territorial power there. Eugenius in general was more concerned with Italian affairs, and was less aware of the threat which the Hussites were posing to Christendom north of the Alps, where their campaigns into Germany had inflicted considerable damage. Martin, some three weeks before his death, had nominated as his legate to the council Cardinal Cesarini, who had been involved in a crusade against the Hussites and was well aware of their power, and his support gave considerable moral authority to the council in face of papal opposition. From the start Eugenius distrusted it, so it was not surprising that its first concern was to justify its own position in terms of *Frequens,* which it reaffirmed at its first plenary session. About the same time, the pope attempted to dissolve it, but this merely hardened the council's attitude; it justified its legitimacy in terms of *Haec Sancta,* while still treating the pope with respect, and requesting him to revoke the bull of dissolution. The absence of any response led them to affirm that the dissolution was invalid, and to dismiss the alternative council which Eugenius had called to Bologna as an act of schism on the pope's part.[24] Both sides dug in their heels, and had it not been for mediation by Sigismund, who had an interest in keeping on good terms with both sides – the council could assist him in Bohemia, but he also wished for imperial coronation from the pope – a schism would almost certainly have occurred. Throughout 1433 conciliar decrees continued to reassert the terms of *Frequens,* and threaten the pope with suspension and later with deprivation.[25] Eventually, the pope's resistance cracked and he had to acknowledge that the council had been legitimate from the start, announcing his adherence to the council in February 1434. This same period also saw the writing of the most eloquent, but also reasoned and moderate, apologia for the council, the *De Concordantia Catholica* of Nicholas of Cusa. He was willing to accept that the pope had superior standing to other prelates, but asserted that the universal council of the whole Church was greater than any part of it, and that the power of infallibility was given to it rather than to the pope. While he claimed that the council could depose the pope for offences other than heresy, as had been done at Constance, and declared that Eugenius was bound to obey *Frequens,* he had some reservations on the extent of conciliar powers and urged the council to act gently towards the pope.[26]

The mistrust engendered by this early struggle did not disappear, and although the council secured a major success by coming to terms with the Bohemians, paradoxically this was the beginning of its downfall, by removing its main *raison d'être* as far as Sigismund was concerned. The council lost its unanimity, splitting into moderate and radical wings; although most members talked of reform, they envisaged it in different ways – some saw the most pressing task being to purify individual lives and inculcate greater piety, while others focussed their attention on removing corruption from the curial bureaucracy and others again wished to impose constitutional controls on papal authority. Fundamentally the Council of Basel lacked the unifying focus which its predecessor at Constance had had in the desire to end the schism, and as no one wished to bring back the divisions of the 1378–1417 period, action against Eugenius did not attract the same level of support which the rebel cardinals had secured against Urban VI.

Eugenius secured a further advantage when the Byzantine emperor, threatened by the advance of the Ottoman Turks, persuaded the Greek Church to enter into discussions with the West by which military support could be forthcoming in return for a negotiated reunion of the Eastern and the Western churches. On the face of it, one might have expected that the Greeks would have found the council, which was trying to curb the overwhelming power of the pope, a more congenial partner for such discussions, but in the end they perhaps felt that the pope's position was more clear-cut. Furthermore, Eugenius could offer better financial guarantees to support them during the negotiations, so they joined him, first at Ferrara and then at Florence, where a short-lived union of the churches was proclaimed in 1439. Perhaps the effects of this were more important in the West than in the East (where the hard-line traditionalists repudiated the concessions made at Florence), because reactions to the Greek question split the Council of Basel. A minority of the council fathers felt that the prospect of a settlement of the East–West schism was more important than putting further pressure on Eugenius for reform, and transferred their support to the pope. This was all the more important because the minority contained some highly respected men, including Cardinal Cesarini and Nicholas of Cusa.

The departure of such men left the balance of influence in the council in the hands of the radicals, who in 1439 declared Eugenius deposed on grounds of heresy and elected as a new pope of their own Duke Amadeus of Savoy, who took the title of Felix V. But this schism did not have the same effect as that of 1378 because of the attitude of the lay powers. Although the rulers of Christendom exploited the council's actions in their own interests – the French king adopted various reform decrees and promulgated them as French law in the Pragmatic Sanction of Bourges – they had no desire to split the Church in two. Even rulers who opposed Eugenius politically were reluctant to take the final step of supporting an antipope. The short-lived emperor Albert II appointed a protector of the council in 1438, when he was at odds with Eugenius, but this made little impact.[27] After Felix's election, he had little support, and in the course of the 1440s Germany and France, which had adopted a neutral position, were won back to the papal side. At the popular level the *Journal of the Bourgeois of Paris* reflects the shift in opinion – in 1444 the writer commented that 'there were still two popes in Holy Church', but in 1447 he described the antipope as 'Pope Felix, Duke of the Savoyards'.[28] The council remained in existence until 1449, but became increasingly irrelevant to the affairs of the Church. Eventually, after

Eugenius IV's death, a face-saving formula was found by which it dissolved itself and elected as pope the man who had already been chosen by the cardinals. A few years later, the papal point of view was asserted by Pius II, himself a former conciliarist, in his bull *Execrabilis* which forbade appeals to a future general council.[29] In practical terms this did not prevent such appeals, but it reflects the strength of the papal recovery that it could be issued at all.

The legacy of conciliarism

In the final analysis, the conciliar movement failed to impose controls on the Papacy for both theoretical and practical reasons. Because men still believed that it was desirable that the spiritual unity of the Church in cosmic terms should be mirrored in a unitary Church on earth, and saw the authority of the pope as a temporal image of the sovereign power of God, lip service at any rate was paid to his power as a channel of divine authority. Councils could be seen as having a useful function, and even the popes were not averse to calling them, provided that they could control them. At Florence, Eugenius IV not only proclaimed the reunion of the Eastern and Western churches, but also affirmed the papal primacy and condemned the rump assembly at Basel.[30] In the early sixteenth century, a French attempt to call a council to take action against Julius II was effectively nullified when the pope called his own council to the Lateran. The claims of the two great decrees of Constance were effectively set aside, although intermittently enemies of the late fifteenth-century popes called for further meetings in terms of *Frequens,* while pro-papal theoreticians argued that *Haec Sancta* could not be regarded as a legitimate decree of a general council because it (unlike the later *Frequens)* had been approved by the council of a single obedience, not by one representing the Church as a whole.

Intellectual and popular attitudes to conciliar claims remained ambiguous. Even men who were critical of some papalist theory could still accept that the pope was superior to all – this is well exemplified in Lorenzo Valla's devastating demolition of the *Donation of Constantine,* written about 1440, in which he accepted the existence of a papal prerogative which could enable him to impose order on warring Christians.[31] On the other hand, when the French were threatening to call a council in 1479, the Florentine diarist Luca Landucci did not apparently regard this action as improper.[32] Even at the end of the fifteenth century, some writers still justified conciliar authority, at least in theory, and declared the bull *Execrabilis* to be unlawful.[33]

In practical terms, much authority in the Church throughout Christendom rested in the hands of local rulers, whose political ideals tended towards an authoritarian enhancement of royal power. There was nothing which could attract them in conciliar political theory, particularly in the more radical forms espoused by some members of the Council of Basel, who saw ultimate power reposing in the whole body of the faithful, rather than in the clergy and more particularly in the bishops.[34] It was also easier for them to negotiate with a single pope rather than with a council over the practical issues which concerned them most, such as appointments to benefices, legal appeals and the taxation of the clergy. It was only when they could see the possibility of utilising opposition to a pope to further their own ends (which might well relate more to political than to ecclesiastical matters) that they were willing to play the conciliar card. Because their motivation was prompted by such factors, it was natural that in these circumstances their political enemies would rally to the pope. There was never any danger that the Papacy would face a mass desertion of the lay rulers of Europe. Only in the highly abnormal circumstances of the Great Schism, when it was not even clear who was the lawful pope, did the conciliar model of church government have any real chance of being taken seriously.

| 14 |

Intellectual and theological controversies

Diversity of theological thought

As recent chapters have shown, the controversies affecting the late medieval Papacy aroused intellectual as well as political debate, as the contending parties sought to justify their views on the right order in the Church. But it was not simply church government which was called in question, for the later Middle Ages was also a period of philosophical and theological ferment. While it is true that there were some arid controversies, which had little relevance either to the fundamental doctrines of the faith or to the nature of the Christian life (such as how many angels could dance on the point of a needle), many debates were concerned with central issues such as the nature of salvation and the intellectual foundations of theological belief, and foreshadowed the disputes of the Reformation. This is not surprising, because the questions which attracted the attention of the leading sixteenth-century reformers were based on the debates of the previous two centuries. The nature of late medieval theological thought has been subject to considerable debate in recent years, particularly as studies of some of the lesser scholars of the period have shown that earlier classifications of the old and the new schools of thought (*via antiqua* and *via moderna*), in which adherence to particular views was associated with different universities, do not always possess the coherence to stand up to close scrutiny. Indeed, it is increasingly clear that there was considerable eclecticism in theological thought, particularly from the mid-fourteenth century onwards, and that it is impossible to say to which tradition certain writers belonged. In late medieval Oxford, Duns Scotus was the main influence on the theology faculty, although it did not formally adhere to a Scotist syllabus in the way that some German faculties were Thomist or nominalist.[1] Nevertheless, while there was a tendency to eclecticism, there is a modicum of substance in the older interpretations; intellectual struggles could lead to heresy charges being bandied about; an argument at the University of Louvain over divine foreknowledge and the contingency of future events extended to Paris and Köln, and was eventually taken to the papal Curia for decision. In the aftermath of this struggle the French king restricted the range of philosophical teaching at Paris to upholders of older school.[2]

During the thirteenth century scholastic theology had made a bold attempt to incorporate Aristotelian philosophy into a synthesis with Christian doctrine, but this had created intellectual tensions, and, as already noted, a substantial number of propositions advanced in the universities, including some in the writings of Aquinas, were condemned at Paris in 1270 and 1277.[3] The condemnations did not inhibit future intellectual debate, but they did lead to some reorientation of theological speculation, more particularly in the abandonment of attempts to produce comprehensive accounts of Christian belief, such as that of the *Summa* of Aquinas. Debates tended to focus on particular areas of belief, and the controversies engendered in these affected the Church down to and indeed after the Reformation. Much of this theological debate was confined to academic circles, and the problems did not concern a wider public, but in two notable cases, in England and Bohemia, the teachings of John Wyclif and Jan Hus had at least some part in laying the foundations for popular heretical movements. These will be considered later,[4] but it is important to set them in their academic context, because later medieval theological speculation was rooted in the universities. The number of these proliferated in the later Middle Ages, as individual rulers, and sometimes also bishops, apparently regarded the existence of a university within their lands as something of a status symbol, as well as a means of training men who could serve in their administrations. The fourteenth-century establishment of the University of Prague was followed by other foundations in eastern Europe, various German principalities acquired them in the years around 1400, and even as remote a country as Scotland saw its first university at St Andrews in the early fifteenth century, and two more, at Glasgow and Aberdeen, before 1500. The division of Christendom during the Great Schism probably gave an incentive to new foundations, as kings and bishops wished to save their subjects from the dangers of studying in institutions which lay within the obedience of a man whom they regarded as an antipope. Paris retained a certain primacy in the world of learning, but Oxford became more of a national and less of a supranational institution than it had been previously.[5] In the context of the Schism, it is hardly surprising that university-trained scholars also played a crucial role in the debates of the Councils of Constance and Basel.

God's power and salvation

At the heart of the controversies in the 1270s was the question of how far Christian thought could draw on the skills of pagan philosophy, a matter on which the Parisian condemnations were severely critical. One effect of these was that later theologians laid more stress on the revealed teachings of Scripture and a greater emphasis on faith at the expense of reason. It was felt that an emphasis on reason restricted the freedom of God, whereas by contrast later medieval theology was concerned with vindicating the freedom and omnipotence of the divine will. The first great theologian to stress this was the Franciscan Duns Scotus, but his ideas were taken further by William of Ockham. These two in some senses represented a reaction against Aquinas, and his belief in divine reason, and were the most important influence on later writers. Aquinas was still respected and his teaching made a significant contribution to many theological debates of the period. In order to avoid claiming that God could be completely irrational, the theologians of the period drew a distinction between two aspects of God's power, *potentia absoluta* (absolute power) and *potentia ordinata* (ordained power). The former represented God as totally free, subject only to the logical principle of contradiction (e.g. that God could not both save and damn an individual), while the latter represented the normal exercise of divine power, because God had of his own free will bound himself to act in accordance with a consistent natural law. Significantly, this self-restriction of God was connected with the biblical concept of a covenant, which left the initiative in divine hands. While there was an agreement on the existence of a covenant, however, there was still disagreement about its precise terms. This meant that while many theologians of the period started from similar metaphysical foundations, they could still come to diverse conclusions. The belief, however, that God acted within his own rules left some freedom of human action in the spheres of religion and ethics. While God might theoretically save a man who had not received grace and not save one who had, as Ockham argued that he could, he would not normally do so.[6]

Indeed, some of the most controversial issues in the theological disputes of the period were bound up with the doctrine of salvation. This belief was crucial, and depended on the doctrine of the fall, that man, because of Adam's disobedience to God, was unable not to sin. This was not a matter of purely academic concern, because it was also related to the Church's pastoral activity and to the eternal destiny of individual members of the faithful, who were themselves concerned with it. If God could predestine individuals to salvation irrespective of anything which they had done, two important questions followed: what was the role of the Church and its sacraments in the process of salvation, and why should its pastoral teachings inculcate moral behaviour? The more purely philosophical theologians tended to lay stress on the intellectual arguments for God's power, while preachers and theologians with a stronger pastoral interest gave greater weight to the part which an individual had in establishing his or her own destiny.

Indeed, the development of a more educated lay public throughout Western Christendom had led to a growth among the laity of a tendency to a do-it-yourself religion. This had already emerged in both orthodox and heretical circles, posing problems in the thirteenth century,[7] and had repercussions in the academic debates as to how the processes of salvation operated. This was nothing new – the question of man's participation in his salvation had been debated between Augustine and Pelagius in the fifth century, with the former affirming that only God could save and the latter asserting that each individual had a responsibility for his own destiny. The teaching of the church had sided with Augustine, affirming that three things were necessary to justify fallen man, the infusion of healing grace (reliance on the Church and the sacraments), the free turning of the will to God and away from sin (the participation of the individual with grace), and the remission of sin by priestly absolution. In the fourteenth-century debates, it was the second of these issues which provoked the most bitter controversies, because the affirmation of God's omnipotence had as a corollary the belief that man could not be free. The Oxford theologian Thomas Bradwardine, who died in 1349, attacked as 'plaguey Pelagians' (*pelagiani pestiferi*) those men, essentially of the Ockhamist tradition, who tried to defend the idea of human moral autonomy. The question of free will had been a major topic of discussion at Oxford from the 1330s onwards.[8] The Ockhamist tradition, relying on a covenant theology, asserted that by his *potentia ordinata* God had voluntarily accepted human participation in the process of salvation – Robert Holcot still affirmed the freedom of God (even to the extent of asserting that theoretically God could will that man hate him), but by asserting that God acted consistently, he would grant grace to those who disposed themselves to receive it.[9] For theologians of this school, God would not deny grace to individuals who tried to act well according to what was in them (*facere quod in se est*), and that such an infusion of grace was part of the world order established by divine *potentia ordinata*.

Ockham denied that his views were Pelagian – where the fifth-century writer had claimed that individuals could earn salvation by doing their moral best, he claimed that such an effort could only obtain the grace necessary to salvation. These views certainly tended towards Pelagianism, and there was a powerful Augustinian reaction voiced in the works of Gregory of Rimini, whose pessimism about human nature was as deep as his master's. This led him to adopt an extreme predestinarian view, that God could determine the fate of individuals to salvation or damnation as he pleased, irrespective of his foreknowledge of any moral acts which they might or might not perform.[10] In such teachings, one hears the premonitory foreshadowing of Calvinist theology two centuries later.

Scripture and Tradition

The connected themes of justification and predestination run through the theological debates of the later Middle Ages, and, of course, surfaced again in the controversies of the Reformation. The same was true of another long-standing controversy, over the respective roles of Scripture and Tradition as the foundations of Christian orthodoxy. As long as the two were seen as coherent there was no problem; Augustine had declared, 'I should not have believed the Gospel, had not the authority of the universal Church moved me to do so', but he also raised the issue of what was to be done on matters where the Scriptures gave no guidance, because such questions had not arisen in biblical times. Here Tradition was seen as a means of supplementing the Scriptures. By the fourteenth century, however, it was no longer accepted that Scripture and Tradition necessarily cohered, and Ockham was generally sympathetic to the idea that there were truths which were neither explicitly stated in the Scriptures nor could be logically deduced from the Bible. On the other hand, Thomas Bradwardine at Oxford upheld the principle of *sola Scriptura* (Scripture alone), and although he himself was never suspected of heresy, in this he was followed by Wyclif and Hus, both of whom were ultimately condemned by the Church. A stress on *sola Scriptura*, however, did not inevitably lead to an individual being suspected of unorthodoxy – the fifteenth-century Dutch theologian Wessel Gansfort upheld it.[11] The emphasis on Scripture as the sole authority for doctrine reflected the move from a natural theology, supported by reason, to the stress on truth as something which only God could reveal. It also posed something of a challenge to the teaching authority of the Church, if individuals could claim that an infallible text was more dependable than papal pronouncements, and in Wyclif's case this challenge to established authority was all the more serious because he also developed an increasingly virulent hostility to the Papacy.

Wyclif

Wyclif, however, raised two more serious challenges to accepted orthodox belief and practice, when he challenged the doctrine of transubstantiation in the Eucharist which had been formally defined at the Fourth Lateran Council and when he supported the translation of the Scriptures into the vernacular. The former had laid a foundation for the development of the cult of the sacrament, symbolised most clearly by the establishment of the feast of Corpus Christi in the thirteenth century. This had widespread popular appeal, and significantly a number of late medieval religious guilds were dedicated to the sacrament. Wyclif's teaching on this developed gradually, and was influenced by both his realist metaphysics and by his biblicism. It was subtle and intellectual, and did not totally deny traditional doctrine, arguing that the essence of the elements remained even when the body of Christ was present in them. (His less educated followers were to simplify his teachings and take a more fully materialistic view of the sacraments.) Even so, his views served to undermine perceptions of priestly power, as one foundation of this was the belief that only a priest could perform the Eucharistic miracle. His metaphysical views were transmitted to Prague, which had established links with Oxford following the marriage of the young Richard II to Anne of Bohemia, but did not initially lead to the adoption of anti-transubstantiationist teachings there.

The question of whether the Scriptures should be available to all in their native tongues attracted varying answers, and although in England possession of vernacular bibles eventually was regarded as indicating support for heresy, this was not necessarily true in Wyclif's own day. Until at least 1400 writers who criticised his other teachings were still prepared to accept the desirability of making the Bible available to a wider audience. (The subsequent ownership of texts of the so-called 'Wycliffite Bible' shows that the translation which he inspired was used in orthodox quarters.) It was probably because of Wyclif's doctrinal unorthodoxy that the idea of the vernacular Scriptures became and remained unacceptable to the English ecclesiastical establishment, probably to a greater extent than elsewhere in Christendom. The question of the accessibility of the Bible to the people is bound up with popular religion, but the concern for the Scriptures must be understood not only in terms of individuals wishing to have available the basic texts of the faith for their personal devotions but also in relation to the debates on the question of Scripture and Tradition. When Wyclif wrote on the truth of the Scriptures, he had three main aims: to demonstrate the inerrancy of the Bible, which rested on its divine authorship, to emphasise that it must be the touchstone by which other teachings were judged, and to argue that it must be placed at the disposal of all Christians.[12] In the second of these matters he was concerned with a far wider area of theological thought than the simply pastoral one.

Wyclif's teachings were formally condemned by the Church, and earlier papal decrees against him were upheld at the Council of Rome in 1412 and by the Council of Constance in 1415, which also ordered that his body be exhumed and burned.[13] His condemnation may have undermined the prominence of Oxford in the intellectual life of Christendom, as the university was tarred with the brush of his heresy. The council's affirmation of doctrinal orthodoxy can also be seen in the considerable time it spent in proceedings against the Bohemian theologian Jan Hus, and his follower Jerome of Prague, both of whom went to the stake.[14] The council's action stressed the authority of the Church as the guarantor of accepted doctrine, and may have been partly prompted by a desire to depict itself to the world as fundamentally orthodox at a time when it was taking revolutionary steps to challenge another traditional belief by undermining papal authority. It is worth stressing that the council's proceedings represented the most extreme sanction against alleged heresy taken by a central authority in the Church, as it was at the time, at any point in the later Middle Ages. While it would be erroneous to argue that the age was a tolerant one, it must be stressed that the pre-Reformation Church was prepared to accept a wider range of doctrinal opinion than the successor churches of the sixteenth and later centuries, where each sect became liable to insist that its members accepted every jot and tittle of its confession. In the later Middle Ages some debate was acceptable, provided that new teachings were not seen as infringing the substance of the faith. Individuals might overstep acceptable limits, but if they were prepared to accept the condemnation of their views, they were allowed to recant and return to the fold of the Church. Only men such as Wyclif, who obstinately adhered to their views, put themselves beyond the pale. He was exceptional, and most dissidents were prepared to compromise with the authority of the Church.

The Franciscan dissidents

Some areas of theological debate had practical implications. This was most notably true of the Franciscan radicals, whose whole lifestyle was underpinned by a doctrinal belief in the absolute poverty of Christ and the apostles; if their life was to be a true imitation of Christ, they too had to live in this way. From the start, this had posed problems for the order,[15] but a practical compromise had been reached on poverty and property by the Papacy undertaking the role of trustee for it. This had satisfied the majority of the order, but even its less rigorous members became embroiled in controversy in the early fourteenth century, when John XXII made it clear that he was unwilling to maintain the compromise; he not only insisted that the Franciscans should undertake responsibility for their possessions but also declared that it was heretical to believe in the absolute poverty of Christ and the apostles. This latter assertion led to a break between the pope and the order, and to accusations of heresy being made against John by Ockham, who was closely associated with Michael of Cesena, the general of the order. In fact, although the pope was not a theologian by training he clearly fancied himself as such, for he later became involved in another controversy, which further fuelled hostility to him, on the question of whether the blessed enjoyed the Beatific Vision immediately after death or would have to await the Last Judgement. Although his support for the latter view was later set aside, it was never formally condemned as heretical. The episode demonstrates, however, how some theological controversies had little impact on the Church's general teaching.

Mystical theology

While debates continued on the foundations of theological authority, and while the issues posed by the reception of Aristotelian philosophy into the schools remained prominent in scholastic disputation, there was also a reaction against the aridity of some logic-chopping. In addition to the categories of natural and revealed theology, an active school of mystical writing also developed, starting from the premise that man can know God by some form of direct apprehension. While in one sense this represented a flight from the metaphysical approach of the schools, it was not entirely incompatible with contemporary academic thought, because the mystics, who believed in the possibility of a direct apprehension of God, were operating within the framework of believing in God's absolute power, which could break through the normal processes of salvation.

The mystical approach to God was not new, and indeed not exclusively Christian, but the demand for devotional material by an increasingly articulate lay society probably stimulated the production of a wide variety of such works. The writings of the later period looked back to the thought of the twelfth century and beyond, and it is noteworthy that the works of St Bernard, who had been critical of more speculative theology, were an influential source for many of them. What the later Middle Ages saw was less a rise of mystical movements than the fact that they became increasingly articulate and literate. The phenomenon was widespread, and one finds mystical and devotional writings throughout Europe – there was an active school of writers in England, another in the Rhineland, and other similar writers in Italy. Some works were in Latin, others in the vernacular. The authors varied in type, for some were academically trained and wrote in the technical language of the schools, while others wrote (or had written for them) accounts of their personal spiritual experiences in non-learned terms. Their purposes in writing varied, and one should distinguish between mystical works, which attempt to express ideas beyond the scope of normal reason, and devotional manuals which were directed to a wider public among the faithful to try and deepen the quality of the readers' spiritual lives.

As with scholastic philosophy, there is a danger in excessively clear-cut characterisation of mystical schools, because there were considerable overlaps between those who saw the mystic way as an attempt to attain union with the divine will and those who sought union with the divine intellect. A powerful influence on some writers was the writings of 'pseudo-Dionysius', probably a Syrian monk from the early sixth century, but whose works were attributed to Dionysius the Areopagite, St Paul's Athenian convert, and for this reason were viewed as meriting particular respect. Above all, this writer stressed the belief that God transcended reason and that the divine nature remained hidden. Ideas were expressed in terms of paradoxes, that God was best known through unknowing, by going beyond mind and reason. The fourteenth-century English writer of *The Cloud of Unknowing* and the fifteenth-century German Nicholas of Cusa in his *Docta Ignorantia* (Learned Ignorance) were among those influenced by this tradition. Cusa, whose conciliarist writings have already been considered,[16] was perhaps the most outstanding figure in the fifteenth-century Church, both a man of thought and a man of action, but in his theological ideas he stands apart from the mainstream. Possibly this was partly due to his departure from the world of academic theology for the controversies of the later conciliar movement, and later for the responsibilities of a cardinal and a diocesan bishop, but it must also be understood in terms of the nature of his thought, which was individual and personal. It was not accidental that he was also a mathematician, because the characteristic of God which lies at the centre of his thought was his infinity, and the impossibility of the gap between finite and infinite being bridged, except in the person of Jesus, the absolute mediator.[17]

The mystics' writings aroused suspicion, and the ecclesiastical authorities' concerns are understandable. Even if the views expressed were orthodox, the belief that individuals could apprehend God directly made the established sacramental procedures of the Church irrelevant. The mystics normally regarded themselves as loyal members of the Church, and might well play an active part in its life. The great German mystic Meister Eckhart was provincial of the Saxon province of his Dominican order for eight years, was an active preacher to clergy and laity, and certainly regarded himself as orthodox. When accused of heresy he defended himself with the intellectual skill appropriate to his order, protesting that while he might err, he could not be a heretic, because the former act was concerned with the intellect and the latter with the will.[18] He willingly accepted the sacramental demands of the Church, urging frequent communion on the faithful, and saying in his *Talks of Instruction* that it was proper for an individual to go to confession, even if his conscience was clear, but he also urged that a guilty person should admit a fault to God if no opportunity for confession was available, and rest easy until one was.[19] Here perhaps he laid himself open to criticism, because it gave the individual an opportunity to disregard routine ecclesiastical discipline. The authorities may not have been entirely unjustified in their fears because there was a danger that a do-it-yourself religion might lapse into heresy (and thereby lead to eternal damnation) if it were not subject to strict supervision. The problem may well have been that while the writers themselves understood their ideas as orthodox, the problem of trying to express ideas beyond the scope of normal language, particularly if they used the vernacular, left them vulnerable to misinterpretation by their contemporaries. The posthumous condemnation of twenty-eight articles drawn from Eckhart's writings in 1329 may also have been influenced by the atmosphere of tension at the time and a sense of fear within the ecclesiastical establishment which was also facing the critical attacks on the Papacy by Marsilius of Padua and William of Ockham.[20] Most mystical thought, however, was channelled into pious and devotional movements rather than into academic debate, but it had a long-term influence on the writings of some sixteenth-century German reformers, notably Luther, who was well acquainted with the writings of some of Eckhart's successors.

Varieties of theological development

From at least the twelfth century the person of the Virgin Mary had been a focus for devotion, and although the initial impetus to this had come from popular sentiment, theological writings also took up the theme, most notably in the debates over the Immaculate Conception. Here Aquinas had criticised the new teachings (being followed in this by other Dominicans), whereas the Franciscans particularly had popularised the cult of Mary. The first major academic theologian to argue for the Immaculate Conception was Scotus, and by the end of the fourteenth century this doctrine had been accepted by many outside the Franciscan order, including Gerson. The Council of Basel proclaimed the doctrine as the official teaching of the Church in 1439, but doubts about the council's status left the validity of this declaration doubtful after the end of the Basel schism. (Indeed, the Dominicans used the proclamation as a stick with which to beat the council.) It was significantly a Franciscan pope, Sixtus IV, who gave further authority to the doctrine in 1476, by granting indulgences to all who attended services on the feast of the Conception, although this action gave rise to considerable controversy in succeeding years.[21] Although this particular doctrinal issue was out of the mainstream of earlier controversy, the debates on it demonstrate how theology could represent beliefs seeking support as well as faith seeking understanding.

One final influence which coloured late medieval religious thought was Renaissance humanism. The emphasis of the new learning on trying to establish the precise texts of ancient works was something which affected religious thought, not least because of the stress placed on the authority of Scripture. Those influenced by the new scholarship demanded a critical approach to the sacred text, and this had a profound influence on its interpretation. By the fifteenth century, attempts were being made to go back to the precise meaning of the sources. The Italian humanist scholar Lorenzo Valla's philological studies in his *Adnotationes in Novum Testamentum* influenced the Dutchman Erasmus in preparing his new edition of the text, and the Florentine humanist Marsilio Ficino influenced the English churchman John Colet whose scriptural exegesis moved away from the medieval traditions of allegorical reading of the text to an attempt to understand its literal meaning. In Spain, the reforming cardinal Ximénez de Cisneros masterminded the production of the Complutensian Polyglot Bible, which provided editions of Greek, Hebrew and Aramaic texts alongside the traditional Latin of the Vulgate.[22] It was possible to harness the linguistic skills of classical learning to the service of theology, not only in biblical studies but also in preparing new editions of the Church Fathers, whose works were regarded as crucial in the development of ecclesiastical tradition. At the same time the Church repudiated any adherence to the more secular philosophies of the ancient world.

The Church's intellectual life in this period, therefore, should be seen as

active rather than stagnant. While there were no thinkers of outstanding distinction after the death of Ockham, there were still men who were willing to
tackle doctrinal problems, and to respond to questions which were raised.
Different traditions of theological interpretation could co-exist, and only
occasionally did individual writers who overstepped the accepted bounds of
the Church's teaching have to retract or suffer punishment. It is not quite
certain why this was the case, but it may be that the main themes of ecclesiastical debate from the late fourteenth century onwards were focussed less
on questions of doctrine and belief and more on issues of church government, where the conciliar challenge posed more of a threat to stability than
the views of dissident theologians, not least because the Council of
Constance had firmly committed itself to traditional orthodoxy by its
posthumous condemnation of Wyclif and by burning Hus. When one looks
at the circumstances in which the Reformation broke out, the crucial
moment was not Luther's posting of his ninety-five theses on indulgences at
Wittenberg in 1517, but his subsequent burning of the papal bull condemning him. The former had been simply a challenge to academic disputation,
the latter called in question the authority of the ecclesiastical establishment.

|15|

Piety – orthodox and heretical

The pursuit of piety

Although academic theologians were active in debating doctrinal issues, and at times crossed the divide between orthodoxy and heresy, such matters had little concern for most people, who were more concerned to remain faithful, and attain salvation in eternity. It is misleading to differentiate too much between 'lay religion' and clerical ideals, because the underlying principles behind both were the same, and even individuals who remained in the lay world still saw their spiritual ideals in terms of those of the clerical life – ultra-pious members of the laity tried to live lives as close as possible to those of churchmen, with regular prayer and penances, the living of an austere life, and the observance of celibacy (even among the married). Some of the most characteristic religious movements of the period lay on the margins between clerical and lay society, and drew both churchmen and laymen into them. The appearance of the spiritually concerned layman reflected also the growth of a more literate lay society, some members of which wished to follow a pious way of life. The ideal of the *vita mixta* (mixed life), in which an individual lived in the world at the same time as following a spiritual discipline, was characteristic of this period. It reflects an emerging religious individualism, which might be seen as a challenge to the Church establishment, even though the Church had determined the essential parameters of a pious existence. The acceptance of these can be seen in the popular acclamation of certain individuals as saints (some clerical but others lay), of whom some received official approbation from the Church. Charles of Blois, the Duke of Brittany (d. 1364), took a vow of chastity after he had begotten heirs, thus compromising between his social obligations and his religious ideals. He also went regularly to confession and practised the discipline of flagellation. He was popularly regarded as a saint, and was eventually beatified by the Church. Such acclaim is a good barometer of the religious sensibilities of the age, while his beatification demonstrates official approval of them.

The main characteristic of such laity who aspired to a pious life was the pursuit of practices originating in the ideals of the religious orders, notably in their attempts to curb two of the most basic of human instincts, the wish to preserve oneself by maintaining an adequate diet and the desire to perpetuate the species by sexual intercourse. Such austere modes of life were not for the majority, but were regarded as pleasing to God, and significantly were admired even by those who did not wish to participate in them, or at least not all the time. The Florentine merchant Gregorio Dati resolved in 1404 to keep every Friday and the following night as a time of total chastity and abstinence from carnal pleasures in memory of the Passion of Jesus, undertaking a penalty for any failure to observe this vow.[1] The Church's teaching on sex was ambivalent, because God's command in Genesis to living creatures to increase and multiply could not be easily reconciled with St Paul's criticism of sexual acts, mitigated only by his reluctant statement that it was better to marry than to burn. In general it was accepted that procreative sex as such was not sinful, but that associated carnal desire was. Sexual relations, even between spouses, simply for the pleasure of the participants were undoubtedly a sin, although the gravity of the sin might vary according to the nature of the act.[2] Ambivalent attitudes can be seen also among the laity; at the end of the fourteenth century Philippe de Mézières' *Letter to King Richard II,* in which he urged a marriage alliance between the French and English royal houses, to unify Europe for a crusade against the advancing powers of Islam, also spend considerable time praising the virtues of virginity and chastity, which one would have thought might have diminished the effectiveness of any such alliance.[3]

Death and judgement

Behind many spiritual practices lay the belief that man was simply a pilgrim on the earth, and that life's essential purpose was to prepare for eternity. In a late medieval London merchant's will, death was described as 'departing out of this vale of misery'. The 'Four Last Things', heaven, hell, death and judgement, and more particularly the last of these, set the tone of much religious observance. Life, of course, was always vulnerable; the early fourteenth century saw widespread famines and the sense of impending doom may well have been heightened by the Black Death, the outbreak of plague which swept across Western Europe from 1347 onwards, killing perhaps as much as or more than one third of the population, with the disease remaining endemic for generations. Some surviving visual images of the transitory nature of life antedated the plague – *The Triumph of Death,* as depicted in the Camposanto at Pisa, was probably painted before 1347, and that of the 'Three living and the Three dead', in which three travellers or three hunters encounter the same number of corpses, first appeared in the late thirteenth century – but their numbers were multiplied after it. The theme of the Dance of Death, developed in both literary and visual imagery, showing death leading individuals of all social classes, became increasingly widespread throughout Europe in the fifteenth century. The imagery in the cemetery of the Innocents in Paris was copied at St Paul's in London in the 1420s, and a printed edition of it was produced in Paris in 1486, presumably as an aid to devotion.[4] The Scots poet William Dunbar, in his *Lament for the Makars* (poets), written around 1500, with its refrain, *Timor mortis conturbat me* ('the fear of death disquiets my mind'), described how death took all irrespective of their earthly condition. Clearly in one sense this idea was a commonplace, but its significance in the religiosity of the period is demonstrated by the particularly lurid forms in which it was often depicted, notably in the grisly 'cadaver' tombs, such as those of the late fifteenth-century French kings in the abbey of St Denis. The imagery was intended to act as a *memento mori* to the living, so that they in turn would make a good end when their time came. A whole genre of literature was devoted to the art of dying well, the *ars moriendi*, with the soul being depicted as a battleground between God and the devil, where it could remain in danger until the end. Even men who had no particular love for priests would call for them when they were faced with the prospect of eternity. The Florentine Buonaccorso Pitti, who claimed that he had never met an honest priest, still sent for one when he believed that he was dying.[5] Another, and perhaps more pious, Florentine diarist, Gregorio Dati, commented on the deaths of various of his family that they had received the last sacraments before death – in the case of his mother, he said that she had 'returned her soul to her Creator'.[6]

After death, provision was made for intercession for the soul of the departed by friends and relatives, so as to shorten the time that it might have to spend in purgatory. The concept of this intermediate state between heaven and hell had been developed in the thirteenth century, and was finally declared to be an article of faith at the time of the reunion with the Greek Church at the Council of Florence. The formal definition of the doctrine followed the development of popular belief on the subject, an indication of how popular religious attitudes might compel the church authorities to clarify their teaching. It provided a means by which those who had not been so evil as to be damned for eternity might atone for their sins and eventually enter into bliss, though there was some disagreement as to whether the soul would undergo purgation immediately after death or only after the Last Judgement. The doctrine was developed of the 'Treasury of Merits' by which Christ and the saints accumulated grace which could be redistributed in indulgences to relieve others of the pains of purgatory, provided that they had duly confessed their sins and received absolution. In the fifteenth century, however, there was a significant development in indulgence theology when it was officially affirmed that indulgences could be applied to the souls of the dead.[7] The growth of indulgences represented one means of assisting the soul on its way through purgatory, but there were other pious practices devoted to the same end in the endowment of prayers by the living and the celebration of masses for the deceased.

In this the Church's pastoral theology might well be out of line with some of the doctrines taught in the schools, notably that of predestination, which made no allowance for the existence of purgatory. Men were encouraged to perform good works as a religious duty, and in this there were certainly undertones of Pelagianism, for although these could not be held to guarantee salvation such acts were generally assumed to be meritorious. Indeed, they were classified in terms of the seven works of mercy, most of which derived from the parable of the sheep and the goats. Men made provision for their future blessedness by charitable endowments, according to their individual resources. The Church criticised the accumulation of wealth, but if an individual believed that he held his goods as a trust from God, for which he would have to account, wealth need not be a barrier to salvation. Rich men, such as Francesco di Marco Datini of Prato, who died in 1410, left substantial endowments; he bequeathed most of his resources to the commune to meet the needs of the poor.[8] Preachers emphasised the spiritual merits of good social conduct: the thirteenth-century Franciscan St Anthony of Padua stressed particularly the moral significance of the text on which he was preaching, and St Bernardino of Siena, one of the greatest fifteenth-century friars, denounced the tendency of men to pursue vendettas as though it were a moral duty, and launched diatribes against gambling.[9]

Preachers and their followers

Talented preachers could exercise considerable moral influence over the populace as a whole. Perhaps the most extraordinary example of this was the Dominican friar Savonarola, who established himself as a virtual spiritual dictator over the sophisticated citizens of Florence. Even such a wealthy city was willing to accept the idealisation of poverty and austerity, and burn the 'vanities' which were regarded as a symbol of man's corruption. The diarist Luca Landucci, writing of 1494, accepted Savonarola as a prophet and approved the moral principles behind his rule, and when the friar fell from power he lamented the fact, adding 'God be praised that I saw this short period of holiness'.[10] Savonarola's influence was unique in its extent, although it was short-lived, probably because he fell foul of the Papacy, which worked actively to bring him down, but his ideals were similar to those of other preachers; a Franciscan called Brother Richard persuaded the Parisians in 1429 to burn various games and dice, and destroy frivolous articles of clothing. When, after his departure, he was reported to have joined the Armagnacs, pro-Burgundian citizens resumed the games which he had forbidden, to the disgust of a contemporary diarist, who still respected him.[11]

In these cases the preachers influenced the faithful in their own communities, but on other occasions religious movements were more wide-spread. Nowhere was this more conspicuous than in the Flagellant movement, which appeared for the first time in 1260, the year which the followers of Joachim of Fiore had seen as the likely date for the start of the Third Age.[12] The movement survived more strongly in Italy, where various fraternities practised the discipline as a means of identifying with the sufferings of Christ, and had the support of the secular and religious authorities. It seems to have been particularly active at times of apocalyptic expectation – a contemporary diarist records a case of a procession from Naples to Rome in 1500 in which the participants had backs bleeding from the penances which they had inflicted on themselves. In Germany, by contrast, the movement incurred the opposition of the establishment, and when Flagellant groups attempted to enter France in the aftermath of the Black Death, the king forbade them to enter the country, for fear of popular disorder. In this action he was supported by both the pope and the University of Paris.[13] Other movements were less flamboyant; the Bianchi, so-called from the simple white linen which they wore, held processions throughout a large part of Italy, following a Lenten diet and dedicating themselves to nine days of devotion, hearing masses, singing and praying in unison, and listening to sermons. Their activities focussed on devotion rather than on the more ascetic forms of penitence, and they also seem to have tried to bring about reconciliations in their communities, a point noted by Buonaccorso Pitti.[14]

Guilds and corporate religion

Corporate devotional activity was a marked feature of late medieval religious life. In England, most parishes had guilds which provided opportunities for voluntary observances beyond the routine obligations laid on individuals by the Church. Their functions varied according to the desires of the founders and the scale of their resources, but there is no doubt that the increase of worship was the essential element in their activity. This might involve the saying of masses, particularly for the souls of deceased guild members, or the support of specified services in the church. This parallels the groups in Italy known as the Laudesi, which had as their main role the singing of services. In some cases the guilds also provided practical charity in the form of financial support for unemployed members, a clear demonstration of how religious observance was directed into action. It is of course hard to estimate the level of personal devotion among guild members, even though the activity was voluntary, because in some cases guild membership may have been regarded as a symbol of social status. (The Corpus Christi guild at York Minster, for example, probably had a measure of snob appeal as various members of the royal family were also among the guild brothers.) There may also have been attempts to use guilds as instruments of social control, because some Florentine groups from the late fourteenth century were intended to provide spiritual education for young people and to keep them away from 'inane spectacles and games'.

Sacramental obligations

But although such bodies were firmly committed to religious orthodoxy, and might well work in conjunction with the ecclesiastical authorities, their organisation was often kept under lay control, with the guild priests being hired and dismissed by lay wardens. In the Church's routine observances the laity were kept in a subordinate role, because normally only priests could administer the sacraments, although in an emergency a layman could baptise an infant who might die before the priest arrived. The decree of the Fourth Lateran Council in 1215 that all the faithful should confess to their own priest at least once a year, and receive the Eucharist at Easter, unless advised not to do so by their priest, represented an important development in sacramental practice because it strengthened existing obligations on the laity and gave the authorities greater disciplinary sanctions against those who did not comply.[15] It also emphasised the private nature of confession, and may well have influenced the personal character of late medieval religion. The period after 1215 saw the production of manuals for confessors, to enable them to assist penitents to a proper state of contrition, and hence to absolution. These tended to classify offences in various categories, such as breaches of the Ten Commandments or commission of the Seven Deadly Sins. Many offences were subdivided into more specific categories – for example, simony, theft, usury and fraud were among the possible manifestations of avarice. Attempts were made to distinguish between venial and mortal sins (a matter which led to divergence among the moral theologians), and penitents had to be instructed in what precisely these were, because it is evident that some people's moral scruples led them to an excess of confession. The authorities were prepared to recognise the complexity of human nature and, at least in theory, attempted to deal with the neuroses of the over-sensitive.[16]

Pilgrimages and relics

It is easier to identify the Church's teaching on confession and penance than to estimate how far it was followed in practice or to judge how pious the majority of the people were. In many cases their motives were probably mixed, and while one should not take Chaucer's picture as a literal description of what a pilgrimage was, and may suspect that for some pilgrims the break from daily routine was as much a reason for their journey as any desire for spiritual benefits, it is worth stressing that the imaginary journey was set within the framework of a well-attested devotion to St Thomas of

Canterbury. The experiences of the indefatigable English pilgrim, Margery Kempe of Lynn, in the early fifteenth century demonstrate that travel was at best difficult and often dangerous, but such problems did not prevent her from journeying to Palestine, Rome, Spain and the Baltic to visit holy places. As at an earlier period,[17] devotion was often bound up with particular places and with tangible objects such as relics. Increasingly too, with the development of indulgences, visits to holy places were an opportunity to acquire pardons and a release of time in purgatory. An English description of the churches of Rome about 1470 gives details of the indulgences attached to each church.[18] In some cases relics might be displayed to the pilgrims. These were still regarded with awe – during the English invasion of France a monk of St Denis took certain precious relics to the Dauphin at Bourges, so that they should not fall into English hands, and they were restored only after the expulsion of the English, with large numbers of the faithful accompanying them.[19] When the Emperor Frederick III visited Italy, the clergy who met him in procession at Siena carried relics with them. The most conspicuous example of the relic cult in this period was the reception of the head of St Andrew in Rome during the pontificate of Pius II, whose *Commentaries* tell how it was brought from Patras to Italy by the brother of the last Byzantine emperor at the time of the Turkish advance. Many lay princes tried to buy the relic, but Pius declared that the relic should be kept along with those of St Peter. After it was declared genuine, it was received in Rome with great ceremonial.[20]

Such cults attracted some criticism. Satirists, such as Chaucer, poked fun at pardoners with bogus relics, but some leading churchmen also had reservations about such manifestations of popular piety. During Cardinal Nicholas of Cusa's legatine mission to Germany in 1451–2, he was particularly critical of the three so-called 'bleeding hosts' at Wilsnack in Brandenburg. This cult, taken as visible evidence for transubstantiation, attracted widespread devotion as a focus on the miracle of the mass. Nevertheless, when he issued a decree against reverence being paid to them, indulgences were still granted to pilgrims visiting the church, although it was stipulated that a recently consecrated host be exposed for veneration alongside the alleged miraculous ones.[21] The popular appeal of relics is well documented in numerous references to them in the accounts of two Bohemian travellers who toured Europe in the mid-1460s – wherever they went they noted both what relics were preserved in churches and the miracles which they had allegedly worked.[22] The wealthy collected them. English wills record bequests of relics – Philippa, Countess of March, bequeathed a ring containing part of the Cross, and her husband Edmund also had a relic of it. More likely to be genuine were his remains of more recent English saints, a bone of St Richard of Chichester, a finger of St Thomas Cantilupe and a relic of Becket.[23] It is a historical irony that one of the most avid collectors of relics (with their attached indulgences) in the early sixteenth century was Luther's patron, the Elector Frederick of Saxony.

Reform movements – the Devotio Moderna

Although there were many common features in popular devotion throughout Europe, the later Middle Ages did not see the development of great reform movements which spread throughout the whole of the Western Church, comparable to the burgeoning of the Cistercians in the twelfth century or of the friars in the thirteenth. Despite concern at the Council of Constance for reform 'in the members' as well as 'of the head', no individual nor institution took the initiative in reinvigorating the Church's life. Movements for reform in the period tended to be more geographically limited. The reformed Observant wing of the Franciscans spread throughout Europe, but did not develop as a movement on the scale of earlier reforms in the religious orders. More significant were various localised attempts to restore rigorous observance, among the Benedictines at Melk in Austria and at Santa Giustina and Subiaco in Italy, which had some wider repercussions, as monks from reformed houses were sent to revitalise houses which had fallen into decline.

One notable movement for regular reform was the Windesheim congregation, which was closely linked with the most distinctive religious movement of the later Middle Ages, that known as the Devotio Moderna. This again was predominantly local in character, being centred in the Netherlands. It inherited some characteristics from those religious groups which lay on the margin between lay devotion and clerical piety, in that it could not be strictly described as an order, but was rather, originally, a group of devout people who wished to pursue a more pious life. Its inspiration was Gerard Groote (*c*.1340–84), the son of a cloth merchant at Deventer, who had embarked on a clerical career and had studied at Paris, obtaining provisions to canonries at Aachen and Utrecht. Accounts of his life seem like stylised hagiography, which would edify the hearer by stressing his born-again character, but it is probable that he went through some spiritual crisis in a search for personal salvation. He resigned his canonries and gave up his house to a group of poor women, apart from two rooms which he retained for his own use. He also spent two years in a Carthusian house, pursuing a regime of rigid asceticism, and was influenced by the great mystical writer, Jan van Ruysbroeck. He turned his back on contemporary scholastic disputation, drawing his theology from the New Testament and the writings of the Church Fathers. His main concerns were pastoral, and after ordination as a deacon in 1380 he lived the life of an itinerant evangelist preaching to the clergy in Latin and to the people in the vernacular. His actions aroused opposition, and when the bishop of Utrecht forbade deacons to preach he complied with the command, while appealing to Rome to have the decree rescinded. Before any decision was made on his appeal he died of the plague. He was no rebel, but while he could not preach he could still write and give private instruction. He developed a concern for educating boys, in the hope that future leaders of the Church would have a secure

grounding in spiritual matters, and more in these than in intellectual
subtleties.

He was a charismatic figure, so it is not surprising that he attracted followers. The group of poor women to whom he made over his house, and for
whom he compiled a constitution, came to be known as the Sisters of the
Common Life. The pious motivation behind the group was similar to that
which had earlier led women to become beguines, but the sisterhood was
even more informal. The sisters wore no distinctive habit, took no vows on
entering the house, and could leave if they chose, although in this case they
could not return. They were not required to give up their property, but
worked in common, sharing income and expenditure. Groote disapproved
of mendicancy, and believed that the sisters should earn their living by
menial work. But men as well as women were attracted by Groote, and a
brotherhood developed parallel to the sisterhood. Its most notable organiser
was another churchman, Florens Radewijns, whose vicarage served as a
meeting-place for Groote's followers. As the Brethren of the Common Life
developed, Radewijns provided an organisation similar to that of the sisterhood. Again there was no binding vow and an emphasis on labour, particularly the copying of books. The group attempted to combine clergy and laity
in a single community, but increasingly the ordained brothers became
absorbed in a routine of prayer and meditation, and the lay members were
reduced to a subordinate role. The absence of a vow led to criticism and
some attacks on the Brethren, and at the Council of Constance the
Dominican Matthew Grabow, who argued that the life of perfection was
open only to a spiritual elite, who were bound by vows, attempted to accuse
them of heresy. However, they were strongly defended by two of the most
influential figures at the council, Jean Gerson and Pierre d'Ailly.[24]

The Brethren were not opposed to regular observance, and maintained
friendly relations with the Augustinian canons of Windesheim, whose house
was founded in 1387, and which became the driving force behind various
reformed houses in Holland, Belgium and northern Germany. Indeed, many
early recruits to these houses came from the communities of the Brethren,
and the Devotio Moderna's most permanent legacy to the Church came
from one of them. One of the first canons of Windesheim was John à
Kempis, who, like Groote, came from Deventer. He became the first prior of
the house of Agnetenberg, where he was followed by his brother Thomas,
who was professed as a canon in 1407 and took priest's orders in 1413.
Thomas took his share of monastic duties, as subprior and as master of the
novices, but he was above all a writer. Among his works were lives of both
Groote and Radewijns, but he secured literary immortality with his devotional treatise, *The Imitation of Christ,* in which he emphasises that to
follow Christ means taking the way of the Cross, which involved living an
ascetic life. (By the end of the fifteenth century, the young Erasmus reacted
against this.) Its first three books deal with the inner life, and the fourth with
the Eucharist. The work stressed personal faith, based on experience, rather

than theological or philosophical questions, which might be controversial. Thomas accepted the Church's authority, and in this one can see the pervasive influence of Groote, whose belief in obedience had even led him to abandon preaching when commanded to do so. The *Imitation* soon came to be regarded as a spiritual classic, and, a reflection of the social milieu in which it originated, was early translated into the vernacular, as well as being adopted by the religious orders. It is significant that the first English versions of the work were made under Carthusian influence, but they do not appear to have made much of an impression on lay traditions of piety.[25] The Brethren were successful in walking the tightrope between encouraging lay piety and avoiding the suspicions of the authorities, perhaps because they had the support of various influential churchmen. They remained essentially a regional movement, and had little direct influence outside the Low Countries and northern Germany – as far as the wider Church was concerned their most important contribution was the *Imitation of Christ*.

Piety and heresy – the Hussites

Elsewhere, however, parallel movements of popular piety could not always be incorporated within traditional ecclesiastical structures, possibly because the criticisms of spiritual idealists antagonised the hierarchy. The Hussite movement in Bohemia, which ended as the most dangerous heretical challenge to the Church before the Reformation, drew originally on fundamentally orthodox traditions of piety, and many of the early patrons of English Lollardy did not see themselves as rebels. In the pious tract *The Two Ways*, by the Herefordshire knight Sir John Clanvowe, in which he identifies himself with the despised sect of Lollards, he interpreted the commandment 'Honour thy father and thy mother' as an instruction to the devout to worship their ghostly mother, holy Church.[26] The margin between heresy and radical orthodoxy was a narrow one, and both drew from a common stock of popular piety.

In fact, heretical movements in the last century and a half of the medieval Church were less of a threat to the establishment than those of the twelfth and early thirteenth centuries had been, because their activity was geographically more limited, and did not seriously affect the heartlands of ecclesiastical power in Italy, France and Germany. The older heretical movements had largely been suppressed, although there were still some residual Waldensian communities in isolated areas, linked by the activity of itinerant preachers, which the church authorities never succeeded in suppressing.[27] Lollardy in England never had more than a limited appeal, and Hussitism, the only heretical movement which caused widespread alarm to the Church as a whole, was largely confined to Bohemia, not least because the religious movement was closely bound up with a struggle for national identity against the German element in the country.

This had not been true initially in the fourteenth century, for the first major evangelical preacher in the country, Conrad of Waldhauser, whose teachings prepared the way for the later revolt, was of German origin. He denounced clerical abuses, notably simony and the use of false relics, and urged ecclesiastical and moral reform. His most important earlier follower, however, was a native Bohemian, Jan Milíč, who took up many of his ideas, including that of moral reform, setting up an establishment for reformed prostitutes. The latter was an ascetic, who refused meat and wine, and may have been subject to Joachite influences, for he had a particular obsession with Antichrist. Both men incurred hostility, and had to answer charges brought against them at Avignon by clerical opponents, who resented their denunciations. After their deaths, in 1369 and 1374 respectively, the tradition of evangelical reform was taken up by Matthias of Janov, an MA of Paris and a member of the Prague chapter. His doctrines were strictly biblicist, but he also laid great stress on the importance of the Eucharist as a means of grace. Furthermore, he urged its daily reception for the laity as well as for the clergy, and there were pious laymen who supported such ideas. Thomas of Stitny, a country gentleman, wrote a series of pious vernacular treatises, and in 1391 Wenceslas Křiž, a Prague merchant, along with other knights and burgesses, founded the Bethlehem Chapel in the city to provide for two vernacular sermons to be preached there daily. (One should not be misled by the term 'chapel' – the building could hold 3,000 people.[28]) This acquired a new importance when Jan Hus was appointed as preacher there in 1402. Although he was a man of academic importance – he was rector of the University of Prague – he was not an original theologian, and his *Commentary on the Sentences* (1407–9) was a conventional work. His influence was exercised primarily as a preacher against clerical abuses, and this may have aroused hostility to him among the Prague clergy. He did not, however, preach in German, as the earlier reformers had done, but only in Czech, reflecting a division in Bohemian society which was to be crucial for the development of the subsequent religious movement.

The other significant influence on the Bohemian reform movement was the University of Prague, which had been founded in 1346 as the only university in the Empire. It had ties with the reformers, and may have had a wider influence because Radewijns had studied there about the same time as Milíč. International politics also established links between Prague and Oxford, when Anne of Bohemia married Richard II of England, and Czech scholars were affected by some of Wyclif's philosophical ideas, although by no means all the Czech masters were willing to follow the Englishman's unorthodox views on the Eucharist.[29] For a long time Hus opposed Wyclif's views, although by 1412 his opinions became more radical – he denounced a 'crusade' launched by John XXIII against Ladislas of Naples, and compounded his offence by arguing that some of Wyclif's condemned views could be understood in an orthodox sense. Hus was excommunicated, and when threats were made that the place where he was would be laid under an interdict, he left Prague. Attempts to promote a reconciliation between him and his opponents merely demonstrated that while Hus and his followers were concerned with church reform, his opponents concentrated on the question of obedience to the Church. When the Council of Constance met he was given a safe-conduct to defend his orthodoxy, but this was disregarded. He was imprisoned, and after refusing to recant views which he had allegedly expressed – in some cases he denied affirming them but declared that it would be perjury to abjure something which he had not said[30] – he was executed on 6 July 1415. About a year later, his follower Jerome of Prague suffered the same fate.

Another contributory factor to the subsequent revolution was the changing character of the university from the end of the fourteenth century, when other universities were founded in German lands – this led both to a decline in Prague's international importance, and to tensions between the Bohemians and the non-Bohemians there. This culminated in 1409 in the royal decree of Kutna Hora, which gave three votes to the Bohemian nation, which, like the king, supported the Council of Pisa, and left only one to the remaining three nations (the Bavarian, Saxon and Polish) which favoured the archbishop of Prague and Gregory XII. This nationalism gave Hus the status of a Bohemian hero – while he was in custody some leading nobles wrote both to Sigismund urging him to ensure that Hus should not be 'furtively abused, to the dishonour of our nationality and of the Bohemian land', and to the Council affirming his innocence and protesting against the violation of the safe-conduct. After his execution, there was a powerful national reaction. The Estates of Bohemia and Moravia renewed their statement that Hus was innocent, declaring that anyone who said there was heresy in Bohemia was speaking lies, as a malicious heretic and the son of the devil, who is the father of lies. It is hardly surprising that after Jerome's death, the Council launched heresy proceedings against more than four hundred members of the nobility.[31] The lords at the diet concluded a covenant for six years to defend free preaching on their estates, to obey the bishops only as they acted according to the Scriptures, and to acknowledge the University of Prague as the highest authority on disputed matters of faith.

In practice this meant that the Bohemian laity were taking the revolutionary step of setting up a national church, acknowledging a different supreme authority from the rest of Christendom. The first major issue on which the university made a pronouncement, and one which was to be critical in the Hussite revolution, was in March 1417 on the practice known as Utraquism, the granting of communion in both kinds to the laity. As this had been condemned by the Council of Constance in June 1415,[32] the university's declaration may well have been a conscious act of defiance. It is not quite clear why this issue became so prominent, but various factors probably contributed. Matthias of Janov had stressed the importance of the Eucharist and the desirability of frequent communion, and criticism of the clergy by some of the reformers may have given rise to a feeling that the former were claiming a special privilege for themselves. Feeling was not unanimous on the question; some men resisted the demands of the Utraquists, while others had started to give the chalice to the laity even before the university made its position clear. Hus himself had favoured Utraquism in theory, but was willing to compromise, and tried to restrain his more radical supporter Jakoubek of Stříbro who advocated it more strongly. Shortly before his death, however, he wrote to his successor at the Bethlehem Chapel, urging him not to oppose giving the cup to the laity. Certainly from the university's pronouncement onwards, the chalice became the principal symbol of the Hussite movement, and the insistence that the laity should have the right to receive it was a sticking-point in later negotiations.[33]

The Hussite movement was never homogeneous, but many of its different groups were prepared to sink their differences for a time, when the rest of Christendom attempted to suppress them by force. Particularly, there was profound distrust of Sigismund, whose safe-conduct to Hus had been violated, but who also claimed the Bohemian throne after his brother Wenceslas's death in 1419. One of Hus's last letters to his supporters accused Sigismund of acting deceitfully, so if this message was taken back to Bohemia, it is hardly surprising that the emperor faced opposition.[34] Wenceslas had opposed granting the chalice to the laity and had tried to restore orthodox practices, with some support from religious conservatives, who did not wish to become involved in social and political revolution, but the main effect of this had been to leave the radicals as pace-makers in the Hussite camp. One group of these met in southern Bohemia at the mountain they called Tabor, where they not only heard preaching and received communion but also practised simple communism of goods, while in Prague a radical revolution led by the priest Jan Želivsky released imprisoned Utraquist leaders, and defenestrated the king's Catholic councillors. Wenceslas died of apoplexy a fortnight later. The Four Articles of Prague (1420) laid down terms on which the Bohemians were prepared to accept Sigismund, and significantly all were concerned with ecclesiastical issues: (1) free preaching of God's word without impediment, (2) communion in both kinds for the laity, (3) the punishment of mortal sins, and (4) the restoration of the Church to apostolic poverty.[35]

The Four Articles had varying connotations for different groups. For some they were their maximum demand, for others they were a starting-point for religious revolution, which would include a vernacular mass, the destruction of images, the denial of the intercession of the saints, and the end of a hierarchy. There were tensions among the various factions throughout the 1420s, and it was essentially only external pressures which preserved a measure of unity – between 1420 and 1431 there were five major expeditions against them, to which a crusading indulgence was granted. Initially the Hussites had one major advantage in resisting these – they possessed a soldier of genius in Jan Žižka, who proved an effective leader of their armies. Originally, he had come to the fore as an adherent of Tabor, but he later turned on the radicals and suppressed them in 1422. Žižka's death in 1424 was a major setback for the Hussite movement, but it continued to resist attacks successfully until the time of the Council of Basel.

Politics and religion could not be separated. Sigismund had two aims, to recover the kingdom and to restore orthodoxy, and his support for the Council of Basel can be explained by its willingness to try and resolve the problem. It was prepared to do what its predecessor at Constance had not done – in 1433 it made a concession on the issue of the chalice, thereby driving a wedge between the moderate and the radical Hussites, and a year later a conservative alliance of Catholics and Utraquists defeated the radicals at Lipany, giving Sigismund the opportunity to return to Bohemia shortly before his death. Not all the council members were happy about the concessions – Nicholas of Cusa criticised the Bohemian demand for communion in both kinds, compared the Hussites to the Iconoclasts, and exhorted the emperor to bring them back to orthodoxy.[36] The fact that he was German may reflect the element of national tension in the dispute. Sigismund's behaviour seems to have been two-faced, for during the negotiations he promised more, privately, than the council would concede, while after Lipany he worked for a Catholic reaction. Certainly after Lipany the Hussites lost ground. Although their moderate leader Jan Rokycana was elected as archbishop of Prague by the Bohemian Estates in 1435 (presumably in the hope that as such he could guarantee the observance of the Basel agreement), the Papacy never recognised his position. One consequence of this was that the later Hussites had difficulties in securing episcopal ordination for their priests.

Nevertheless a Hussite church survived in Bohemia, the only national church outside the control of Rome before the Reformation. Its survival was due to widespread national support, which was clearly demonstrated when in 1458 a Moravian noble, George of Podiebrad, was elected as a national king. In 1485, religious toleration in the country was formally recognised, making Bohemia the only pluralist religious country in Western Christendom. The country also saw the emergence of a radical pacifist group, the Unity of the Brethren (*Unitas Fratrum*), which took a more detached attitude to political matters. The survival of the Hussites was unique and their strength depended primarily on their identification with a national cause. This, however, was a two-edged weapon, for the national character of Hussitism perhaps explains why it did not spread far beyond Bohemia and Moravia where it had its roots. The only other country where it obtained some limited support was Poland – Hus claimed this in a letter written shortly before his death, and it is worth noting that in the 1420s the Bohemians offered their crown to the Polish prince Korybut. This was partly an attempt to exploit Slav distrust of the Germans, because the Council of Constance had also seen a bitter controversy between the Poles and the Teutonic Knights. However, a small number of cases of Hussitism, including nine executions, were recorded in Poland in the fifteenth century.[37]

Lollardy

This identification of Hussitism with political nationalism contrasts very markedly with the other important heresy of the later Middle Ages, English Lollardy. The two movements had connections with each other; some of Wyclif's ideas influenced teaching in the University of Prague, at first in philosophy and later, although less widely, also in theology. Even Nicholas Biceps, a theologian who was sympathetic to Wyclif's metaphysical realism, opposed his teachings on the Eucharist. But Czech scholars, including Jerome of Prague, visited England and obtained copies of Wyclif's writings – significantly many Wycliffite manuscripts now survive in Czech libraries.[38] Letters were exchanged between English and Bohemian clergy, including Hus, and indeed between evangelically inclined laymen in the two countries. When the Oxford Wycliffite Peter Payne was under threat in England he fled to Bohemia, where he played a prominent part in the Hussite movement down to the time of the Council of Basel. English sympathisers in the late 1420s condemned the attacks being launched against the Bohemians.[39] On the other hand, mainstream Hussitism was not a Wycliffite offshoot, for it had its own distinctive characteristics; most notably it stressed the Eucharist, whereas Wyclif's anti-transubstantiationist doctrines probably diminished the importance of the sacrament. Hussitism too was more populist, seeing church reform as something to be brought about from beneath, while the old royal servant Wyclif looked to the Crown for reform.

Yet in the late fourteenth century there is evidence of English piety similar to that which had provided a fertile seed-bed for the Hussites in Bohemia. Among the nobility and the gentry there were men who wrote religious tracts, and others who sought to pursue the *vita mixta* by regular devotional observances. Some of these extended patronage to priests who were influenced by Wyclif, and incurred the suspicion of contemporary clerical chroniclers. Even so, their unorthodoxy was often muted, and their beliefs were certainly not homogeneous. One statement of Lollard beliefs, the Twelve Conclusions of 1395, contained a strongly pacifist affirmation,[40] but two Lollard knights to whom reasonable suspicion attaches actually died during a campaign against the Turks. Some of Wyclif's clerical followers travelled widely through the country preaching dissident doctrines, but they attracted only a few disciples. Undoubtedly there was criticism of clerical wealth (even proposals for church disendowment) and a fair measure of anti-papalism, but these never came together into a unified movement such as existed in Bohemia. The English church establishment had attacked Wyclif's teachings in Oxford, and although the university resented the interference of successive archbishops of Canterbury, it could not resist them. The intellectual tradition of dissent persisted till the late fourteenth century, and was responsible for the production and copying of a lengthy cycle of Wycliffite sermons, but although a substantial number of manuscripts of this survive, they do not seem to have circulated among the secret heretical communities of the fifteenth century.[41] Only one prominent lay Lollard, Sir John Oldcastle, was prepared to take up arms against the Crown, and then only after he had been charged with heresy by the archbishop of Canterbury. His rising in 1414 had no support from his fellows in the landed class. The Crown was powerful, and loyal to the ecclesiastical establishment – the Lancastrian dynasty, which usurped the throne in 1399, owed much of its strength to the support of prominent churchmen. Indeed, the enactment of a statute in 1401 providing for the burning of heretics may well have been a gesture of gratitude from the king to his ecclesiastical allies.

The consequence of this was that English Lollardy never was more than a minority movement. The ecclesiastical authorities destroyed its intellectual base in Oxford and royal power backed them up. English national sentiment was directed to lay matters such as the war with France, in which the lay nobility and the Crown were united. Lollardy moved into small communities in some towns and certain areas of the countryside, where it probably survived largely in certain families. There was a continuing tradition of heresy in London, Bristol and Coventry, in various places in the lower Thames valley and the Chilterns, and in southern Kent, often in places adjacent to diocesan boundaries, so that suspects could slip quietly away when the local bishop was becoming too inquisitive. Some links were maintained among groups by itinerant evangelists, but these were slight, although they may later have provided a network for the distribution of heretical literature during the Reformation. Their theological beliefs, as far as can be judged, were simple rather than sophisticated; most followed Wyclif's denial of transubstantiation, criticised pilgrimages and the veneration of images, and a small number, especially just before 1500, looked to an imminent Second Coming. Persecution was only sporadic – the English bishops were either unenthusiastic about it or were more preoccupied with other matters – although it did intensify in the early sixteenth century, when records of executions become more common, and the numbers brought to trial also increased. Even so, in the century between the failure of Oldcastle's rising and the first appearance in England of the new teachings of the continental Reformation, the number of recorded executions was less than a hundred and that of abjurations less than a thousand. For most Englishmen, traditional forms of piety sufficed to meet their spiritual aspirations.

16

The age of concordats

Popes and lay rulers

Europe in the later Middle Ages was increasingly dominated by its secular princes, who saw themselves as the sovereign power in their lands.[1] The Great Schism and the conciliar challenge to the Papacy, by contrast, had made it very apparent that the popes could not reassert their predecessors' claims to universal authority. From the Council of Constance onwards, the Papacy lived in the shadow of the conciliar challenge, and if the popes were to reassert their real power, they could do so only by coming to terms with the political system of the time. This involved more systematic compromise than had been seen before 1378, and it was best embodied in various concordats which the Papacy made with the secular rulers. Even churchmen recognised that the lay power had a crucial role to play in church organisation – Nicholas of Cusa in his *De Concordantia Catholica* declared that secular rulers had a responsibility to protect the Church and that the emperor was protector of the Universal Church, as well incidentally as of the council.[2]

The system of concordats necessitated a new perception of ecclesiastical organisation. However much the Church was seen as unified under God, and the widespread desire to restore this unity had been the driving force behind the Council of Constance, while its maintenance had been the most powerful weapon possessed by Eugenius IV in his dealings with the rebels at Basel when they threatened another schism, its practical management existed in the world of national states, in which power rested with the lay rulers. The step from a national state to a national church was small, and the fifteenth century saw an increasing use of such terms as *ecclesia anglicana* or *ecclesia gallicana,* to describe that portion of the Universal Church which existed in a particular geographical area. Lay rulers had, of course, always resisted what they saw as the encroachment of centralised ecclesiastical power on their rights of jurisdiction and of taxation, and they had always tried, often with success, to ensure that their preferred nominees would occupy the leading positions in the Church in their countries. By the fifteenth century, the Papacy had to accept the *de facto* limitations on its powers, although it attempted to resist encroachent on them. Provided its theoretical headship of the Church was recognised, it accepted that it had to find a *modus vivendi* with the secular rulers, and this had some practical implications for the unity of the Church. Some reformers were even willing to envisage regional diversity within the Church being incorporated in its constitutional machinery, possibly as a means of curbing papal claims. In his *De Concordantia Catholica,* Nicholas of Cusa envisaged a structured system of representation, suggesting that the cardinals should be elected by the metropolitans of provinces with the consent of the bishops, and that they should serve as the representatives of their particular part of the Church.[3] Later, Nicholas criticised Pius II when he created new cardinals at his own whim, disregarding an oath he had taken at the conclave not to make new appointments without the consent of the majority of the existing members of the college – it also reflected his pro-conciliar past that he accused the pope of not acting according to the decrees of the Council of Constance. While the pope rebuked Cusa for exceeding his rights by making the criticism, it reflects a recognition of the political framework of Christendom that he also defended the policy of creating cardinals to satisfy various nations.[4]

In fact the fifteenth-century college of cardinals became increasingly dominated by Italians, in whose appointments the pope always had the determining voice. In practice, however, secular rulers could often make representations to Rome for the promotion of one of their leading ecclesiastics to the college. In 1488 Henry VII of England requested a red hat for Archbishop John Morton, 'seeing that they [the English] have been so long without such primary light of ecclesiastical dignity, as much to inconvenience the commonwealth', a somewhat exaggerated statement as the last English cardinal had died only two and a half years previously.[5] Such diplomatic requests in themselves indicate the regionalising of the Church, because princes clearly felt that it was a question of prestige for their realm to have a cardinal, the more so as many recipients of the title remained in their native lands rather than going to the Curia. The emergence of such non-curial cardinals is in itself a measure of a changing attitude to their function in the Church – they were regarded as dignitaries rather than as functionaries in church government. In the early sixteenth century many cardinals remained in their own countries and some were exceedingly influential there – George of Amboise in France, Ximénez de Cisneros in Spain and Wolsey in England. One consequence of this, however, was that the papal Curia was dominated by the college members who resided in Rome, most of them Italian. Many of these too were related to the popes who had appointed them, who saw them as the best way of buttressing their own power.[6]

Issues in the concordats

The stipulations in the various concordats concerned practical questions of church government and areas where there was a possible clash of interests between the Papacy and the local rulers. Probably the most significant issue was appointments to major ecclesiastical offices, because a king could influence the Church in his lands through a well-disposed archbishop, whatever the strict legal position was. Martin V's attempt to secure the revocation of the English statute of Provisors significantly led to a clash between him and Archbishop Chichele of Canterbury, whom he suspected of being lukewarm in support. The concordats at the end of the Council of Constance made elaborate attempts to strike a balance between contrasting interests in the Church, the rights of canonical electors, the claims of patrons and the right of the Papacy to make provisions. It reflects the social divisions in the German Church that the concordat allowed chapters to appoint only men of noble or knightly rank as canons, and more generally, that provisions were made for the rights of graduates, a reflection perhaps of the number of prominent university men at the council. The concordats said little about the rights of secular rulers, probably because their practical influence was already recognised, and compromises were reached between them and the Papacy in individual negotiations. In 1422 the future Charles VII of France requested the power to nominate 500 persons to benefices in the kingdom, as had been granted to his predecessors.[7] The struggle between Eugenius IV and the Council of Basel gave the lay rulers opportunities to assert their influence over the local churches – indeed the French adopted various of the council's reform decrees as law for their church in the Pragmatic Sanction of Bourges of 1438. During the remainder of the century the Papacy made numerous attempts to secure the abandonment of the Pragmatic, because it reflected French royal support for the hated doctrines of conciliar superiority. Twice the French abolished it briefly, probably as an attempt to secure papal political support, but on both occasions it was restored when this was no longer forthcoming. On one of these occasions, Louis XI offered to abrogate the Pragmatic in return for having two Frenchmen promoted to the cardinalate, a concession which Pius II was willing to make.[8]

The French concordat of 1472 laid down that collation of benefices should fall to the ordinary collators in even months, a similar provision to that contained in the Concordat of Vienna of 1448 between the pope and the German nation, following that country's restoration of obedience at the end of the Basel schism. But although in theory these agreements were supposed to restore freedom of election, in practice they were accompanied by a papal willingness to accommodate the lay rulers' wishes. Such secular influence was demonstrated most clearly by the final settlement between the French Crown and the Papacy in the pre-Reformation period, the Concordat of Bologna of 1516, agreed at a time when Francis I was politically dominant in Italy. This effectively delivered the Church into the

Crown's control, and it is noteworthy that the first nine clauses dealt with the issue of appointment to benefices. When a bishopric fell vacant in France, the king had six months in which to nominate a candidate to the pope, and only when he had failed to do so could the pope take the initiative in making an appointment. If the pope refused the nomination, the king could propose an alternative candidate within the next three months. Although attempts were made to safeguard the quality of men appointed to high office, by stipulations about their age and their academic status, these could be waived if the nominee was related to the king, came from a noble family, or was a member of a reformed religious order – only the last of these exempt groups was likely to produce a nominee of notable spirituality. The extension of royal influence incurred some opposition from the Parlement of Paris, which was more favourable to free elections, but the Crown was able to get its way.[9]

If the lay power could win substantial power over ecclesiastical appointments, it was equally successful in other disputed areas of authority, such as taxation of the clergy and rights of jurisdiction. The question of service payments was defined in the concordats at the end of the Council of Constance, and the abolition of annate payments by the Council of Basel gave the lay princes a good pretext for withholding the transmission of taxes to Rome. Significantly, the suppression of annates was incorporated in the Pragmatic Sanction of Bourges, and in the declaration of neutrality between the pope and the council by the German princes at Mainz in 1439. The lay power was sometimes prepared to acknowledge the Papacy's financial needs, and in the Concordat of Vienna the right to annate payments was restored.[10]

Similar attempts were made to regulate the respective rights of ecclesiastical and lay courts in individual countries. Some matters remained incontestably under Church control, notably those dealing with marriage law, penitential matters and questions of conscience; indeed the Penitentiary's activity was virtually unaffected by political tensions, as individuals continued to have recourse to Rome irrespective of relations between their rulers and the pope. On the other hand, a working system was generally developed on the question of the right of the rival courts to proceed against offending churchmen – in general, matters were not remitted to the Curia, but the local church courts still preserved substantial powers. The Spanish and French concordats at the end of the Council of Constance laid down that the importance of the individual case would determine whether it would be heard at the Curia or remitted to the country of origin. Almost a century later, in the Concordat of Bologna, it was made clear that judicial cases should be heard within the realm, except for certain reserved issues, and should proceed up the hierarchy and not be taken to the Holy See until the lower courts had exhausted them. The area of law which probably raised most difficulties was the recognised papal power to grant dispensations for marriage within the prohibited degrees of kinship. Within particular countries landed interests might be affected by the granting or withholding of a dispensation, and when a monarch was affected, it might have implications for international politics. In such circumstances immediate relations between the pope and the particular ruler could affect the decision. Louis XII of France was able to exploit the ambitions of Alexander VI to secure an annulment of his marriage to his cousin, Louis XI's daughter, so that he could marry his predecessor's widow, Anne of Brittany, but Henry VIII of England was unable to secure the annulment of his marriage to Catherine of Aragon.

The organisation of the Penitentiary, however, reflected papal awareness of the divisions of Europe. In 1435 Eugenius IV's regulations for it, which limited the number of minor penitentiaries to eleven, provided that there were to be two each from Italy, France and Spain, and one each from England, Hungary, Upper Germany, Lower Germany, and the Slav lands.[11] This presumably was an attempt to anticipate the number of cases which might be brought to Rome from each of these areas, because it was obviously desirable to have officials who could deal with individual petitioners in their own languages. In this one sees an attempt to provide for the needs of Christians in a world which was breaking up into separate nations. The universality of the Church's role was best displayed in the way in which individuals had recourse to its central institutions for solutions to legal questions which were recognised as essentially spiritual in character, and for grants of graces and dispensations to provide relief on matters where they might feel a sense of guilt.

By comparison, ecclesiastical administrative matters were increasingly devolved to the churches in each country, where the lay power could often influence the local hierarchy. Although there were differences in practical details between various countries, the general pattern of compromise remained very similar throughout Western Christendom. In the last resort the popes needed support from lay rulers if they were to maintain even a theoretical semblance of power, and the price which they had to pay was the concession of administrative authority. Disputed questions were resolved pragmatically, and the extent to which either the Papacy or the local ruler could prevail depended on a wide variety of factors, both political and administrative, affecting both sides. On the whole the lay rulers were reasonably happy to accept papal claims to theoretical (though not perhaps practical) supremacy in the Church, not least because the constitutional arguments of the conciliarists could be easily taken over by their own subjects, and applied to a lay monarchy as well as to an ecclesiastical one.

Reform proposals

Constitutional reform had been the fundamental issue of the conciliar period, but the councils had talked about the reform of the Church in its members as well as in the head. The power struggles during the Council of

Basel pushed other reform issues into the background, but the question was not entirely forgotten. Proposals were put forward for various reforms during the reigns of both Pius II and Sixtus IV, but nothing much came of them, probably because their main emphasis, on curbing ecclesiastical bureaucracy, faced too many vested interests. The reform of moral standards in monasteries was encouraged, but for implementation this required action in the localities rather than words at the centre.[12] A further set of reform proposals was produced in 1497 by a commission which Alexander VI appointed, perhaps prompted by feelings of guilt, after the murder of his son the Duke of Gandia. Some proposals attacked the behaviour of the Borgia court, but many were again directed against the elaboration of the bureaucracy. In practice little came of the suggestions put forward.[13] The fate of reform in the period demonstrates that it could not be imposed from the centre, but depended essentially on local initiatives. Certainly the impetus given to reform by the Papacy from the eleventh century onwards was now something of the past. It was more likely to come from individual activity in particular areas or in relatively limited contexts – one sees the latter in the growth of the Observant wing of the Franciscans, where reform spread successfully throughout Western Christendom, but in a manner which did not threaten the accepted order of the Church. In fifteenth-century Europe, where kings were asserting their authority ever more autocratically, reform had to accommodate itself to what was politically acceptable (and some kings were prepared to extend patronage to moral reform at any rate). The local churches, however, were not likely to rebuke their temporal masters, and individual churchmen did so only at their own risk. When leading churchmen fell foul of their kings and action was taken against them, the Papacy could do nothing to protect them.

Political rivalries and church government

Even if the Papacy could have confined its attention to matters of ecclesiastical government, the lay rulers' power would have posed problems, but in the thirteenth and fourteenth centuries it also was deeply involved in politics,[14] and could not avoid the problems caused by the European powers' competing interests in the affairs of the Italian peninsula. In times of crisis, it was easy to use matters of church government as bargaining counters for political support. The extent of external intervention in Italy varied from time to time, depending on how highly the lay rulers of Christendom rated their other concerns, and indeed on what pretexts they had to intervene in Italy. The rival claims of Aragonese kings and French princes to the succession in Naples, after the extinction of the first Angevin line in 1434, gave rise to civil wars there, and as the Papacy was nominally the king's overlord it was inevitably drawn into the ensuing conflicts. These were not continuous, because the Aragonese line established itself firmly in the kingdom for much of the second half of the fifteenth century (not least because the French kings were more concerned with pursuing ambitions on the frontiers of their own kingdom and were not disposed to further the ambitions of a cadet line of the royal house), but from 1494 rival political interests in the peninsula compelled the Papacy to concentrate on its territorial interests. Indeed, it was almost essential for the pope to be a man whose skills were more appropriate for diplomacy and administration rather than for spiritual leadership.

The return of the Papacy to Italy after the conciliar crisis led to the election of a series of popes of Italian origin, or at least with predominantly Italian interests, which they shared with the other territorial rulers of the peninsula. The popes must be regarded as monarchs, who differed from their lay counterparts only in the fact that their position was elective rather than hereditary. Indeed, one can see a virtual hereditary element creeping into the Papacy, for the tendency to nepotism in the appointments of cardinals resulted in the virtual establishment of clerical dynasties; no fewer than four men elected to rule the Church between 1417 and 1517 were nephews of earlier popes. (Paul II was the nephew of Eugenius IV, Alexander VI of Calixtus III, Pius III of Pius II, and Julius II of Sixtus IV.) Indeed, some struggles for influence in the conclaves reflected a feud between two such families, the Borgia and the della Rovere, because both Rodrigo Borgia, later Alexander VI, and Giuliano della Rovere, later Julius II, were men of great influence in the college, not only during their uncles' pontificates, but also after them. Both were men of considerable ability, but they were also strong personal and political rivals. The dangers of nepotism were recognised by the cardinals, who attempted to restrict it in capitulations drawn up at the conclaves of 1464 and 1471, by including a proviso that only one papal relative could be appointed to the college, but this was neglected – Paul II and Sixtus IV, the popes elected, named respectively three and six relatives to it. Perhaps significantly, no such restriction was set on the relatives of existing cardinals, other than those related to the pope.[15] Such factional divisions within the college, however, prevented the cardinals from preserving a unified front and enabled the popes to play off potential rivals for influence against each other. It also gave scope for lay powers to intrigue for the choice of a pope who might be deemed politically sympathetic to them, by lobbying members of the college. With the political role of the Papacy being so important, it is hardly surprising that Italian *signori* and later also European kings were interested in who might be elected as pope. If one may believe Pius II's account of his own election, there was intense overnight intrigue among the cardinals, in which national sentiment among the Italian cardinals was exploited to block the candidature of the archbishop of Rouen, Cardinal d'Estouteville.[16]

The only real exception to Italian domination of the Papacy was the Spaniard Alonso Borgia, who took the title of Calixtus III (1455–8). His election was essentially a compromise, and, at the age of 77, he may well have been chosen primarily as a stopgap in a conclave which was divided both between the Italian and non-Italian cardinals, and among different factions in each of these groups. His moral reputation was high and he may well have had a particular appeal to the college because of the Spanish tradition of crusading against Islam at a time when the Turkish threat to Christendom had been highlighted by the fall of Constantinople in 1453 – significantly, while attempts were made in other conclaves to bind newly elected popes to make concessions to the college, the only oath sought in 1455 had been to pursue the war against the Turks. After his election too, he took steps to mount campaigns against the Turks in the Eastern Mediterranean.[17] Despite his background, Calixtus was prepared to resist the power of the Aragonese king of Naples, and by the end of his pontificate he had effectively shifted the focus of his interests to Italy. In doing so, he furthered the interests of his family, the most notorious of whom was his nephew Rodrigo, who became pope as Alexander VI in 1492. As Rodrigo spent his adult life in Italy, he should be regarded as more Italian than Spanish in outlook.

In moral terms, Alexander has rightly been seen as a reflection of papal decline in the period, but his election must be understood in the light of Italian political circumstances in 1492. His predecessor, Innocent VIII, had been politically inept and the temporal power of the Papacy had suffered serious decline; also, three months before the conclave, the death of Lorenzo de' Medici, the most skilful figure in Italian inter-state diplomacy, had led to increasing divisions among the various states of the peninsula. It was in the Papacy's interests to maintain a balance of power within Italy and prevent the intervention of the ultramontane powers, but in practice this was impossible. Contending families within the lands of the Church looked for support to Italian princes, whose own rivalries led them to seek external assistance from France and Aragon. The Aragonese already had a foothold in Naples, where the French also had a claim. And while the Papacy was sufficiently powerful to play a significant role in relation to the other Italian states, like all of them it lacked political clout in dealing with the greater powers of Christendom, when they tried to secure power and influence in the peninsula.

The Florentine historian Guicciardini commented on Alexander VI that he was wise and attentive in political matters, but that this was balanced by his shamelessness, impiety and avarice.[18] As his policies were undoubtedly directed primarily to aggrandising his family, notably his sons Juan, Duke of Gandia, and Cesare, one can see the combination of both his positive and his negative qualities. Cesare had originally been destined for the Church, and had been created a cardinal at the age of 19, but after his brother's murder he was released from his clerical status to become one of the greatest and most unscrupulous military leaders of the time, who dominated Italian politics for much of his father's pontificate. Substantial parts of the papal states were brought under Cesare's control, and it is clear that the Church's resources were being systematically despoiled in the interests of the Borgia family. Alexander's successor, the elderly and frail Pius III, survived for less than a month, and the next conclave brought to power Julius II, a man fairly described in a recent life as the 'warrior pope'. Although his activities aroused criticism, voiced most forcefully in the brilliant and witty vision of judgement by the Dutch humanist Erasmus, entitled *Julius Exclusus,* in which he imagined an encounter between the pope and St Peter at the heavenly gates,[19] Julius gave good service to the temporal interests of the Papacy, where he effectively refounded the papal states. Guicciardini said of him that he would have deserved the highest glory if he had been a secular prince.[20] His prime political objective was to restore the Church's power, and he recovered many lands which had been usurped by local tyrants. Although his diplomacy saw frequent changes of alignment in his choice of allies, his basic strategy remained constant. Most markedly, he eschewed the family aggrandisement which had been the hallmark of Alexander's reign.

The authority and image of the papal monarchy

The popes' political interests had various implications for the Church. As long as the Papacy had to maintain a substantial administrative bureaucracy, it needed the resources to sustain it, and although fees payable by litigants and supplicants at the Curia met some costs, a substantial part of the Church's resources were drawn from its territorial power base. The maintenance of this in itself imposed extra demands on the papal finances, as well as the involvement in political manoeuvres resulting from the popes' position as territorial princes. This role was unavoidable, unless the Papacy abandoned the administrative structures which had been developed in previous centuries, an action which would have been totally unrealistic. The Papacy was generally regarded as a monarchy, and an ecclesiastical monarch was expected to maintain a court just as much as a lay ruler. The ways in which the popes asserted their dignity varied – Nicholas V was a bibliophile and a patron of scholarship as well as of the visual arts, and Pius II had himself been a humanist of distinction before his election as pope. Paul II fell foul of the humanists, because he suspected that some of them were cultivating pagan ideals, but he still supported some scholars and installed the first printing press in Rome. Perhaps the most notable cultural patron among the late fifteenth-century popes was Sixtus IV, who widened the streets of Rome and built new churches, including the Sistine Chapel, which still bears his name. He also founded the choir for the chapel. Julius II was also a patron of the arts, employing both Michelangelo and Raphael, and commissioning Bramante to design the new St Peter's. He was present when the foundation stone was laid in 1506, and also arranged for the sale of indulgences to help in defraying the costs, an action which provoked criticism later. The popes were concerned with the visible power of their office, and it is hard to judge how far this was prompted by considerations of vanity and how far by the feeling that without this assertion of their status they would lose credibility in the eyes of Europe. In either case, it shows how far the Papacy had been secularised.

The popes' spiritual role was less visibly threatened. Individual holders of the papal office might not be respected, but their spiritual and jurisdictional powers meant that the faithful needed to have recourse to Rome from all over Christendom. Furthermore, it was not simply the need to secure a dispensation or some other favour that attracted visitors, for Rome was still a place of voluntary pilgrimage for Christians, particularly in the years of Jubilee which were consciously developed by the Papacy as a means of attracting pilgrims, and their money. And the popes may well have hoped that the visible power and the ceremonial of their court would impress those visiting it with their power and dignity, irrespective of how little relevance it might have to the spiritual aspects of the Church's life. In practice, however, for most people the two sides of the Church were able to co-exist.

|17|

The Church in the early sixteenth century

The Western Church before the Reformation

The Reformation was such a crucial watershed in the Church's history that historians risk viewing events immediately before it simply in terms of its occurrence. Furthermore, as both sides in the Reformation were concerned with justifying their position in the eyes of the Christian world, many events of this period have been viewed in a strongly confessional light. But the character of the Church just after 1500 must be understood in its own terms, rather than with the benefit of hindsight. One cannot overlook the fact that the Reformation occurred, but one should not assume that it was inevitable. It was brought about by a combination of factors, which may have been foreshadowed in the previous century, but none of which on their own would necessarily have led to the disintegration of the Western Church.

The limits of the West Christian world

What then was the character of the Western Church in organisation and faith around 1500 and how great was its power? It had inherited traditions and organisation which had developed over more than a thousand years, and dominated the mental world of Western Europe. European paganism had finally ended in the late fourteenth century with the conversion of Lithuania (1385), and the problems of its relationship with the Eastern Church were no longer a major factor in its life. The fall of Constantinople to the Turks in 1453 had confined the traditions of Orthodox Christianity to the Russian world, and to some small areas in the Balkans, where it was struggling to survive under Moslem rule. The Roman tradition was firmly established in the West, and had indeed extended its influence in Spain, where the Moorish kingdom of Granada had been destroyed in 1492. This success was welcomed outside the Iberian peninsula; the Florentine diarist

Luca Landucci described it as a great acquisition for the faith of Christ and, more optimistically, as a first step to recovering the Levant and Jerusalem.[1] Spanish and Portuguese voyages across the Atlantic had been followed by the setting up of the first bishoprics in the New World.

In the Mediterranean world and in Eastern Europe on the other hand, however, Islam was gaining ground. The fall of Constantinople had sounded a tocsin of alarm throughout the West, and was recorded in lurid terms even by the chronicler of Crowland Abbey in England, while the future pope Pius II lamented the fall of the city, the enslavement of its people and the pollution of St Sophia by 'Moslem filth'.[2] Despite this language Pius actually made an effort to bring about the Sultan's conversion in a letter of 1460. In this he suggested that if he were baptised he would be the greatest man of his time, and could be called emperor of the East. Essentially this plea was made on the same grounds as those which had persuaded the barbarians of the sixth century to accept Christianity, but because Islam was itself a cultured and intellectual religion, the pope attempted to strengthen his letter by setting out both the areas of common ground and the differences between it and Christianity.[3] One doubts if Pius ever expected this letter to accomplish anything, and significantly about the same time attempts were made to resurrect crusading activity. Although this had some verbal support, no one was prepared to turn it into action. In Germany a diet at Ratisbon approved a crusade, and a subsequent meeting at Frankfurt eventually endorsed this, after some complaints were made that the pope and the emperor were using the crusade simply as a pretext for raising money. Pius II faced some opposition from the cardinals when he called a congress at Mantua in 1460, although he had some support from a Spanish and a Greek member of the college.[4] His attempt to mount an expedition to the East, however, ended at his death. The southern frontier of Christendom remained under severe pressure until the sixteenth century. In the Eastern Mediterranean, there were still isolated Christian outposts – Rhodes survived a siege in 1480 but was to fall in 1522, and the advance of Islam was not decisively checked until the defence of Malta in 1565 and the defeat of the Turkish fleet at Lepanto in 1571. Even in Italy itself, the Turks were able to secure and retain a base at Otranto for thirteen months in 1480–1.

Even more serious a threat was the steady Turkish advance from the late fourteenth century through the Balkans, following the collapse of the Serbian Empire. An attempt to unite Christendom against the Turks during the schism period ended in military disaster at Nicopolis in 1396, and further expeditions were launched against the Turks in the fifteenth century. The fortunes of war varied and the armies of Christendom secured some successes in the Danube valley, as in 1456 when a force under the military leadership of the Hungarian Janos Hunyadi, and spiritually inspired by the Franciscan St John Capistrano, compelled them to withdraw from Belgrade.[5] Crusading remained a pervading ideal of knightly society in the later Middle Ages, but actual military activity against the Moslem world was largely confined to men from those countries immediately vulnerable to it.[6] The actual Turkish threat to Christendom varied with the ambitions of successive Sultans, some of whom were more concerned with campaigning in the Middle East than with trying to extend their power in Europe. But the threat remained present and was renewed in the 1520s, when the Hungarian king was defeated and killed at the battle of Mohacs in 1526, and most of his lands fell under Turkish control. The fear of Islam too remained in the consciousness of Christian Europe – when Sir Thomas More, in prison for his opposition to Henry VIII, wrote his *Dialogue of Comfort against Tribulation*, he set it in the context of the Turkish advance – but at the same time attitudes to the Turks were increasingly determined by considerations of Realpolitik, even to the extent of Western rulers seeking alliances with them.

North and South

The frontiers of Western Christendom were therefore fluid, but within them, people's perceptions of its nature varied. More particularly, there was considerable mutual antagonism between North and South. Pius II accused Cardinal Jouffroy of Arras both of deception and of accumulating benefices and described Nicholas of Cusa as 'a German too devoted to his nation'. Over half a century later, Guicciardini clearly regarded the Papacy as essentially an Italian institution and was apprehensive about the election of the Dutchman Adrian VI.[7] Italian dislike of the northerners was reciprocated. In *The Praise of Folly,* Erasmus claimed that the Italians, particularly the Romans and the Venetians, congratulated themselves on being the only civilised race of men.[8] Complaints were made about Roman rapaciousness and the corruption of the Curia in the mid-fifteenth century, and although this attitude was not new, it took a more distinctively national character. By the early sixteenth century there was conscious resentment at Italian prejudices. In 1518 a young German theologian, Franz Friedlieb, complained about Italians who called Germans barbarians.[9] The development of such an attitude helped to prepare the ground for Luther's criticisms of Rome, and it is noteworthy that one of his most influential early works was addressed to 'the Christian Nobility of the German Nation'.

In an age of increasing political rivalry in Western Europe, particularly when rulers had conflicts of interest in Italy, the Papacy's political role could not be totally separated from its function as the administrative and spiritual head of the Western Church. Much effective power over the local churches had already passed into lay rulers' hands, although their authority affected only the Church's temporal rights over lands and revenues, and set limits to the extent to which the Papacy could control higher ecclesiastical appointments and exercise jurisdictional authority. Where the latter was seen as having spiritual connotations, canon law remained intact, but in other areas it was curtailed. But kings were quite prepared to blackmail the Papacy by playing on its fear of internal challenges to its authority, and this was never demonstrated more clearly than in the action of Louis XII of France and the Emperor Maximilian in backing the discontent of a group of rebel cardinals in calling a council to Pisa against Julius II in 1511.[10] The pope, however, rose to the challenge, assisted perhaps by the fact that his political allies showed no willingness to join the revolt, and effectively called the bluff of this neo-conciliarism by summoning a council of his own to meet at the Lateran to carry out reforms in the Church. Fundamentally, the Papacy was prepared to tolerate meetings of councils if they were held in places where they could be influenced – what was unacceptable were meetings which asserted their autonomy of the papal monarchy.

The Fifth Lateran Council

The Fifth Lateran Council was the last great ecclesiastical assembly in the West before the Reformation crisis, and its proceedings illuminate some of the Church's main preoccupations in the early sixteenth century. The first five sessions were held during Julius II's lifetime, and were concerned primarily with asserting the pope's rights against the claims of the rebel council, which was condemned, along with any continuations of it. An interdict was imposed on France for supporting the rebels, and the Pragmatic Sanction of Bourges was revoked as displeasing to God. Even a decree against simony, which might be regarded as a reform measure, affirmed papal authority in its preamble; 'The supreme maker of things, the creator of heaven and earth, has willed by his ineffable providence that the Roman pontiff preside over Christian people in the chair of pastoral supremacy.'[11] After Julius' death, the new pope, Leo X, was better able to restore peace with France, and later sessions of the council were more concerned with questions of reform. Many measures were traditional, providing for the reform of the Curia, laying down educational qualifications for major prelates, stipulating that the cardinals should lead sober, chaste and godly lives and be mirrors of moderation and frugality, and imposing penalties for clerical concubinage. In 1513 it was affirmed that once peace had been restored within Christendom a campaign should be launched against the infidel, and at the concluding session of the council in 1517, the pope reaffirmed the need to crush the Turks. The restoration of Christian unity in another way was reflected in the instructions to the cardinal legate to Hungary and Bohemia to try to restore the Hussites to the Church.[12]

There were, however, also various provisions which reflect the new circumstances of the early sixteenth century. At the eighth session, the council condemned certain propositions which were contrary to the Christian faith, such as ideas of the mortality of the soul or of the eternity of the world. References to the 'infected sources of philosophy and poetry' show concern at the ideas circulating among some Italian humanists. Another measure provided for sanctions against 'false Christians and those with evil sentiments towards the faith' as well as against heretics. This again probably alluded to pagan and perhaps also pantheist ideas among humanists, because it was stipulated that offenders should be expelled from any position which they held, particularly from the Curia. The maintenance of orthodoxy was also the objective of a bull on preaching, to ensure that it did not contain fraud and error, based on the false testimony of alleged miracles; it provided for preachers to be examined by their superiors, whose sermons were to be consistent with the words of Scripture and the interpretations of the doctors of the Church. There was also a stress on ethical matters, for preachers were to reject vices and commend virtues.[13] Perhaps the most interesting bull issued at the council, at its tenth session in 1515, referred to printing, and the implications which this had for the maintenance of orthodoxy. The new technology was accepted in principle, being described as invented and perfected with God's assistance, and it was noted that the extension of learning had had good results, but the bull sounded a warning note in that some printers had published books containing errors opposed to the faith and pernicious views contrary to the Christian religion. The bull provided for the imposition of censorship – new books were to be examined by the local bishop or someone delegated by him and by the local inquisitor of heresy. Breaches of these rules were to be punished by the burning of offending books, financial penalties on those responsible and the suspension of their right to print.[14]

Such allusions to heresy in the council's decrees are perhaps surprising, because it was not a serious problem in Europe around 1500. Apart from the Hussites in Bohemia, who were formally tolerated, the English Lollards, who were increasingly being pursued by the authorities, and a few isolated Waldensians, there were no heretical groups of any importance. Indeed, heresy was probably a less serious problem for the Church in 1500 than it had been three centuries before. The last persecution of Waldensians in the German lands took place in Brandenburg between 1478 and 1483, after which the fugitives migrated to Moravia.[15] The council's measures were probably directed more against the fear of philosophical innovations than against traditional unorthodoxy. Most piety was firmly based on the Church's teachings, and there were no widespread popular movements of dissent. It is worth stressing that the council's condemnations did not single out any alleged heresiarchs by name, but simply attacked certain beliefs in general terms.

Christian Humanism

The most significant influence on religious developments around this period was that which historians have called Christian Humanism. One cannot call it a movement, for it was not organised, nor indeed was there any homogeneity among its supporters' views; it was rather a state of mind shared by many leading scholars of the day, who sought to harness to the Church's needs the linguistic skills developed in the renewed study of the classics. Among these writers there was a confidence that they could reconcile their philosophical views with the Church's teaching – the Florentine Marsilio Ficino not only translated the works of Plato into Latin, but also composed an apologetic treatise on the Christian religion. His translation of the works of pseudo-Dionysius suggests, furthermore, that he was sympathetic to aspects of mystical religion. He became a priest himself in 1473 when he was about 40, and for a time at any rate was an admirer of Savonarola.[16]

In the North, ideals of humanist education were followed in the schools set up by the Brethren of the Common Life – Alexander Hegius, rector of the schools at Emmerich and Deventer in the late fifteenth century, was willing to study both pagan authors and the Church Fathers, and believed strongly in clerical education as a means of furthering the restoration of the Church. He encouraged the study of Greek, but, in the tradition of the Brethren, did not despise the vernacular.[17] Humanism belonged to the intellectual elite, both lay and clerical, rather than to the people as a whole, although the educational objectives of its supporters were not confined to a limited group, but extended through a wider part of Christian society than a small number of scholars. This concern for spreading Christian teaching reflected increasing literacy in society as a whole, a social change which itself affected religious attitudes. On the other hand, humanist criticism of the existing order and of popular practices may well have made it less rather than more popular with the majority of the people, who sought salvation in traditional practices such as pilgrimages, the cult of relics and the pursuit of indulgences.

There was always, however, some tension between questioning intellectuals and more conservative teachers. In England, the Dean of St Paul's, John Colet, who attempted to strip scriptural exegesis of some of its allegorical accretions and return to examining the meaning of the text, fell foul of his bishop, the old Scotist Richard Fitzjames, and a more sinister quarrel broke out in Germany in 1509, when a converted Jew, Johann Pfefferkorn, petitioned the emperor to order the surrender of Jewish books for examination on anti-Christian opinions; the matter was referred to the inquisitors and to the leading German Hebraist, Johann Reuchlin, whose protests against the plan led to charges of heresy being brought against him. For a time his views were upheld, both by a papal judge-delegate and by a committee of cardinals, but the inquisitors persisted and pamphlets written by Reuchlin in defence of the value of Hebrew literature were condemned. Reuchlin had support from two humanists, who tried to depict his opponents as pseudo-scholars in the satirical letters called the *Letters of Obscure Men*. In fact even among the humanists, Reuchlin's views were not always supported, but after the outbreak of the Reformation, many of his supporters recognised that Luther's opponents were drawn from the same circle of men as his had been. This may have won Luther some initial support in humanist circles, although he himself was more influenced by traditional scholastic theology than by the values of the new learning.[18]

The laity's ability and desire to read challenged the Church's monopoly of teaching and its status as the guarantor of orthodoxy, as the contrasting views of two prominent humanists to Bible translations make clear. Their respective backgrounds conditioned their views. The Netherlands had no active tradition of heresy, and in the introduction to his edition of the New Testament the Dutchman Erasmus expressed a wish that the Gospels and the Epistles should be accessible to all, women and men, Scots and Irish, Turks and Saracens, and that they should inspire the farmer at his plough and the weaver at his loom, people in other words who might not be expected to participate in intellectual activity.[19] Erasmus saw learning as a means of pastoral activity, and its development as potentially beneficial to the Church. By contrast Sir Thomas More, coming from a country where there was an active heretical sect in the Lollards (and admittedly writing after the outbreak of the Lutheran revolt), violently criticised the whole idea of making the Scriptures available to all and sundry; his attack on such a translation by the reformer William Tyndale was significantly entitled the *Dialogue of Heresies*.

Christian humanist learning was international, and it is not surprising that some of its earliest examples came from Italy. Lorenzo Valla's *Adnotationes in Novum Testamentum* were a landmark in critical studies, and indeed were used by Erasmus, and Gianozzo Manetti was the first humanist to master Hebrew. The work of Ximénez de Cisneros in Spain was directed to restoring the text of the Vulgate.[20] This represented Christian learning at its highest level, but Christian works were becoming accessible to a wider public by other means also. The humanists' scholarship was furthered by the activity of the printers, with whom they were closely associated, and who made both their original works and their editions of early Christian texts available to a wider public. The printing revolution began in the mid-fifteenth century – the earliest work printed by movable type was the Bible published at Mainz by Johann Gutenberg in 1453 – and rapidly spread throughout Western Christendom. By the 1470s there were presses in Germany, Italy, Bohemia, Switzerland, France, Spain, England and the Low Countries, and the productions of these publishers generated their own market. Many publishers had close ties with their authors, as can be seen from the association between Erasmus and Johann Froben at Basel.

The nature of the book market is less clear. Booksellers' lists and early surviving books both show a heavy weighting towards religious works, including both Bibles and Bible commentaries, liturgical texts, books of sermons and saints' lives, and devotional tracts, in other words a very similar range of works to those which had earlier been produced by copying manuscripts. The whole character of publication, however, meant that works could be produced in multiple copies, and the publisher might well not be aware of who would purchase his products.[21] Many books were probably bought by churchmen, but it was always possible that works might pass into lay hands, and it was the fear that writings of dubious orthodoxy or books critical of the ecclesiastical establishment might reach an audience which would not approach them with sufficient awareness of this, that lies behind the censorship decree of the Fifth Lateran Council.[22]

This fear of subversion was not wholly unjustified. In Italy some philosophers held views which were hardly compatible with traditional Christian doctrine, and in the North Erasmus at any rate was highly intolerant and critical of many aspects of the contemporary Church. In his waspish and humorous satire, *The Praise of Folly,* he attacked aspects of both academic thought and popular religion. He launched a savage diatribe against the various schools of scholastic philosophers and theologians, criticising the terminology of both as barbarous, and the irrelevance to the Christian life of some issues debated by the latter.[23] He also satirised the popular practice of making votive offerings to saints, and the superstitions attached to their cult, claiming that such follies were encouraged by the venality of priests who saw them as a means of making a profit. The religious life was equally attacked, with many of the regulars being described as hypocrites who relied on formal ceremonies.[24] What made such views more dangerous was that the work achieved widespread popularity among the literate public. It was published nineteen times between 1511 and 1516, and twenty more editions appeared by 1525. He should not, however, be seen purely as a negative critic, because in other writings his approach was more positive, and reflected the balance between mind and soul for which he strove, which he described by the term 'the Philosophy of Christ'. In his earlier *Enchiridion Militis Christiani* (the Handbook of a Christian Knight), published in 1503, he urged that the classics should be studied as an intellectual training for a higher purpose, namely studying the Scriptures, which should be approached with reverence as well as with the intellect. Furthermore, despite his general hostility to the religious orders and their members, he was influenced in writing the work by the Franciscan mystic and reformer Jean Vitrier. Initially it made less impression than *Folly* was to do, but later it surpassed it in the number of published editions, not only in Latin but also in various vernacular translations. No fewer than twenty-three editions appeared between 1515 and 1521.[25] In his later *Education of a Christian Prince,* he again stressed that learning must serve moral and spiritual ends. There was an optimistic element in such ideas, that man could contribute to his own spiritual betterment, so it is not surprising that after the outbreak of the Reformation Luther, nurtured in an Augustinian tradition which emphasised the innate sinfulness of humanity, which could be rescued only by God's grace, attacked Erasmus's views as Pelagian. On many matters there was common ground between Erasmus and Luther – both welcomed the idea of the Scriptures being available in the vernacular, both criticised indulgences, and Erasmus recognised that many of Luther's enemies were also his own – but the Dutchman lacked the German's spiritual agonies, which led the latter to find relief in a doctrine of salvation by faith alone.

Many of Erasmus's contemporaries shared his attitude to learning. The greatest of the French humanists, Jacques Lefèvre d'Étaples, declared that human knowledge was vain, if God did not illuminate the eyes of the heart, and the ideals of many scholars represented a perennial characteristic of Christian thought, the desire to interpret the Scriptures in intellectual terms compatible with the accepted philosophy of the age. The outbreak of the Reformation, however, forced the humanists to take sides, and probably affected attitudes to Erasmus. Where previously his criticisms might have been accepted with wry amusement, after 1517 these could be seen as subversive. Among the humanists there were those who had always been more sympathic to traditional religion; in Germany Willibald Pirckheimer was attached to traditional cults and Ulrich von Hutten wished a friend well in going on pilgrimage to Jerusalem, and the criticisms of such men were directed more at where old ideals had failed rather than at the ideals themselves.[26] In England, where the young Thomas More was for a time drawn towards the Carthusian order before he eventually settled for a lay career, it reflects the continuing appeal of the old ideals of monastic austerity that it was the most rigorous of the orders to which he was drawn. The idealism of men with strong spiritual principles was well demonstrated by the fact that it was the Carthusians, along with the Observant wing of the Franciscans, who refused to yield to the demands of Henry VIII in the 1530s, accepting instead the full horrors of a traitor's death. More died on the scaffold, as did another noted English humanist, bishop Fisher of Rochester.

Manifestations of piety

Loyalty to the traditional faith in face of persecution testifies to the fact that it still met the needs of pious men. Although some humanist criticism may have weakened the traditional defences of the Church, it represented a positive desire for reform, like many other movements throughout the centuries, and cannot be equated with a desire for revolt. It should be seen as one aspect of the intellectual vigour of ecclesiastical thought at the time, which provided the background to the theological debates between reformers and traditionalists in the sixteenth century. Despite differences between individuals, they were essentially seeking the same objective, the betterment of the Church. At the popular level too, there is evidence of widespread positive loyalty to the Church and its teaching. The response to Savonarola's preaching in Florence demonstrates that audiences not only listened to sermons but tried to respond to their content. The late fifteenth century saw massive amounts of church building in Germany, and a similar phenomenon can be seen in England.[27] This represented a corporate religious act, and the integration of the Church and Society can also be seen in the activity of English religious guilds which offered an opportunity for pious activity beyond the formal requirements of canon law. Similar guilds were established in Italy, with titles such as 'Divine Love' and the 'Name of Jesus', and this movement culminated in the establishment of the Oratory of Divine Love, which combined personal sanctification and the practice of charity. Some of these bodies survived beyond the division of the Church in the mid-sixteenth century and made a substantial contribution to the movements for Catholic reform.[28] Lay piety was undoubtedly active, and perhaps the greatest failure of late medieval churchmen was their inability to channel this into support for the established order. Lay groups within the Church might be tolerated, indeed encouraged, as an outlet for religious enthusiasm but they remained peripheral to its central activities. The celebration of the sacraments was the prerogative of the clergy, and the role of the laity was to observe and receive.

Late medieval religion, however, allowed scope for individual as well as corporate devotion. The development of the works called Books of Hours provided something of a private liturgy, setting out a sequence of readings and prayers (significantly, many connected with devotion to the Virgin Mary) for private devotion. This at any rate provided a form of private worship, at least for the literate.[29] Such contemplation might focus on the suffering of Christ, something also reflected in the art of the period. The woodcarvings of men such as Veit Stoss and Tilman Riemenschneider stressed both the humanity and the sufferings of Christ,[30] and the agonies of the crucifixion have seldom been more graphically depicted than in Grünewald's Isenheim altarpiece. The development of new liturgies for special feasts included those of the Five Wounds of Christ and of the Holy Name, as well as others for various aspects of the life of the Virgin Mary. In these at any rate, the Church gave formal endorsement to popular cults.

The background to the Reformation

It was a combination of popular religiosity and political pressures which provided the seed-bed for the Reformation. The former reflected the increasing sophistication of a more literate society, and as some laity certainly were better educated than many of the lesser clergy, this resulted at times in a measure of anti-clericalism, directed against the attitudes of a clerical order which saw itself not simply as the ruling class in the Church but also as something qualitatively distinct from other men. In practice, however, there were many situations in which the laity could exercise *de facto* control over churchmen (as for example in the hiring and dismissal of guild priests) in a manner which provided a precedent for the kind of lay control that was developed in the sixteenth century. Most conspicuously, the Church at its highest administrative levels had to accept the existence of two masters in the pope and the local lay ruler. The Papacy could no longer exercise the kind of dominance sought by the reformers of the eleventh and twelfth centuries, but had reached a compromise in which its theoretical supremacy was still acknowledged, but in which the lay power could call the tune on many matters, such as the appointment of higher clergy and the restriction of appeals outside its land.

If the Western Church could still be recognised as a unity in 1500, this was essentially in matters of faith and worship. With the exception of a very few heretics, most people accepted the same formal beliefs which were regarded as the essence of orthodoxy, but this reflected a willingness to limit those matters of doctrine which were seen as the substance of the faith. Academic theologians differed in their understanding of details of belief, but still acknowledged the Church's right to make the final decision as to what was and what was not acceptable, and on such matters the lay power made no claim to intervene. There were also tensions between the older scholastic traditions of theology and newer styles of interpretation of the Scriptures influenced by the linguistic disciplines of humanism, but again these could generally be comprehended within the fold of the Church. It was this unity which was broken in the sixteenth century, when the lay rulers (sometimes kings and princes, at other times civic rulers) also took decisions on which doctrines were to be considered as orthodox, and the religious divisions of Europe were determined by the principle of *cuius regio, eius religio* ('to each region, its own faith'). It was the lay powers' combination of administrative authority with control over belief that marked the decisive difference between the Church of the Middle Ages and that of the post-Reformation period. Even where rulers still accepted the Papacy as the final authority over doctrine, this decision in itself was an act of lay power, which marked the final fragmentation of the ideal of ecclesiastical unity which had been the hallmark of the central Middle Ages.

Appendix I:
Table of significant events

312	Constantine's Edict of Toleration
324	Council of Nicaea
380	Edict of Theodosius enforcing Nicaean Christianity as the orthodox religion of the Roman Empire
late 4th c.	Activity of St Martin at Tours
early 5th c.	Foundation of monasteries at Lérins (Honoratus) and Marseilles (Cassian)
410	Sack of Rome by the Visigoths
451	Council of Chalcedon
476	Fall of the Roman Empire in the West
c.500	The Frankish king Clovis accepts Catholic rather than Arian Christianity
early 6th c.	Probable writing of the Rule of St Benedict
565	Mission of St Columba from Ireland to Iona
568	Lombard invasion of Italy and restriction of Byzantine power in peninsula
c.586	Spanish Visigoths abandon Arianism for Catholic Christianity
590ff.	Mission of St Columbanus to the Frankish lands
597	Mission of St Augustine to England
632	Death of Mohammed
641	Fall of Egypt and Syria to Islam
663	Last visit of Byzantine emperor to Rome
664	Synod of Whitby
690	Mission of St Willibrord to Frisia
711	Moslem invasion of Spain
716–54	Missions of St Boniface to the German lands (732 Creation of archbishopric at Mainz)
726–87	Iconoclast controversy
732	Defeat of Moslems near Poitiers

751	End of the Merovingian dynasty and establishment of the Carolingians
late 8th c.	Establishment of political connections between the Papacy and the Frankish rulers, probable date of the *Donation of Constantine*. Adoptionist movement in Spain
800	Imperial coronation of Charlemagne
early 9th c.	Monastic reforms of St Benedict of Aniane
848/849	Condemnation of Gottschalk of Orbais
c.850	Pseudo-Isidorian writings
850ff.	Missions to the Slavs, pagan Viking settlements in England and Gaul
c.874	Conversion of Bohemia
883	Sacking of Monte Cassino by the Saracens
897	'Cadaver' synod condemns Pope Formosus
901ff.	Rise of the Theophylact family in Rome
909	Foundation of the monastery of Cluny
962	Imperial coronation of Otto I
989	Council of Charroux tries to establish Peace Movement
1000ff.	Enforcement of Christianity in Scandinavia
c.1020	Completion of the *Decretum* of Burchard of Worms
1025	Heresy proceedings in the diocese of Cambrai-Arras
1046	Synod of Sutri – imperial deposition of rival popes
1054	Schism between the Eastern and the Western Churches. Abjuration of Berengar of Tours
1059	Election decree of Nicholas II gives cardinals responsibility for choosing pope
1071	Seljuk Turks defeat the Byzantines at Manzikert
1073, 1075	Papal decrees against clerical marriage
1076	Gregory VII excommunicates Emperor Henry IV
1077	Emperor does penance at Canossa
1084	Foundation of the abbey of the Grande Chartreuse
1085	Supersession of Mozarabic by Roman rite in Spain at Council of Burgos
c.1090	Anselm formulates ontological argument for the existence of God
1095	Council of Clermont, proclamation of the First Crusade
1098	Foundation of the abbey of Cîteaux
1099	Fall of Jerusalem to the Crusaders
1112	Bernard enters abbey of Cîteaux
1115	Foundation of the abbey of Clairvaux
1121	Council of Soissons condemns Abelard
1122	Concordat of Worms
1123	First Lateran Council
1130	Schism of Papacy
1139	Second Lateran Council

1140	Council of Sens – further condemnation of Abelard
c.1140	Completion of the *Decretum* of Gratian
1140ff.	Heresy trials in Rhineland, possibly of Cathars
1147	Second Crusade
c.1150	Completion of Peter Lombard's *Book of Sentences*
1159	Papal schism between pro- and anti-imperial claimants
1165	Debate at Lombers between Cathars and church authorities
1170	Murder of Archbishop Thomas Becket
c.1176	Conversion of Valdes of Lyons to a life of poverty
1179	Third Lateran Council
1184	Condemnation of Waldensians and Humiliati
1187	Fall of Jerusalem to Saladin
1189	Third Crusade
1204	Fall of Byzantium to the Fourth Crusade
1205	Split between moderate and radical Waldensians
1208	Murder of papal legate by Cathars leads to proclamation of crusade against them
1209	Recognition of Francis and his followers as an order by Innocent III
1212	Christian Spaniards defeat the Moors at Las Navas de Tolosa
1213	Defeat of the southerners by the Albigensian crusaders at Muret
1215	Fourth Lateran Council
1227	Excommunication of Emperor Frederick II
1231	Bull *Parens scientiarum* authorises University of Paris to regulate its own constitution
1233	'The Great Devotion' revivalist movement in Italy
1239	Renewed excommunication of Emperor Frederick II
1244	Fall of Cathar stronghold of Montségur
1245	Bull *Ordinem vestrum* by which the Papacy assumed legal ownership of the goods of the Franciscan order. First Council of Lyons
c.1248–57	Bonaventura teaching in Paris
1250	Death of Frederick II
1252–9	Thomas Aquinas teaching at Köln and Paris
1260	Outbreaks of Flagellant activity prompted by Joachite prophecy
1266	Papal forces defeat Hohenstaufen Manfred at Benevento
1268	Papal and French forces defeat Hohenstaufen Conradin at Tagliacozzo
1268–71	Papal vacancy of two and three-quarter years
1268–72	Aquinas again teaching in Paris
1270	Condemnation of thirteen philosophical propositions at Paris

1274	Second Council of Lyons proclaims reunion of Eastern and Western Churches. Death of Aquinas
1277	Condemnation of 219 philosophical propositions at Paris (also at Oxford)
1279	Bull *Exiit qui seminat* attempts to reach a compromise between radical and moderate wings of the Franciscan order
1282	Sicilian Vespers
1283	Annulment of the Union of the Eastern and Western Churches
1291	Fall of Acre and end of crusading states in Palestine
1294	Election and abdication of Pope Celestine V
1296	Bull *Clericis laicos* forbids lay taxation of clergy
1302	Bull *Unam sanctam* affirms supremacy of spiritual over temporal power
1303	French attack on Pope Boniface VIII
1307	Philip IV of France attacks the Templar Order
1309	Papacy settles at Avignon
1310	Execution of Marguerite Porete
1311	Council of Vienne
1318	Execution of four Spiritual Franciscans at Marseilles
1322	Bull *Ad conditorem*, by which Papacy relinquishes trusteeship of the goods of the Franciscan order
1323	Bull *Cum inter nonnullos*, declaring doctrine of the absolute poverty of Christ and the apostles to be heretical
1324	Completion of Marsilius of Padua's *Defensor Pacis*
1327–30	Imperially supported schism
1328	Flight of Franciscan leaders from Avignon
1329	Posthumous condemnation of twenty-eight articles from the writings of Meister Eckhart
1334–42	Pontificate of Benedict XII sees start of building of papal palace at Avignon
1346	Foundation of the University of Prague
1347–9	First outbreak of the Black Death
1352	First papal election capitulation
1367	Temporary return of the Papacy to Rome
1377	Papacy returns again to Rome
1378	Outbreak of the Great Schism
1379–83	Active preaching career of Gerard Groote
1385	Final conversion of Lithuania
1387	Foundation of Augustinian abbey of Windesheim
1391	Foundation of the Bethlehem Chapel in Prague
1396	Crusade of Nicopolis
1398	First French withdrawal of obedience
1402	Hus appointed preacher at the Bethlehem Chapel

1409	Meeting of the Council of Pisa, and election of conciliar pope
1414	Lollard rebellion in England. Meeting of the Council of Constance
1415	Decree *Haec Sancta*. Deposition of John XXIII and resignation of Gregory XII. Condemnation of the writings of Wyclif. Execution of Hus
1416	Withdrawal of Spanish obedience from Benedict XIII
1417	Deposition of Benedict XIII by the Council. Decree *Frequens*. Election of Martin V
1418	Concordats between the Papacy and Spain, France, Germany and England
1420	Four Articles of Prague
1420–31	Anti-Hussite crusades
1423	Council of Pavia-Siena
before 1427	Writing of *The Imitation of Christ*
1431	Meeting of the Council of Basel
1434	Eugenius IV adheres to the council. Defeat of Hussite radicals
1438	Pragmatic Sanction of Bourges
1439	Division in the Council of Basel. German princes declare neutrality between the pope and the council. Election of antipope by the radical party. Council of Ferrara-Florence agrees reunion of the Eastern and Western churches
c.1440	Lorenzo Valla demonstrates that the *Donation of Constantine* was a forgery
1448	Concordat of Vienna
1449	Council of Basel dissolves itself
1451–2	Legatine mission of Nicholas of Cusa to Germany
1453	Fall of Constantinople to the Turks. Gutenberg's printed edition of the Bible
1456	Repulse of the Turks from Belgrade
1460	Bull *Execrabilis* forbids appeals to a future council
1472	Concordat between the Papacy and France
1480	Siege of Rhodes by the Turks
1480–1	Turks occupy Otranto
1485	Formal recognition of religious toleration in Bohemia
1492	Fall of the Moorish kingdom of Granada
1494	French invasion of Italy
1494–8	Savonarola dominates religious life of Florence
1509	Erasmus writes *The Praise of Folly*
1511	Anti-papal council summoned to Pisa. Fifth Lateran Council meets (till 1517)
1514	Printing of the *Complutensian Polyglot* edition of the Bible
1516	Concordat of Bologna between Papacy and France. Publication of Erasmus' edition of the New Testament
1517	Luther's ninety-five theses

Appendix II: Chronological list of Popes, 312–1517

(Antipopes' names and dates are shown in *italics*)

311–14	Miltiades (or Melchiades)
314–35	Sylvester I
336	Mark
337–52	Julius I
352–66	Liberius
355–65	*Felix II*
366–84	Damasus I
366–7	*Ursinus*
384–99	Siricus
399–401	Anastasius I
401–17	Innocent I
417–18	Zosimus
418–19	*Eulalius*
418–22	Boniface I
422–32	Celestine I
432–40	Sixtus III
440–61	Leo I 'the Great'
461-8	Hilarus
468–83	Simplicius
483–92	Felix III
492–6	Gelasius I
496–8	Anastasius II
498–514	Symmachus
498–9, 501–16	*Lawrence*
514–23	Hormisdas
523–6	John I
526–30	Felix IV
530	*Dioscorus*

530–2	Boniface II
533–5	John II
535–6	Agapitus I
536–7	Silverius
537–55	Vigilius
556–61	Pelagius I
561–74	John III
575–9	Benedict I
579–90	Pelagius II
590–604	Gregory I 'the Great'
604–6	Sabinian
607	Boniface III
608–15	Boniface IV
615–18	Deusdedit (later Adeodatus I)
619–25	Boniface V
625–38	Honorius I
640	Severinus
640–2	John IV
642–9	Theodore I
649–53	Martin I
654–7	Eugenius I
657–72	Vitalian
672–6	Adeodatus II
676–8	Donus
678–81	Agatho
682–3	Leo II
684–5	Benedict II
685–6	John V
686–7	Conon
687	*Theodore*
687	*Paschal*
687–701	Sergius I
701–5	John VI
705–7	John VII
708	Sisinnius
708–15	Constantine
715–31	Gregory II
731–41	Gregory III
741–52	Zacharias
752	Stephen (II) (Died before consecration)
752–7	Stephen II (III)
757–67	Paul I
767–8	*Constantine*
768	*Philip*
768–72	Stephen III (IV)

772–95	Hadrian I
795–816	Leo III
816–17	Stephen IV (V)
817–24	Paschal I
824–7	Eugenius II
827	Valentine
827–44	Gregory IV
844	*John*
844–7	Sergius II
847–55	Leo IV
855–8	Benedict III
855	*Anastasius Bibliothecarius*
858–67	Nicholas I
867–72	Hadrian II
872–82	John VIII
882–4	Marinus I
884–5	Hadrian III
885–91	Stephen V (VI)
891–6	Formosus
896	Boniface VI
896–7	Stephen VI (VII)
897	Romanus
897	Theodore II
898–900	John IX
900–3	Benedict IV
903–4	Leo V
903–4	*Christopher*
904–11	Sergius III
911–13	Anastasius III
913–14	Lando
914–28	John X
928	Leo VI
928–31	Stephen VII (VIII)
931–6	John XI
936–9	Leo VII
939–42	Stephen VIII (IX)
942–6	Marinus II
946–55	Agapitus II
955–64	John XII
963–5	Leo VIII
964	Benedict V
965–72	John XIII
973–4	Benedict VI
974, 984–5	*Boniface VII*
974–83	Benedict VII

983–4	John XIV
985–96	John XV
996–9	Gregory V
997–8	*John XVI*
999–1003	Sylvester II
1003	John XVII
1003–9	John XVIII
1009–12	Sergius IV
1012–24	Benedict VIII
1012	*Gregory VI*
1024–32	John XIX
1032–44, 1045, 1047–8	Benedict IX
1045	Sylvester III
1045–6	Gregory VI
1046–7	Clement II
1048	Damasus II
1049–54	Leo IX
1055–7	Victor II
1057–8	Stephen IX (X)
1058–9	*Benedict X*
1058–61	Nicholas II
1061–73	Alexander II
1061–4	*Honorius II*
1073–85	Gregory VII
1080, 1084– 1100	*Clement III*
1086–7	Victor III
1088–99	Urban II
1099–1118	Paschal II
1100–1	*Theodoric*
1101	*Albert (or Adalbert)*
1105–11	*Sylvester IV*
1118–19	Gelasius II
1118–21	*Gregory VIII*
1119–24	Calixtus II
1124–30	Honorius II
1124	*Celestine II*
1130–43	Innocent II
1130–8	*Anacletus II*
1138	*Victor IV*
1143–4	Celestine II
1144–5	Lucius II
1145–53	Eugenius III
1153–4	Anastasius IV

1154–9	Hadrian IV
1159–81	Alexander III
1159–64	*Victor IV*
1164–8	*Paschal III*
1168–78	*Calixtus III*
1179–80	*Innocent III*
1181–5	Lucius III
1185–7	Urban III
1187	Gregory VIII
1187–91	Clement III
1191–8	Celestine III
1198–1216	Innocent III
1216–27	Honorius III
1227–41	Gregory IX
1241	Celestine IV
1243–54	Innocent IV
1254–61	Alexander IV
1261–4	Urban IV
1265–8	Clement IV
1271–6	Gregory X
1276	Innocent V
1276	Hadrian V
1276–7	John XXI (No pope took designation John XX)
1277–80	Nicholas III
1281–5	Martin IV (No popes were designated Martin II and III)
1285–7	Honorius IV
1288–92	Nicholas IV
1294	Celestine V
1294–1303	Boniface VIII
1303–4	Benedict XI
1305–14	Clement V
1316–34	John XXII
1328–30	*Nicholas V*
1334–42	Benedict XII
1342–52	Clement VI
1352–62	Innocent VI
1362–70	Urban V
1370–8	Gregory XI
1378–89	Urban VI
1378–94	*Clement VII*
1389–1404	Boniface IX
1394–1417/23	*Benedict XIII (Deposed in 1417 but refused to accept deposition)*
1404–6	Innocent VII
1406–15	Gregory XII

1409–10	Alexander V (Conciliar pope)
1410–15	John XXIII (Conciliar pope)
1417–31	Martin V
1423–9	*Clement VIII*
1425	*Benedict XIV*
1431–47	Eugenius IV
1439–49	*Felix V*
1447–55	Nicholas V
1455–8	Calixtus III
1458–64	Pius II
1464–71	Paul II
1471–84	Sixtus IV
1484–92	Innocent VIII
1492–1503	Alexander VI
1503	Pius III
1503–13	Julius II
1513–21	Leo X

(Details from J. N. D. Kelly, *The Oxford Dictionary of Popes*)

Appendix III:
Glossary of terms

Accidents: the visible and variable elements which could differentiate individual examples of the same species (*see also* **Substance**)

Adoptionism: eighth-century heresy in Spain which stressed the humanity of Christ as an adopted son of God

Anchorites: religious who lived as solitaries

Annates: a payment of the first year's revenues made by a cleric to the Papacy on his appointment to a non-elective benefice (one other than a bishopric or an abbey) reserved to the Holy See. The term was also used loosely to include **Services** (*see below*)

Antinomianism: denial of an obligation to keep the moral law

Arianism: doctrine of a fourth-century heretic that the Son was of like nature but not of the same nature as the Father

Camera: the financial department of the papal **Curia**

Catharism: heretical doctrine which affirmed the competing powers of good and evil gods, and which rejected the material world as inherently evil

Cenobites: religious who lived in a community

Conclaves: the meetings (from 1059 of the cardinals) which elected popes

Concordat: agreement between the Papacy and a secular power to regulate matters of ecclesiastical administration in a particular territory

Curia: the papal court

Excommunication: exclusion of an individual from receiving the sacraments of the Church

Humiliati: late twelfth-century movement on the fringes of heresy which idealised poverty

Iconoclasm: destruction of images because veneration shown to them was considered to be idolatry

Indulgences: originally the remission of a temporal penalty incurred as a canonical penance for a sin. By the late Middle Ages, it had come to mean the commutation of an act of penance for a payment of money

Interdict: papal ban on the performance of church services in a particular area

Joachimism: term applied by historians to the teachings of Abbot Joachim of Fiore, who put forward a theory of three ages of history, the last of which would be preceded by the coming of Antichrist

Lay investiture: the conferment of a spiritual office on a churchman by a layman

Lollardy: heretical movement in late medieval England

Monophysitism: doctrine (condemned in 451) that Christ had only a single nature

Monotheletism: doctrine (condemned in 680–1) that while Christ had both a divine and a human nature, he had only one will

Nominalism: philosophical teaching that the universal (the concept of something) was purely a name and had no real existence (*see below*, **Realism**)

Ockhamist: school of theologians following the teachings of William of Ockham

Pallium: vestment conferred on archbishops by the Papacy

Patarenes: originally a radical reform movement in eleventh-century Milan, but later the term was used to designate heretics there

Peace Movement: an attempt in the tenth and eleventh centuries by the Church and by pious laity to establish greater social order

Pelagianism: doctrine of a fifth-century heretic that man might attain to salvation through his own free will without the aid of grace

Penitentiary: the branch of the Curia which heard cases concerning spiritual irregularities

Perfecti: full members of the Cathar sect

Provision: a papal appointment to a benefice normally in the patronage of someone else

Realism: philosophical teaching that the universal had a real existence (*see above*, **Nominalism**)

Reservation: action of Papacy reserving the right to make a future appointment to a benefice

Scotist: school of theologians following the teachings of Duns Scotus

Services: payments made to the Papacy on their appointment by bishops and abbots, if their benefices were assessed at more than 100 florins *per annum*

Simony: the offence of paying money to obtain a spiritual office

Substance: the essential being in something which underlies its appearance and gives it its real nature. This contrasts with **Accidents** (*see above*)

Thomism: school of theologians following the teachings of St Thomas Aquinas

Transubstantiation: the doctrine that in the Eucharist the substance of the elements was transmuted from bread and wine, which were annihilated, into the body and blood of Christ, although the accidents of the elements remained unaltered (*see also above*, **Accidents, Substance**)

Utraquism: Hussite practice of giving communion in both kinds (bread and wine) to the laity

Waldensians: followers of Valdes of Lyons, who believed in a life of poverty, and who eventually were condemned by the Church

Bibliography

Primary Sources

Adam of Bremen, *History of the Archbishops of Hamburg-Bremen,* trans. F. J. Tschau (New York, 1959).

Adomnan's Life of Columba, trans. A. O. and M. O. Anderson (Edinburgh, 1961).

Alcuin, *The Bishops, Kings and Saints of York,* trans. P. Godman (Oxford, 1982).

Anglo-Saxon Missionaries in Germany, trans. C. H. Talbot (London, 1954).

The Annals of Fulda, trans. T. Reuter (Manchester, 1992).

The Annals of St. Bertin, trans. J. L. Nelson (Manchester, 1991).

Asser, *Life of Alfred* (various editions available, cited by chapter).

G. Barraclough, ed., *Modus et forma procedendi ad executionem seu protestationem gratiae alicui factae per dominum papam* (Milan, 1938).

Bede, *Ecclesiastical History* (various editions available, cited by chapter).

Bede, *Life of St. Cuthbert* (various editions available, cited by chapter).

J. F. Benton, ed., *Self and Society in Medieval France* (Medieval Academy of America Reprints 15, *The Memoirs of Abbot Guibert of Nogent*) (Toronto, 1984).

Bernard of Clairvaux, *The Letters of St. Bernard of Clairvaux,* trans. B. S. James (London, 1953).

Bernard of Clairvaux, *The Works of St. Bernard of Clairvaux, I, Treatises, I,* intro. J. Leclercq (Cistercian Fathers Series, 1) (Shannon, 1970).

R. B. Blakney, trans., *Meister Eckhart* (New York, 1957).

U.-R. Blumenthal, *The Early Councils of Pope Paschal II* (PIMS, 43) (Toronto, 1978).

L. Boisset, *Un concile provincial au treizième siècle* (Paris, 1973).

The Book of Pontiffs, trans. R. Davis (Liverpool, 1989).

The Book of St. Gilbert, trans. R. Foreville and G. Keir (Oxford, 1987).

Boso's Life of Alexander III, trans. G. M. Ellis, intro. P. Munz (Oxford, 1973).

The Burgundian Code, trans. K. F. Drew (Philadelphia, PA, 1972).

Calendar of Papal Registers (London and Dublin, 1893–1994).

Canterbury Professions, ed. M. Richter, Canterbury and York Society, 67 (London, 1973).

Carolingian Chronicles, trans. B. W. Scholz (Ann Arbor, MI, 1972).

Charlemagne's Cousins, trans. A. Cabaniss (Syracuse, NY, 1967).

Chronicle of Battle Abbey, trans. E. Searle (Oxford, 1980).

Chronicle of the Election of Hugh, Abbot of Bury St. Edmunds and later Bishop of Ely, trans. R. M. Thomson (Oxford, 1974).

Chronicle of Fredegar, see Fredegar, *The Fourth Book of the Chronicle of Fredegar with its Continuations*.

Chronicle of Jean de Venette, see Jean de Venette, *Chronicle*.

Chronicle of Jocelin of Brakelond, trans. H. E. Butler (Edinburgh and London, 1949).

Chronicles of Matthew Paris, trans. R. Vaughan (Gloucester, 1986).

The Cistercian World, trans. P. Matarosso (Harmondsworth, 1993).

C. B. Coleman, *The Treatise of Lorenzo Valla on the Donation of Constantine* (Renaissance Society of America Reprint Texts, 1) (Toronto, 1993).

Conquerors and Chroniclers of Early Medieval Spain, trans. K. B. Wolf (Liverpool, 1990).

The Correspondence of Pope Gregory VII, trans. E. Emerton (New York, 1932).

C. M. D. Crowder, *Unity, Heresy and Reform, 1378–1460* (London, 1977).

Dante, *The Divine Comedy* (various editions available, cited by canto and line).

The Deeds of Frederick Barbarossa, trans. C. C. Mierow (New York, 1953).

Dino Compagni's Chronicle of Florence, trans. D. E. Bornstein (Philadelphia, PA, 1993).

P. Dubois, *The Recovery of the Holy Land*, trans. W. I. Brandt (New York, 1956).

Eadmer, *Eadmer's History of Recent Events in England*, trans. G. Bosanquet (London, 1964).

Eadmer, *The Life of St. Anselm, Archbishop of Canterbury by Eadmer*, ed. R. W. Southern (Edinburgh and London, 1962).

The Earliest English Poems, trans. M. Alexander (Harmondsworth, 1966).

Early Charters of St. Paul's Cathedral, ed. M. Gibbs, Camden Third Series, 58 (London, 1939).

Eddius Stephanus, *Life of Wilfrid* (various editions available, cited by chapter).

Einhard, *Life of Charlemagne* (various editions available, cited by chapter – see also *Two Lives of Charlemagne*).

English Historical Documents, I. ed. D. Whitelock, II. ed. D. C. Douglas and G. W. Greenaway (London, 1953–5).

Epistolae Vagantes of Pope Gregory VII, trans. H. E. J. Cowdrey (Oxford, 1972).

Erasmus, *Julius Exclusus,* trans. P. Pascal (Bloomington, IN, 1968).

Erasmus, *The Praise of Folly* (various editions available, cited by chapter).

Fredegar, *The Fourth Book of the Chronicle of Fredegar with its Continuations,* trans. J. M. Wallace-Hadrill (London, 1960).

Fulbert of Chartres, *The Letters and Poems of Fulbert of Chartres,* trans. F. Behrends (Oxford, 1976).

Fulcher of Chartres, *A History of the Expedition to Jerusalem,* trans. H. S. Fink (Knoxville, TN, 1969).

Galbert of Bruges, *The Murder of Charles the Good, Count of Flanders,* trans. J. B. Ross (New York, 1960).

J. Gerson, *Oeuvres Complètes,* ed. P. Glorieux (Paris, 1960–73).

Gesta Francorum, ed. R. Hill (Edinburgh, 1962).

Rodulfus Glaber, *Opera,* ed. J. France, N. Bulst and P. Reynolds (Oxford, 1989).

Gregory of Tours, *The Glory of the Confessors,* trans. R. van Dam (Liverpool, 1988).

Gregory of Tours, *The Glory of the Martyrs,* trans. R. van Dam (Liverpool, 1988).

Gregory of Tours, *The History of the Franks,* trans. L. Thorpe (Harmondsworth, 1974).

Gregory of Tours, *The Life of the Fathers,* trans. E. James (Liverpool, 1991).

B. Gui, *Manuel de l'inquisiteur,* ed. G. Mollat (Paris, 1964).

F. Guicciardini, *History of Italy,* trans. S. Alexander (Princeton, NJ, 1969).

J. Hillgarth and G. Silano, eds, *Register 'Notule Communium' 14 of the Diocese of Barcelona 1345–1348* (PIMS, Subsidia Medievalia 13) (Toronto, 1983).

Historia Pontificalis, see John of Salisbury, *Historia Pontificalis.*

A. Hudson, *Selections from English Wycliffite Writings* (Cambridge, 1978).

A. Hudson and P. Gradon, eds, *English Wycliffite Sermons,* 5 vols (Oxford, 1983–96).

Hugh the Chantor, *History of the Church of York,* trans. C. Johnson (Edinburgh and London, 1961).

Hugh of Poitiers, *The Vézelay Chronicle,* trans. J. Scott and J. O. Ward (Binghamton, NY, 1992).

Imperial Lives and Letters of the Eleventh Century, trans. T. E. Mommsen and K. Morrison, ed. R. L. Benson (New York and London, 1962).

Ingulph's Chronicle, trans. H. T. Riley (London, 1854).

B. Jarrett, *The Emperor Charles IV* (London, 1935).

John of Salisbury, *Historia Pontificalis,* trans. M. Chibnall (Edinburgh and London, 1956).

John of Salisbury, *The Letters of John of Salisbury,* trans. W. J. Millar and C. N. L. Brooke, 2 vols (Edinburgh and London, 1955–79).

John of Salisbury, *Metalogicon,* trans. D. D. McGarry (Berkeley, CA, 1955).

Joinville and Villehardouin, *Chronicles of the Crusades,* trans. M. R. B. Shaw (Harmondsworth, 1963).

Jonas, *Life of St. Columban* (Felinfach, 1993).

M. Kantor, *Medieval Slavic Lives of Saints and Princes* (Ann Arbor, MI, 1983).

M. Kantor, *The Origins of Christianity in Bohemia* (Evanston, IL, 1990).

L. Landucci, *A Florentine Diary from 1450 to 1516,* trans. A. Jervis (repr. New York, 1969).

Lanfranc, *The Letters of Lanfranc, Archbishop of Canterbury,* trans. H. Clover and M. Gibson (Oxford, 1979).

Lanfranc, *The Monastic Constitutions of Lanfranc,* trans. D. Knowles (Edinburgh and London, 1951).

The Letters of Abelard and Heloise, trans. B. Radice (Harmondsworth, 1974).

The Letters and Poems of Fulbert of Chartres, see Fulbert of Chartres, *The Letters.*

The Letters of Gerbert, with his Papal Privileges as Sylvester II, trans. H. P. Lattin (New York, 1961).

The Letters of John of Salisbury, see John of Salisbury, *The Letters.*

The Letters of Lanfranc, see Lanfranc, *The Letters.*

The Letters of St. Bernard of Clairvaux, see Bernard of Clairvaux, *The Letters.*

Libellus de diversis ordinibus et professionibus qui sunt in Aecclesia, trans. G. Constable and B. Smith (Oxford, 1972).

Liber Augustalis or Constitutions of Melfi, trans. J. M. Powell (Syracuse, NY, 1971).

The Lives of the Eighth Century Popes, trans. R. Davis (Liverpool, 1992).

The Lives of the Ninth Century Popes, trans. R. Davis (Liverpool, 1995).

The Lombard Laws, trans. K. F. Drew (Philadelphia, PA, 1973).

L. S. Loomis, ed., *The Council of Constance* (New York, 1961).

Medieval Handbooks of Penance, trans. J. T. McNeill and H. M. Gamer (repr. New York, 1990).

Memoirs of a Renaissance Pope, trans. F. A. Gragg (London, 1960).

A. Mercati, *Raccolta di Concordati su materie ecclesiastiche tra la Santa Sede e le Autorità Civili,* I (Vatican, 1954).

The Metalogicon of John of Salisbury, see John of Salisbury, *Metalogicon.*

Philippe de Mézières, *Letter to King Richard II,* trans. G. W. Coopland (Liverpool, 1975).

The Mirror of Simple Souls, trans. E. L. Babinsky (New York, 1993).

The Monastic Constitutions of Lanfranc, see Lanfranc, *The Monastic Constitutions.*

The Monks of Redon, trans. C. Brett (Woodbridge, 1989).

G. R. Murphy, *The Saxon Savior* (Oxford and New York, 1989).

Nicholas of Cusa, *The Catholic Concordance,* trans. P. E. Sigmund (Cambridge, 1991).

Nicholas of Cusa, *The Vision of God,* trans. E. G. Salter (London, 1928).

Odo of Deuil, *De Profectione Ludovici VII in Orientem,* trans. V. G. Berry (New York, 1948).

Orderic Vitalis, *The Ecclesiastical History,* trans. M. Chibnall, 6 vols (Oxford, 1969–80).

E. Peters, *Heresy and Authority in Medieval Europe* (Philadelphia, PA, 1980).

Petrarch's Book without a Name, trans. N. P. Zacour (Toronto, 1973).

Aeneas Sylvius Piccolomini, *De Gestis Concilii Basiliensis Commentariorum Libri II,* ed. and trans. D. Hay and W. K. Smith (Oxford, 1967).

The Register of Eudes of Rouen, trans. S. M. Brown, ed. J. O'Sullivan (New York and London, 1964).

Regularis Concordia, trans. T. Symons (Edinburgh and London, 1953).

The Rule of St. Benedict (various editions available, cited by chapter).

Saint Odo of Cluny, trans. G. Sitwell (London, 1958).

Sainted Women of the Dark Ages, trans. J. A. McNamara (Durham, NC, 1992).

V. J. Scattergood, ed., *The Works of Sir John Clanvowe* (Cambridge, 1965).

Scripta Leonis, Rufini et Angeli, Sociorum S. Francisci, ed. R. B. Brooke (Oxford, revised edn, 1990).

Selected Letters of Pope Innocent III concerning England, trans. C. R. Cheney and W. H. Semple (Edinburgh and London, 1953).

J. Shirley, trans., *A Parisian Journal* (Oxford, 1968).

Son of Charlemagne, trans. A. Cabaniss (Syracuse, NY, 1961).

M. Spinka, ed., *Advocates of Reform* (London, 1953).

M. Spinka, ed., *John Hus at the Council of Constance* (New York, 1965).

G. Strauss, ed., *Manifestations of Discontent in Germany on the Eve of the Reformation* (Bloomington, IN, 1971).

Suger, trans. E. Panofsky, *On the Abbey Church of St. Denis* (Princeton, NJ, 2nd edn, 1979).

Sulpicius Severus, *The Life of St. Martin,* trans. B. M. Peebles, in *The Fathers of the Church,* VII (Washington, 1949). (Also contains Sulpicius Severus, *Dialogues.*)

N. P. Tanner, ed., *Decrees of the Ecumenical Councils* (London, 1990).

Testamenta Vetusta, ed. N. H. Nicolas (London, 1826).

B. Tierney, ed., *The Crisis of Church and State, 1050–1300* (Englewood Cliffs, NJ, 1964).

The Travels of Leo of Rozmital, 1465–67, ed. M. Letts, Hakluyt Society, Second Series, 108 (Cambridge, 1957).

Two Lives of Charlemagne, trans. L. Thorpe (Harmondsworth, 1969).

Two Memoirs of Renaissance Florence, ed. G. Brucker, trans. J. Martines (New York, 1967).

Jean de Venette, *Chronicle*, trans. R. A. Newhall (New York, 1953).

Vézelay Chronicle, see Hugh of Poitiers.

W. L. Wakefield and A. P. Evans, *Heresies of the High Middle Ages* (New York, 1991).

William of Newburgh, *The History of English Affairs*, I, trans. P. G. Walsh and M. J. Kennedy (Warminster, 1988).

William of Ockham, *A Short Discourse on Tyrannical Government* (Cambridge, 1992).

D. Williman, ed., *Calendar of the Letters of Arnaud Albert, Camerarius Apostolicus, 1361–1371* (PIMS, Subsidia Medievalia, 20) (Toronto, 1992).

C. E. Woodruff, trans., *A XVth Century Guide-Book to the Principal Churches of Rome, compiled c.1470 by William Brewyn* (London, 1933).

Wulfstan of Winchester, *The Live of St. Aethelwold*, trans. M. Lapidge and M. Winterbottom (Oxford, 1991).

Secondary Sources

M. Aston and C. Richmond, eds, *Lollardy and the Gentry in the Later Middle Ages* (Stroud, 1997).

R. N. Bailey, 'A crucifixion plaque from Cumbria', in J. Higgitt, ed., *Early Medieval Sculpture in Britain and Ireland*.

D. Baker, ed., *Medieval Women* (*SCH*, Subsidia, 1) (Oxford, 1978).

M. Barber, *The New Knighthood* (Cambridge, 1994).

M. Barber, *The Trial of the Templars* (Cambridge, 1978).

M. W. Barley and R. P. C. Hanson, eds, *Christianity in Britain, 300–700* (Leicester, 1968).

G. Barraclough, ed., *Medieval Germany, 911–1250* (Oxford, 1948).

G. Barraclough, *Papal Provisions* (Oxford, 1935).

G. W. S. Barrow, *Kingship and Unity* (London, 1981).

J. Barrow, 'Hereford bishops and married clergy, c. 1130–1240', in *Historical Research*, 60 (1987).

M. Baxandall, *The Limewood Sculptors of Renaissance Germany* (Newhaven, CT, 1970).

J. Beckwith, *Early Christian and Byzantine Art* (Newhaven, CT, 1970).

R. F. Bennett, *The Early Dominicans* (Cambridge, 1937).

H. Bett, *Nicholas of Cusa* (London, 1932).

P. Biller, 'The Cathars of Languedoc and written materials', in P. Biller and A. Hudson, eds, *Heresy and Literacy, 1000–1530*.

P. Biller and A. Hudson, eds, *Heresy and Literacy, 1000–1530* (Cambridge, 1994).

P. Binski, *Medieval Death* (London, 1996).

J. Blair and R. Sharpe, eds, *Pastoral Care before the Parish* (Leicester, 1992).

U.-R. Blumenthal, *The Investiture Controversy* (Philadelphia, PA, 1988).

T. S. R. Boase, *Boniface VIII* (London, 1933).

T. S. R. Boase, *Death in the Middle Ages* (London, 1972).

B. Bolton, 'Innocent III's treatment of the Humiliati', in *SCH*, 8 (1972).

B. Bolton, 'Tradition and temerity: papal attitudes to deviants', in *SCH* 9 (1972).

D. E. Bornstein, *The Bianchi of 1399* (Ithaca, NY, 1993).

C. N. L. Brooke, 'The Church in the towns', in *SCH*, 6 (1970).

C. N. L. Brooke, 'Monk and canon: some patterns in the religious life of the twelfth century', in *SCH*, 22 (1985).

A. D. Brown, *Popular Piety in Late Medieval England* (Oxford, 1995).

D. C. Brown, *Pastor and Laity in the Theology of Jean Gerson* (Cambridge, 1987).

J. A. Brundage, *Medieval Canon Law* (London, 1995).

M. Bull, *Knightly Piety and the Lay Response to the First Crusade* (Oxford, 1993).

D. Burr, *Olivi and Franciscan Poverty* (Philadelphia, PA, 1989).

C. W. Bynum, *Holy Feast and Holy Fast: The Religious Significance of Food to Medieval Women* (Berkeley, CA, 1987).

E. Cameron, *The European Reformation* (Oxford, 1991).

E. Cameron, *The Reformation of the Heretics* (Oxford, 1984).

J. Campbell, ed., *The Anglo-Saxons* (Oxford, 1982).

B. Cassidy, ed., *The Ruthwell Cross* (Princeton, NJ, 1992).

G. Cattin, trans. S. Botterill, *Music of the Middle Ages,* I (Cambridge, 1984).

J. I. Catto and T. A. R. Evans, eds, *History of the University of Oxford,* II (Oxford, 1992).

E. Christiansen, *The Northern Crusades* (London, 1980).

N. Cohn, *The Pursuit of the Millenium* (London, 1957, 1962).

R. Collins, 'Mérida and Toledo, 550–585', in E. James, ed., *Visigothic Spain.*

J. J. Contreni, 'The Carolingian renaissance: education and literary culture', in *New CMH*, II.

I. B. Cowan, ed. J. Kirk, *The Medieval Church in Scotland* (Edinburgh, 1995).

H. E. J. Cowdrey, 'The Papacy, the Paterenes and the church of Milan', in *TRHS,* 5th ser., 18 (1968).

M. Creighton, *History of the Papacy, 5* vols (London, 1892–4).

C. Cubitt, 'Unity and diversity in the early Anglo-Saxon liturgy', in *SCH,* 32 (1996).

M. Deanesly, *History of the Medieval Church* (London, 1925).

M. De Jong, 'Carolingian monasticism: the power of prayer', in *New CMH*, II.

M. C. Diaz y Diaz, 'Literary aspects of the Visigothic liturgy', in E. James, ed., *Visigothic Spain*.

A. G. Dickens and W. R. D. Jones, *Erasmus the Reformer* (London, 1994).

M. Dilworth, *Scottish Monasteries in the Late Middle Ages* (Edinburgh, 1995).

R. B. Dobson, ed., *The Church, Politics and Patronage* (Gloucester, 1984).

C. R. Dodwell, *Painting in Europe, 800–1200* (Harmondsworth, 1971).

E. Duffy, *The Stripping of the Altars* (Newhaven, CT and London, 1992).

C. Duggan, 'Richard of Ilchester, royal servant and bishop', in *TRHS*, 5th ser., 16 (1966).

M. Dunn, 'Mastering Benedict: monastic rules and their authors in the early medieval west', in *EHR*, 105 (1990).

M. Dunn, 'The Master and St. Benedict: a rejoinder', in *EHR*, 107 (1992).

E. L. Eisenstein, *The Printing Revolution in Early Modern Europe* (Cambridge, 1983).

G. R. Evans, *The Thought of Gregory the Great* (Cambridge, 1986).

R. T. Farrell, ed., *Bede and Anglo-Saxon England* (BAR, 46) (Oxford, 1978).

R. T. Farrell, 'The construction, deconstruction and reconstruction of the Ruthwell Cross', in B. Cassidy, ed., *The Ruthwell Cross*.

R. A. Fletcher, *The Episcopate in the Kingdom of León in the Twelfth Century* (Oxford, 1978).

S. Foot, 'Parochial ministry in early Anglo-Saxon England', in *SCH*, 26 (1989).

P. Fouracre, 'The work of Audoenus of Rouen and Eligius of Noyon in extending episcopal influence from the town to the country in seventh century Neustria', in *SCH*, 16 (1979).

W. H. C. Frend, 'The winning of the countryside', in *JEH*, 18 (1967).

D. Ganz, 'The debate on predestination', in M. T. Gibson and J. L. Nelson, eds, *Charles the Bald, Court and Kingdom*.

D. Ganz, 'Theology and the organisation of thought', in *New CMH*, II.

P. J. Geary, *Furta Sacra* (revised edn, Princeton, NJ, 1990).

M. Gervers, ed., *The Second Crusade and the Cistercians* (New York, 1992).

A. Gewirth, *Marsilius of Padua* (New York, 1951).

M. T. Gibson, *'Artes' and Bible in the Medieval West* (Aldershot and Brookfield, VT, 1993).

M. T. Gibson, *Lanfranc of Bec* (Oxford, 1978).

M. T. Gibson, 'Latin commentaries on logic before 1200', in *Bulletin de philosophie médiévale*, 24 (1982).

M. T. Gibson and J. L. Nelson, eds, *Charles the Bald, Court and Kingdom* (BAR-I, 101) (Oxford, 1981).

J. Gill, *The Council of Florence* (Cambridge, 1959).

E. Gilson, *History of Christian Philosophy in the Middle Ages* (London, 1955).

B. Guillemain, *La cour pontificale d'Avignon* (Paris, 1966).

E. M. Hallam, *Capetian France* (London, 1980).

G. Halsall, *Early Medieval Cemeteries* (Skelmorlie, 1995).

B. Hamilton, *The Latin Church in the Crusader States* (London, 1980).

B. Hamilton, *The Medieval Inquisition* (London, 1981).

B. Hamilton, *Religion in the Medieval West* (London, 1986).

B. Hamilton, 'Wisdom from the East: the reception by the Cathars of Eastern dualist texts', in P. Biller and A. Hudson, eds, *Heresy and Literacy, 1000–1530.*

M. Haren, *Medieval Thought* (2nd edn, Toronto, 1992).

D. Hay, *The Church in Italy in the Fifteenth Century* (Cambridge, 1977).

T. Head, 'The judgment of God: Andrew of Fleury's account of the peace league of Bourges', in T. Head and R. Landes, eds, *The Peace of God.*

T. Head and R. Landes, eds, *The Peace of God* (Ithaca, NY, 1992).

Y. Hen, 'Unity in diversity: the liturgy of Frankish Gaul before Charlemagne', in *SCH,* 32 (1996).

J. Herbert, 'The transformation of hermitages into Augustinian priories in twelfth-century England', in *SCH,* 22 (1985).

J. Higgitt, ed., *Early Medieval Sculpture in Britain and Ireland* (BAR, 152) (Oxford, 1986).

C. Holdsworth, 'Boniface the Monk', in T. Reuter, ed., *The Greatest Englishman.*

N. Housley, *The Avignon Papacy and the Crusades, 1305–78* (Oxford, 1986).

N. Housley, *The Italian Crusades* (Oxford, 1982).

N. Housley, *The Later Crusades* (Oxford, 1992).

A. Hudson, *Lollards and their Books* (London, 1985).

K. Hughes, 'The Celtic Church and the Papacy', in C. H. Lawrence, ed., *The English Church and the Papacy.*

N. Hunt, ed., *Cluniac Monasticism* (London, 1971).

A. Hyma, *The Christian Renaissance* (2nd edn, Hamden, CT, 1965).

E. James, ed., *Visigothic Spain* (Oxford, 1980).

H. Jedin, *History of the Council of Trent,* I (London and Edinburgh, 1957).

A. H. M. Jones, 'The Western Church in the fifth and sixth centuries', in M. W. Barley and R. P. C. Hanson, eds, *Christianity in Britain, 300–700.*

G. Jones, *The Vikings* (Oxford, 1968).

H. Kaminsky, *A History of the Hussite Revolution* (Berkeley, CA, 1967).

H. Kaminsky, *Simon de Cramaud and the Great Schism* (Rutgers, NJ, 1983).

J. N. D. Kelly, *The Oxford Dictionary of Popes* (Oxford, 1986).

E. W. Kemp, 'Pope Alexander III and the canonization of saints', *TRHS,* 4th ser., 27 (1945).

B. Kempers, *Painting, Power and Patronage* (Harmondsworth, 1993).

A. Kenny, *Aquinas* (Oxford, 1980).

A. Kenny, *Wyclif* (Oxford, 1985).

R. Kieckhefer, *Unquiet Souls* (Chicago and London, 1984).

D. P. Kirby, 'The genesis of a cult: Cuthbert of Farne and ecclesiastical politics in Northumbria in the late seventh and early eighth centuries', in *JEH,* 46 (1995).

M. D. Knowles, *The Episcopal Colleagues of Archbishop Thomas Becket* (Cambridge, 1951).

M. D. Knowles, *The Evolution of Medieval Thought* (London, 1962).

M. D. Knowles, *From Pachomius to Ignatius* (Oxford, 1966).

P. Kras, 'Hussitism and the Polish nobility', in M. Aston and C. Richmond, eds, *Lollardy and the Gentry in the Later Middle Ages.*

P. O. Kristeller, *Renaissance Thought,* II (New York, 1965).

M. Lambert, *Medieval Heresy* (2nd edn, Oxford, 1992).

P. Lasko, *Ars Sacra, 800–1200* (Harmondsworth, 1972).

P. Lasko, *The Kingdom of the Franks* (London, 1971).

C. H. Lawrence, ed., *The English Church and the Papacy* (London, 1965).

C. H. Lawrence, *The Friars* (London, 1994).

C. H. Lawrence, *Medieval Monasticism* (2nd edn, London, 1989).

G. Leff, *Heresy in the Later Middle Ages* (Manchester, 1967).

E. Le Roy Ladurie, trans. B. Bray, *Montaillou* (London, 1978).

D. R. Lesnick, *Preaching in Medieval Florence* (Athens, GA, 1989).

H. Leyser, *Hermits and the New Monasticism* (London, 1984).

P. Linehan, *The Spanish Church and the Papacy in the Thirteenth Century* (Cambridge, 1971).

R. W. Lovatt, 'The *Imitation of Christ* in late medieval England', in *TRHS,* 5th ser., 18 (1968).

J. H. Lynch, *The Medieval Church* (London, 1992).

J. H. Lynch, *Simoniacal Entry into Religious Life from 1000 to 1260* (Columbus, OH, 1976).

M. Mallett, *The Borgias* (London, 1969).

H. E. Mayer, trans. J. Gillingham, *The Crusades* (Oxford, 1972).

H. M. R. E. Mayr-Harting, *The Coming of Christianity to Anglo-Saxon England* (London, 1972).

H. M. R. E. Mayr-Harting, *Two Conversions to Christianity, the Bulgarians and the Anglo-Saxons* (Reading, 1994).

P. Meyvaert, 'A new perspective on the Ruthwell Cross; Ecclesia and Vita Monastica', in B. Cassidy, ed., *The Ruthwell Cross.*

B. Moeller, 'Piety in Germany around 1500', in S. E. Ozment, ed., *The Reformation in Medieval Perspective.*

G. Mollat, *Les papes d'Avignon* (9th edn, Paris, 1949).

R. I. Moore, *The Origins of European Dissent* (London, 1977).

J. R. H. Moorman, *A History of the Franciscan Order* (Oxford, 1968).

C. Morris, *The Papal Monarchy: The Western Church from 1050 to 1250* (Oxford, 1989).

J. L. Nelson, 'Queens as Jezebels', in D. Baker, ed., *Medieval Women.*

J. L. Nelson, 'Women and the Word', in *SCH,* 27 (1990).

New Cambridge Medieval History, II, ed. R. McKitterick (Cambridge, 1995).

D. Nimmo, *Reform and Division in the Franciscan Order, 1226–1538* (Rome, 1987).

D. E. Nineham, 'Gottschalk of Orbais: reactionary or precursor of the Reformation', in *JEH,* 40 (1989).

J. M. Noiroux, 'Les deux premiers documents concernant l'hérésie aux Pays-Bas', in *RHE,* 49 (1954).

F. Oakley, *The Western Church in the Later Middle Ages* (Ithaca, NY, 1979).

H. A. Oberman, *The Harvest of Medieval Theology* (Cambridge, MA, 1963).

I. Origo, *The World of San Bernardino* (New York, 1962).

S. E. Ozment, *The Age of Reform, 1250–1550* (Newhaven, CT and London, 1980).

S. E. Ozment, ed., *The Reformation in Medieval Perspective* (Chicago, 1971).

L. Paolini, 'Italian Catharism and written culture', in P. Biller and A. Hudson, eds, *Heresy and Literacy, 1000–1530.*

P. Partner, *The Lands of St. Peter* (London, 1972).

P. Partner, *The Papal State under Martin V* (London, 1958).

L. Pastor, *History of the Popes,* trans. F. I. Antrobus and R. Kerr, vols I–VII (London, 1891–1908).

A. Patchovsky and F. Smahel, eds, *Eschatologie und Hussitismus* (Prague, 1996).

F. S. Paxton, *Christianizing Death* (Ithaca, NY, 1990).

J. Percival, 'Villas and monasteries in Late Roman Gaul', in *JEH,* 48 (1997).

D. Phillips, *Beguines in Medieval Strasburg* (Stanford, CA, 1941).

M. Reeves, *The Influence of Prophecy in the Later Middle Ages* (Oxford, 1969).

A. Renaudet, *Préréforme et humanisme à Paris pendant les premières guerres d'Italie* (Paris, 1953).

T. Reuter, ed., *The Greatest Englishman* (Exeter, 1980).

T. Reuter, 'St. Boniface and Europe', in T. Reuter, ed., *The Greatest Englishman.*

R. E. Reynolds, 'The organisation, law and liturgy of the Western Church, 700–900', in *New CMH,* II.

J. S. C. Riley-Smith, *The Crusades: A Short History* (London, 1987).

J. S. C. Riley-Smith, *The First Crusade and the Idea of Crusading* (London, 1986).

I. S. Robinson, *Authority and Resistance in the Investiture Contest* (Manchester, 1978).

I. S. Robinson, *The Papacy, 1073–1198* (Cambridge, 1990).

D. W. Rollason, *Saints and Relics in Anglo-Saxon England* (Oxford, 1989).

G. Rosser, 'The cure of souls in English towns before 1000', in J. Blair and R. Sharpe, eds, *Pastoral Care before the Parish.*

M. Rubin, *Corpus Christi* (Cambridge, 1991).

S. Runciman, *A History of the Crusades,* 3 vols (Cambridge, 1951–5).

S. Runciman, *The Sicilian Vespers* (Cambridge, 1958).

R. Rusconi, 'L'escatologia negli ultimi secoli del Medioevo', in A. Patchovsky and F. Smahel, eds, *Eschatologie und Hussitismus.*

J. C. Russell, *The Germanization of Early Medieval Christianity* (Oxford, 1994).

J. E. Sayers, *Innocent III* (London, 1994).

C. Shaw, *Julius II, the Warrior Pope* (Oxford, 1993).

D. J. Smith, 'Sancho Ramírez and the Roman Rite', in *SCH,* 32 (1996).

R. W. Southern, *The Making of the Middle Ages* (London, 1953).

R. W. Southern, *St. Anselm* (Cambridge, 1990).

R. W. Southern, *Scholastic Humanism and the Unification of Europe,* I (Oxford, 1995).

R. W. Southern, *Western Society and the Church in the Middle Ages* (Harmondsworth, 1970).

R. W. Southern, *Western Views of Islam in the Middle Ages* (Cambridge, MA, 1962).

C. E. Stancliffe, 'The Christianisation of the Touraine', in *SCH,* 16 (1979).

M. Stroll, *The Jewish Pope* (Leiden, 1987).

U. Stutz, 'The Proprietary Church', in G. Barraclough, ed., *Medieval Germany, 911–1250.*

R. N. Swanson, *Religion and Devotion in Europe, c.1215–c.1515* (Cambridge, 1995).

C. H. Talbot, 'St. Boniface and the German Mission', in *SCH,* 6 (1970).

G. Tellenbach, trans. T. Reuter, *The Church in Western Europe from the Tenth to the Early Twelfth Century* (Cambridge, 1993).

A. Tenenti, *La vie et la mort à travers l'art du XVe siècle* (Paris, 1952).

T. N. Tentler, *Sin and Confession on the Eve of the Reformation* (Princeton, NJ, 1977).

C. Thomas, *The Early Christian Archaeology of North Britain* (Oxford, 1971).

A. Thompson, *Revival Preachers and Politics in Thirteenth-Century Italy* (Oxford, 1992).

E. A. Thompson, *The Goths in Spain* (Oxford, 1969).

J. A. F. Thomson, 'Knightly piety and the margins of Lollardy', in M. Aston and C. Richmond, eds, *Lollardy and the Gentry in the Later Middle Ages.*

J. A. F. Thomson, *The Later Lollards* (Oxford, 1965).

J. A. F. Thomson, *Popes and Princes, 1417–1517* (London, 1980).

J. A. F. Thomson, '"The Well of Grace": Englishmen and Rome in the fifteenth century', in R. B. Dobson, ed., *The Church, Politics and Patronage.*

S. Twyman, 'Papal *adventus* at Rome in the twelfth century', in *Historical Research,* 69 (1996).

W. Ullmann, *The Growth of Papal Government in the Middle Ages* (3rd edn, London, 1970).

W. Ullmann, *The Origins of the Great Schism* (London, 1948).

J. H. Van Engen, *Rupert of Deutz* (Berkeley, CA, 1983).

A. Vauchez, *La sainteté en occident aux derniers siècles du moyen age* (Rome, 1981).

A. P. Vlasto, 'The mission of SS. Cyril and Methodios and its aftermath in Central Europe', in *SCH*, 6 (1970).

A. de Vogüé, 'The Master and St. Benedict: a reply to Marilyn Dunn', in *EHR*, 107 (1992).

W. L. Wakefield, *Heresy, Crusade and Inquisition in Southern France, 1100–1250* (London, 1974).

D. Waley, *The Papal State in the Thirteenth Century* (London, 1961).

D. Walker, *Medieval Wales* (Cambridge, 1990).

J. M. Wallace-Hadrill, *The Frankish Church* (Oxford, 1983).

B. Ward, *Miracles and the Medieval Mind* (Aldershot, 1982).

J. A. Watt, *The Theory of Papal Monarchy in the Thirteenth Century* (London, 1965).

D. M. Wilson, *Anglo-Saxon Art* (London, 1984).

D. Wood, *Clement VI* (Cambridge, 1989).

C. P. Wormald, 'Bede, *Beowulf,* and the conversion of the Anglo-Saxon aristocracy', in R. T. Farrell, ed., *Bede and Anglo-Saxon England.*

Notes

Chapter 1. The spread and consolidation of Christianity

1 *The Book of Pontiffs,* 53; *Conquerors and Chroniclers of Early Medieval Spain,* 116, 127. The Spanish writers of the period remained well informed about events in the Byzantine world.
2 Bede, *EH,* I. cc.8, 10, 17–20.
3 Gregory of Tours, *History of the Franks,* 7–8, 11; *Life of the Fathers,* 43, 47–8.
4 J. L. Nelson, 'Queens as Jezebels', in D. Baker, ed., *Medieval Women,* 52.
5 R. Collins, 'Mérida and Toledo, 550–585', in E. James, ed., *Visigothic Spain,* 194–5, 201, 211–12. E. A. Thompson, *The Goths in Spain,* 32–6, 78–87. *Conquerors and Chroniclers of Early Medieval Spain,* 67, 76, 99, 103–4.
6 Thompson, *The Goths in Spain,* 107.
7 T. Reuter, 'St. Boniface and Europe', in T. Reuter, ed., *The Greatest Englishman,* 74.
8 Sulpicius Severus, *Life of St. Martin,* in *The Fathers of the Church,* VII. 120–2. Gregory of Tours, *Glory of the Confessors,* 19.
9 W. H. C. Frend, 'The Winning of the Countryside', in *JEH,* 18 (1967), 10–11.
10 C. E. Stancliffe, 'The Christianisation of the Touraine', in *SCH,* 16 (1979), 52.
11 A. H. M. Jones, 'The Western Church in the Fifth and Sixth Centuries', in M. W. Barley and R. P. C. Hanson, eds, *Christianity in Britain, 300–700,* 15. Thompson, *The Goths in Spain,* 310.
12 P. Fouracre, 'The Work of Audoenus of Rouen and Eligius of Noyon in Extending Episcopal Influence from the Town to the Country in Seventh Century Neustria', in *SCH,* 16 (1979), 77, 82.
13 *The Lombard Laws,* 180. *Medieval Handbooks of Penance,* 389–90.
14 Bede, *EH,* I. c.30. *The Book of Pontiffs,* 62. Admittedly the Pantheon, although earlier a pagan temple, was probably no longer associated with pagan worship.
15 G. R. Murphy, *The Saxon Savior,* 79–80.
16 Adam of Bremen, *History,* 87.
17 *Sainted Women of the Dark Ages,* 200, n. 18.
18 Bede, *EH,* II. c.16.
19 C. P. Wormald, 'Bede, *Beowulf,* and the Conversion of the Anglo-Saxon Aristocracy', in R. T. Farrell, ed., *Bede and Anglo-Saxon England,* 45.
20 Bede, *EH,* IV. c.13.

21 Ibid., II. c.13. Bede's account gave Coifi a prominent role in rejecting traditional paganism, but a later writer, Alcuin, significantly gave greater weight to the part played by the king. Alcuin, *Bishops, Kings and Saints of York*, 19.
22 *Anglo-Saxon Missionaries in Germany*, 76–7.
23 *Medieval Handbooks of Penance*, 198, 227, 229.
24 Reuter, 'St. Boniface and Europe', in Reuter, ed., *The Greatest Englishman*, 74–5. J. M. Wallace-Hadrill, *The Frankish Church*, 63–9, 147.
25 *Sainted Women of the Dark Ages*, 178, 181–2.
26 Wallace-Hadrill, *The Frankish Church*, 144–7.
27 *Anglo-Saxon Missionaries in Germany*, 10–11.
28 Wallace-Hadrill, *The Frankish Church*, 151. Reuter, 'St. Boniface and Europe', 77.
29 Wallace-Hadrill, *The Frankish Church*, 152, 154, 156. Reuter, 'St. Boniface and Europe', 79; C. Holdsworth, 'Boniface the Monk', in Reuter, ed., *The Greatest Englishman*, 59–62.
30 *Anglo-Saxon Missionaries in Germany*, 70, 99, 117. C. H. Talbot, 'St. Boniface and the German Mission', in *SCH*, 6 (1970), 54.
31 Reuter, 'St. Boniface and Europe', 79.
32 *Anglo-Saxon Missionaries in Germany*, 46, 139–40, 145.
33 *Two Lives of Charlemagne*, 61, 63.
34 Murphy, *The Saxon Savior*, 11, 33, 75.
35 *Chronicle of Fredegar*, 90–1, 93–5; Rodulfus Glaber, *Opera*, 18–21.
36 M. Kantor, *Medieval Slavic Lives of Saints and Princes*, 65, 92.
37 *Annals of Fulda*, 58–60, 64–5.
38 Kantor, *Medieval Slavic Lives of Saints and Princes*, 69.
39 Ibid., 127, 138. A. P. Vlasto, 'The Mission of SS. Cyril and Methodios and its Aftermath in Central Europe', in *SCH*, 6 (1970), 2.
40 Kantor, *Medieval Slavic Lives of Saints and Princes*, 143, 157. Vlasto, 'The Mission of SS. Cyril and Methodios', 4.
41 M. Kantor, *The Origins of Christianity in Bohemia*, 103, 158, 176, 250.
42 Adam of Bremen, *History*, 83, 105–6.
43 Ibid., 71, 215.
44 *Imperial Lives and Letters of the Eleventh Century*, 84–5.
45 *Lives of the Ninth Century Popes*, 253. The respective claims of Byzantium and Rome were debated at a council in 870, where the Roman delegates asserted the power of the pope. Ibid., 283–7. See also H. M. R. E. Mayr-Harting, *Two Conversions to Christianity, the Bulgarians and the Anglo-Saxons*, which contains some valuable general comments on the character of the various conversions.
46 Vlasto, 'The Mission of SS. Cyril and Methodios', 16.
47 Adam of Bremen, *History*, 61–2, 66–7.
48 G. Jones, *The Vikings*, 107–8.
49 Adam of Bremen, *History*, 29–30, 32.
50 Ibid., 49–51. Jones, *Vikings*, 112–14, 125–7.
51 Adam of Bremen, *History*, 94–5, 97–8, 210. Jones, *Vikings*, 74.
52 Adam of Bremen, *History*, 197, 210.
53 Jones, *Vikings*, 132, 134–5.
54 Ibid., 377–8, 385.
55 *Correspondence of Pope Gregory VII*, 136–7, 152–4, 184–5.
56 E. Christiansen, *The Northern Crusades*, 134, 137.
57 Ibid., 157. B. Jarrett, *The Emperor Charles IV*, 52, 63.
58 N. Housley, *The Later Crusades*, 352.
59 *Infra*, chapter 7.
60 *The Burgundian Code*, 86.

61 *Conquerors and Chroniclers of Early Medieval Spain*, 106.
62 *Chronicle of Fredegar*, 54.
63 Thompson, *The Goths in Spain*, 53–4.
64 Ibid., 165–6, 178, 186, 196, 205–7, 225, 234–7, 246, 315–16.

Chapter 2. Religion and ideas of holiness

1 Sulpicius Severus, *Life of St. Martin*, 118–19.
2 *Conquerors and Chroniclers of Early Medieval Spain*, 89.
3 *Annals of St. Bertin*, 64–5.
4 Gregory of Tours, *Glory of the Martyrs*, 45–6; c.27.
5 C. Thomas, *The Early Christian Archaeology of North Britain*, 136–7, 191, 194.
6 D. Rollason, *Saints and Relics in Anglo-Saxon England*, 26.
7 N. P. Tanner, ed., *Decrees of the Ecumenical Councils*, I. 145.
8 P. J. Geary, *Furta Sacra*, 35, 37.
9 J. F. Benton, *Self and Society in Medieval France*, 85 and n.4.
10 *Charlemagne's Cousins*, 150. See *infra*, p.24.
11 *Carolingian Chronicles*, 50.
12 Eddius Stephanus, *Life of Wilfrid*, c.33. He collected further relics on a later visit. Ibid., c.55.
13 *Anglo-Saxon Missionaries in Germany*, 8, 49.
14 *St. Odo of Cluny*, 163. Adam of Bremen, *History*, 60–1.
15 Eadmer, *History of Recent Events in England*, 112–13.
16 Rodulfus Glaber, *Opera*, 180–5, 274–5.
17 Geary, *Furta Sacra*, 53.
18 *The Monks of Redon*, 180–1. *Son of Charlemagne*, 84.
19 Bede, *EH*, III. cc. 9, 11; *Life of St. Cuthbert*, cc. 41, 43, 45. Alcuin, *The Bishops, Kings and Saints of York*, 31–3, 37.
20 Gregory of Tours, *History of the Franks*, Bk III, c.28; Bk IV, c.49; Bk V, c.4.
21 Ibid., Bk VII, c.42. *Sainted Women of the Dark Ages*, 76.
22 Rodulfus Glaber, *Opera*, 76–7.
23 D. P. Kirby, 'The Genesis of a Cult: Cuthbert of Farne and Ecclesiastical Politics in Northumbria in the Late Seventh and Early Eighth Centuries', in *JEH*, 46 (1995), 395–7.
24 *The Monks of Redon*, 170–3, 196–203. *Sainted Women of the Dark Ages*, 95.
25 *Chronicle of Fredegar*, 14–15. *Annals of Fulda*, 36.
26 *Adomnan's Life of Columba*, 179, 187.
27 *Chronicle of Fredegar*, 4, 10.
28 Ibid., 67–8, 97, 121. In the twelfth century, St Bernard of Clairvaux, in a letter to Abbot Suger of St Denis, referred to the martyrs who ennobled the place with their relics. *The Letters of St. Bernard of Clairvaux*, 113.
29 Benton, *Self and Society in Medieval France*, 124. *Letters of John of Salisbury*, I. 54, II. 802–7.
30 Odo of Deuil, *De Profectione Ludovici VII in Orientem*, 17.
31 E. Hallam, *Capetian France*, 234–5, 261.
32 Tanner, *Decrees of the Ecumenical Councils*, I. 263–4.
33 Bede, *EH*, Bk V, c.7. M. Kantor, *The Origins of Christianity in Bohemia*, 80, 149, 186.
34 *EHD*, I. 231, 310, 558; II. 206.
35 *Letters of Gerbert*, 73–4, no. 36. Rodulfus Glaber, *Opera*, 36–7, 132–7.
36 Glaber, *Opera*, 60–1, 198–201, 212–15. *EHD*, II. 127, 209.

37 R. A. Fletcher, *The Episcopate in the Kingdom of León in the Twelfth Century*, 9.
38 *Sainted Women of the Dark Ages*, 81, 88, 207, 227, 287, 314.
39 Gregory of Tours, *Life of the Fathers*, 2.
40 Wulfstan of Winchester, *Life of St. Aethelwold*, ci.
41 *Sainted Women of the Dark Ages*, 143, 157–8, 185, 205, 257, 310.
42 Sulpicius Severus, *Life of St. Martin*, 117.
43 There is a valuable discussion of the different and changing ways in which monastic communities developed in J. Percival, 'Villas and Monasteries in Late Roman Gaul', in *JEH*, 48 (1997), 1–21. *Rule of St. Benedict*, c.1.
44 *Anglo-Saxon Missionaries in Germany*, 5–6, 30, 35.
45 G. R. Evans, *The Thought of Gregory the Great*, 43.
46 Gregory of Tours, *History of the Franks*, VIII. cc. 15, 34.
47 Bede, *Life of St. Cuthbert*, cc. 6, 17. Alcuin, *The Bishops, Kings and Saints of York*, 55–7, 127.
48 Eddius, *Life of Wilfrid*, c.64.
49 Gregory of Tours, *Glory of the Confessors*, 38–9, 85–8; *Life of the Fathers*, 67, 81, 86, 91, 96–7.
50 Gregory of Tours, *Life of the Fathers*, 69, 91.
51 Ibid., 4–7.
52 Ibid., 84.
53 *Supra*, p.24.
54 C. P. Wormald, 'Bede, *Beowulf*, and the Conversion of the Anglo-Saxon Aristocracy', in R. T. Farrell, ed., *Bede and Anglo-Saxon England*, 51–3, 62.
55 M. Dunn, 'Mastering Benedict: Monastic Rules and Their Authors in the Early Medieval West', in *EHR*, 105 (1990), 567–94; 'The Master and St. Benedict: A Rejoinder', ibid., 107 (1992), 104–11. The second article is a reply to A. de Vogüé, 'The Master and St. Benedict: A Reply to Marilyn Dunn', ibid., 107 (1992), 95–103.
56 C. H. Lawrence, *Medieval Monasticism*, 60, 62.
57 *Anglo-Saxon Missionaries in Germany*, 191, 213.
58 *St. Odo of Cluny*, 71 and n.1.
59 Lawrence, *Medieval Monasticism*, 77–9. *Son of Charlemagne*, 64.
60 *Charlemagne's Cousins*, 64, 197.
61 Asser, *Life of Alfred*, c.81. Lay interference with monastic property was not, of course, new: see p. 29, *supra*.
62 Ibid., cc.78, 92–4, 98.
63 D. Knowles, *From Pachomius to Ignatius*, 11.
64 *St. Odo of Cluny*, 82.
65 Lawrence, *Medieval Monasticism*, 97. This monastery had a particularly high standing, because it possessed the body of St Benedict, allegedly stolen, with the saint's compliance, from Monte Cassino. Geary, *Furta Sacra*, 120–2.
66 *Letters of Fulbert*, 108–9, 177. *Letters of Gerbert*, 365–6.
67 Lawrence, *Medieval Monasticism*, 87, 103–4.
68 Wulfstan of Winchester, *Life of St. Aethelwold*, lii, lxxx–lxxxi, 27.
69 *Regularis Concordia*, 3, 30, 62. Lawrence, *Medieval Monasticism*, 104.
70 Wulfstan of Winchester, *Life of St. Aethelwold*, 19, 21, 29, 43, 61.
71 *Regularis Concordia*, 5, 7, 13–14, 21–2.
72 *Infra*, chapter 8.
73 *Letters of Gerbert*, 114–15, 124–5, 127–9, 131–3, 180.
74 Ibid., 305–6, 307, 320–2, 328–9.
75 *Letters of Fulbert*, 3–9.
76 Orderic Vitalis, *Ecclesiastical History*, II. 9–13.

77 Rodulfus Glaber, *Opera*, 268–73, 276–7, 296–7. Orderic Vitalis, *Ecclesiastical History*, II. 75.
78 Orderic Vitalis, *Ecclesiastical History*, II. 65–7, 91, 95.
79 Ibid., 95–101, 109–15, 128 n.1.

Chapter 3. The rise of the Papacy

1 The classic study of this is W. Ullmann, *The Growth of Papal Government in the Middle Ages*.
2 Ibid., 5, 7.
3 K. Hughes, 'The Celtic Church and the Papacy', in C. H. Lawrence, ed., *The English Church and the Papacy*, 13–16.
4 *St. Odo of Cluny*, 146.
5 G. R. Murphy, *The Saxon Savior*, 4, 72, 103.
6 *Lives of the Ninth Century Popes*, 152.
7 M. Lambert, *Medieval Heresy*, 9.
8 J. L. Nelson, 'Queens as Jezebels', in D. Baker, ed., *Medieval Women*, 42.
9 *Sainted Women of the Dark Ages*, 180.
10 *The Book of Pontiffs*, 71–2.
11 Ibid., 52–3, 90–1.
12 Gregory of Tours, *History of the Franks*, II.1, V.20, pp. 105–6, 285.
13 P. Partner, *The Lands of St. Peter*, 6–7.
14 Ibid., 11–12.
15 *Lives of the Eighth Century Popes*, 56, 61.
16 *Chronicle of Fredegar*, 96, 102, 104, 106–7. *Eighth Century Popes*, 58, 64. *Carolingian Chronicles*, 39.
17 *Eighth Century Popes*, 63, 71.
18 Partner, *The Lands of St. Peter*, 23.
19 *Ninth Century Popes*, 212–13, 221–3, 270–6. N. P. Tanner, ed., *Decrees of the Ecumenical Councils*, I. 182.
20 The *Liber Pontificalis* does not specifically note that the pope resisted election, but does state that it had been the Roman clergy and people who had created him. *Ninth Century Popes*, 6.
21 *Carolingian Chronicles*, 102. *Son of Charlemagne*, 62. *Annals of St. Bertin*, 57. *Annals of Fulda*, 99.
22 Ullmann, *Growth of Papal Government*, 173. *Charlemagne's Cousins*, 180, 183, 187–9. *Ninth Century Popes*, 236.
23 *Vézelay Chronicle*, 99. It is worth noting that this commendation to the Papacy antedates that of Cluny by about half a century, and reflects a belief in its moral authority.
24 *Carolingian Chronicles*, 117.
25 *Annals of St. Bertin*, 110, 112–17, 142. *Annals of Fulda*, 52. *Ninth Century Popes*, 225–31.
26 *Annals of St. Bertin*, 123–4. The *Liber Pontificalis* gives a picture of this crisis from the papal point of view. *Ninth Century Popes*, 234–7.
27 *The Monks of Redon*, 178–9. *Annals of St. Bertin*, 207–12.
28 *St. Odo of Cluny*, 28, 78.
29 *Letters of Gerbert*, 326–8, 333–4, 345–7, 350–2.
30 Rodulfus Glaber, *Opera*, 62–5, 252–3.
31 *Letters of Fulbert of Chartres*, 17, 75, 111, 115.
32 Ibid., 161.
33 *EHD*, I. 165, 168, 170, 172, 215, 229, 239.

34 C. Morris, *The Papal Monarchy: The Western Church from 1050 to 1250*, 92–3.

Chapter 4. The Church in the localities

1 S. Foot, 'Parochial Ministry in Early Anglo-Saxon England: The Role of the Monastic Communities', in *SCH*, 26 (1989), 43, 49.
2 G. Rosser, 'The Cure of Souls in English Towns before 1000', in J. Blair and R. Sharpe, eds, *Pastoral Care before the Parish*, 284.
3 I. B. Cowan, *The Medieval Church in Scotland*, 1, 5, 9–10.
4 Sulpicius Severus, *Life of St. Martin*, 115; *Second Dialogue*, 201.
5 Bede, *EH*, III. cc.14, 17.
6 Eddius Stephanus, *Life of Wilfrid*, c.12. H. Mayr-Harting, *The Coming of Christianity to Anglo-Saxon England*, 113. In Visigothic Spain, Bishop Masona of Mérida was surrounded by pomp and ceremony: R. Collins, 'Mérida and Toledo', in E. James, ed., *Visigothic Spain*, 197.
7 *Son of Charlemagne*, 64.
8 Gregory of Tours, *Life of the Fathers*, 106; *History of the Franks*, IV. cc.6–7.
9 *Chronicle of Fredegar*, 34, 48, 63–4, 71, 75.
10 N. P. Tanner, ed., *Decrees of the Ecumenical Councils*, I. 140, 175.
11 Bede, *EH*, III. c.7, IV. c.1. Alcuin, *The Bishops, Kings and Saints of York*, 99, 101, 117.
12 *Conquerors and Chroniclers of Early Medieval Spain*, 78, 125, 160, 162.
13 E. A. Thompson, *The Goths in Spain*, 163, 275.
14 *Life of Charlemagne*, c.26. *Life of Alfred*, c.88.
15 *Charlemagne's Cousins*, 155.
16 *Letters of Gerbert*, 9–12, 157–8, 188, 192–4, 197, 199, 202–5, 213–23, 234, 236–62, 289–90.
17 *Letters of Fulbert*, 48–51, 93, 95.
18 Ibid., 52–3, 103.
19 Rodulfus Glaber, *Opera*, 36–7.
20 *Letters of Fulbert*, 231–7. Glaber, *Opera*, 70–1.
21 Glaber, *Opera*, 158–9, 244–7.
22 Adam of Bremen, *History*, 74, 102. Archbishop Adalbert of Bremen had to rely on the emperor for support against his more immediate lord, Bernhard of Saxony, and repaid him in service at court. Ibid., 118–19.
23 *Supra*, chapter 3.
24 *Annals of St. Bertin*, 194. *Annals of Fulda*, 112.
25 *Annals of St. Bertin*, 123–4, 191.
26 R. E. Reynolds, 'The Organisation, Law and Liturgy of the Western Church, 700–900'; J. J. Contreni, 'The Carolingian Renaissance: Education and Literary Culture', in *New CMH*, II. 617, 750–1.
27 *Letters of Gerbert*, 235, 267, 268. Glaber, *Opera*, 64–5.
28 *Letters of Fulbert*, 129–31, 231–7.
29 U. Stutz, 'The Proprietary Church', in G. Barraclough, ed., *Medieval Germany, 911–1250*, 42, 44–5. For aristocratic influence over abbeys, see chapter 2, *supra*.
30 Stutz, 'The Proprietary Church', 62.
31 M. Deanesly, *History of the Medieval Church*, 31.
32 G. Tellenbach, *The Church in Western Europe from the Tenth to the Early Twelfth Century*, 28. C. N. L. Brooke, 'The Church in the Towns', in *SCH*, 6 (1970), 72.
33 Tellenbach, *Church in Western Europe*, 29.

34 Brooke, 'The Church in the Towns', 64–7.
35 Ibid., 82.
36 A. D. Brown, *Popular Piety in Late Medieval England*, 116.
37 Glaber, *Opera*, 194–9. A recent collection of essays considers many of the issues connected with the Peace Movement, and gives a valuable picture of the current debate: T. Head and R. Landes, eds, *The Peace of God*.
38 Glaber, *Opera*, 236–9, and 238 n. 1.
39 T. Head, 'The Judgment of God: Andrew of Fleury's Account of the Peace League of Bourges', in Head and Landes, eds, *The Peace of God*, 221–6.

Chapter 5. Belief and worship

1 B. Kempers, *Painting, Power and Patronage*, 21. The images would have had to be regarded as a means of reminding the worshippers of the stories, as they would have had little meaning unless they knew them first.
2 *Lives of the Eighth Century Popes*, 151, 153.
3 M. Lambert, *Medieval Heresy*, 9. D. Ganz, 'Theology and the Organisation of Thought', in *New CMH*, II. 775–7.
4 *Annals of Fulda*, 102.
5 *The Book of Pontiffs*, 44, 48, 97–9.
6 J. Beckwith, *Early Christian and Byzantine Art*, 49.
7 *The Book of Pontiffs*, 47, 49–50.
8 Gregory of Tours, *Glory of the Martyrs*, 103–6.
9 *Chronicle of Fredegar*, 7. Jonas, *Life of St. Columban*, 98.
10 J. M. Wallace-Hadrill, *The Frankish Church*, 210.
11 E. Peters, *Heresy and Authority in Medieval Europe*, 52–6. *Carolingian Chronicles*, 70, 73, 189.
12 *Annals of St. Bertin*, 67, 91, 94; *Annals of Fulda*, 28. D. Ganz, 'The Debate on Predestination', in M. Gibson and J. Nelson, eds, *Charles the Bald, Court and Kingdom*, 358–9. D. E. Nineham, 'Gottschalk of Orbais: Reactionary or Precursor of the Reformation', in *JEH*, 40 (1989), 2–6, 15. M. Haren, *Medieval Thought*, 77.
13 *Annals of Fulda*, 26–7. The implications of this case are discussed by J. L. Nelson, 'Women and the Word', in *SCH*, 27 (1990), 73–4.
14 *Annals of St. Bertin*, 42, 64. *Letters of Fulbert*, 51 and 50 n. 1.
15 *Medieval Handbooks of Penance*, 101–16.
16 Ibid., 184–6, 195–8.
17 Ibid., 112, 309.
18 Ibid., 102–5.
19 *Letters of Gerbert*, 224–5.
20 *Medieval Handbooks of Penance*, 111, 177, 195, 308–10.
21 Ibid., 278.
22 *Monastic Constitutions of Lanfranc*, 90–2.
23 These developments are discussed very thoroughly by M. Gibson, *Lanfranc of Bec*, 71–81. The fact that Gregory VII had not supported a literal belief in transubstantiation was used as a weapon against him by the Emperor Henry IV in his attempt to depose the pope at the synod of Brixen in 1080, at which Gregory was accused of being a follower of Berengar of Tours. *Imperial Lives and Letters of the Eleventh Century*, 159.
24 *Historia Pontificalis*, 11.
25 N. P. Tanner, ed., *Decrees of the Ecumenical Councils*, I. 244.
26 Y. Hen, 'Unity in Diversity: The Liturgy of Frankish Gaul before Charlemagne', in *SCH*, 32 (1996), 22–3, 26–7.

27 Ibid., 26. G. Cattin, *Music of the Middle Ages*, I. 14–16.
28 *Lives of the Ninth Century Popes*, 11.
29 *Two Lives of Charlemagne*, 102–4. R. E. Reynolds, 'The Organisation, Law and Liturgy of the Western Church, 700–900', in *New CMH*, II. 618–20. *Ninth Century Popes*, 108, 293.
30 C. Cubitt, 'Unity and Diversity in the Early Anglo-Saxon Liturgy', in *SCH*, 32 (1996), 45, 47.
31 Cattin, *Music of the Middle Ages*, 17, 22.
32 M. Kantor, *Medieval Slavic Lives of Saints and Princes*, 77, 94–5, 113. J. N. D. Kelly, *Dictionary of Popes*, 111, 113.
33 *Correspondence of Gregory VII*, 148.
34 M. Kantor, *The Origins of Christianity in Bohemia*, 12–14, 20, 22.
35 M. C. Diaz y Diaz, 'Literary Aspects of the Visigothic Liturgy', in E. James, ed., *Visigothic Spain*, 61.
36 R. A. Fletcher, *The Episcopate in the Kingdom of León in the Twelfth Century*, 182–3. *Correspondence of Gregory VII*, 29, 177. Cattin, *Music of the Middle Ages*, I. 42. D. J. Smith, 'Sancho Ramírez and the Roman Rite', in *SCH*, 32 (1996), 100–3.
37 Fletcher, *Episcopate*, 209–10.
38 Adam of Bremen, *History*, 102, 137.
39 *Charlemagne's Cousins*, 41.
40 C. H. Lawrence, *Medieval Monasticism*, 32–3, 100–1.
41 M. De Jong, 'Carolingian Monasticism: The Power of Prayer', in *New CMH*, II. 640–4.
42 Orderic Vitalis, *Ecclesiastical History*, II. 29, 41, 77, 133.
43 *Supra*, chapter 2.
44 *Supra*, chapter 1. J. C. Russell, *The Germanization of Early Medieval Christianity*, 195.
45 For developments in the liturgy of death see F. S. Paxton, *Christianizing Death*, *passim*.
46 G. Halsall, *Early Medieval Cemeteries*, 9, 13, 15, 21, 24–5, 62.
47 *The Earliest English Poems*, 106–9. J. Campbell, ed., *The Anglo-Saxons*, 90–1.
48 G. R. Murphy, *The Saxon Savior*, 17, 29 n. 8, 58, 62.
49 C. P. Wormald, 'Bede, *Beowulf*, and the Conversion of the Anglo-Saxon Aristocracy', in R. T. Farrell, ed., *Bede and Anglo-Saxon England*, 56.
50 R. T. Farrell, 'The Construction, Deconstruction and Reconstruction of the Ruthwell Cross', in B. Cassidy, ed., *The Ruthwell Cross*, 36, 45. The crucifixion panel is badly damaged, so it is impossible to discern its precise style: ibid., pl. 19. D. M. Wilson, *Anglo-Saxon Art*, 72, 138, 174–5.
51 P. Meyvaert, 'A New Perspective on the Ruthwell Cross; Ecclesia and Vita Monastica', in Cassidy, *Ruthwell Cross*, 107.
52 Beckwith, *Early Christian and Byzantine Art*, pl. 126.
53 P. Lasko, *Ars Sacra, 800–1200*, pls. 31, 33, 56, 82.
54 Ibid., pl. 143.
55 C. R. Dodwell, *Painting in Europe, 800–1200*, pls. 59–60, 72.
56 R. N. Bailey, 'A Crucifixion Plaque from Cumbria', in J. Higgitt, ed., *Early Medieval Sculpture in Britain and Ireland*, 12–13, 18–19.
57 Dodwell, *Painting in Europe, 800–1200*, 68, pls. 82–4. Gospel books, however, which were for more private use, would be less influential in forming popular beliefs than crucifixes on altars or in wall paintings.
58 R. W. Southern, *The Making of the Middle Ages*, 237–8.
59 Beckwith, *Early Christian and Byzantine Art*, 66, pl. 122.
60 P. Lasko, *The Kingdom of the Franks*, 100–1.
61 Rodulfus Glaber, *Opera*, 92–3, 116–17.

62 *Charlemagne's Cousins*, 52.
63 Glaber, *Opera*, 88–91.
64 R. I. Moore, *The Origins of European Dissent*, 9–20. Lambert, *Medieval Heresy*, 29. J.-M. Noiroux, 'Les deux premiers documents concernant l'hérésie aux Pays-Bas', in *RHE*, 49 (1954), 842–55.

Chapter 6. Gregorian reform – the clerical order

1 I. S. Robinson, *Authority and Resistance in the Investiture Contest*, 7–9.
2 Rodulfus Glaber, *Opera*, 70–1. *Imperial Lives and Letters of the Eleventh Century*, 74. G. Tellenbach, *The Church in Western Europe from the Tenth to the Early Twelfth Century*, 169.
3 C. Morris, *The Papal Monarchy*, 86–7, 101–3. It is noteworthy that Adam of Bremen's account of the Council of Mainz stresses that simony and clerical marriage were the main targets, but does not mention lay investiture. Adam of Bremen, *History*, 138.
4 *Correspondence of Gregory VII*, 1–3.
5 *Imperial Lives and Letters of the Eleventh Century*, 149, 158.
6 *Correspondence of Gregory VII*, 9, 11–12.
7 For the cross-currents of faction and the involvement of both Papacy and Empire, see H. E. J. Cowdrey, 'The Papacy, the Patarenes and the Church of Milan', in *TRHS*, 5th ser., 18 (1968), 25–48.
8 *Correspondence of Gregory VII*, 80–1, 84, 102. *Epistolae Vagantes of Pope Gregory VII*, 38–9, 47, 101–3, 109–15.
9 *Correspondence of Gregory VII*, 143. Morris, *The Papal Monarchy*, 102.
10 N. P. Tanner, ed., *Decrees of the Ecumenical Councils*, I. 190, 197, 214–15, 217.
11 *Libellus de diversis ordinibus*, 35.
12 *Eadmer's History of Recent Events*, 150–1.
13 *EHD*, II. 134–5, 274. Orderic Vitalis, *Ecclesiastical History*, II. 173.
14 *Epistolae Vagantes*, 151–2. Fulcher of Chartres, *History of the Expedition to Jerusalem*, 104.
15 Tanner, *Decrees of the Ecumenical Councils*, I. 244.
16 J. F. Benton, *Self and Society in Medieval France*, 156–7.
17 R. A. Fletcher, *The Episcopate in the Kingdom of León in the Twelfth Century*, 81. *Chronicle of Jocelin of Brakelond*, 55.
18 *Chronicle of Jean de Venette*, 65, 86, 220.
19 Ibid., 125.
20 *Chronicle of the Election of Hugh, Abbot of Bury St. Edmunds*, 58–9.
21 J. A. F. Thomson, '"The Well of Grace": Englishmen and Rome in the Fifteenth Century', in R. B. Dobson, ed., *The Church, Politics and Patronage*, 103–4.
22 L. Boisset, *Un concile provincial au treizième siècle*, 288–9.
23 Orderic Vitalis, *Ecclesiastical History*, IV. 117, 133, 135. Benton, *Self and Society in Medieval France*, 176.
24 Galbert of Bruges, *The Murder of Charles the Good*, 211.
25 Boisset, *Un concile provincial au treizième siècle*, 294–7.
26 *EHD*, I. 437.
27 Orderic Vitalis, *Ecclesiastical History*, III. 121–3. Benton, *Self and Society in Medieval France*, 151.
28 *The Book of St. Gilbert*, 25–7.
29 *Medieval Handbooks of Penance*, 360.
30 Morris, *The Papal Monarchy*, 114.

31 *Epistolae Vagantes*, 15–27, 161.
32 Ibid., 85–7, 103.
33 Orderic Vitalis, *Ecclesiastical History*, II. 201.
34 Ibid., III. 25–7.
35 *Correspondence of Gregory VII*, 63.
36 *Letters of Lanfranc*, 135. *Eadmer's History of Recent Events*, 150, 198–9. Continuing attempts were made to enforce celibacy at later dates, but the reiteration of measures suggests that they bore little fruit: ibid., 207–8, 227–9.
37 Adam of Bremen, *History*, 138–9.
38 *Early Charters of St. Paul's Cathedral*, 193–4.
39 Orderic Vitalis, *Ecclesiastical History*, V. 13–15.
40 U.-R. Blumenthal, *The Early Councils of Pope Paschal II*, 91–2, 97.
41 Tanner, *Decrees of the Ecumenical Councils*, I. 191, 198, 201–2, 217–18.
42 Orderic Vitalis, *Ecclesiastical History*, VI. 291–3, 389. *Letters of John of Salisbury*, I. 153–6.
43 *Correspondence of Gregory VII*, 117.
44 Benton, *Self and Society in Medieval France*, 51.
45 Fletcher, *Episcopate*, 175. J. Barrow, 'Hereford Bishops and Married Clergy, c.1130–1240', in *Historical Research*, 60 (1987), 1–8.
46 *Selected Letters of Pope Innocent III*, 82.
47 *Calendar of Papal Registers*, passim. *Travels of Leo of Rozmital*, 75, 113.
48 *Register of Eudes of Rouen*, 16, 234, 429–30, 544.
49 J. N. Hillgarth and G. Silano, eds, *Register 'Notule Communium' 14 of the Diocese of Barcelona 1345–48*, 94, 97, 103, 113, 125–8, 136.
50 P. Dubois, *The Recovery of the Holy Land*, 56, 118–19 and 119 n. 18.
51 Tanner, *Decrees of the Ecumenical Councils*, I. 473, 485–7. Aeneas Sylvius Piccolomini, *De Gestis Concilii Basiliensis Commentariorum Libri II*, 249.
52 Tanner, *Decrees of the Ecumenical Councils*, I. 623.
53 Morris, *The Papal Monarchy*, 171. J. H. Lynch, *Simoniacal Entry into Religious Life from 1000 to 1260*, passim.
54 W. Ullmann, *The Growth of Papal Government in the Middle Ages*, 375–6, 378.

Chapter 7. Gregorian reform – Popes and the lay world

1 *Imperial Lives and Letters of the Eleventh Century*, 67, 70.
2 Adam of Bremen, *History*, 184.
3 Ibid., 35–6, 43, 46. *Imperial Lives and Letters of the Eleventh Century*, 140.
4 Orderic Vitalis, *Ecclesiastical History*, II. 145–7.
5 *Supra*, chapter 6.
6 *Letters of John of Salisbury*, II. 474–5.
7 C. Morris, *The Papal Monarchy*, 114–17.
8 *Imperial Lives and Letters of the Eleventh Century*, 108.
9 Ibid., 117–21.
10 *Epistolae Vagantes*, 131, 133.
11 Orderic Vitalis, *Ecclesiastical History*, IV. 79.
12 *Correspondence of Gregory VII*, 182. In fact, Lanfranc was pragmatic rather than rigorous on this. *Supra* , chapter 6.
13 *Epistolae Vagantes*, 129.
14 *Eadmer's History of Recent Events in England*, 10.
15 Ibid., 53–64. *Eadmer's Life of St. Anselm*, 85–7.
16 U.-R. Blumenthal, *The Investiture Controversy*, 160, 161–2.
17 *Epistolae Vagantes*, 57–9, 119.

18 Morris, *The Papal Monarchy*, 155. Blumenthal, *The Investiture Controversy*, 140.
19 Ibid., 137.
20 *Imperial Lives and Letters of the Eleventh Century*, 175–6. Indeed, in a letter of 1102 to the abbot of Cluny, he admitted that the disunity in the Church had been caused by his sins: ibid., 177.
21 U.-R. Blumenthal, *The Early Councils of Pope Paschal II*, 17. *Eadmer's History of Recent Events in England*, 134–6, 141–2.
22 *Hugh the Chantor's History of the Church of York*, 13–14, 22, 48, 65–6.
23 Orderic Vitalis, *Ecclesiastical History*, VI. 173–5.
24 *Eadmer's History of Recent Events in England*, 211.
25 Morris, *The Papal Monarchy*, 158.
26 *Imperial Lives and Letters of the Eleventh Century*, 102.
27 G. Tellenbach, *The Church in Western Europe from the Tenth to the Early Twelfth Century*, 276. *Imperial Lives and Letters of the Eleventh Century*, 194.
28 Blumenthal, *The Early Councils of Pope Paschal II*, 65. Morris, *The Papal Monarchy*, 158.
29 Blumenthal, *The Early Councils of Pope Paschal II*, 83, 97, 103, 119–20.
30 Blumenthal, *The Investiture Controversy*, 169.
31 Ibid., 172–3.
32 Orderic Vitalis, *Ecclesiastical History*, I. 170, 199, V. 197–9.
33 *Deeds of Frederick Barbarossa*, 28–9.
34 M. D. Knowles, *The Episcopal Colleagues of Archbishop Thomas Becket*, chapters 1–2.
35 I. S. Robinson, *The Papacy, 1073–1198*, 443.
36 The historiography of the schism is well summarised by M. Stroll, *The Jewish Pope*, 1–20.
37 Orderic Vitalis, *Ecclesiastical History*, I. 161, 200, VI. 421.
38 *The Letters of St. Bernard of Clairvaux*, 188, 190–3, 198, 210, 223.
39 M. Dilworth, *Scottish Monasteries in the Late Middle Ages*, 8.
40 Galbert of Bruges, *The Murder of Charles the Good, Count of Flanders*, 79, 81.
41 *EHD*, II. 721–2.
42 *Letters of John of Salisbury*, II. 20–3, 48–9, 210–11.
43 *Boso's Life of Alexander III*, 115–16.
44 R. A. Fletcher, *The Episcopate in the Kingdom of León in the Twelfth Century*, 54–5, 77, 80, 150.
45 *Historia Pontificalis*, 65–7. *Deeds of Frederick Barbarossa*, 169, 190, 267.
46 *Chronicle of Battle Abbey*, 135, 141–3. *EHD*, II. 721.
47 C. Duggan, 'Richard of Ilchester, Royal Servant and Bishop', *TRHS*, 5th ser., 16 (1966), 13–14. *Letters of John of Salisbury*, II. 776–81.
48 *Chronicle of Battle Abbey*, 285. *Chronicle of Jocelin of Brakelond*, 16–23.
49 *Selected Letters of Pope Innocent III concerning England*, 199–201.
50 J. Riley-Smith, *The First Crusade and the Idea of Crusading*, 21–2, 44, 121, 124–5, 128.
51 *Correspondence of Gregory VII*, 23, 25; *Epistolae Vagantes*, 11–13.
52 *Correspondence of Gregory VII*, 6. Fulcher of Chartres, *History of the Expedition to Jerusalem*, 269–70.
53 *Correspondence of Gregory VII*, 94.
54 *Gesta Francorum*, 17, 32, 40, 75, 85.
55 Orderic Vitalis, *Eccl. Hist.*, IV. 167. Fulcher of Chartres, *History of the Expedition to Jerusalem*, 61, 69–70, 75.
56 Orderic Vitalis, *Eccl. Hist.*, V. 29–191, 325–39, VI. 105–37, 395–419, 495, 509.
57 Fulcher of Chartres, *History of the Expedition to Jerusalem*, 65–6.

58 B. Hamilton, *The Latin Church in the Crusader States*, 4, 8–9. *Gesta Francorum*, 69, 87. Riley-Smith, *The First Crusade and the Idea of Crusading*, 105, 125.
59 *Gesta Francorum*, 3, 6, 9.
60 Orderic Vitalis, *Eccl. Hist.*, V. 327, 335–9, 357. Fulcher of Chartres, *History of the Expedition to Jerusalem*, 111, 192. Hamilton, *The Latin Church in the Crusader States*, 17.
61 Odo of Deuil, *De Profectione Ludovici VII in Orientem*, 15, 55, 57, 69ff., 81, 87, 91, 133–5.
62 William of Newburgh, *The History of English Affairs*, I. 93–5.
63 N. P. Tanner, ed., *Decrees of the Ecumenical Councils*, I. 235–6. Allegations of the Greeks washing altars were also made by James of Vitry, the Latin bishop of Acre from 1216. Hamilton, *The Latin Church in the Crusader States*, 316. M. Kantor, *Medieval Slavic Lives of Saints and Princes*, 293, 304.
64 *Vézelay Chronicle*, 308. Riley-Smith, *The First Crusade and the Idea of Crusading*, 133.
65 Tanner, *Decrees of the Ecumenical Councils*, I. 191–2, 201.
66 *Letters of John of Salisbury*, II. 622–3, 692–5, 754–5.
67 *Selected Letters of Pope Innocent III concerning England*, 58, 184, 207–8.
68 Joinville and Villehardouin, *Chronicles of the Crusades*, 163.

Chapter 8. Regular ideals in a changing world

1 *Infra*, chapter 9.
2 *Supra*, chapter 2.
3 *Epistolae Vagantes*, 4–7.
4 Ibid., 97–9.
5 C. H. Lawrence, *Medieval Monasticism*, 150–2.
6 Ibid., 153.
7 J. F. Benton, *Self and Society in Medieval France*, 58–9, 60–2. Odo of Deuil, *De Profectione Ludovici VII*, 15.
8 Lawrence, *Medieval Monasticism*, 154, 178–81. Orderic Vitalis, *Ecclesiastical History*, IV. 13–23, gives the figure as twelve, but this number may be symbolic to mirror that of the apostles.
9 *The Cistercian World*, 20–2, 35.
10 *The Letters of St. Bernard of Clairvaux*, 203.
11 *The Deeds of Frederick Barbarossa*, 71, 73.
12 *The Cistercian World*, 40. *The Letters of St. Bernard of Clairvaux*, 212, 215, 286.
13 *The Letters of St. Bernard of Clairvaux*, 275–6, 354.
14 *The Cistercian World*, 28.
15 *The Letters of St. Bernard of Clairvaux*, 310–12.
16 Ibid., 230–1.
17 Ibid., 518.
18 Ibid., 1–10, 95–9.
19 *The Works of St. Bernard of Clairvaux*, I. 37–8, 42–3.
20 Ibid., I. 52–62.
21 *The Letters of St. Bernard of Clairvaux*, 378–80, 427–8. Peter's achievement at Cluny was noted also by Orderic Vitalis, who commented on the new statutes which he issued for his house: Orderic Vitalis, *Ecclesiastical History*, VI. 425.
22 Suger, *On the Abbey Church of St. Denis*, 62–5, 72–3, 124–7, 199.
23 *The Works of St. Bernard of Clairvaux*, I. 64–6.

24 *The Letters of St. Bernard of Clairvaux,* 112–13, 480–1.
25 Ibid., 241–2, 294–6, 331–2, 345–8, 437–9, 452–5, 463–4, 469, 484–6, 493–4, 495.
26 Orderic Vitalis, *Ecclesiastical History,* III. 339–41.
27 M. D. Knowles, *From Pachomius to Ignatius,* 24–8. Lawrence, *Medieval Monasticism,* 187.
28 William of Newburgh, *The History of English Affairs,* I. 75, 79, 81. *The Book of St. Gilbert,* 41–3.
29 C. N. L. Brooke, 'Monk and Canon: Some Patterns in the Religious Life of the Twelfth Century', in *SCH,* 22 (1985), 112.
30 *The Cistercian World,* 172, 197.
31 *Chronicle of Jocelin of Brakelond,* 40–1.
32 Lawrence, *Medieval Monasticism,* 164–5.
33 J. Herbert, 'The Transformation of Hermitages into Augustinian Priories in Twelfth-century England', in *SCH,* 22 (1985), 135–6, 139.
34 Lawrence, *Medieval Monasticism,* 170.
35 Ibid., 171. Knowles, *From Pachomius to Ignatius,* 32.
36 *Libellus de diversis ordinibus,* 99.
37 Ibid., 37, 39, 43, 97.
38 N. P. Tanner, ed., *Decrees of the Ecumenical Councils,* I. 240–2.
39 *Letters of John of Salisbury,* II. 574–7.
40 For these, see *infra,* chapter 9.
41 *Scripta Leonis,* 88–91.
42 Ibid., 272–3.
43 C. H. Lawrence, *The Friars,* 30–4. J. R. H. Moorman, *A History of the Franciscan Order,* 13.
44 Lawrence, *The Friars,* 66–9.
45 Ibid., 79–80.
46 Knowles, *From Pachomius to Ignatius,* 51–3.
47 Ibid., 46–8.
48 *Scripta Leonis,* 210–13.
49 The details of these disputes and the attempts to find solutions to the problem are fully covered in Moorman, *History of the Franciscan Order,* chapters 10–13.
50 *Infra,* chapter 9.
51 R. F. Bennett, *The Early Dominicans,* 50–1.

Chapter 9. Heresy and orthodoxy

1 G. Leff, *Heresy in the Later Middle Ages,* I. 1.
2 *Supra,* chapter 5. M. Lambert, *Medieval Heresy,* 44–6, 50–2.
3 N. P. Tanner, ed., *Decrees of the Ecumenical Councils,* I. 187–203, 224–5.
4 E. Peters, *Heresy and Authority in Medieval Europe,* 170–3.
5 *Infra,* pp. 127–8.
6 Tanner, *Decrees of the Ecumenical Councils,* I. 231, 233–5.
7 W. L. Wakefield and A. P. Evans, *Heresies of the High Middle Ages,* 120, 125, 130–1.
8 Lambert, *Medieval Heresy,* 62–4. Wakefield and Evans, *Heresies,* 200–10.
9 *Supra,* chapter 8.
10 Lambert, *Medieval Heresy,* 65–6. B. Bolton, 'Innocent III's Treatment of the Humiliati', in *SCH,* 8 (1972), 74; 'Tradition and Temerity: Papal Attitudes to Deviants, 1159–1216' in *SCH,* 9 (1972), 80–1.
11 Bolton, 'Humiliati', 75–7, 80. J. Sayers, *Innocent III,* 143–50.

12 Wakefield and Evans, *Heresies*, 220–30, 277.

13 Lambert, *Medieval Heresy*, 76, 93–4. Wakefield and Evans, *Heresies*, 283–4.

14 B. Gui, *Manuel de l'inquisiteur*, I. 38–9. Lambert, *Medieval Heresy*, 147–71.

15 Wakefield and Evans, *Heresies*, 240.

16 B. Hamilton, 'Wisdom from the East: The Reception by the Cathars of Eastern Dualist Texts', in P. Biller and A. Hudson, eds, *Heresy and Literacy, 1000–1530*, 42–5, 59.

17 Ibid., 45–6.

18 Wakefield and Evans, *Heresies*, 244–7, 256–8. Lambert, *Medieval Heresy*, 106.

19 Hamilton, 'Wisdom from the East', 58.

20 Wakefield and Evans, *Heresies*, 194, 196–7, 200.

21 *Supra*, chapter 8.

22 Tanner, *Decrees of the Ecumenical Councils*, I. 224.

23 C. Morris, *The Papal Monarchy*, 445–7.

24 Lambert, *Medieval Heresy*, 133–5.

25 The classic account of rural Catharism in the Pyrenees as late as the early fourteenth century is in E. Le Roy Ladurie, *Montaillou*.

26 *Register of Eudes of Rouen*, 175. L. Boisset, *Un concile provincial au treizième siècle*, 235–7.

27 Lambert, *Medieval Heresy*, 143. *Liber Augustalis*, 4, 7–9. Those who simply supported heretics, described as *credentes*, were condemned to the lesser, although still severe, penalty of exile and confiscation of goods: ibid., 10.

28 Lambert, *Medieval Heresy*, 144.

29 P. Biller, 'The Cathars of Languedoc and Written Materials', and L. Paolini, 'Italian Catharism and Written Culture', in Biller and Hudson, eds, *Heresy and Literacy, 1000–1530*, chapters 4, 5.

30 Wakefield and Evans, *Heresies*, 186.

31 Ibid., 512, 531, 570.

32 Ibid., 329–46, esp. 336–9, 343.

33 Ibid., 270–1, 308, 312, 358–61.

34 Morris, *The Papal Monarchy*, 472–5.

35 *Supra*, p. 132. B. Hamilton, *The Medieval Inquisition*, 76–9.

36 A. Thompson, *Revival Preachers and Politics in Thirteenth-Century Italy*, 29–33.

37 There is a valuable summary of these periods of crisis in R. Rusconi, 'L'escatologia negli ultimi secoli del Medioevo', in A. Patchovsky and F. Smahel, eds, *Eschatologie und Hussitismus*, 7–24.

38 M. Reeves, *The Influence of Prophecy in the Later Middle Ages*, 59–60.

39 Leff, *Heresy in the Later Middle Ages*, I. 83–4. J. R. H. Moorman, *A History of the Franciscan Order*, 180–1.

40 Moorman, *History of the Franciscan Order*, 188. D. Burr, *Olivi and Franciscan Poverty*, 27. This latter book gives a full account and analysis of the debates within the order.

41 Moorman, *History of the Franciscan Order*, 197, 313. B. Gui, *Manuel de l'inquisiteur*, I. 108–93.

42 Lambert, *Medieval Heresy*, 202–3. Gui, *Manuel de l'inquisiteur*, I. 84–107.

43 Morris, *The Papal Monarchy*, 468–70. Lambert, *Medieval Heresy*, 182–3. Tanner, *Decrees of the Ecumenical Councils*, I. 242. D. Phillips, *Beguines in Medieval Strasburg*, 11, 217, 219, 224. *Register of Eudes of Rouen*, 734.

44 Lambert, *Medieval Heresy*, 184–5. The gradations of divine love are described in terms of their intoxicating qualities, God is described as 'the Ravishing Most High', and the free soul was said not to need the sacraments of the Church. *The Mirror of Simple Souls*, 106, 155, 160.

45 Tanner, *Decrees of the Ecumenical Councils*, I. 374, 383–4.

46 Lambert, *Medieval Heresy*, 186–7.
47 For this see E. Cameron, *The Reformation of the Heretics*.
48 *Infra*, chapter 15.

Chapter 10. Logic, theology and law

1   *Supra* , chapter 5.
2   M. D. Knowles, *The Evolution of Medieval Thought*, 95–6.
3   R. W. Southern, *St. Anselm*, 77–9.
4   J. H. Van Engen, *Rupert of Deutz*, 78–9, 87–8. One may be sceptical of Rupert's
    'brevity' – his commentary on St. John's Gospel ran to fourteen books and 800
    pages! Ibid., 95.
5   For example, Otto of Freising records the proceedings against Abelard: *Deeds of
    Frederick Barbarossa*, 83–8.
6   *The Cistercian World*, 90.
7   *Letters of St. Bernard of Clairvaux*, 345.
8   *Letters of Abelard and Heloise*, 270.
9   *Historia Pontificalis*, 16–17.
10 *Letters of John of Salisbury*, II. 318–19, 332–3.
11 M. T. Gibson, 'Latin Commentaries on Logic before 1200', in *Bulletin de
    philosophie médiévale*, 24 (1982), 54, 62–4, reprinted in M. T. Gibson, *'Artes'
    and Bible in the Medieval West*.
12 *The Metalogicon of John of Salisbury*, 167.
13 *Letters of Abelard and Heloise*, 58–9.
14 R. W. Southern, *Scholastic Humanism and the Unification of Europe*, I. 167.
15 *The Metalogicon of John of Salisbury*, 95–9.
16 Knowles, *Evolution of Medieval Thought*, 179–83.
17 J. A. Brundage, *Medieval Canon Law*, 32–3, 38.
18 C. Morris, *The Papal Monarchy*, 30–1, 401–3.
19 Knowles, *Evolution of Medieval Thought*, 236–54.
20 The best brief introduction to Aquinas' life and thought is A. Kenny, *Aquinas*,
    1–31. Knowles, *Evolution of Medieval Thought*, 257, 261, 264, 268.
21 Knowles, *Evolution of Medieval Thought*, 272.
22 Dante, *Paradiso*, canto 10, lines 136–8.
23 E. Gilson, *History of Christian Philosophy in the Middle Ages*, 405–7, 728.

Chapter 11. Authority and government

1   *Supra*, chapter 7.
2   J. A. Watt, *The Theory of Papal Monarchy in the Thirteenth Century*, 95–6.
3   E. W. Kemp, 'Pope Alexander III and the Canonization of Saints', in *TRHS*, 4th
    ser., 27 (1945), 14, 23.
4   *Letters of John of Salisbury*, II. 736–7, 750–1.
5   *Selected Letters of Innocent III concerning England*, 31–2.
6   *Boso's Life of Alexander III*, 83.
7   Ibid., 14, 43–5.
8   S. Twyman, 'Papal *adventus* at Rome in the Twelfth Century', in *Historical
    Research*, 69 (1996), 234–7.
9   C. Morris, *The Papal Monarchy*, 190–3.
10 Ibid., 193–4, 402–3. Morris quotes figures of 12 decretals in six years surviving

from Eugenius III, 8 from five years under Hadrian IV, and 713 from Alexander's 22-year pontificate, but notes that these need minor adjustments in the light of more recent work. The change, however, still demonstrates overwhelmingly that the Papacy was responding far more extensively than previously to the demands of Christendom.

11 *Letters of John of Salisbury*, II. 114–15, 420–1.
12 R. W. Southern, *Western Society and the Church in the Middle Ages*, 109.
13 *Epistolae Vagantes of Pope Gregory VII*, 29, 63.
14 Ibid., 57–9.
15 *Correspondence of Gregory VII*, 13–14.
16 *Eadmer's History*, 131–2.
17 *Historia Pontificalis*, 75–8.
18 *Chronicle of Jocelin of Brakelond*, 83.
19 *Letters of Lanfranc*, 153.
20 Ibid., 67–73, 155–61, 161–3.
21 *Canterbury Professions*, 29, 31, 34–5, 39, 42.
22 G. W. S. Barrow, *Kingship and Unity*, 69–70. D. Walker, *Medieval Wales*, 78. An unsuccessful attempt was made to make St Andrews an archbishopric in the 1120s. *Hugh the Chantor's History of the Church of York*, 126–7, 129.
23 Fulcher of Chartres, *History of the Expedition to Jerusalem*, 267.
24 *Correspondence of Gregory VII*, 142–3.
25 John of Salisbury, *Historia Pontificalis*, 4–6, 50.
26 Ibid., 67–8 and 67, n. 2.
27 *Epistolae Vagantes*, 91, 117.
28 *Selected Letters of Pope Innocent III concerning England*, 70.
29 *Eadmer's History*, 208–9.
30 *Supra*, chapter 7.
31 J. E. Sayers, *Innocent III*, 17–23.
32 P. Partner, *The Lands of St. Peter*, 235.
33 Morris, *The Papal Monarchy*, 428–9.
34 *Supra*, chapter 7.
35 N. P. Tanner, ed., *Decrees of the Ecumenical Councils*, I. 230–71.
36 D. Waley, *The Papal State in the Thirteenth Century*, 134–6.
37 Morris, *The Papal Monarchy*, 547.
38 *Chronicles of Matthew Paris*, 128, 156. P. Linehan, *The Spanish Church and the Papacy in the Thirteenth Century*, 292.
39 G. Barraclough, *Papal Provisions*, 60.
40 *Register of Eudes of Rouen*, 262, 263–4, 310–12.

Chapter 12. From victory to captivity

1 N. Housley, *The Italian Crusades*, 16–17. The fullest narrative of these wars is in S. Runciman, *The Sicilian Vespers*.
2 Housley, *The Italian Crusades*, 20.
3 L. Boisset, *Un concile provincial au treizième siècle*, 298–301, 304–5, 306–7.
4 J. A. Watt, *The Theory of Papal Monarchy in the Thirteenth Century*, 99–103.
5 *Dino Compagni's Chronicle of Florence*, 24, 60.
6 B. Tierney, ed., *The Crisis of Church and State, 1050–1300*, 175–6.
7 N. P. Tanner, ed., *Decrees of the Ecumenical Councils*, I. 221, 255.
8 Tierney, *The Crisis of Church and State, 1050–1300*, 176–9. Housley, *The Italian Crusades*, 23. Dante, *Inferno*, canto 27, lines 85–8.
9 P. Partner, *The Lands of St. Peter*, 292.

10 T. S. R. Boase, *Boniface VIII*, 121, 297–9.
11 Tierney, *The Crisis of Church and State, 1050–1300*, 185–6.
12 Ibid., 188–9.
13 Tanner, *Decrees of the Ecumenical Councils*, I. 317.
14 Tierney, *The Crisis of Church and State, 1050–1300*, 124–6.
15 Dante, *Inferno*, canto 19, lines 52–3; *Purgatorio*, canto 20, lines 86–90.
16 P. Dubois, *The Recovery of the Holy Land*, 70.
17 M. Barber, *The Trial of the Templars*, 45–6. This book gives a full account and assessment of the proceedings.
18 *Dino Compagni's Chronicle of Florence*, 86. A reverse sense of national prejudice can be seen in Pierre Dubois, who had said, albeit somewhat inaccurately, that the supreme prelacy had been withheld from the French by 'the craft and cunning of the Romans': Dubois, *The Recovery of the Holy Land*, 168.
19 *Petrarch's Book without a Name*, 58–9, 67, 71–3, 85–6, 91, 93, 97, 108–13.
20 This is demonstrated by the genealogical tables of papal relations in B. Guillemain, *La cour pontificale d'Avignon*.
21 *Chronicle of Jean de Venette*, 38, 56. D. Wood, *Clement VI*, 197–8.
22 The form of this is printed in G. Barraclough, ed., *Modus et forma procedendi ad executionem seu protestationem gratiae alicui factae per dominum papam*.
23 D. Williman, ed., *Calendar of the Letters of Arnaud Aubert*, 354–5; nos 681–2.
24 Ibid., 122, 131, 197–8, 303; nos 150, 177, 318, 559.
25 Ibid., 192–7, 251–3, 264–5; nos 315, 451, 472.
26 Ibid., 434–5; nos 860–1.
27 Ibid., 128–9; no. 169.
28 J. N. Hillgarth and G. Silano, eds, *The Register 'Notule Communium' 14 of the Diocese of Barcelona*, 24, 193; nos 10, 532.
29 *Infra*, chapter 14; *supra*, chapter 9.
30 William of Ockham, *A Short Discourse on Tyrannical Government*, 44.
31 A. Gewirth, *Marsilius of Padua*, I. 21.
32 B. Jarrett, *The Emperor Charles IV*, 51.
33 G. Mollat, *Les papes d'Avignon*, 400–1.
34 Williman, *Calendar of the Letters of Arnaud Aubert*, 104.

Chapter 13. Schism and councils

1 There is no reason to doubt the official curial account of the election, later set out in the document called the *Factum Urbani*, as its key points can be corroborated in other sources. W. Ullmann, *The Origins of the Great Schism*, 11–25.
2 Ibid., 45–6, 48.
3 Ibid., 69–75.
4 Ibid., 57–8.
5 The political negotiations during this period are discussed in detail in H. Kaminsky, *Simon de Cramaud and the Great Schism*.
6 *Two Memoirs of Renaissance Florence*, 82, 84.
7 *Supra*, chapter 12.
8 Substantial excerpts from Langenstein's *Epistola concilii pacis* are printed in M. Spinka, ed., *Advocates of Reform*, 106–39.
9 C. M. D. Crowder, *Unity, Heresy and Reform, 1378–1460*, 41–5.
10 Gerson, *Oeuvres Complètes*, VI. 45.
11 Ibid., VI. 98.
12 Kaminsky, *Simon de Cramaud and the Great Schism*, 277–80.

13 Some of the proceedings of the council are printed in Crowder, *Unity, Heresy and Reform, 1378–1460*, 58–64.
14 Ibid., 76–82.
15 L. S. Loomis, ed., *The Council of Constance*, 222–4, 229. N. P. Tanner, ed., *Decrees of the Ecumenical Councils*, I. 407–10.
16 Loomis, *The Council of Constance*, 466–7, 471, 474, 479, 484.
17 Ibid., 495, 497, 499.
18 Ibid., 227–8, 491.
19 *Calendar of Papal Registers*, XVII. i. 112, 270, 281. For Amadeus of Savoy, see *infra*, p. 190.
20 Tanner, *Decrees of the Ecumenical Councils*, I. 438–43.
21 Loomis, *The Council of Constance*, 426–8.
22 J. A. F. Thomson, *Popes and Princes, 1417–1517*, 81, 125.
23 *Infra*, chapter 15.
24 Tanner, *Decrees of the Ecumenical Councils*, I. 455, 456–60, 464–5.
25 Ibid., I. 466–72.
26 Nicholas of Cusa, *The Catholic Concordance*, 102–3, 118, 122–4, 139–41, 146.
27 Aeneas Sylvius Piccolomini, ed. and trans. D. Hay and W. K. Smith, *De Gestis Concilii Basiliensis Commentariorum Libri II*, 11, 17.
28 J. Shirley, trans., *A Parisian Journal*, 352, 365.
29 Crowder, *Unity, Heresy and Reform, 1378–1460*, 179–81.
30 Tanner, *Decrees of the Ecumenical Councils*, I. 523–8, 529–34.
31 C. B. Coleman, *The Treatise of Lorenzo Valla on the Donation of Constantine*, 24–5, 178–9, 182–3. Nicholas of Cusa had also, a few years earlier, expressed scepticism about the validity of the *Donation: The Catholic Concordance*, 217.
32 Landucci, *Diary*, 26.
33 Thomson, *Popes and Princes, 1417–1517*, 21–4.
34 The debates on authority are fully reported in Aeneas Sylvius Piccolomini, *De Gestis Concilii Basiliensis Commentariorum Libri II*, 99–151.

Chapter 14. Intellectual and theological controversies

1 There is a good summary of the debate in D. C. Brown, *Pastor and Laity in the Theology of Jean Gerson*, 79–83. J. I. Catto and T. A. R. Evans, eds, *History of the University of Oxford*, II. 270.
2 A. Renaudet, *Préréforme et humanisme à Paris pendant les premières guerres d'Italie*, 90–2.
3 *Supra*, chapter 10.
4 *Infra*, chapter 15.
5 Catto and Evans, *History of the University of Oxford*, II. 178.
6 S. Ozment, *The Age of Reform, 1250–1550*, 37.
7 *Supra*, chapter 9.
8 Catto and Evans, *History of the University of Oxford*, II. 28–9.
9 F. Oakley, *The Western Church in the Later Middle Ages*, 131. M. D. Knowles, *The Evolution of Medieval Thought*, 329.
10 Ozment, *The Age of Reform*, 41–2.
11 H. A. Oberman, *The Harvest of Medieval Theology*, 408–12.
12 A. Kenny, *Wyclif*, 59.
13 N. P. Tanner, ed., *Decrees of the Ecumenical Councils*, I. 411–16, 421–6.
14 Ibid., I. 426–31, 433–4.

15 *Supra,* chapters 8, 9.
16 *Supra,* chapter 13.
17 Nicholas of Cusa, *The Vision of God,* chapter 19.
18 R. B. Blakney, trans., *Meister Eckhart,* 259.
19 Ibid., 27–31.
20 Ozment, *The Age of Reform,* 133–4.
21 Oberman, *The Harvest of Medieval Theology,* 284–5.
22 Oakley, *The Western Church in the Later Middle Ages,* 251–6. Ozment, *The Age of Reform,* 306–7.

Chapter 15. Piety – orthodox and heretical

1   *Two Memoirs of Renaissance Florence,* 124. As Dati was married four times, and had twenty-eight children in all, such a vow must have required considerable resolution.
2   T. N. Tentler, *Sin and Confession on the Eve of the Reformation,* 162–86.
3   Philippe de Mézières, *Letter to King Richard II,* 36, 109.
4   R. N. Swanson, *Religion and Devotion in Europe, c.1215–c.1515,* 199–200. A. Tenenti, *La vie et la mort à travers l'art du XVe siècle,* 27–8. T. S. R. Boase, *Death in the Middle Ages,* 104–6. P. Binski, *Medieval Death,* 128, 134–40, 153–9.
5   *Two Memoirs of Renaissance Florence,* 25, 46.
6   Ibid., 108, 112, 130, 132.
7   Swanson, *Religion and Devotion in Europe, c.1215–c.1515,* 36–8.
8   F. Oakley, *The Western Church in the Later Middle Ages,* 271.
9   D. R. Lesnick, *Preaching in Medieval Florence,* 140. I. Origo, *The World of San Bernardino,* 137–8, 147.
10 Landucci, *Diary,* 101, 130–1.
11 J. Shirley, trans., *A Parisian Journal,* 230–1, 238–9.
12 *Supra,* chapter 9.
13 D. E. Bornstein, *The Bianchi of 1399,* 36–7. Landucci, *Diary,* 168. *Chronicle of Jean de Venette,* 52.
14 Bornstein, *Bianchi,* 41, 44–5, 49. *Two Memoirs of Renaissance Florence,* 62.
15 N. P. Tanner, ed., *Decrees of the Ecumenical Councils,* I. 245. Tentler, *Sin and Confession on the Eve of the Reformation,* 22.
16 Tentler, *Sin and Confessions,* 136, 144–7, 159.
17 *Supra,* chapter 2.
18 C. E. Woodruff, trans., *A XVth Century Guide-Book to the Principal Churches of Rome, passim.* The production of a number of pilgrim guides at this time reflects the market for them.
19 Shirley, *A Parisian Journal,* 357–8.
20 *Memoirs of a Renaissance Pope,* 61, 185, 242–59.
21 H. Bett, *Nicholas of Cusa,* 44–5.
22 *Travels of Leo of Rozmital,* 22–3, 25, 52–3, 67, 74, 101, 116–17, 126, 143.
23 *Testamenta Vetusta,* I. 101, 111.
24 Oakley, *The Western Church in the Later Middle Ages,* 106, 297. D. C. Brown, *Pastor and Laity in the Theology of Jean Gerson,* 47.
25 R. W. Lovatt, 'The *Imitation of Christ* in Late Medieval England', in *TRHS,* 5th ser., 18 (1968), 97–123.
26 V. J. Scattergood, ed., *The Works of Sir John Clanvowe,* 70, 74.
27 M. Lambert, *Medieval Heresy,* 156–68.
28 Ibid., 289–92.

29 *Supra,* chapter 14.
30 M. Spinka, ed., *John Hus at the Council of Constance,* 269–71, 292.
31 Ibid., 123–5, 153–4, 158–62. L. S. Loomis, ed., *The Council of Constance,* 288–9.
32 Tanner, *Decrees of the Ecumenical Councils,* I. 418–19.
33 H. Kaminsky, *A History of the Hussite Revolution,* 97–136. Spinka, *John Hus at the Council of Constance,* 277.
34 Spinka, *John Hus at the Council of Constance,* 286.
35 Kaminsky, *A History of the Hussite Revolution,* 369–75.
36 Nicholas of Cusa, *The Catholic Concordance,* 162–3, 281.
37 Spinka, *John Hus at the Council of Constance,* 258. P. Kras, 'Hussitism and the Polish Nobility', in M. Aston and C. Richmond, eds, *Lollardy and the Gentry in the Later Middle Ages,* 183–98.
38 See the extensive bibliography in A. Hudson, *Lollards and their Books.*
39 J. A. F. Thomson, *The Later Lollards,* 145.
40 A. Hudson, *Selections from English Wycliffite Writings,* 28.
41 A. Hudson and P. Gradon, eds, *English Wycliffite Sermons* (5 vols).

Chapter 16. The age of concordats

 1 J. A. F. Thomson, *Popes and Princes,* chapter 2.
 2 Nicholas of Cusa, *The Catholic Concordance,* 238, 257.
 3 Ibid., 125–6.
 4 *Memoirs of a Renaissance Pope,* 228, 238–40.
 5 Thomson, *Popes and Princes,* 57–60.
 6 Ibid., 62–3.
 7 Ibid., 146–7, 152.
 8 *Memoirs of a Renaissance Pope,* 225, 231.
 9 Thomson, *Popes and Princes,* 153, 160–1, 163–4. The full text of the concordat is printed in A. Mercati, *Raccolta di Concordati,* I. 233–51.
10 Mercati, *Raccolta di Concordati,* I. 180.
11 Thomson, *Popes and Princes,* 184.
12 Some examples are noted *supra,* chapter 15.
13 Thomson, *Popes and Princes,* 107–9.
14 *Supra,* chapter 12.
15 Thomson, *Popes and Princes,* 62–3, 68.
16 *Memoirs of a Renaissance Pope,* 80–7.
17 M. Mallett, *The Borgias,* 69–72.
18 F. Guicciardini, *History of Italy,* 10.
19 Erasmus, trans. P. Pascal, *Julius Exclusus.*
20 Guicciardini, *History of Italy,* 273.

Chapter 17. The Church in the early sixteenth century

 1 Landucci, *Diary,* 52.
 2 *Ingulph's Chronicle,* 417–18. *Memoirs of a Renaissance Pope,* 65.
 3 R. W. Southern, *Western Views of Islam in the Middle Ages,* 100–2.
 4 *Memoirs of a Renaissance Pope,* 66–8, 120.

5 N. Housley, *The Later Crusades*, 103–4.
6 Ibid., chapters 13–14.
7 *Memoirs of a Renaissance Pope*, 364–5, 372. F. Guicciardini, *History of Italy*, 329.
8 Erasmus, *The Praise of Folly*, chapter 42.
9 G. Strauss, ed., *Manifestations of Discontent in Germany on the Eve of the Reformation*, 51, 74.
10 C. Shaw, *Julius II, the Warrior Pope*, 284–5.
11 N. P. Tanner, ed., *Decrees of the Ecumenical Councils*, I. 595–603.
12 Ibid., I. 607–8, 651.
13 Ibid., I. 606, 625, 634–8.
14 Ibid., I. 632–3.
15 B. Moeller, 'Piety in Germany around 1500', in S. E. Ozment, ed., *The Reformation in Medieval Perspective*, 52, 65.
16 P. O. Kristeller, *Renaissance Thought*, II. 91–2.
17 A. Hyma, *The Christian Renaissance*, 125–9.
18 E. Cameron, *The European Reformation*, 105–6.
19 A. G. Dickens and W. R. D. Jones, *Erasmus the Reformer*, 61.
20 See also *supra*, chapter 14.
21 The influence of printing on learning is best set out in E. L. Eisenstein, *The Printing Revolution in Early Modern Europe*.
22 *Supra*, p. 234.
23 Erasmus, *The Praise of Folly*, chapters 52–3.
24 Ibid., chapters 40–1, 54.
25 Dickens and Jones, *Erasmus the Reformer*, 52–4. F. Oakley, *The Western Church in the Later Middle Ages*, 258.
26 Cameron, *The European Reformation*, 65, 67.
27 Moeller, 'Piety in Germany around 1500', in Ozment, ed., *The Reformation in Medieval Perspective*, 53. English examples of this and the relation between them and worship are demonstrated by E. Duffy, *The Stripping of the Altars*.
28 D. Hay, *The Church in Italy in the Fifteenth Century*, 79. H. Jedin, *History of the Council of Trent*, I. 146.
29 R. N. Swanson, *Religion and Devotion in Europe, c.1215– c.1515*, 97.
30 M. Baxandall, *The Limewood Sculptors of Renaissance Germany*, plates 24–6, 34, 40, 48.

Index

Printed in the United States
40686LVS00005B/130-177